The Great Treatise on the Stages of the Path to Enlightenment

The Lamrim Chenmo Translation Committee

José Ignacio Cabezón
Daniel Cozort
Joshua W. C. Cutler
Natalie Hauptman
Roger R. Jackson
Karen Lang
Donald S. Lopez, Jr.
John Makransky
Elizabeth S. Napper
Guy Newland
John Newman
Gareth Sparham
B. Alan Wallace
Joe B. Wilson

The Great Treatise on the Stages of the Path to Enlightenment

by
Tsong-kha-pa

Volume One

Translated by
The Lamrim Chenmo Translation Committee

Joshua W. C. Cutler, Editor-in-Chief
Guy Newland, Editor

Snow Lion
Boston & London

Snow Lion
An imprint of Shambhala Publications, Inc.
Horticultural Hall
300 Massachusetts Avenue
Boston, Massachusetts 02115
www.shambhala.com

15 14 13 12 11 10 9 8 7

Printed in the United States of America

♾ This edition is printed on acid-free paper that meets the American National Standards Institute Z39.48 Standard.
♻ Shambhala Publications makes every effort to print on recycled paper. For more information please visit www.shambhala.com.
Distributed in the United States by Random House, Inc., and in Canada by Random House of Canada Ltd

Library of Congress Cataloging-in-Publication Data

Tsoṅ-kha-pa Blo-bzaṅ-grags-pa, 1357–1419.
[sKyes bu gsum gyi rnyams su blaṅ ba'i rim pa thams cad tshaṅ bar ston pa'i byaṅ chub lam gyi rim pa/ Lam rim chen mo. English]
The great treatise on the stages of the path to enlightenment / by Tsong-kha-pa; translated by the Lamrim Chenmo Translation Committee; Joshua W. C. Cutler, editor-in-chief; Guy Newland, editor.
p. cm.
Includes bibliographical references and index.
ISBN 978-1-55939-152-8 (alk. paper)
1. Lam-rim—Early works to 1800. I. Title.
BQ7950.T754.L34413 2000
294.3'444—dc21
00-044664

TABLE OF CONTENTS

DEDICATION

We dedicate this translation to
His Holiness the Fourteenth Dalai Lama
and the people of Tibet.

Editor's Preface

This book is the first of a three-volume series that presents a complete translation of the *Great Treatise on the Stages of the Path to Enlightenment (Byang chub lam rim che ba)*. The first volume sets forth all of the preliminary practices for developing the spirit of enlightenment (*bodhicitta, byang chub kyi sems*). The subsequent volumes focus on the motivation and practice of the bodhisattva, with the final volume offering a detailed presentation of meditative serenity (*śamatha, zhi gnas*) and insight (*vipaśyanā, lhag mthong*).

This translation has been done under the auspices of the Tibetan Buddhist Learning Center (TBLC), which was founded in 1958 by the late Geshe Ngawang Wangyal in Washington, New Jersey. Geshe-la was the trailblazer in the teaching of Tibetan Buddhism in this country and gave his students a broad spectrum of teachings from all the Tibetan traditions, including various short presentations of the stages of the path (*lam rim*) written by Tsong-kha-pa, some of which were published before his death in 1983. The *lam rim* presentation of the teachings as a graduated path to enlightenment has also become one of the core topics of study at the TBLC, as it has for many other centers of Tibetan Buddhism around the world. For the busy members of our modern society the stages of the path literature gives a concise and easily grasped picture of the Buddhist path. All the books on the stages of the path according to the Ge-lug tradition published until now are derived from the *Great Treatise on the Stages of the Path to Enlightenment*, and carry an inherent assumption that the reader can refer to this primary source. However, to date there has been no complete English translation of this text.

In 1991 Loling Geshe Yeshe Tapkay and Donald Lopez, then visiting teachers at the TBLC, proposed that the TBLC organize a group of translators to make a complete translation of the *Great Treatise*. I enthusiastically embraced their idea. As Geshe Wangyal's student I had always wanted to undertake a translation of one of Tsong-kha-pa's major works, because Geshe-la had inspired me with his reverence for Tsong-kha-pa. He once told me that he was especially interested in Tsong-kha-pa's writings because Tsong-kha-pa had received many personal instructions from Mañjuśri in visionary experiences. I was further impressed by this when I read in Losang Yeshe's *Quick Path* (*Lam rim myur lam*) that Mañjuśri had made sure that Tsong-kha-pa wrote the *Great Treatise* with the special feature of blending the three types of persons (*skyes bu gsum*)—the persons of small, medium, or great capacities—with the three principal aspects of the path (*lam gyi gtso bo rnam gsum*)—the determination to be free (*nges byung*), the spirit of enlightenment (*byang chub kyi sems*), and correct view (*yang dag pa'i lta ba*). Furthermore, as the TBLC had many qualified translators associated with it, this plan seemed feasible. The text was divided amongst fourteen translators, and thus was born the Lamrim Chenmo Translation Committee. In the summer of 1992 several meetings were held at the TBLC to agree on a list of technical terminology. By looking at the ensuing introductory material, the reader will see that reaching agreement on Buddhist technical terms is itself a monumental task.

For the ease of the reader the translators have arranged the text for Volume One in twenty-four chapters adapted from the Tibetan outline. The entire outline of this first section of the text is appended at the end of the volume.

The translators have approached the task of translation with the general reader in mind. Thus, although Tsong-kha-pa almost invariably uses an abbreviation when citing a text, here a rough English equivalent of a fuller name of the text is provided. At the first occurrence of a text's citation, the fuller title is provided in its original language. The full name of the text as it is found in *The Tibetan Tripiṭaka, Peking Edition* edited by D.T. Suzuki (1955-61) is given in the note at the first citation of each work. In those cases in which Tsong-kha-pa does not provide the author's name when quoting a text, the name of its author—as identified by traditional Tibetan authorities, even when modern scholarship has not determined the author or has identified another author—is added in the translation. The translators have given the location of the citation in Suzuki where possible in an effort to provide a reference for scholars who wish to pursue more detailed research into the Tibetan text. Additional bibliographic information about these texts is provided in the bibliography.

The translators have not attempted an exhaustive bibliography, but supply information about the original language editions and translations they have generally used. Readers seeking more detailed information about translations and other works in English are directed to Pfandt (1983), de Jong (1987), Nakamura (1989) and Hirakawa (1990).

The translators have used an approximate English phonetic equivalent for the names of Tibetan authors, orders, and places. The correct Tibetan spelling in accordance with Wylie (1959) is given in parentheses at the first occurrence. The translators have also added a short glossary of Tibetan technical terms at the end.

The members of the Lamrim Chenmo Translation Committee who worked on this volume are Elizabeth S. Napper, Joshua W. C. Cutler, John Newman, Joe B. Wilson, and Karen Lang. They used the edition published by the Tso Ngön (Qinghai) People's Press in 1985 which was based on the Ja-kyung (Bya khyung) block prints. The Tibetan page numbers of this edition are included throughout the translation in brackets and bold typeface for ease of reference. The translators used the Ganden Bar Nying edition as a reference since it is regarded as the oldest set of wood blocks of the text. No exact date for the carving of the wood blocks appears in the text, but another important text in the same set of wood blocks, the *Great Treatise on the Stages of the Mantra Path (sNgags rim chen mo)*, was carved in 1426. His Holiness the Dalai Lama graciously lent Elizabeth Napper the Ganden Bar Nying manuscript from his private library. She then had it microfilmed under the auspices of the Library of Tibetan Works and Archives. The translators compared the Tso Ngön and Ganden editions and found no significant variants. The translators also referred to the commentary *Four Interwoven Annotations (Lam rim mchan bzhi sbrags ma)* and used it consistently to interpret citations. The editors have read through the text and discussed the interpretation of difficult passages with the eminent contemporary Tibetan Buddhist scholars Denma Lochö Rimbochay and Loling Geshe Yeshe Tapkay.

As with any project of this size, there were many other helpers and supporters. First and foremost, I would like to give both my gratitude and deepest respect to the one who made this project possible, the great patriarch of Tibetan Buddhism in this country, the late Geshe Ngawang Wangyal, who revealed life to me through the eyes of the Buddha. Next, I am very grateful to all the above-mentioned translators and Tibetan scholars for their immense contributions to this project. I am especially grateful to my editorial collaborator Guy Newland for so energetically providing his essential contributions. I also thank Don Lopez for his editorial suggestions and helpful advice, and Brady Whitton, Carl Yamamoto, and Paul Coleman for their editing work. I am also very grateful to Snow Lion editor Susan Kyser for her unfailing efforts to polish this work. I deeply appreciate the many efforts of the TBLC geshes, Thupten Gyatso, Ngawang Lhundup, Lozang Jamspal, and Lobzang Tsetan, who all helped in locating the citation references and clarifying the text. I also thank David Ruegg and Robert Thurman for their cogent contributions to the introductory material. Among the translators I especially thank Elizabeth Napper for her extra efforts and for so willingly supplying the project with all the work that she had already done on the text. I am also grateful to Natalie Hauptman and Gareth Sparham for their kind efforts on the notes and bibliography. This project would not have gone forward without the generous financial support of Buff and Johnnie Chace and Joel McCleary, whose friendship I equally appreciate. I am deeply indebted to my parents, Eric and Nancy Cutler, for their inestimable kindnesses to me and the work of the TBLC. Finally, I thank my wife Diana for her constant support and unwavering assistance in bringing this project to completion.

Joshua W.C. Cutler
Tibetan Buddhist Learning Center
Washington, New Jersey

Foreword

Jey Tsong-kha-pa's *Great Treatise on the Stages of the Path to Enlightenment* is one of the greatest religious or secular works in the library of our human heritage. It presents a stunning vision of the timeless origin and infinite permutations of all life forms, locating the precious jewel of an individual human embodiment at a critical moment of personal evolution. It provides this revelation in such a way that individual readers can be moved to achieve a fundamental paradigm shift in their vision of their lives: from having been a self-centered, this-life-oriented personal agent struggling with the currents and obstacles around them, anxiously seeking some security and happiness before hopefully finding peaceful obliteration in death; to becoming a magnificent awakening being soaring out of an infinite past experience in marvelous evolutionary flight toward an unimaginably beautiful destiny of wisdom, love, and bliss—Buddhahood, or simply the supreme evolutionary glory attainable by any conscious being.

The *Great Treatise* did not originate this vision, of course. It is the very vision propounded by Shakyamuni Buddha and his enlightened followers, in all the Asian civilizations for almost two millennia, through a vast literature with many branches in many languages, that reveals humans to themselves as participant in this magnificent and meaningful evolutionary process.

The *Great Treatise* gathers the threads of story, image, and teaching from this luminous literature and weaves them into a concentrated pattern, a fabric so rich and comprehensive and versatile it can be fashioned into useful and beautiful raiment adaptable to any person who seeks to wear it. It is sometimes said that Jey Tsong-kha-pa took the Dharma teachings of the Buddha at a time when they were due to fade into neglect and essential disuse as beings everywhere quarreled and struggled over the formalities and properties associated with enlightenment, penetrated their quintessential truths, and revitalized their practice in so powerful a manner they would energize millions of open-minded people over the subsequent five hundred years.

Once readers have achieved the axial shift of perception systematically revealed in this symphonic work, the *Great Treatise* gives them detailed and specific practical methods to implement their vision in the transformative practices needed to aid them in their flight. These practices are skillfully arranged to awaken the worldly person obsessed with success in this life and lead any one of the three types of spiritual persons from evolutionary stage to evolutionary stage. The stages run from reliance on the spiritual mentor, through the themes that free the spirit in transcendent renunciation—the preciousness of human embodiment endowed with liberty and opportunity, immediacy of death, evolutionary causality, and pervasiveness of suffering of unenlightened living; into the themes that open the heart—compassion, love, and the altruistic spirit of enlightenment; and finally into the profound and definitively liberative intricacies of the transcendent wisdom of subjective and objective selflessness. Students and practitioners can use these themes and methods over and over, taking them ever more deeply into their hearts, and their lives will slowly but surely improve.

It is crucial to remember that the *Great Treatise* is not a work of gradualism, a mere set of preliminary practices aiming to prepare the reader for some higher esoteric teaching somehow waiting there out beyond its teachings of the path. It is an exoteric—open—teaching, to be sure, and its path is even referred to by its author as the "shared" (*thun mong*) path, the path shared by both exoteric and esoteric teachings. It is the fullest, highest teaching, the concentrated quintessence of the entirety of the Buddhist path from all the ocean of its literature, concentrated by its integration with the supreme esoteric teachings of the Tantras every single step of its way. For example, the beginning stage, the reliance on the spiritual mentor, is indeed a foundational stage in every Buddhist teaching. But the *Great Treatise* does not teach it with preliminary methodology. The visualization of the refuge field, the heavenly host of the Mentor and all the Buddhas, Bodhisattvas, deities, angels, and spiritual ancestors—this vision is drawn from the most esoteric tantric methodologies and made freely available in an unerringly useful way without exposing the uninitiated practitioner to the danger of formal tantric performance. The way transcendence is taught, the way compassion and the spirit of enlightenment are taught, and even the way wisdom is taught as the inexorable indivisibility of voidness and relativity—all this makes the power of Tantra accessible in a generous, transformative, and dynamic, but safe and sound, perhaps we could say fail-safe, way. This is the genius of the *Great Treatise*.

Some practitioners are so overwhelmed when they experience the shift of vision from this-worldly self-centeredness to cosmically altruistic evolutionary expansiveness, they feel a powerful need to purify their bodies by hundreds of thousands of prostrations, pilgrimages, asceticisms, and complex rituals, their speech by millions of mantra repetitions, and their minds by hundreds of thousands of mentor-worship bonding rituals. These are powerful gateway practices. Jey Tsong-kha-pa himself, after deeply studying all the earlier versions of the stages of the path teachings from all traditions, performed 3,500,000 prostrations, offered 10,000,000 mandala-universe give-aways, recited countless Vajrasattva purification mantras, performed countless mentor rituals, and did fourteen other kinds of practices. And finally he achieved his aim. Thereupon, he wrote the *Great Treatise* to help all other kinds of persons reach their aims, in whichever way they need to go, but in the easiest manner possible for them, always with the optimal efficiency of perfect adaptation to their specific evolutionary situation. So many people achieved this new vision in the centuries following, the whole of Tibetan culture completed its transformation into a vehicle of the enlightenment-orientation for all its people, and its unique atmosphere spilled over from the Himalayan plateau onto the steppes of Inner Asia.

During the nearly 600 years since its writing, the beneficiaries of the *Great Treatise* have mainly been Tibetans and Mongolians, still numbering in the millions. In this century there have been tentative translations into Russian and into Chinese, neither of which has yet spread widely in those cultures. Parts of, and commentaries on, the work have been translated into English in recent decades.

It is thus a historic occasion that the students of the late Venerable Geshe Wangyal have gathered together a team of scholars to create a complete English translation of this masterpiece. They pooled their efforts, analyzed the texts with intellectual rigor, searched their hearts with great sincerity, experimented for the best terminologies, and produced this labor of love. We must hope that the prediction of the five-hundred-year-long usefulness of the teaching of the *Great Treatise* was too conservative, and that this new English version will extend its benefits for many generations to come, leading to further translations into many other languages.

It is my honor and delight in this foreword to congratulate the translators and rejoice in their achievement, a product of their own effort to repay the great kindness of our true spiritual friend, our *Kalyāṇamitra*, the Holy Mentor Geshe Wangyal, who came out here to our wild and woolly savage land, haunted by generations of conquest and enslavement and ongoing violence without and within, and brought us the undimmed lamp of the Enlightenment Path, alive in him as cheerful hope, courageous kindness, incisive wisdom, absolutely adamantine practical concern, and an all-embracing miraculous determination that lives on. Thank you, Geshe-la indivisible from Jey Rimpochey! Thank you all translators for accomplishing this work! And welcome one and all to this *Great Treatise*!

Robert A. F. Thurman
President, Tibet House
Jey Tsong Khapa Professor of Indo-Tibetan Buddhist Studies
Columbia University

INTRODUCTION

The Contents, Antecedents and Influence of Tsong-kha-pa's *Lam rim chen mo*

The Great(er) Treatise on the Stages of the Path to Enlightenment—the *Byang chub lam rim chen mo/ chen po/ che ba* to give it its Tibetan title in its three attested forms—by Tsong-kha-pa Blo-bzang-grags-pa (1357-1419) is one of the world's great monuments of philosophy and spirituality as well as one of the most renowned works of Buddhist thought and practice to have been composed in Tibet.[1] It is perhaps the best known work by Tsong-kha-pa—the source of the New bKa'-gdams-pa or dGa'-ldan-pa/dGe-lugs-pa order[2]—who completed it in his forty-sixth year (1402). This he did at the monastery of Rva-sgreng, a center for the old bKa'-gdams-pa tradition which goes back to the Indian master Atisha (982-1054) and his great Tibetan pupil, the lay disciple 'Brom-ston-pa, and to their numerous Tibetan followers in the eleventh–twelfth centuries such as the graded path (*lam rim*) masters dGon-pa-ba dBang-phyug-rgyal-mtshan and Po-to-ba Rin-chen-gsal.

The *Great Treatise* is made up of sections which are further divided into subsections and individual rubrics. First comes a metrical prologue paying homage to the great masters of the *lam rim* spiritual tradition beginning with the Buddha and passing through Maitreya and Mañjughoṣa—the Bodhisattva patrons of the twin great departments of deep philosophical theory (*zab mo'i lta ba, darśana*) and of extensive spiritual practice (*rgya chen spyod pa, caryā*)—together with the masters Ārya Nāgārjuna and Ārya

Asaṅga, who by their teaching opened up the way for this pair of philosophical-spiritual disciplines **[1-2]**.[3]

The main body of the *Great Treatise* opens with a preamble setting out the instruction to be treated in it (*gdams pa'i sngon 'gro*) **[3-32]**. The following section expounds the progressive method by which the student is to be guided through this instruction, consisting in attending on the spiritual friend (*dge bshes, kalyāṇamitra*) and in the practicer-disciple's mind-training and purification **[33-97]**.[4] The next section is concerned with the graded path suitable for the last, or lowest, category of persons (*skyes bu chung ngu/ tha ma*), namely those who delight in the pleasures of the round of existences (*'khor ba, saṃsāra*) and strive merely for a fortunate future existence in a heavenly world still belonging to the world of saṃsāra **[98-205]**. The following section deals with the middling category of persons (*skyes bu 'bring*), those who develop a distaste for existences and seek liberation for their own sake **[206-280]**. These two paths are nevertheless described as being nonspecific or "common" (*thun mong ba*), for to a very large degree they remain applicable to all Buddhist exercitants. The following sections of the *Great Treatise* are all devoted in principle to the highest category of persons (*skyes bu chen po*), that is, to those who are characterized by compassion (*snying rje, karuṇā*) and therefore strive to achieve awakening (*byang chub, bodhi*) in order to bring an end to the pain of all sentient beings. They accordingly train themselves in generating the mind of awakening (*byang chub kyi sems, bodhicitta*) in its two forms of aspirational vow (*smon pa'i sems, praṇidhāna-citta*) and engagement (*'jug pa'i sems, prasthāna-citta*) **[281-468]**.

This high form of training relates in particular to the first four perfections (*pāramitā*) of the bodhisattva, namely generosity (*sbyin pa, dāna*; "liberality"), ethical discipline (*tshul khrims, śīla*), patient receptivity (*bzod pa, kṣānti*), and energy (*brtson 'grus, vīrya*).

The last two in this classic set of six perfections, meditation (*bsam gtan, dhyāna*) and discriminative understanding (*shes rab, prajñā*), have then been treated in two very long and detailed sections of the *Great Treatise*. In them is carefully examined the true nature of fixation-meditation (*'jog sgom*) as Tsong-kha-pa understands it—and which he shows to be far removed from any simple quietism or ataraxia and from cataleptic fixation or trance (*har sgom, had de 'jog pa*)—and of analytical meditative realization (*dpyad sgom*) made up of *prajñā* or analytical investigation (*so sor rtog pa = pratyavekṣā*)—as opposed to unbridled intellection and mental activity—together with the two corresponding factors of tranquillity (*zhi gnas, śamatha*) and insight (*lhag mthong, vipaśyanā*) and their very close interrelation. These twin sections on tranquillity and insight are thus the most detailed, the most difficult and doubtless also the most ground-breaking in the *Great Treatise*. It is here above all that the very remarkable contribution made by Tsong-kha-pa to Buddhist thought, and to philosophy and spirituality in general, is revealed.

The first of these two sections is accordingly nothing less than a searching and penetrating treatise on the subject of tranquillity (*zhi gnas, śamatha*) involving both bodily and mental calm (*shin sbyangs, praśrabdhi*)—the contrary of turbulence (*gnas ngan len, dauṣṭhulya*)—that examines *śamatha* in the greatest detail with a view to defining its relation to insight (*lhag mthong, vipaśyanā*) and to establishing just how these two factors alternate at certain stages of practice and then mutually reinforce each other **[468-563]**. Major topics treated in this context are attention or mindfulness (*dran pa, smṛti*), awareness (*shes bzhin, samprajanya*), mentation (*yid la byed pa, manasikāra*), composure or equanimity (*btang snyoms, upekṣā*), natural quietude (*rnal du 'dug pa, praśaṭhavāhitā*), aptitude for spiritual and philosophical operation (*las su rung ba, karmaṇyatā*), and non-conceptualization (*[cir yang] mi rtog pa, nirvikalpa*). Special attention is given to the practicer's need to avoid torpor and drowsiness (*rmug pa* and *gnyid, styānamiddha*) and laxness (*bying ba, laya;* "accidie") marked by slackness (*glod pa, lhod drags pa*) as well as agitation (*rgod pa, auddhatya*) marked by excessive tension (*sgrim pa, grims drags pa*) or effort (*rtsol ba*). The appropriate procedure for cultivating tranquillity has here been illustrated by the classical comparison with the training of an elephant **[506-507]**. The nine forms of stabilization of mind (*sems gnas pa, cittasthiti*) associated with tranquillity are also discussed at length. This section reflects Tsong-kha-pa's understanding of the teaching of Asaṅga, and it therefore quotes extensively from this master's *Abhidharma-samuccaya* and, in particular, from his *Śrāvaka-bhūmi*. Other major sources often cited in this section are the *Saṃdhi-nirmocana-sūtra* and Ratnākaraśānti's *Prajñāpāramitopadeśa*.

The second of this pair of sections is an even longer, and virtually independent, study on insight (*lhag mthong, vipaśyanā*), which is often quoted, and sometimes commented upon separately, under the title of *Great [Treatise on] Insight* (*lHag mthong chen mo*) **[564-809]**. Toward its beginning we find a discussion of the question as to how to differentiate between sūtra-texts that are considered, in the doctrinal frame of the Madhyamaka, to be of final, definitive meaning (*nges pa'i don, nītārtha*) and those that are on the contrary regarded, in the same frame, as being of provisional meaning and as therefore requiring to be further interpreted, or "elicited," in a sense other than the obvious surface one (*drang ba'i don, neyārtha*). Also briefly discussed in this context is the distinction in the hermeneutics of the Madhyamaka between a *nītārtha* text and one that is of literal, word-for-word meaning (*sgra ji bzhin pa, yathā-ruta*) and between a *neyārtha* text and one that is non-literal (*sgra ji bzhin ma yin pa*). Buddhist hermeneutics was several years afterwards to be the subject of a major independent work by Tsong-kha-pa completed in his fifty-second year (1408), the *Drang nges legs bshad snying po*. A careful consideration of the nature of the two "principles" of ultimate reality (*don dam pa'i bden pa, paramārthasatya*) and the surface-level (*kun rdzob bden pa, saṃvṛtisatya*), or transactional/pragmatic usage (*tha snyad [bden pa], vyavahāra[satya]*), is pertinent here. Essentially, this section of the *Great Treatise* is concerned with the object of *vipaśyanā*, namely the theory of emptiness (*stong pa nyid, śūnyatā*) in its twin aspects of absence of self-nature (*rang bzhin med pa*) or self-existence (*ngo bo nyid med pa, niḥsva-bhāvatā*)—i.e. the "aseitas" of any entity (*dngos po, bhāva*) posited as hypostatically established (*bden par grub pa*)—and origination in dependence (*rten cing 'brel bar 'byung ba, pratītyasamutpāda*)[5] as expounded by Nāgārjuna and his great successors in the Madhyamaka school. These are in particular Buddhapālita (c. 500 C.E.), Bhavya (Bhā[va]viveka, sixth century) and Candrakīrti (seventh century). Tsong-kha-pa's discussion involves among other things a consideration of the coordinate pair made up of presentation-appearance and the empty (*snang stong*), it being concluded that it is in fact by presentation-appearance in dependent origination that the philosophical extreme of eternal existence (*yod mtha', astitā*) is eliminated while the philosophical extreme of nihilistic nonexistence (*med mtha', nāstitā*) is eliminated by emptiness. This procedure allows the Mādhyamika to keep to the philosophical middle path (*dbu ma'i lam, madhyamā pratipat*), and it answers to the theory that the transactional/pragmatic (*vyavahāra*) is established on its own level through right knowledge or *pramāṇa* (*tha snyad tshad [mas] grub [pa]*). (Compare the idea in Western thought of saving the phenomenal: *sôzein tà phainómena, salvare phaenomena*, "to save [phenomenal] appearances.") This section furthermore includes a discussion of the negandum for the path (*lam gyi dgag bya/ lam goms pa'i dgag bya*, i.e. the *bden 'dzin gyi ma rig pa* or subjective misknowledge that engages in hypostatization or reification) and the negandum for reasoning (*rigs pa'i dgag bya*, i.e. the *bden grub* or objective hypostatic establishment **[651 ff.]**). It is also demonstrated how the negandum must be delimited neither too widely (*dgag bya ngo 'dzin [ha cang] khyab ches pa*) nor too narrowly (*khyab chung ba/ chungs pa*).[6] This discussion also involves an examination of the methods of the two main branches of the Madhyamaka, namely Bhavya's "Svātantrika" (the Rang-rgyud-pa or "Autonomist" branch which on its own account admits an autonomous probative inference, *svatantrānumāna*, and a formal "syllogism," *svatantraprayoga*) and Buddhapālita's and Candrakīrti's "Prāsaṅgika" (the Thal-'gyur-ba or "Apagogist" branch which instead relies on apagogical reasoning that serves to point up an occurrence or "eventuation," *prasaṅga*, which is undesired by the opponent himself). There is also a detailed and fundamental discussion of the question whether the Prāsaṅgika-Mādhyamika (as distinct from the Svātantrika) can legitimately entertain, within the frame of his philosophy, any thesis (*dam bca', pratijñā*), assertion (*khas len pa, abhyupagama*) or position (*rang gi phyogs, svapakṣa* or *rang lugs, svamata*) of his own, Tsong-kha-pa concluding that he in fact can and does. This analysis comprises some very important observations on the place in Madhyamaka thought of right knowledge (*tshad ma, pramāṇa*, definable in terms of a cognition that is reliable, veridical and indefeasible), and it leads to the conclusion that even if such a *pramāṇa* is not established in ultimate reality it still has a fundamental role to play on the level of transactional/pragmatic usage (*tha snyad, vyavahāra*).[7] Next comes an examination of how Madhyamaka theory (*lta ba, darśana*) is generated in the philosopher-practicer's mental continuum (*rgyud, saṃtāna*), including an exposition of the comprehension (*rtogs pa, adhigama*), or ascertainment (*nges pa, niścaya*), of the non-substantiality (*bdag med pa, nairātmya*) of the individual (*gang zag, pudgala*) and of all factors of existence (*chos, dharma*) **[719-769]**. This treatment of emptiness, or non-substantiality, is followed by a very detailed exposition on the forms of insight (*vipaśyanā*) and of how it is realized **[769-808]**. Here Tsong-kha-pa has once again discussed the nature of fixation-meditation (*'jog sgom*) and analytical meditation (*dpyad sgom*) and the relation between these two forms of realization.

This final major section of the *Great Treatise* closes with a very brief reference to the Vajrayāna **[808-809]**. It is to be noticed that from time to time throughout his treatise Tsong-kha-pa has alluded to the question of how the "exoteric" Sūtranaya or Pāramitāyāna of the scholastic (*mtshan nyid pa*) and the philosopher-exercitant, to which the *Lam rim chen mo* is essentially devoted, links up with the "esoteric" Mantrayāna or Vajrayāna of the mantrin (*sngags pa*) and yogin (*rnal 'byor pa*).[8]

The *Great Treatise* concludes with a short metrical epilogue **[810-812]** and a colophon **[812-813]**.

Tsong-kha-pa presents his *Great Treatise* as inspired (especially in its earlier sections) by the *Lamp on the Path to Enlightenment* (*Byang chub lam gyi sgron ma* or *Bodhi-patha-pradīpa*), composed by the renowned Bengali master Atisha Dīpaṃkaraśrījñāna (982-1054), who migrated from India to Tibet where he became the source of the Tibetan bKa'-gdams-pa tradition. Atisha's relatively brief work takes as its point of departure the above-mentioned division of three ascending spiritual categories of person (*skyes bu gsum*).

As a composition that presents a synthesis of very many of the spiritual and philosophical traditions of Buddhism constituting the Path of Awakening, Tsong-kha-pa's *Great Treatise* cites, often at very considerable length, a large number of sources drawn from Buddhist scriptural (*sūtra*) and, above all, exegetical (*śāstra*) literature. The first place is occupied by numerous Mahāyānist (i.e. Pāramitāyāna and, accessorily, Vajrayāna) sources. But works belonging to the path of the *śrāvaka*, and the Vinaya, are also frequently quoted or referred to; these include a number of scriptural works, Vasubandhu's *Abhidharma-kośa* along with its autocommentary which pertain to the Vaibhāṣika and Sautrāntika schools, and the *Śrāvaka-bhūmi* (which is one of the main sources for Tsong-kha-pa's treatment of tranquillity). It is to be observed that references to the latter Śrāvakayānist works are found not only in the sections concerned with the two lower categories of person but also in those devoted to the highest category constituted by the Bodhisattva and aspirant Mahāyānist. This feature is of course perfectly regular and normal in the Tibetan Buddhist tradition which is certainly Mahāyānist, but not in the exclusive sense sometimes supposed (especially in the West) since it embraces the entirety of the Word of the Buddha inclusive of the Śrāvakayāna as well as of the Mahāyāna, and because it encompasses not only the two disciplines (*saṃvara*) of the Bodhisattva and the Mantrin (or Vajrayānist) but also the *prātimokṣa* discipline of the ordained monk or *bhikṣu* following the Vinaya. Tsong-kha-pa as well as most of his teachers and his disciples were indeed monks following the Vinaya of the Mūlasarvāstivādin order, which was the Vinaya school (or Nikāya) adopted in Tibet.

The *Great Treatise* is no mere commentary on these sources but, rather, an independent *summa* and synthesis of Buddhist ethical, religious, and philosophical thought and practice. In its language, style, and presentation it is no doubt slightly less scholastic than several of Tsong-kha-pa's other major works; but it is nonetheless a theoretically grounded treatise on soteriology and gnoseology that always requires the reader's very close, and informed, attention. Tsong-kha-pa's tradition indeed never claimed that the Buddhist path could be an easy one amenable to any kind of "quick fix"; and if certain *lam rim* texts have sometimes been described by their authors as a *bde lam* or *myur lam*, the path set out in them is describable as "easy" or "convenient" and as "rapid" only relatively to other, more detailed and technical, expositions.

Moreover, although not properly speaking a polemical work, the *Great Treatise* does not avoid thorny, and sometimes controversial, issues. But only seldom does it explicitly name the scholars whose views it opposes after a critical examination. In particular, in his sections on tranquillity and insight—but also in earlier sections of this work—Tsong-kha-pa has often referred, either explicitly or tacitly, to certain vexed issues of theory and practice that had arisen in Tibet as early as the end of the eighth century in connection with the "Great Debate of bSam yas"; and on a number of occasions he has mentioned "the view, or method, of the Ho-shang" (*hva shang gi lta ba/ lugs*). This is a reference to the opinion that all effort, all mental activity and discursive intellection and all conceptualization—indeed anything that is not entirely natural and spontaneous—is nothing but an obstacle to spiritual understanding, a view ascribed—no doubt somewhat emblematically and with perhaps only limited justice—to the Chinese Ho-shang Mo-ho-yen (Mahāyāna).[9] By Tsong-kha-pa this view is treated as a case where the negandum (*rigs pa'i dgag bya*) in philosophical analysis has been delimited by its propounders in a way that is too wide, thus leading in effect to a form of philosophical (and spiritual) negativism or nihilism. Another target of criticism is the doctrine of the "empty of the heterogeneous" (*gzhan stong*) which was advocated by the Tibetan Jonang-pa school, the masters of which Tsong-kha-pa does not here mention by name. This doctrine—which is opposed to that of the "empty of self-existence" (*rang stong, svabhāvaśūnya*) linked with Candrakīrti and his Tibetan followers amongst whom Tsong-kha-pa is himself included—is connected with a philosophical view where (as in the case just mentioned) the negandum (*dgag bya*) has been delimited too widely by being made to include the whole of the *saṃvṛti* level of pragmatic usage, so that it too might be regarded as negativist or nihilist. But, first and foremost, the *gzhan stong* doctrine is regarded as a kind of substantialism—a *dngos por smra ba*—because it is understood to posit an absolute that is empty of all that is heterogeneous or different from itself (*gzhan stong*) without, however, being itself empty of self-existence (*rang stong*), the negandum being then delimited too narrowly. In addition, the "Svātantrika" doctrine of the Indian master Bhavya and his followers in India and above all in Tibet is the object of criticism in so far as it is held by Tsong-kha-pa to postulate entities which, although ultimately empty of self-existence, are nevertheless describable as being established by self-characteristic (*rang gi mtshan nyid kyis grub pa*) on the surface level. And, following Candrakīrti, Tsong-kha-pa rejects the addition of the specification "in the ultimate sense" (*don dam par, paramārthatas*) before the four great propositions with which Nāgārjuna has begun his *Madhyamaka-kārikās*, and which proclaim the non-production of a self-existent entity (*dngos po, bhāva*) from (i) itself, (ii) another such entity, (iii) both, and (iv) neither (i.e. from no cause at all). This is because the notion of origination by self-existence on the surface level of *saṃvṛti* alone is considered to be incoherent **[668 f.]**. In various contexts in the *Great Treatise*, other theories too have been examined and criticized in more or less detail. For example, as already noted above, a topic of controversy examined at some length is the question whether—in addition to the Svātantrika (Rang-rgyud-pa)—the advocate of the purely deconstructive method of apagogical reduction (*prasaṅga*)—the so-called Prāsaṅgika (Thal-'gyur-ba)—may entertain a philosophical position (*pakṣa*) of his own, and whether he may formulate a thesis (*pratijñā*) and a corresponding assertion (*abhyupagama*), while still remaining faithful to his school's *prasaṅga*-method. Unlike some other authorities who have considered this problem, Tsong-kha-pa's conclusion is that the "Prāsaṅgika" does indeed maintain such a philosophical position and thesis; to show this he has examined critically even the views of certain earlier Mādhyamika masters regarded as "Prāsaṅgikas" who were active in Tibet such as the Kashmirian master Jayānanda, Khu Mdo-sde-'bar and rMa-bya.[10]

Even though the *Great Treatise* has in effect inaugurated a distinct genre in Tibetan religio-philosophical writing, Tsong-kha-pa's work on the *lam rim* was certainly not without antecedents and parallels in Sanskrit and Tibetan texts. Total innovation was indeed not his aim.

On the Indian side, beside the above-mentioned *Bodhi-patha-pradīpa* by Atisha dating from the eleventh century, which was itself based in part on instruction its author received from Dharmakīrti of Suvarṇadvīpa (gSer-gling-pa), mention is to be made in particular of Śāntideva's *Śikṣā-samuccaya* (seventh–eighth century), a work described as a *Bodhisattva-vinaya* comprising some nineteen topics in Buddhist practice and thought and constituting an anthology of relevant canonical texts, and of the same author's *Bodhi(sattva)-caryāvatāra*, which is structured round an exposition of the six perfections (*pāramitā*) and which thus parallels Tsong-kha-pa's treatment of the same perfections in the sections of his *Great Treatise* devoted to the highest category of person (*skyes bu chen po*) and the path of the bodhisattva. Of special relevance also are Kamalaśīla's three *Bhāvanā-krama*s (eighth century) and Ratnākaraśānti's *Prajñāpāramitopadeśa* (eleventh century), which are often quoted in the *Great Treatise.* In support of his exposition Tsong-kha-pa has made a point of citing, and often of quoting at length, a very large body of Indian sūtra and *śāstra* sources.

Among the most renowned Tibetan compositions that may be cited as predecessors (if not precisely as models) of the *Great Treatise*, mention should in the first place be made of the *bstan rim* texts composed by rNgog Blo-ldan-shes-rab (1059–1109) and by his pupil Gro-lung-pa Blo-gros-'byung-gnas.[11] Another important predecessor was the *Dam chos yid bzhin gyi nor bu thar pa rin po che'i rgyan zhes bya ba theg pa chen po'i lam rim gyi bshad pa (Dvags po'i lam rim thar rgyan)* by sGam-po-pa bSod-nams-rin-chen (Dvags-po-lha-rje, 1079–1153), a master who combined traditions of the bKa'-gdams-pa and bKa'-brgyud-pa orders; justly famous though it is, this last treatise is considerably shorter than Tsong-kha-pa's *Lam rim chen mo.*[12] Other renowned early works from the bKa'-gdams-pa tradition—the *dPe chos rin chen spungs pa* by Po-to-ba Rin-chen-gsal (1027/1031–1105), the *Be'u bum sngon po* by Rog Shes-rab-rgya-mtsho (Dol-pa dMar-zhur-ba, 1059–1131), a *lam rim* known as the

Be'u bum dmar po by Sha-ra-ba/ Shar-ba-pa Yon-tan-grags (1070–1141) and further texts of the *dpe chos* and *be'u bum* class by other masters of this school which are assignable also to the *blo sbyong* (mind-training) literature closely allied to the *lam rim* literature[13]—prefigure important parts of the *Great Treatise*.

From the Sa-skya-pa order there are the *sNang gsum* and *(Blo sbyong) Zhen pa bzhi bral* teachings of Virūpa's path-and-fruit (*lam 'bras*) doctrine.[14] And even though they are somewhat different in contents from Tsong-kha-pa's *Lam rim chen mo*, the *sDom gsum rab dbye* and the *Thub pa'i dgongs gsal* by Sa-skya-paṇḍi-ta Kun-dga'-rgyal-mtshan (1182-1251) might also be cited in the present context since they provide a comprehensive synthesizing exposition of Buddhist teachings.[15] Later another Sa-skya-pa master, Rong-ston Śākya-rgyal-mtshan (1367-1449), wrote a *lam rim*-type work based in particular on the Prajñāpāramitā, the *Shes rab kyi pha rol tu phyin pa nyams su len pa'i lam gyi rim pa*. In the Jo-nang-pa tradition, Tāranātha (b. 1575) composed a *bsTan pa la 'jug pa'i rim pa skyes bu gsum gyi man ngag gi khrid yig bdud rtsi'i nying khu*. From the rNying-ma order a recent counterpart of the *lam rim* literature is provided by the *rDzogs pa chen po klong chen snying thig gi sngon 'gro'i khrid yig Kun bzang bla ma'i zhal lung* by Dza dPal-sprul O-rgyan 'Jigs-med-chos-kyi-dbang-po (1808-1887),[16] a work expounding the new *snying t(h)ig* teaching of 'Jigs-med-gling-pa (1729-1798) entitled *rNam mkhyen lam bzang* which is itself linked with the older *sNying t(h)ig* and the *Ngal gso skor gsum* cycle of Klong-chen Dri-med-'od-zer (1308-1363). Already contained in the earlier *Bla ma'i thugs sgrub rdo rje drag rtsal* treasure-text (*gter ma*) connected with Padmasambhava there is the *Zhal gdams lam rim ye shes snying po*.[17] Finally, amongst modern Bon-po works on rDzogs-chen, reference can be made to the *'Od gsal rdzogs pa chen po'i lam gyi rim pa'i khrid yig Kun tu bzang po'i snying tig* by Shar-rdza bKra-shis-rgyal-mtshan (1859-1933).[18]

These works concerning the path, its stages and grades of course represent a quite diverse collection of texts with respect not only to their times of composition but also to their extent and to their method of presentation and contents. (The works listed here represent only a small selection of compositions on the graded path. On some further *lam rim*-type works connected mainly with the Vajrayāna, see below.)

In the extensive list of more ancient works of the *lam rim* and *blo sbyong* class forming the second section in his valuable bibliography of older and rarer works of Tibetan literature, A-khu Shes-rab-rgya-mtsho (1803-1875) has enumerated some 250 Tibetan works.

Not all of them are, however, directly comparable with Tsong-kha-pa's *Great Treatise*; and in addition to independent compositions this list includes commentarial works on Āryaśūra's *Jātaka-mālā*, on the *Suhṛl-lekha* ascribed to Nāgārjuna, on Candragomin's *Bodhisattva-saṃvara-viṃśaka*, on Śāntideva's *Bodhi(sattva)-caryāvatāra* and *Śikṣā-samuccaya*, and on Atisha's *Bodhi-patha-pradīpa*.[19]

Among works of the Theravāda tradition of Buddhism in the Pali language, the closest parallel to Tsong-kha-pa's *Great Treatise* is probably provided by Buddhaghosa's *Visuddhimagga* (c. 400 C.E.), a voluminous treatise concerned with the three main divisions into which it divides the path: ethical discipline (*sīla*), meditative concentration (*samādhi*) and discriminative understanding (*paññā*). But unlike the other earlier texts just mentioned, many of which were doubtless known to Tsong-kha-pa, the *Visuddhimagga*, never rendered into Tibetan, would not have been available to him. A small part of a work which the author of the *Visuddhimagga* knew and used, Upatissa's *Vimuktimārga/Vimuttimagga*, was, however, translated into Tibetan.[20]

In addition to the *Lam rim chen mo,* which he completed in 1402, Tsong-kha-pa also composed the *Shorter Treatise on the Graded Path of Awakening* (*Lam rim chung ba*, also known as the *Lam rim 'bring* or "Middling Graded Path") completed at Ri-bo dGe-ldan (or dGa'-ldan) Monastery in 1415.[21] And included amongst Tsong-kha-pa's miscellaneous works (*bKa' 'bum thor bu,* contained in the second volume of his Collected Works) there is a short prose *Lam gyi rim pa mdo tsam du bstan pa* or "Condensed Graded Path" (sometimes referred to as the *Lam rim chung ngu* or "Small Graded Path")[22] as well as an even shorter metrical work on practice entitled *Byang chub lam gyi rim pa'i nyams len gyi rnam gzhag mdor bsdus te brjed byang du bya ba*.[23] Reference should furthermore be made to Tsong-kha-pa's *Byang chub lam gyi rim pa'i brgyud pa rnams la gsol ba 'debs pa'i rim pa Lam mchog sgo 'byed*, a metrical hymn of invocation to the masters who have transmitted the *lam rim* teaching, in which is included his well-known *Yon tan gzhir gyur ma*.[24]

Beside the genre of *lam rim* text digesting and synthesizing a vast body of sūtra and *śāstra* literature, there exist in Tsong-kha-pa's dGa'-ldan-pa / dGe-lugs-pa school two related, but nevertheless distinct, categories of works devoted to grades on the path of spiritual realization. The first is composed of a large number of theoretical manuals, generically known as *Sa lam rnam bzhag*, which are concerned with the stages (*sa, bhūmi*) and paths (*lam, mārga*) whose main source lies in the Prajñāpāramitā literature and which have been set out in the *Abhisamayālaṃkāra* and its commentaries (a tradition on which Tsong-kha-pa composed his compendious *Legs bshad gser phreng*, begun in his late twenties).[25] The second category comprises works expounding the path of Mantra, a subject on which Tsong-kha-pa himself composed the voluminous *sNgags rim chen mo* (the *Rgyal ba khyab bdag rdo rje 'chang chen po'i lam gyi rim pa gsang ba kun gyi gnad rnam par phye ba*), completed in his forty-ninth year (1405). In this second category are also to be found treatises devoted to the stages of the path as defined in accordance with individual tantric cycles of the Vajrayāna (Guhyasamāja, Vajrabhairava, etc.).

Over the succeeding centuries followers of Tsong-kha-pa's dGa'-ldan-pa/dGe-lugs-pa tradition produced many works that are based on or derive from his *lam rim* compositions. His direct disciple Hor-ston Nam-mkha'-dpal (1373-1447) composed a mind-training (*blo sbyong*) manual for the Mahāyāna. And two guides (*'khrid yig*) to the *lam rim* were composed by another of Tsong-kha-pa's pupils, sPyan-snga Blo-gros-rgyal-mtshan (1402-1471/2), who was born in the very year his master completed the *Lam rim chen mo*. Two further early works on the subject are the *Lam rim legs gsung nying khu* and the *Byang chub lam gyi rim pa'i dka' gnad ngag 'don du dril ba* by Dvags-po-mkhan-chen Ngag-dbang-grags-pa (born in the fifteenth century).

To be mentioned next are several important instructions on practical spiritual guidance (*khrid yig, dmar khrid*): the *Byang chub lam gyi rim pa'i khrid yig gser gyi yang zhun (Lam rim gser zhun ma)* by bSod-nams-rgya-mtsho (Dalai Lama III, 1543-1588) which is linked with Tsong-kha-pa's *Yon tan gzhir gyur ma*;[26] the highly renowned *Byang chub lam gyi rim pa'i dmar khrid thams cad mkhyen par bgrod pa'i bde lam (dMar khrid bde lam)* by Blo-bzang-chos-kyi-nyi-ma (Paṇ chen I, 1567?-1662); the also very famous *Byang chub lam gyi rim pa'i 'khrid yig 'jam pa'i dbyangs kyi zhal lung ('Jam dpal zhal lung)* by Ngag-dbang Blo-bzang-rgya-mtsho (Dalai Lama V, 1617-1682);[27] and the *Byang chub lam gyi rim pa'i dmar khrid thams cad mkhyen par bgrod pa'i myur lam (Lam rim myur lam)* by Blo-bzang-ye-shes (Paṇ-chen II, 1663-1737).

Connected with Tsong-kha-pa's *lam rim* either directly or indirectly—frequently through the second, third or fourth of the four *lam rim khrid yig* works just enumerated—are a very large number of further *lam rim* and *sbyor ba'i chos drug* (sixfold preparatory practice) treatises by Tibetan and Mongol authors. These are for example the *Byang chub lam gyi rim pa'i gdams pa'i tshigs su bcad pa kun mkhyen bde lam* and other *lam rim* texts by Ngag-dbang Blo-bzang-chos-ldan (lCang-skya I, 1642-1714); the *Byang chub lam gyi rim pa'i dmar khrid 'jam dpal zhal lung gi snying po bsdus pa'i nyams len 'khyer bde bla ma'i gsung rgyun* ascribed to 'Jam-dbyangs-bzhad-pa I Ngag-dbang-brtson-'grus (1648-1721) and the same author's *Lam rim che chung gi dris lan nor bu'i phreng ba*; the *Byang chub lam rim las brtsams pa'i dris lan* by Phur-lcog Ngag-dbang-byams-pa (1682-1762); the *Byang chub lam gyi rim pa'i dmar khrid gzhan phan bdud rtsi'i bum pa* by Blo-bzang-dpal-ldan-ye-shes (Paṇ-chen III, 1738-1780); the *Byang chub lam gyi rim pa'i snying po'i gsal byed yang gsal sgron ma* and the *Byang chub lam gyi rim pa'i snying po bsdus pa dngos grub kun 'byung* by Tshe-mchog-gling-rin-po-che Yongs-'dzin Ye-shes-rgyal-mtshan (1713-1793), as well as the *Byang chub lam gyi rim pa'i dmar khrid thams cad mkhyen par bgrod pa'i lam gyi nyams khrid las skyes bu chung ngu'i skor gyi zin tho* recording a lecture given by the same Ye-shes-rgyal-mtshan[28] and also the record by Gung-thang dKon-mchog-bstan-pa'i-sgron-me (1762-1823/4) of this author's instructions entitled *Yongs 'dzin rin po che ye shes rgyal mtshan nas bde lam gyi khrid gnang ba rje btsun dkon mchog bstan pa'i sgron me dpal bzang pos zin bris su gnang ba gdung sel bdud rtsi'i thigs pa*; the *Byang chub lam gyi rim pa'i dmar khrid 'jam dpal zhal lung gi sngon 'gro sbyor ba'i chos drug nyams su len tshul* and the *Byang chub lam gyi rim pa'i dmigs skor mdor bsdus pa byin rlabs kyi gter mdzod* by dKon-mchog-'jigs-med-dbang-po ('Jam-dbyangs-bzhad-pa II, 1728-1791); the *Byang chub lam gyi rim pa'i sngon 'gro sbyor ba'i chos drug skal ldan 'jug ngogs* by A-kya-yongs-'dzin dByangs-can-dga'-ba'i-blo-gros (1740-1827); the *Byang chub lam gyi sngon 'gro sbyor ba'i chos drug gi khrid yig chen mo 'jam dbyangs bla ma'i dgongs rgyan* and the *Byang chub lam rim gyi rim pa chung ngu'i zin bris blo gsal rgya mtsho'i 'jug ngogs* by Ke'u-tshang Blo-bzang- 'jam-dbyangs-smon-lam (1750-1827); the *Byang chub lam gyi rim pa'i sngon 'gro'i sbyor ba'i chos drug lag tu len tshul gsal bar bkod pa lam bzang sgrub pa'i 'jug ngogs* and the *Byang chub bde lam gyi dmigs skor cha tshang bar tshigs bcad du bsdebs pa lam mchog snying po* by the above-mentioned Gung-thang dKon-mchog-bstan-pa'i-sgron-me (1762-1823/4); works by dPal-mang dKon-mchog-rgyal-mtshan (1764-1853) on the *bDe lam*, one of them based on Gung-thang's lectures; the *Khri chen rdo rje 'chang chen pos bde lam stsal skabs kyi gsung bshad zin bris* recording instructions given by Rva-sgreng Blo-bzang-ye-shes-bstan-pa-rab-rgyas (1759-1816?); several shorter works by dNgul-chu Dharmabhadra (1772-1851) including the *Byang chub lam gyi rim pa'i dmar khrid thams cad mkhyen par bgrod pa'i bde lam gyi lhan thabs nag 'gros su bkod pa*; the *Byang chub lam rim chen mo'i sa bcad kyi thog nas skyes bu gsum gyi lam gyi rim pa'i man ngag gi gnad bsdus gsal ba'i sgron me* by Chu-bzang Ye-shes-rgya-mtsho;[29] the *Byang chub lam gyi rim pa'i dmar khrid myur lam gyi sngon 'gro'i ngag 'don gyi rim pa khyer bde bklag chog bskal bzang mgrin rgyan* by (Dvags-po) 'Jam-dpal-lhun-grub (1845-1919);[30] the *lHag mthong chen mo'i dka' gnad rnams brjed byang du bkod pa dgongs zab snang ba'i sgron me* and the *Byang chub bde lam gyi khrid dmigs skyong tshul shin tu gsal bar bkod pa dge legs 'od snang 'gyed pa'i nyin byed (Zhva dmar lam rim)* by Zhva-dmar dGe-'dun-bstan-'dzin-rgya-mtsho (1852-1912); the *rNam sgrol lag bcangs su gtod pa'i man ngag zab mo tshang la ma nor ba mtshungs med chos kyi rgyal po'i thugs bcud byang chub lam gyi rim pa'i nyams khrid kyi zin bris gsung rab kun gyi bcud bsdus gdams ngag bdud rtsi'i snying po* that records teachings given by Pha-bong-kha-pa Byams-pa-bstan-'dzin-'phrin-las-rgya-mtsho (1878-1941) as edited by his disciple Khri-byang Blo-bzang-ye-shes-bstan-'dzin-rgya-mtsho (1901-1981),[31] Pha-bong-kha-pa's *rJe'i lam rim chung ngu dang myur lam dmar khrid sbrags ma'i gsung bshad stsol skabs kyi zin bris mdo tsam du bkod pa zab rgyas snying po*, his *Byang chub lam gyi rim pa'i sngon 'gro sbyor ba'i chos drug nyams su len tshul theg mchog 'phrul gyi shing rta*, his *Byang chub lam gyi rim pa'i dmar khrid 'jam dpal zhal lung gi khrid rgyun rgyas pa dbus brgyud lugs kyi sbyor chos kyi ngag 'don khrigs chags su bkod pa rgyal ba'i lam bzang*, and his *Byang chub lam gyi rim pa'i snying po bsdus pa yon tan gzhir gyur ma'i zab khrid gnang skabs kyi brjed byang mdor bsdus pa blang dor lta ba'i mig rnam par 'byed pa* (commenting on Tsong-kha-pa's *Yon tan gzhir gyur ma*);[32] the *Byang chub lam gyi rim pa'i mtha' dpyod gzhung lugs rgya mtshor 'jug pa'i gru gzings zhes bya ba las lhag mthong gi mtha' dpyod* by Blo-bzang-rdo-rje (twentieth century); the *bDe lam zhal shes blo bzang dgongs rgyan* and the *'Jam dpal zhal lung gi dmigs rim* by Brag-dkar-dka'-bcu-pa Ngag-dbang-grags pa; and the *Byang chub lam gyi rim pa'i dmar khrid thams cad mkhyen par bgrod pa'i bde lam gyi zin bris* by Shes-rab-rgya-mtsho (twentieth century).[33]

Further related works that derive from a teaching of Tsong-kha-pa treat of the three essentials for the path (*lam gyi gnad*, i.e. the *lam gyi gtso bo rnam gsum*), namely (i) release or detachment (from clinging to the round of existence, *nges 'byung*, a term that may render Sanskrit *niḥsaraṇa, niryāṇa,* and *naiṣkramya*), (ii) mind of awakening (*byang chub kyi sems, bodhicitta*) and (iii) right view (*yang dag pa'i lta ba, samyagdṛṣṭi*, on the understanding of origination in dependence and emptiness).[34]

Of special importance for the interpretation of the *Lam rim chen mo* is its annotated edition—originally from the Tshe-mchog-gling monastery and reprinted at the Zhol printing house in Lhasa—in two parts bearing the titles *Byang chub lam rim chen mo'i dka' ba'i gnad rnams mchan bu bzhi'i sgo nas legs par bshad pa theg chen lam gyi gsal sgron*. The first part contains the text of the earlier sections of the *Great Treatise* accompanied by numerous short notes; and the second part contains the text of the last two sections on tranquillity and insight (*zhi lhag gnyis*), the notes on the former being fairly concise while the section on insight is accompanied by especially copious comment and explanation. The four authors of these notes and explanations are the 6th dGa'-ldan abbot Ba-so Chos-kyi-rgyal-mtshan (1402-1473); sDe-drung-mkhan-chen Ngag-dbang-rab-brtan, who brought together explanations given by the 30th dGa'-ldan abbot sTag-lung-brag-pa Blo-gros-rgya-mtsho (1546-1618) as compiled by his own teacher, the 35th dGa'-ldan abbot 'Jam-dbyangs dKon-mchog-chos-'phel (1573-1646); Ngag-dbang-brtson-'grus ('Jam-dbyangs-bzhad pa'i-rdo-rje I, 1648-1721); and Bra-ti-dge-bshes Rin-chen-don-grub (late seventeenth century). This edition of the *Great Treatise* along with its four sets of annotations is also known as the *Lam rim chen mo mchan bu bzhi sbrags* or *Lam rim mchan bzhi sbrags ma*.[35]

On the lexicography and exegesis of the first part only of the *Great Treatise*, we have the helpful but relatively short *Byang chub lam gyi rim pa chen po las byung ba'i brda bkrol nyer mkho bsdus pa* by A-kya-yongs-'dzin dByangs-can-dga'-ba'i-blo-gros (1740-1827).

Since the time when it attracted the attention (in a still rather unsatisfactory manner) of the Italian Jesuit Ippolito Desideri during his missionary sojourn in Tibet in the early eighteenth century,[36]

Tsong-kha-pa's *Lam rim chen mo* has come to be known to a number of interested persons in the West. The first published translation into a European language of a substantial part of the *Great Treatise,* a partial Russian rendering by the Mongol scholar G. Tsybikov (Cybikov/Zybikow) made from its Mongolian version, appeared in 1910-13 at Vladivostok together with the corresponding text of this Mongolian version (*Lam rim chen po,* vol. 1, nos. 1-2).[37] In English there is a two-volume rendering of a substantial portion by Alex Wayman (*Calming the Mind and Discerning the Real,* New York, 1978; and *Ethics of Tibet,* Albany, 1991). And in French there is a partial translation, also in two volumes, by Georges Driessens prepared under the direction of Yon-tan-rgya-mtsho, a scholar from Bla-brang bKra-shis-'khyil (*Le grand livre de la progression vers l'Éveil,* Jujurieux, 1990 and Saint-Jean-le-Vieux, 1992). Neither of these versions is, however, yet complete. There also exists a Japanese translation of the insight section by G. M. Nagao (Tōkyō, 1954).

Translations of various important materials stemming from or connected with Tsong-kha-pa's *Lam rim* have been published by Geshe Wangyal in *The Door of Liberation* (New York, 1973) and *The Jewelled Staircase* (Ithaca, 1986).

For the present writer, who was introduced to *lam rim* traditions by Geshe Wangyal many years ago in India, it is a special pleasure to welcome the present new, and complete, translation of the *Great Treatise* being brought out under the auspices of the Tibetan Buddhist Learning Center (Labsum Shedrub Ling), an institute for Buddhist study and practice founded soon after his arrival in America by this learned and wise West Mongol scholar-monk born in Kalmykia and educated at the Gomang College of Drepung Monastery near Lhasa.[38]

D. Seyfort Ruegg
School of Oriental and African Studies
London

PROLOGUE

Homage to the guru Mañjughoṣa.

I bow my head to the chief of the Śākyas,
Whose body was formed by ten million perfect virtues,
Whose speech fulfills the hopes of limitless beings,
Whose mind sees precisely all objects of knowledge.

I bow down to Ajita [Maitreya] and to Mañjughoṣa,
The supreme heirs of the unequaled teacher [the Buddha].
Having assumed the burden of all the Conqueror's deeds,
They emanate in innumerable buddha-realms.

I bow to the feet of Nāgārjuna and Asaṅga,
Thoroughly renowned throughout the three levels,
Ornaments of Jambudvīpa[1] who wrote exact commentaries on the intent
Of the Mother of Conquerors,[2] so difficult to fathom.

I bow to Dīpaṃkara [Atisha], bearer of the treasury of instructions
That comprise the key points, unmistaken and complete,
Of the paths of the profound view and vast deeds,
Transmitted well from those two great trailblazers.

I bow with respect to the teachers
Who, with deeds of skill in means moved by loving concern,
Illuminate for the fortunate the gateway leading to liberation,
The eye for viewing all the limitless scriptures.

Nowadays those making effort at yoga have studied few [of the classic texts],
While those who have studied much are not skilled in the key points of practice.

They tend to view the scriptures through the eyes of partisanship,
Unable to use reason to discriminate the meaning of the scriptures.

Therefore, having seen that they lack the path pleasing to the wise,
The supreme complete instructions, the key points of the teaching, **[2]**
I was inspired to explain
This path of the great trailblazers.

All those fortunate ones who are unobscured by the darkness of partisanship,
Who have the mental capacity to differentiate good and bad,
And who wish to make meaningful this good life of leisure
Should listen with one-pointed attention. **[3]**

Here the teaching that I will explain is how fortunate beings are led to buddhahood by way of the stages of the path to enlightenment that (1) contain the key points of all of the Conqueror's scriptures, (2) are the pathways forged by two great trailblazers, Nāgārjuna and Asaṅga, (3) are the system for supreme beings progressing to the state of omniscience, and (4) fully comprise all the stages practiced by the three types of persons.

The scholars of glorious Nālanda (Nā-lendra) are said to have explained the teaching by way of three purities—the purity of speech of the master, the purity of mind of the disciple, and the purity of the teaching that will be explained. At a later time the teaching spread to Vikramalaśīla (Bri-kā-ma-la-shī-la);[3] it is said that it was important for its scholars to begin with three topics—the greatness of the author of the teaching, the greatness of the teaching, and how one should explain and listen to that teaching. Between these two renowned methods, here I will follow the latter in my explanation.

This explanation of the stages of the path to enlightenment has four parts:[4]

1. Showing the greatness of the teaching's author in order to establish that it is of noble origin (Chapter 1)
2. Showing the greatness of the teaching in order to engender respect for the instructions (Chapter 2)
3. How to listen to and explain the teachings (Chapter 3)
4. How to lead students with the actual instructions (Chapters 4 and on)

1

ATISHA

I. Showing the greatness of the teaching's author in order to establish that it is of noble origin
   A. How he took rebirth in an excellent lineage
   B. How upon that basis he gained good qualities
      1. How, knowing many texts, he gained the good qualities of scriptural knowledge
      2. How, engaging in proper practice, he gained the good qualities of experiential knowledge
         a. That Atisha possessed the training in ethics
            1) How Atisha possessed superior vows of individual liberation
            2) That Atisha possessed the bodhisattva vows
            3) That Atisha possessed the vows of the Vajrayāna
         b. That Atisha possessed the training in concentration
            1) The training in concentration common to sūtra and tantra
            2) The training in the uncommon concentrations
         c. That Atisha possessed the training in wisdom
            1) The common training in wisdom
            2) The uncommon training in wisdom
   C. Having gained those good qualities, what Atisha did to further the teachings
      1. What he did in India
      2. What he did in Tibet

I. Showing the greatness of the teaching's author in order to establish that it is of noble origin

These instructions, in general, are those of the *Ornament for Clear Knowledge (Abhisamayālaṃkāra)*,[5] composed by the venerable Maitreya. **[4]** In particular, the text for this work is Atisha's *Lamp for the*

Path to Enlightenment (*Bodhi-patha-pradīpa*); hence, the very author of the *Lamp for the Path to Enlightenment* is also the author of this [work].[6]

The other name by which the great master Dīpaṁkaraśrījñāna is widely renowned is the glorious Atisha.

A. **How he took rebirth in an excellent lineage**

As is set forth in the *Eighty Verses of Praise (bsTod pa brgyad cu pa)* composed by the great translator Nag-tso (Nag-tsho):[7]

> In the excellent land of Za-hor [Bengal] in the east,
> Is a great city, Vikramanipūra.
> In its center is a royal residence,
> A palace extremely vast,
> Called the "Golden Banner."
> Its resources, might, and fortune
> Were like that of the eastern emperor of China.[8]
>
> The king of that country was Kalyanaśrī,
> The queen was Śrīprabhā.
> They had three sons, Padmagarbha,
> Candragarbha, and Śrīgarbha.
> Prince Padmagarbha had five queens and nine sons.
>
> His eldest son, Puṇyaśrī,
> Is a great scholar of our time
> Known as Dha-na-shrī.[9]
> The youngest, Śrīgarbha,
> Is the monk Viryācandra.
> The middle [son], Candragarbha,
> Is our present venerable guru [Atisha].

B. **How upon that basis he gained good qualities**

How he gained good qualities is explained in two parts:

1. How, knowing many texts, he gained the good qualities of scriptural knowledge
2. How, engaging in proper practice, he gained the good qualities of experiential knowledge

1. **How, knowing many texts, he gained the good qualities of scriptural knowledge**

Nag-tso's *Eighty Verses of Praise* says:[10]

> At the age of twenty-one,
> He had mastered the sixty-four arts,[11]

All forms of crafts,
The Sanskrit language,
And all philosophy.

As it states here, by the time he was twenty-one, he had become a full-fledged scholar after training in the topics of knowledge common to Buddhists and non-Buddhists, the four knowledges—of grammar, logic, the crafts, and medicine.[12] **[5]** More specifically, the great Dro-lung-ba (Gro-lung-pa) said that at age fifteen, after hearing Dharmakīrti's *Drop of Reasoning (Nyāya-bindu-prakaraṇa)* one time, Atisha debated with a famous scholar, a non-Buddhist logician, and defeated him, whereby his fame spread everywhere.

Then, he received complete initiation from the guru Rāhulagupta, lord of contemplation of the Black Mountain Temple,[13] who had a vision of the glorious Hevajra and had received prophecies from Vajraḍākinī. He was given the secret name Jñānaguhyavajra. By training through his twenty-ninth year in the Vajrayāna with many gurus who had achieved spiritual attainments, he became skilled in all the tantric texts and instructions. When the thought occurred to him, "I alone am skilled in the mantra vehicle,"[14] his pride was subdued by *ḍākinīs*[15] in a dream showing him many volumes of the mantra path that he had not seen before.

Then, his gurus and chosen deities, either in person or in dreams, urged him to become a monk, saying that if he did so, it would benefit vastly the teaching and many beings. Upon their urging, he became a monk, receiving ordination from an abbot who had attained a meditative concentration in which he engaged reality from one perspective, having reached the path of preparation.[16] This abbot was a Mahāsaṃghika elder, a great upholder of the texts on discipline, called Śīlarakṣita. As it states in Nag-tso's *Eighty Verses of Praise*, "Your abbot was renowned by all as having attained the path of preparation."[17] Furthermore, Atisha was given the name Śrī Dīpaṃkarajñāna.

Then, until he was thirty-one, Atisha trained in the higher and lower scriptural collections of Buddhist knowledge within the tradition of philosophy. In particular, at O-tan-ta-pū-ri,[18] he heard teachings for twelve years from the guru Dharmarakṣita on the *Great Detailed Explanation (Mahā-vibhāṣā)*.[19] Through becoming very skilled in the texts of the four basic schools,[20] he came to know according to the different schools and without confusion even the finest details of what behavior should be adopted and what avoided in such rules of monastic discipline as those regarding how to give and receive things such as food. **[6]**

Thus, through crossing over the oceanlike tenets of our own and others' schools, he came to know accurately all the key points of the scriptural teaching.

2. **How, engaging in proper practice, he gained the good qualities of experiential knowledge**

In general, the three precious scriptural collections[21] include all of the scriptural teachings of the Conqueror. Thus, the three precious trainings must also include the teachings as they are realized.[22] With respect to that, the scriptures and their commentaries repeatedly praise training in ethical discipline as the basis for all good qualities, such as the trainings in concentration and wisdom. Therefore, at the outset you must have the good qualities of knowledge that occur in the context of training in ethical discipline.

a. **That Atisha possessed the training in ethics**[23]

That Atisha possessed the training in ethics is explained in relation to three aspects:

1. The superior vows of individual liberation
2. The bodhisattva vows
3. The vows of the Vajrayāna

1) **How Atisha possessed superior vows of individual liberation**

Nag-tso's *Eighty Verses of Praise*:[24]

> I bow down to the elder upholder of the texts on discipline,
> Supreme of monks, possessing the glory of pure deeds.
> You, having entered the door of the *śrāvaka* vehicle,[25]
> Guarded ethical discipline as a yak guards its tail.

A yak is so attached to the hairs of its tail that when a single hair gets caught in brush, it will risk its life to guard that no hair be lost, even if it sees that it might be killed by a hunter. Likewise, Atisha, after receiving the complete vows of a monk, guarded at the risk of his life every minor fundamental training, not to mention the major fundamental trainings to which he was committed. Therefore, as it is said in Nag-tso's *Eighty Verses of Praise*, he was an elder who was a great upholder of the texts on discipline.

2) **That Atisha possessed the bodhisattva vows**

Nag-tso's *Eighty Verses of Praise*:[26]

> You, having entered the door of the perfection vehicle,
> Developed the pure wholehearted resolve, and due to your

Spirit of enlightenment, you would not desert living beings—
I bow down to you, intelligent and compassionate one.

Thus, it says that he trained in many instructions for developing the spirit of enlightenment, which is rooted in love and compassion. In particular, relying on Ser-ling-ba (gSer-gling-pa),[27] he had trained for a long time in the supreme instructions transmitted from the venerable Maitreya and Mañjughoṣa to Asaṅga and Śāntideva, respectively. **[7]**

Through this, as the *Eighty Verses of Praise* says:[28]

The one who set aside his own interests and took up
The burden of others' interests is my guru [Atisha].

There arose in his heart the spirit of enlightenment that cherishes others more than oneself. That aspirational spirit induced in him the engaged spirit of enlightenment. He then learned the practices pursuant to his promise to train in the great waves of bodhisattva deeds, and with those good actions he never transgressed the boundaries of the code of conquerors' children.[29]

3) **That Atisha possessed the vows of the Vajrayāna**

Nag-tso's *Eighty Verses of Praise*:[30]

Having entered the door of the Vajrayāna,
You saw yourself as a deity and possessed the *vajra* mind.[31]
Lord of contemplation, Avadhūtipa,[32]
I bow down to you who engaged in the secret conduct.

Nag-tso expresses praise in general, calling Atisha a chief of yogis due to his reaching the concentration of the stage of generation, in which he saw his body as divine, and the concentration of the stage of completion, whereupon he attained the *vajra* state of mind. In particular, with respect to his guarding properly the pledges and not transgressing the boundaries of the tantric rules, the *Eighty Verses of Praise* says:[33]

Because you had mindfulness and vigilance,
You had no unethical thoughts.
Conscientious and alert, with no deceit or pretension,
You were not stained by the faults of infractions.

Thus, Atisha was not only courageous in promising to train in the ethical discipline of the three vows,[34] but he also guarded that ethical discipline by keeping his promises and not transgressing the boundaries of the rules. Even when he slightly transgressed, he immediately purified that infraction with the appropriate rite for restoring the vow. Know that this biography delights scholars who understand the key points of the scriptures; emulate such excellent beings. **[8]**

b. **That Atisha possessed the training in concentration**

1) **The training in concentration common to sūtra and tantra**

His mind became serviceable by means of meditative serenity.

2) **The training in the uncommon concentrations**

He reached a very stable stage of generation due to having practiced the deeds of proficient conduct for six or three years.[35] At that time, after hearing the secret tantric songs sung by *ḍākinīs* in Oḍḍiyāna, he committed them to memory.

c. **That Atisha possessed the training in wisdom**

1) **The common training in wisdom**

He gained a concentration of insight that was a union of meditative serenity and insight.

2) **The uncommon training in wisdom**

He gained a special concentration of the stage of completion. *Eighty Verses of Praise*:

> It is clear that you achieved the path of preparation
> In accordance with the texts of the mantra vehicle.

C. **Having gained those good qualities, what Atisha did to further the teachings**

1. **What he did in India**

In the palace of the great enlightenment at the glorious Bodh-gayā, he upheld the Buddhist teaching three times by using the teachings to vanquish the poor instruction of non-Buddhist philosophers. With regard to the higher and lower of our own Buddhist schools, he furthered the teachings through clearing away the corruptions of ignorance, wrong ideas, and doubts. So it is that all of the schools, without partisanship, consider him a crown jewel. *Eighty Verses of Praise*:[36]

> In the palace of the great enlightenment
> When all were assembled together,
> With speech like a lion's roar
> You confounded the minds of all
> Who argued for the poor tenets
> Of our own and others' schools.

Also:[37]

At Otantapūri there were
Two hundred fifty monks,
At Vikramalaśīla
There were almost a hundred.
All four root schools[38] were present.
You did not take up the boasts of the various schools
But became the crown jewel of all
Four followers of the Teacher[39]
In all of the areas
Of the land of Magadha. **[9]**
Because you stayed with the general teachings
Of all eighteen sects [and thus were nonpartisan],
Everyone received teachings from you.

2. **What he did in Tibet**

The royal renunciates, uncle and nephew,[40] sent to India in succession the two translators, Gya-dzön-seng (brGya-brtson-seng)[41] and Nag-tso Tshul-trim-gyal-wa (Nag-tsho-tshul-khrims-rgyal-ba). Because they made great efforts to invite him again and again, Atisha went to Upper Nga-ri (mNga'-ris) during the time of Jang-chup-ö (Byang-chub-'od).

When they welcomed him there, his hosts prayed that he might purify the Buddhist teaching. Based on this prayer, he furthered the teaching through activities such as composing the *Lamp for the Path to Enlightenment*, a text that brings together the stages of practice, condensing all the key points of the sūtra and mantra vehicles. Moreover, for three years at Nga-ri, nine years at Nye-tang (sNye-thang), and five years at other places in Ü (dBus) and Tsang (gTsang), he taught all the instructions for the texts of the sūtra and mantra vehicles to fortunate students.[42] The result was that he re-established the practices of the Buddhist system that had disappeared; he reinvigorated those that remained only slightly; and he removed corruption based on misconceptions. Thus he made the precious teachings free of defilement.

In general, the glorious Śāntarakṣita and Padmasambhava introduced the practices of the Buddhist system to the Land of Snow [Tibet] during the early dissemination of the teaching. However, the Chinese abbot Ha-shang (Hva-shang) caused the teaching to decline. He did not understand emptiness correctly and thereby denigrated the factor of method and negated bringing anything to mind, even virtues. The great master Kamalaśīla, after refuting Ha-shang well, established the Conqueror's intent; hence, his kindness was most great.

In the later dissemination of the teaching to Tibet, some who fancied that they were scholars and yogis misconstrued the meaning of the collections of tantras. Because of this, they did great damage to the maintenance of ethical discipline, the root of the teachings. This excellent being [Atisha] refuted them well. Moreover, he caused their erroneous conceptions to disappear and then reinvigorated the flawless teaching. **[10]** Thus, his kindness reached all those of the Land of Snow.

Furthermore, there are three ideal qualifications for an author of texts that elucidate the intent of the Sage in this way. The author (1) should have mastered the five topics of knowledge;[43] (2) should possess instructions that are the key points for practicing the meaning of the topics of Buddhist knowledge which have been transmitted in an unbroken lineage through excellent beings from the perfect Buddha; and (3) should receive permission to compose the text in a vision of his or her chosen deity. If someone with any one of these qualifications can compose a text, then when all three are present it is ideal. This great master was endowed with all three as follows:

1. With regard to how his chosen deities looked after him, *Eighty Verses of Praise*:[44]

> Due to having visions and receiving permission
> From the glorious Hevajra,
> Trisamayavyūharāja,
> The hero Lokeśvara [Avalokiteśvara],
> The noble and venerable Tārā, and so forth,
> He listened always to the excellent teaching
> Of the profound view and the vast deeds of compassion
> Either in dreams or in person.

2. With regard to the lineages of gurus, there are two lineages: that of the vehicle common [to both the Hīnayāna and Mahāyāna] and that of the Mahāyāna. Within the latter, there are again two: those of the perfection vehicle and those of the mantra vehicle. Within the perfection vehicle, there are two more divisions—the lineage of the view and the lineage of deeds—and within the lineage of deeds, there are lineages descended from Maitreya and from Mañjughoṣa, making three lineages in the perfection vehicle. Further, with respect to the mantra vehicle, there are five systems of lineages.[45] In addition, there are such lineages as the lineages of tenets, the lineages of blessings, and the lineages of various

instructions. Atisha was endowed with instructions from these many lineages. The gurus from whom Atisha received teachings directly are as Nag-tso says:[46]

> The gurus on whom you always relied
> Had achieved spiritual attainments; they were many:
> Śānti-pa and Ser-ling-ba,
> Bhadrabodhi, and Jñānaśrī.
> And, in particular, you possessed
> Instructions on the profound view and the vast deeds
> Passed down over the generations from Nāgārjuna. **[11]**

It is well known that he had twelve gurus who had achieved spiritual attainments, and there were many others as well.

3. His mastery of the five topics of knowledge has already been explained.

Therefore, this master was able to determine well the intent of the Conqueror.

This master who had such qualities had an inconceivable number of students in India, Kashmir, Oḍḍiyāna, Nepal, and Tibet. To mention the chief of these, in India, there were the four great scholars Bi-do-ba (Bi-to-pa), Dharmākāramati, Madhyasinha, and Kṣitigarbha, all equal in knowledge to the Elder [Atisha]. Some also include Mitraguhya as a fifth. From Nga-ri, there were the translator Rin-chen-sang-bo (Rin-chen-bzang-po), the translator Nag-tso, and royal renunciate Jang-chup-ö. From Tsang, there were Gar-gay-wa ('Gar-dge-ba) and Gö-kuk-ba-hlay-dzay ('Gos-khug-pa-lhas-btsas). From Hlo-drak (lHo-brag), there were Chak-ba-tri-chok (Chag-pa-khri-mchog) and Gay-wa-gyong (dGe-ba-skyong). From Khams, there were Nal-jor-ba-chen-bo (rNal-'byor-pa-chen-po), Gön-ba-wa (dGon-pa-ba), Shay-rap-dor-jay (Shes-rab-rdo-rje), and Chak-dar-dön-ba (Phyag-dar-ston-pa). From central Tibet, there were the three, Ku-dön Dzön-dru-yung-drung (Khu-ston-brtson-'grus-gyung-drung), Ngok Lek-bay-shay-rap (Ngog-legs-pa'i-shes-rab), and Drom-dön-ba Gyel-way-jung-nay ('Brom-ston-pa-rgyal-ba'i-'byung-gnas).[47]

From among these, the great holder of the lineage who furthered the activities of the guru [Atisha] himself was Drom-dön-ba Gyel-way-jung-nay who was prophesied by Tārā.

This, in brief, is the greatness of the author. It can be known in detail from the great biographical literature.[48]

2

THE GREATNESS OF THE TEACHING

II. Showing the greatness of the teaching in order to engender respect for the instructions
  A. The greatness of enabling one to know that all of the teachings are free of contradiction
  B. The greatness of enabling one to understand that all of the scriptures are instructions for practice
  C. The greatness of enabling one easily to find the Conqueror's intent
  D. The greatness of enabling one to refrain automatically from great wrongdoing

Concerning the teaching to be explained, the root text of these instructions is the *Lamp for the Path to Enlightenment.* There are many texts composed by the Elder, but the *Lamp for the Path to Enlightenment* is comprehensive and fundamental. Since it teaches by drawing together the key points of both the sūtra and mantra vehicles, its subject matter is comprehensive; since it emphasizes the stages of disciplining the mind, it is easy to put into practice; and since it is adorned with the instructions of two gurus who were skilled in the systems of the two great trailblazers,[49] it is superior to other systems. **[12]**

II. **Showing the greatness of the teaching in order to engender respect for the instructions**

The greatness of the teaching is indicated by four qualities it elicits in the student:

1. Knowing that all of the teachings are free of contradiction
2. Coming to understand that all of the scriptures are instructions for practice
3. Easily finding the Conqueror's intent
4. Automatically refraining from great wrongdoing

A. **The greatness of enabling one to know that all of the teachings are free of contradiction**

With regard to the teachings, Avalokitavrata's *Commentary on the "Lamp for Wisdom" (Prajñā-pradīpa-ṭīkā)* says:[50]

> Concerning "teachings," the scriptures of the Bhagavan[51] accurately teach that which is to be thoroughly known, that which is to be eliminated, that which is to be manifested, and that which is to be cultivated by deities and humans who wish to attain the ambrosial state [of a nonabiding nirvāṇa].

Thus the teachings are what the Conqueror explained well. Here, [in the context of the *Lamp for the Path to Enlightenment*] to know that all the teachings are free of contradiction means to understand that they are the path by which one person becomes a buddha. Some are the main points of the path; some are the various branches of the path.

Bodhisattvas make it their goal to accomplish the good of the world [all living beings]. Since bodhisattvas must take care of students who are followers of all three lineages [those of *śrāvakas*, *pratyekabuddhas*, and bodhisattvas], they must train in the paths of those three lineages. For, as Nāgārjuna's *Essay on the Spirit of Enlightenment (Bodhicitta-vivaraṇa)* says:[52]

> Because they engender in others
> Certain knowledge that accords with their own,
> The wise apply themselves
> Always and without mistake.

And, Dharmakīrti's *Commentary on the "Compendium of Valid Cognition" (Pramāṇa-vārttika-kārikā)* says:[53]

> It is difficult to explain to others
> The results of causes that are obscure to oneself.

Therefore, if you have not ascertained something exactly, you cannot teach it to others.

By stating, "Those benefactors of beings who accomplish the good of the world through the knowledge of paths...," Ajita indicates in the *Ornament for Clear Knowledge* that knowing the paths of the three vehicles is the method for bodhisattvas to achieve the goal they have set.[54] Also the Mother of Conquerors [*The Eighteen-Thousand-Verse Perfection of Wisdom Sūtra*] says:[55] **[13]**

> Bodhisattvas should produce all paths—whatever is a path of a *śrāvaka*, a *pratyekabuddha*, or a buddha—and should know all paths. They should also perform the deeds of these paths and bring all of them to completion.

Thus, it is contradictory to propound that you should not train in the scriptural collections of the Hīnayāna because you are a Mahāyāna practitioner.

There are shared and unshared paths to enter the Mahāyāna. Since the shared are those things that come from the scriptural collections of the Hīnayāna, how could they be something to set aside? Therefore, Mahāyāna followers must practice all those things taught in the Hīnayāna scriptural collections, with only a few exceptions, such as diligently seeking a blissful peace for oneself alone. This is the reason for extensively teaching all three vehicles in the very vast scriptural collections of the bodhisattvas.

Furthermore, a perfect buddha has not extinguished just a portion of faults and accomplished a mere portion of good qualities, but rather has extinguished all types of faults and accomplished all types of good qualities. Mahāyāna practitioners seek to achieve this. Since they will then eliminate all faults and develop all good qualities, all the different types of good qualities derived from the elimination of faults and the acquisition of knowledge within every other vehicle are included in the Mahāyāna path. Therefore, every scripture is included as a branch of the Mahāyāna path for achieving buddhahood. For, there is no saying of the Sage that does not extinguish some fault or develop some good quality, and, of all those, there is none that a Mahāyāna practitioner does not practice.

Qualm: In order to enter the perfection vehicle of the Mahāyāna, you do need the paths that are explained in the Hīnayāna scriptural collections. However, in order to enter into the Vajrayāna, the paths of the perfection vehicle are not shared in common with the paths of the Vajrayāna, because the paths are incompatible.[56] **[14]**

Reply: This too is most unreasonable. The substance of the path of the perfection vehicle comprises the *thought* that is the development of the spirit of enlightenment and the *deeds* of training in the six perfections. That those must be relied upon on all occasions is set forth in the *Vajra Climax Tantra (Vajra-śikhara)*:[57]

> Even to save your life,
> Do not give up the spirit of enlightenment.

And:

> The deeds of the six perfections
> Should never be cast aside.

Further, such is said in many tantric texts.

Such texts also state that on frequent occasions of entering maṇḍalas of highest yoga tantra, you must take both the shared and the unshared tantric vows. The former are simply the vows of a bodhisattva, and taking the vows means promising to apply yourself to the trainings of a bodhisattva, such as the three forms of ethical discipline.[58] Therefore, the perfection vehicle has no path other than the trainings that accord with your promise to practice the bodhisattva deeds after developing the spirit of enlightenment.

Moreover, the above qualm is most unreasonable because you must promise to uphold all aspects of the teaching when you take the tantric vow. This is in accordance with what is said in the *Diamond Ḍāka Tantra (Vajra-ḍāka), Integration Tantra (Saṃpuṭi),* and *Vajra Climax Tantra* on the occasion of taking the pledges of Amitābha:

> Uphold all of the excellent teachings:
> The three vehicles, the external, and the secret.[59]

Some see a slight discrepancy in terms of what you are and are not to do and conclude that these are in complete contradiction, like hot and cold. Obviously, this is a cursory assessment. Apart from certain points about what is or is not to be done, the scriptures are very much in agreement. Therefore, upon entering the higher levels of the three vehicles or the five paths, for instance, you must have all the good qualities of the lower vehicles and paths.

With regard to the path of the perfections, the *Verse Summary of the Perfection of Wisdom in Eight Thousand Lines (Ratna-guṇa-sañcaya-gāthā)* says:[60]

> The path of all the conquerors of the past,
> Of those who have not come, and of those now present
> Is the perfections, nothing else. **[15]**

The path of the perfections is like the center post for the path that leads to buddhahood. Hence, it is unsuitable to cast it aside. As this is said many times even in the Vajrayāna, the path of the perfections is the path common to both sūtra and tantra.

By adding to this shared path the unshared paths of the mantra vehicle—initiations, pledges, vows, the two stages, and their attendant practices—progress to buddhahood is rapid. However, if you cast aside the paths shared with the perfection vehicle, you make a great mistake.

If you do not gain such an understanding, then, each time you gain what seems to be an understanding of an isolated teaching, you will abandon other teachings. When you develop a supposed interest in the higher vehicles, you will abandon in succession the scriptural collections of the Hīnayāna and the perfection vehicle. Even within the mantra vehicle you will abandon the three lower tantras and the like. Thus, you will accumulate the great karmic obstruction of having abandoned the teachings, which has a very grave fruition. In this context, this obstruction readily arises and is in danger of doing so. The source for this is indicated below.

Therefore, having relied upon an excellent protector, solidify your certainty about the way that all the scriptures are causal factors for one person to become a buddha. Then practice those things that you can practice now. Do not use your own incapacity as a reason to repudiate what you cannot actually engage in or turn away from. Rather, think with anticipation, "When will I practice these teachings by actually doing what should be done and turning away from what should not be done?" Work at the causes for such practice—accumulating the collections, clearing away obscurations, and making aspirational prayers. Before long your mental power will become greater and greater, and you will be able to practice all of the teachings that you were previously unable to practice.

The Precious Teacher [Drom-dön-ba] said, "My guru [Atisha] is the one who knows how to bring all of the teachings within a four-sided path."[61] These words are very meaningful.

Because these instructions in the *Lamp for the Path to Enlightenment* guide students by gathering all the key points of the sūtra and mantra vehicles into the path for one person to become a buddha, they have the greatness of producing the certainty that all of the teachings are free of contradiction. **[16]**

B. The greatness of enabling one to understand that all of the scriptures are instructions for practice

In general, only the scriptures of the Conqueror provide the means to achieve all temporary and ultimate benefit and happiness for those who desire liberation, for only the Buddha is free from all error in teaching what is to be adopted and what is to be cast aside. Thus the *Sublime Continuum (Uttara-tantra)* says:[62]

> Because there is no one in this world more wise than the Conqueror—
> No other who knows precisely with omniscience all [phenomena of the world] and the supreme reality—
> [illegible] the collections of sūtra set forth by the [illegible]
> By destroying the system of the Sage, you will harm the sacred teachings.

Therefore, the words of the Conqueror, the precious collections of sūtra and tantra, are the supreme instructions. Nonetheless, since students in this later time will not discover the intent of those words by delving into them on their own without depending on valid commentaries and the personal instructions of excellent beings, the great trailblazers composed treatises and personal instructions that comment on their intended meaning.

Therefore, for something to be a pure personal instruction, it must bestow certain knowledge of the classic texts. No matter how well you learn it, a personal instruction is only something to be cast aside if it cannot bestow certain knowledge of the meaning of the Buddha's words and the great commentaries on their intent, or if it teaches a path incompatible with these.

There are those who conclude that any classic text should be considered only an explanatory teaching, therefore lacking the key points for practice. They hold that there are separate personal instructions that teach the core meanings that are the heart of practice. They then imagine that there are two separate forms of the excellent teaching—a teaching that is explained to you and a teaching that you practice. Know that this attitude precludes the development of great respect for the stainless sūtras and tantras as well as the flawless treatises that comment on their intent. **[17]** Know also that you accumulate the karmic obstruction of abandoning the teaching when you see those classic texts as objects of contempt and say, "Those are merely for promoting one's superficial knowledge and eliminating others' misconceptions; they do not teach the deep meaning."

Therefore, for those who desire liberation, the supreme and authentic instructions are indeed the classic texts. However, due to your limited intelligence and so forth, you may be unable to recognize those texts as the supreme instructions through depending on them alone. Thus, you must seek out personal instructions, thinking, "I will seek certain knowledge of those texts based on the personal instructions of an excellent being." But do not think, "The texts are without substance, since they merely promote a superficial knowledge and eliminate others' misconceptions; yet the personal instructions, since they reveal the deep meaning, are supreme."

The great yogi Chang-chup-rin-chen (Byang-chub-rin-chen) said:

> Concerning instructions, complete mastery does not mean gaining ascertainment of a mere small volume that fits in the palm of one's hand; it means understanding all of the scriptures as instructions for practice.

Also, the great Elder's student Gom-ba-rin-chen-la-ma (sGom-pa-rin-chen-bla-ma) said that he understood all of the texts as instructions for practice by "grinding to dust" all wrong actions of body, speech, and mind during one session of meditation on Atisha's instructions. You too must come to such an understanding.

The Precious Teacher [Drom-dön-ba] said that it is a mistake if, after studying many teachings, you feel a need to look elsewhere for how to practice the teaching. Thus, there are those who have studied many teachings for a long time, but do not know at all how to practice the teaching. When they wish to practice, they must look elsewhere. Their error is in not understanding what I have already explained.

Here, the teachings are as set forth in Vasubandhu's *Treasury of Knowledge (Abhidharma-kośa)*:[63]

> The excellent teaching of the Teacher [Buddha] is twofold:
> Those teachings having a nature of scripture and those having
> a nature of realization.

As this says, there are no more than two types of teaching—scriptural and realized. The scriptural teachings determine the way that you take the teachings in hand, the procedures for practice; the teachings as they are realized are your practice of these procedures in accordance with how you have already determined them. **[18]**

Thus, these two serve as cause and effect. For example, it is like showing a horse the racecourse before you race. Once you have shown it, you then race there. It would be ridiculous to show the horse one racecourse and then race on another. Similarly, why would you determine one thing by means of study and reflection, and then, when you go to practice, practice something else? In this vein, the last of Kamalaśīla's three *Stages of Meditation (Bhāvanā-krama)* says:[64]

> Further, what you meditate on with the wisdom arisen from meditation is just that which you know with the wisdom that has arisen from study and reflection. You do not meditate on something else. This is similar to how you show a horse a racetrack, and then race it there.

Thus, these instructions include, in complete form, all the key points of the path from the scriptures and their commentaries—from how to rely on a teacher through serenity and insight. They then lead you through concise stages of practice in which you engage in stabilizing meditation on that which requires stabilizing meditation, and you analyze with discerning wisdom that which requires analytical meditation.

By doing this, you will understand that all of the scriptures are instructions for practice. Otherwise, you will spend your entire life without discerning wisdom, practicing just some incomplete portion of the path and not the complete corpus. Thus you will not understand that the classic texts are instructions for practice, but you will abandon them, seeing them as merely promoting superficial knowledge and eliminating others' misconceptions. It is evident that the topics explained in the classic texts are, for the most part, only things that require analysis with discerning wisdom. If you cast them aside when you practice, then how can you develop an understanding that sees them as the supreme instructions? If these are not the supreme instructions, then could you find a master whose instructions surpass these?

Therefore, when it becomes clear to you that the profound and vast scriptural collections along with their commentaries are instructions for practice, you will quickly understand that the classic texts of the profound tantric collections along with their commentaries are also instructions for practice. **[19]** You will then become certain that they are the supreme instructions. You will completely overcome the misconceptions that consider these tantras to be only teachings that should be cast aside because they are not actual instructions for practice.

C. **The greatness of enabling one easily to find the Conqueror's intent**

The classic texts—the scriptures along with their commentaries—are the supreme instructions. Yet, even if beginners—persons without extensive training—delve into them, they will not discover their intended meaning without depending on the personal instructions of an excellent being. Even if they find the intended meaning, their search will require a very long time and a great deal of effort. However, if they depend on the personal instructions of a guru, they will easily come to know the intended meaning.

These instructions of the *Lamp for the Path to Enlightenment* will readily bestow certain knowledge of the key points of the Buddha's word and the treatises. I will explain at length how this is done in the appropriate sections below.

D. **The greatness of enabling one to refrain automatically from great wrongdoing**

The *Lotus Sūtra (Sad-dharma-puṇḍarīka-sūtra)*[65] and the *Chapter of the Truth Speaker (Satyaka-parivarta)*[66] explain that all of the Buddha's words directly or indirectly teach methods for becoming a buddha. There are those with misunderstanding who hold that some teachings are methods for becoming a buddha and some teachings are obstacles to becoming a buddha. They then differentiate the words of the Buddha into good and bad, reasonable and unreasonable, and great and small vehicles. Finally, they hold that some teachings are to be cast aside, saying, "A bodhisattva should train in this and should not train in that." Thus, they abandon the teachings.

The *Sūtra Gathering All the Threads (Sarva-vaidalya-saṃgraha-sūtra)*[67] says:

> Mañjuśrī, the karmic obstruction of abandoning the excellent teaching is subtle. Mañjuśrī, whoever distinguishes some of the words spoken by the Tathāgata[68] as good and some as bad abandons the teaching. One who abandons the teaching, by having abandoned it, deprecates the Tathāgata and speaks badly of the community. **[20]**
>
> If you say, "This is reasonable; this is unreasonable," you abandon the teaching. If you say, "This was set forth for the sake of bodhisattvas; this was set forth for the sake of *śrāvakas*," you

> abandon the teaching. If you say, "This was set forth for the sake of *pratyekabuddhas*," you abandon the teaching. If you say, "This is not a training of bodhisattvas," you abandon the teaching.

The fault of having abandoned the teaching is very grave. The *King of Concentrations Sūtra (Samādhi-rāja-sūtra)* says:[69]

> The wrongdoing of one who abandons the collections of sūtras is far greater than that of one who causes the destruction of all of the *stūpas*[70] here in Jambudvīpa. The wrongdoing of one who abandons the collections of sūtras is far greater than that of one who kills arhats equal in number to the sands of the Ganges.

In general, there are many ways that abandoning the teaching can occur. However, the way indicated above is the worst, so take pains to eliminate it. Moreover, since you overcome abandonment by merely gaining certain knowledge of the first two greatnesses as indicated above, you automatically are kept from wrongdoing. Seek such knowledge through extensive reading of the *Chapter of the Truth Speaker* and the *Lotus Sūtra*. In the *Sūtra Gathering All the Threads* you will find other ways of abandoning the teaching.

3

How to Listen to and Explain the Teachings

III. How to listen to and explain the teachings
- A. How to listen to a teaching in which both the teaching and its author are great
  1. Contemplating the benefits of hearing the teaching
  2. Developing reverence for the teaching and the instructor
  3. How you actually listen
     - a. Abandoning the three faults of a vessel
     - b. Relying on the six ideas
- B. How to explain a teaching in which both the teaching and its author are great
  1. Contemplating the benefits of explaining the teaching
  2. Developing reverence for the Teacher and the teaching
  3. With what sort of thoughts and behavior you should explain the teaching
  4. Differentiating between those to whom you should and should not explain the teaching
- C. How a session should be concluded in relation to both hearing and explaining the teaching

---

A. **How to listen to a teaching in which both the teaching and its author are great**

How to listen to the teachings is explained in three parts:

1. Contemplating the benefits of hearing the teaching
2. Developing reverence for the teaching and the instructor
3. How you actually listen

1. Contemplating the benefits of hearing the teaching

The *Verses about Hearing* (*Śruti-varga*) in the *Collection of Indicative Verses* (*Udāna-varga*) says:[71]

> Through hearing, phenomena are understood,
> Through hearing, wrongdoing is overcome,
> Through hearing, what is meaningless is eliminated,
> Through hearing, nirvāṇa is attained. **[21]**

Also:

> Just as someone dwelling inside a house
> Enshrouded in complete darkness
> Has eyes but does not see
> The forms that are there,
>
> So, also, a person born of noble lineage
> Although possessing intelligence,
> Does not know until told
> What is virtuous and what is not.
>
> Just as one with eyes
> Sees forms by using a lamp,
> So through hearing what is virtuous and what is not,
> You will understand what should be done.

Also, the *Garland of Birth Stories* (*Jātaka-mālā*) says:[72]

> Through hearing, you become faithful
> And your delight in virtue becomes steadfast;
> Wisdom arises and delusion will vanish—
> This is worth buying even with your flesh.
>
> Hearing is a lamp that dispels the darkness of delusion,
> The supreme wealth that cannot be carried off by thieves,
> A weapon that vanquishes the foe of confusion;
> It is the best of friends, revealing personal instructions, the techniques of method.
>
> It is the friend who does not desert you in times of need,
> A harmless medicine for the illness of sorrow,
> The supreme battalion to vanquish the troops of great misdeeds,
> It is the best fame, glory, and treasure.
>
> It is the supreme gift when you meet with noble beings.
> Among an assemblage, it delights the wise.

Also:

> The result of hearing is to engage in substantive practice;
> You will be released with little difficulty from the fortress of rebirth.

Develop enthusiasm from the depths of your heart with regard to these benefits of hearing.

Moreover, Asaṅga's *Bodhisattva Levels (Bodhisattva-bhūmi)*[73] says that you should listen with five ideas in mind; that is, with (1) the idea of a jewel, due to the fact that the teachings are rare because buddhas seldom appear nor do their teachings; (2) the idea of an eye, since the wisdom that arises together with hearing the teachings becomes greater and greater; (3) the idea of illumination, since the eye of wisdom that has arisen will see the real nature [emptiness] and the diversity [of all phenomena]; (4) the idea of great benefit, since in the end the teachings bestow the results of nirvāṇa and great enlightenment; **[22]** and (5) the idea of being beyond reproach, since from this very moment you will attain the bliss of meditative serenity and insight, the causes of nirvāṇa and great enlightenment. To contemplate this is to contemplate the benefits of hearing the teaching.

2. **Developing reverence for the teaching and the instructor**

The *Sūtra of Kṣitigarbha (Kṣitigarbha-sūtra)* says:[74]

> Listen to the teachings with one-pointed faith and respect.
> Do not censure or deride the speaker;
> Honor your instructors—
> Develop the idea that they are like a buddha.

Thus, as this says, view the instructor as being like a buddha. Eliminate disrespect; honor him or her with homage and goods by offering a lion throne and the like.

Also, as the *Bodhisattva Levels* sets forth, listen without the afflictions [of arrogance and contempt] and without bringing to mind the five conditions of an instructor.[75] *Being free from arrogance* means to listen with the following six attributes: (1) listening at an appropriate time, (2) showing homage, (3) showing deference, (4) not being resentful, (5) practicing according to the instructor's words, and (6) not looking for the chance to argue. *Being free from contempt* means to respect the teaching and the one who gives it and not to belittle these two. *Not bringing to mind the five conditions* means to cast away the thought, "I will not listen to this person because he or she (1) has fallen from ethical discipline, (2) is of poor lineage,

(3) has an unattractive physical appearance, (4) is inarticulate, (5) or speaks harshly and unpleasantly."

Also, it is as is said in the *Garland of Birth Stories*:[76]

> Stay on a low seat.
> Show the glory of discipline.
> Look with an eye of delight.
> Show respect and one-pointed obeisance,
> As if drinking a nectar of words.
> Show reverence and listen to the teaching
> With clear delight and a mind undefiled,
> Like a patient listening to the words of a doctor.

3. **How you actually listen**

How to listen has two parts:

1. Abandoning the three faults of a vessel
2. Relying on the six ideas

a. **Abandoning the three faults of a vessel**

A vessel might have the following three faults: (1) being upside down; or (2) though held right side up, being dirty; or (3) though clean, having a leaky bottom. If it has these faults, then even though a rainfall from clouds assembled by the deities falls on it, the rain will (1) not go inside; **[23]** or, (2) go inside, but be unable to fulfill its function—to be drunk, etc.—because it is contaminated by filth; or, (3) not be polluted by filth, yet not remain inside and drain away. Similarly, even though you are staying in a place where the teachings are being explained, there is no great purpose in your hearing the teachings if you (1) do not pay attention; or, (2) though paying attention, misunderstand what is heard or listen with a bad motivation such as attachment; or, (3) though lacking these faults, do not solidify the words and meanings taken in at the time of hearing but let them fade due to forgetting them and so forth. Therefore, free yourself from all of these faults.

The remedies for these three faults are indicated in the sūtras in three phrases: "Listen well, thoroughly, and hold it in mind!"[77] Moreover, as the *Bodhisattva Levels* sets forth,[78] listen while wanting to understand everything, staying one-pointed, attentive, with your mind focused, and reflecting with complete composure.

b. **Relying on the six ideas**

1. *Think of yourself as a sick person.* Śāntideva's *Engaging in the Bodhisattva Deeds (Bodhisattva-caryāvatāra)* says:[79]

Since you must follow a doctor's advice,
Even when stricken by ordinary illness,
What need is there to mention those who are constantly
stricken
With the illness of so many faults, attachment and the like?

As Śāntideva says, you have been sick for a long time with the illness of the afflictions such as attachment—an illness that is long-lasting, intractable, and causes strong suffering. Therefore, you must recognize this to be your situation. Ga-ma-pa (Ka-ma-ba) said that if we were not in fact sick, then meditating on our sick condition would be misguided. However, stricken with the virulent and chronic disease of the three mental poisons [attachment, hostility, and ignorance], we are extremely sick, but we are completely unaware that we are ill.

2. *Think of the instructor as a doctor.* For example, when you are stricken by a severe illness such as a wind or bile disorder, you seek a skilled doctor. Upon consulting your doctor, you are greatly delighted and listen to whatever your doctor says, revering him or her respectfully. Likewise, seek in this way a teacher who imparts the teachings. **[24]** Once you have found your teacher, venerate your teacher with respect and do what he or she says. While doing this consider it a privilege, not a burden. For, as the *Verse Summary of the Perfection of Wisdom in Eight Thousand Lines* says:[80]

> Therefore, wise bodhisattvas, who have a strong thought to seek sublime enlightenment, vanquish pride decisively. Just as the sick rely on doctors in order to cure their illnesses, so you should rely on a teacher, applying yourself enthusiastically.

3. *Think of the instructor's explications as medicine.* Just as a sick person has a high regard for the medicine prescribed by a doctor, so too, you should view the instructions and explications that the instructor gives as very important, taking great pains to hold them in high esteem, and not squandering them by lapses such as forgetting them.

4. *Think of earnest practice as the way to cure your disease.* Sick persons know that their illness cannot be cured without taking the medicine prescribed by the doctor. They then take the medicine. Likewise, earnestly engage in practice after you have seen that you cannot vanquish such afflictions as attachment without putting into practice the instructions given by the instructor. Do not devote yourself just to piling up words in great numbers without engaging in practice.

Moreover, one or two doses of medicine will not do anything at all for lepers who have lost their hands and feet. Similarly, to put the meaning of the instructions into practice just once or twice is insufficient for us who from beginningless time have been stricken with the virulent illness of the afflictions. Therefore, analyze with discerning wisdom the entirety of every aspect of the path and make effort that is like a river's current. As the great master Candragomin's *Praise of Confession (Deśanā-stava)* says:[81]

> Our minds are constantly confused;
> We have been ill for a very long time.
> What is achieved by the lepers
> Who have lost their arms and legs and only occasionally take medicine? **[25]**

Thus, the idea of yourself as a sick person is extremely important, for if you have this idea, the other ideas will follow. However, if this idea is mere words, then you will not put the meaning of the instructions into practice in order to clear away the afflictions, and you will have been merely listening to these instructions. This is like sick persons who seek out a doctor. If they apply themselves only to getting the medicine prescribed, but not to taking it, they will not be freed from their illness. For, as the *King of Concentrations Sūtra* says:[82]

> Some people are ill, their bodies tormented;
> For many years there is not even temporary relief.
> Afflicted with illness for a very long time,
> They seek a doctor, in search of a cure.
>
> Searching about again and again,
> They at last find a physician with skill and knowledge.
> Treating the patients with compassion,
> The doctor gives medicine, saying, "Here, take this."
>
> This medicine is plentiful, good, and valuable.
> It will cure the illness, but the patients do not take it.
> This is not a shortcoming of the doctor, nor the fault of the medicine;
> It is just the fault of those who are ill.
>
> Likewise, after you have left the householder's life for the sake of these teachings
> And have come to know the powers, meditative stabilizations, and faculties,
> How can you attain nirvāṇa without making effort
> At meditation, an effort at what is right?

Also:

> I have explained this very good teaching.
> Yet if you, having heard it, do not practice correctly,
> Then just like a sick person holding on to a bag of medicine,
> Your illness cannot be cured.

Also, Śāntideva's *Engaging in the Bodhisattva Deeds* says:[83]

> Physically, put these instructions into practice;
> What will be accomplished by mere talk?
> Will sick persons be helped
> By merely reading a medical treatise?

Therefore, "earnest practice" in the statement, "Think of earnest practice as what clears away the illness of the afflictions," refers to putting into practice the lessons that a teacher has imparted to you on what should be adopted and what should be cast aside. To do that, you need to know the lessons; for this, you need study. The purpose of knowing them through study is to do them. Therefore, it is vital to put the meaning of what you have heard into practice as much as you are able. **[26]** In this vein, the *Verses about Hearing* says:[84]

> Even if you have heard a great deal,
> If you are not well restrained by ethical discipline,
> Then because of your ethical discipline you are scorned,
> And your hearing is not excellent.
>
> Even though you have heard very little,
> If you are well restrained by ethical discipline,
> Then because of your ethical discipline you are praised,
> And your hearing is excellent.
>
> Persons who have not heard much
> And are also not well restrained by ethical discipline
> Are scorned on both accounts,
> And their conduct is not excellent.
>
> Those who have heard a great deal
> And are also well restrained by ethical discipline
> Are praised on both accounts,
> And their conduct is excellent.

Also:

> Though you might understand the heart of the scriptures
> through hearing,
> And might know the core of meditative concentration,
> Such hearing and knowledge are of little import
> If wildly you engage in coarse behavior.

> Those who delight in the teachings taught by noble beings
> And practice accordingly with body and speech,
> Who have patience, delight their friends, and are restrained—
> They will attain the perfection of hearing and knowledge.

Also the *Exhortation to Wholehearted Resolve (Adhyāśaya-saṃcodana-sūtra)* says:[85]

> The foolish are sorrowful at the time of death,
> Saying, "My practice was poor. Now what is to be done?"
> Not having found depth, they will suffer greatly;
> Such are faults of delighting in just the words.

Also:

> Like an actor before an audience watching a show
> Or like describing the good qualities of someone else who is a
> hero,
> You fall from earnest practice yourself—
> Such are the faults of delighting in just the words.

Also:

> The husk of a sugarcane stalk has no substance at all,
> The taste that delights is inside.
> Through eating the husk,
> The delicious taste of molasses cannot be found.
>
> Just as it is with the husk, so it is with the words;
> The "taste" is in contemplating the meaning.
> Therefore, give up delighting in just the words,
> Always be conscientious, and reflect on the meaning. **[27]**

5. Think of the Tathāgatas as excellent beings. Develop respect by remembering the one who set forth the teaching, the Bhagavan [Buddha].

6. Wish that the teaching will endure for a long time. Think, "How wonderful if, in dependence upon studying such teachings, the Conqueror's teachings would remain in the world for a long time!"

Furthermore, when you explain or hear the teachings, if your mind and the teachings remain separate, then whatever is explained will be inconsequential. Hence, listen in such a way that you determine how these teachings apply to your mind. For example, when you want to find out whether or not there is some smudge, dirt, or whatever, on your face, you look in a mirror and then remove whatever is there. Similarly, when you listen to the teachings, your faults such as misconduct and attachment appear in the mirror of the teachings. At that time, you regret that your mind has become like this, and you then work to clear away those faults and establish good qualities. Hence, you must train in the teachings. The *Garland of Birth Stories*:[86]

> When I see the form of my misconduct
> Clear in the mirror of the teachings
> I develop a feeling of regret
> And turn my mind toward the teachings.

With this statement Saudasa requested that Prince Sutasoma bestow the teachings. Thereupon, the bodhisattva prince, knowing Saudasa's state of mind—that is, knowing that Saudasa had become suitable for hearing the teachings—gave him the teachings.

In brief, develop the spirit of enlightenment, thinking:

> For the sake of all living beings, I will attain buddhahood. In order to attain this, I must train in its causes; for this, I must know those causes. For this, it is evident that I must hear the teachings. Therefore, I will listen to the teachings.

Remember the benefits of hearing. Eliminate the faults of a vessel, and so forth, and listen with great delight.

B. **How to explain a teaching in which both the teaching and its author are great**

There are four parts to the explanation:

1. Contemplating the benefits of explaining the teaching
2. Developing reverence for the Teacher and the teaching
3. With what sort of thoughts and behavior you should explain the teaching
4. Differentiating between those to whom you should and should not explain the teaching

1. **Contemplating the benefits of explaining the teaching [28]**

It is very beneficial to impart the teachings without concern for worldly things—profit, honor, fame, and the like. For, as the *Exhortation to Wholehearted Resolve* says:[87]

> Maitreya, there are twenty benefits of the generosity with which you give a gift of the teaching without concern for material things, profit, or honor. What are the twenty? They are as follows. You will come to have (1) recollection; (2) intelligence; (3) understanding; (4) stability; (5) wisdom; (6) supramundane wisdom; (7) little desire; (8) little hatred; and (9) little ignorance. Also, (10) demons

> will not find an opportunity to harm you; (11) the *bhagavan* buddhas will think of you as a precious, only child; (12) nonhumans will guard you; (13) deities will bestow charisma and power on you; (14) enemies will find no opportunity to harm you; (15) friends will remain steadfast; (16) your words will be trusted; (17) you will attain fearlessness; (18) you will have abundant happiness; (19) you will be praised by the wise; and (20) your gift of the teaching will be worthy of remembrance.

Develop belief in the benefits of explaining the teachings from the depths of your heart as they are set forth in many collections of sūtra.

With regard to the fourth benefit above, "you will come to have stability," it is translated in the new translation of Śāntideva's *Compendium of Trainings (Śikṣā-samuccaya)* as, "you will come to have belief," and in some old translations as, "you will come to have diligence."

2. **Developing reverence for the Teacher [Śākyamuni Buddha] and the teaching**

When the Bhagavan [Buddha] set forth the Mother of Conquerors [the *Prajñāpāramitā*], he performed such acts of respect as arranging the throne himself.[88] **[29]** Likewise, since the teachings are respected even by buddhas, when you explain the teachings, be very respectful of the teachings and the Teacher [Śākyamuni Buddha] as well, remembering his good qualities and kindness.

3. **With what sort of thoughts and behavior you should explain the teaching**

With regard to your thoughts, develop the five ideas set forth in the *Questions of Sāgaramati Sūtra (Sāgaramati-paripṛcchā-sūtra)*—think of yourself as a doctor, the teachings as medicine, those listening to the teachings as sick persons, and the *tathāgatas* as excellent beings, and wish that the teachings remain for a long time.[89]

Cultivate love for those who have gathered to listen. Give up jealousy that fears the superiority of others; the laziness of procrastination; the dispiritedness of being tired due to explaining something again and again; praising yourself and listing the faults of others; stinginess with regard to explaining the teaching; and concern for material things such as food and clothing. Then think, "Just this merit from teaching in order that others and I attain buddhahood is a favorable condition for my happiness."

With regard to your behavior, wash and make yourself clean. Then, after putting on unsoiled clothing, sit upon a teaching seat and cushion in a place that is clean and attractive. It is said in the *Questions of Sāgaramati Sūtra* that if you recite the mantra for overcoming demons,[90] then demons and deities of the demon class within a radius of one hundred leagues will not come. Even if they do come, they will be unable to cause difficulties. Therefore, recite that mantra. Then, with a radiant face, teach, using examples, reasons, and scriptural citations and other accessories for ascertaining the meaning.

The *Lotus Sūtra* says:[91]

> The learned always give without jealousy
> Sweet-sounding teachings with manifold meanings.
> Having thoroughly cast aside laziness as well,
> They are not dispirited to repeat teachings again and again.
> The learned give up all that is repugnant
> And cultivate the power of love toward those around them.
> Day and night they cultivate the supreme teachings. **[30]**
> Using millions of examples, the learned
> Bring joy and delight to those listening to their teachings.
> They never have the slightest desire for worldly gain:
> Not thinking of sustenance—hard or soft foods, or drink,
> Of clothing, or bedding, or religious robes,
> Or even of medicine to cure an illness—
> They ask nothing at all from those listening to their teachings.
> Rather, the learned always think, "May I myself
> And all living beings achieve buddhahood," and,
> "Whatever teaching I impart in order to help the world
> Is a completely favorable condition for my happiness."

4. **Differentiating between those to whom you should and should not explain the teaching**

Do not explain the teachings without being requested to do so; as Guṇaprabha's *Sūtra on the Discipline (Vinaya-sūtra)* says,[92] "It should not be done without request." Even when requested, it is necessary to investigate to see whether or not the potential student is suitable to receive the teachings. And even when not requested, it is appropriate to explain the teachings to someone only if you know them to be a suitable recipient.

Concerning this, the *King of Concentrations Sūtra* says:[93]

> Should someone request you
> To bestow the teachings, first say,
> "I am not trained extensively."
> Then say, "You are knowledgeable and wise.
> How can I explain the teachings
> To one as great as you?"

> Do not impart the teachings casually,
> But only after you have investigated whether the listener is a suitable recipient.
> If you know that the listener is a suitable recipient,
> Explain the teachings even without a request.

Further, Guṇaprabha's *Sūtra on the Discipline* says:[94]

> While standing, do not explain the teachings to one who is seated; while seated, do not explain the teachings to one who is lying down; while you are seated on a low seat, do not explain the teachings to someone on a high seat. It is the same also with regard to bad and good seats. Do not explain them to someone walking in front while you walk behind. Do not explain them to someone walking on the path while you walk on the edge. **[31]** Do not explain them to someone whose head is covered or whose upper or lower robe is pulled up, whose upper robe is folded and placed on the shoulder, or whose arms are crossed in front with the hands on the shoulders, or whose hands are clasped behind the neck. Do not explain them to someone with a topknot, wearing a hat, wearing a tiara, or whose head is wrapped in cloth. Do not explain the teachings to someone riding an elephant or a horse, to someone sitting in a sedan chair or carriage, or to someone wearing shoes or boots. Do not explain them to someone holding a staff, an umbrella, a spear, a sword, or other arms, or to someone wearing armor.

It is suitable to explain the teachings to those who are the opposite of these. Further, these instructions apply to persons who are not sick.

C. **How a session should be concluded in relation to both hearing and explaining the teaching**

With strong aspiration dedicate the virtues that have arisen from explaining and hearing the teachings to your temporary and final objectives.

If you explain and listen to the teachings in such a manner, then you will unquestionably receive the aforesaid benefits even from a single session. You will clear away all the karmic obstructions that have accumulated through not taking to heart the instructions on hearing and explaining the teachings and that result from not respecting the teachings and the teacher and so forth. Further, you stop new accumulation of these obstructions. Also, insofar as you have taken to heart this way of explaining and listening to the teaching, the instructions that are explained will benefit your mind. In general, after all the former excellent beings realized this, they practiced earnestly; in particular, the former gurus in the lineage of these instructions made very earnest and great effort in this activity.

This is a great instruction. You will not transform your mind without being certain about this. Without that certainty, no matter how extensively you explain the profound teachings, these very teachings often serve to assist your afflictions, like a helpful deity that becomes a demon. Consequently, it is said, "If you mistake the date from the first day of the lunar month, the error lasts until the fifteenth day." Thus, those with intelligence should work at this way of successfully hearing and explaining the teachings and should have at least a portion of these qualifications every time that they explain or listen to the teachings. **[32]** This is the most important prerequisite for teaching these instructions.

Wary of excessive verbiage, I have condensed the most important points. Understand them more extensively by using other sources. This concludes the explanation of the prerequisites for the instructions.

4

Relying on the Teacher

IV. How to lead students with the actual instructions
- A. How to rely on the teacher, the root of the path
  - 1. A somewhat elaborate explanation for developing certain knowledge
    - a. The defining characteristics of the teacher to be relied upon
    - b. The defining characteristics of the student who relies upon the teacher
    - c. How the student relies upon the teacher
      - 1) How to rely in thought
        - a) A general indication of the attitudes needed to rely on the teacher
        - b) In particular, training in faith, the root
        - c) Remembering the teacher's kindness and being respectful
      - 2) How to rely in practice
    - d. The benefits of relying on the teacher
    - e. The faults of not relying on the teacher
    - f. A summary of the meaning of the previous five parts

IV. How to lead students with the actual instructions [33]

The actual instructions are explained in two parts:

1. How to rely on the teacher (Chapters 4–6)
2. How the students train their minds after having relied on the teacher (Chapters 7 and on)

A. How to rely on the teacher, the root of the path

There are two parts to the explanation of how to rely on the teacher:

1. A somewhat elaborate explanation for developing certain knowledge (Chapter 4)

2. A brief indication of how to sustain the meditation (Chapters 5–6)

1. **A somewhat elaborate explanation for developing certain knowledge**

Atisha's *Digest (Hṛdaya-nikṣepa-nāma)* states:[95]

> One who abides in the lineage of the Mahāyāna
> Has relied on an excellent teacher.

Also Döl-wa's (Dol-ba) arrangement of *Bo-do-wa's Method of Explaining* (*Po to ba'i gsung sgros*) says:

> Of all the personal instructions, "Do not give up the excellent teacher" is the prime instruction.

Thus, the excellent teacher is the source of all temporary happiness and certain goodness, beginning with the production of a single good quality and the reduction of a single fault in a student's mind and eventually encompassing all the knowledge beyond that. Therefore, the way you initially rely on the teacher is important, for the *Scriptural Collection of the Bodhisattvas (Bodhisattva-piṭaka)* states:[96]

> In short, attaining and bringing to completion all the bodhisattva deeds, and, likewise, attaining and bringing to completion the perfections, levels, forbearances, concentrations, superknowledges, retentions of teachings heard, dedications, aspirational prayers, confidence to speak, and all the qualities of a buddha are contingent upon the guru. The guru is the root from which they arise. The guru is the source and creator from which they are produced. **[34]** The guru increases them. They depend upon the guru. The guru is their cause.

Also, Bo-do-wa said:

> For attaining freedom there is nothing more important than the guru. It is sufficient to learn the activities of this life by watching others, but you will not learn them well without an instructor. Likewise, without a guru, how can we succeed in traveling to a place where we have never been, having just been reborn from a miserable realm?

a. **The defining characteristics of the teacher to be relied upon**

Generally, in the scriptures and commentaries many defining characteristics of the teacher are taught from the viewpoint of the individual vehicles. However, the following is a description of a teacher who instructs you in the stages on the paths of the three persons of different capacities and guides you to the Mahāyāna, which is the path to buddhahood. With respect to this, Maitreya says in his *Ornament for the Mahāyāna Sūtras (Mahāyāna-sūtrālaṃkāra)*:[97]

> Rely on a Mahāyāna teacher who is disciplined, serene, thoroughly pacified;
> Has good qualities surpassing those of the students; is energetic; has a wealth of scriptural knowledge;
> Possesses loving concern; has thorough knowledge of reality and skill in instructing disciples;
> And has abandoned dispiritedness.

Thus Maitreya says that a student must rely on a teacher who has these ten qualities.

It is said that those who have not disciplined themselves have no basis for disciplining others. Therefore, gurus who intend to discipline others' minds must first have disciplined their own. How should they have been disciplined? It is not helpful for them to have done just any practice, and then have the result designated as a good quality of knowledge. They need a way to discipline the mind that accords with the general teachings of the Conqueror. The three precious trainings are definitely such a way. Therefore, Maitreya indicated them with these three terms: "disciplined," "serene," and "thoroughly pacified."

With respect to what Maitreya said, "disciplined" refers to the training in ethical discipline. The *Sūtra on the Vows of Individual Liberation (Prātimokṣa-sūtra)* states:[98] **[35]**

> These vows of individual liberation
> Are the bridle set with sharp nails.
> With constant effort they are fit
> For the difficult-to-rein horse of the straying mind.

Also the *Exegesis of the Discipline (Vinaya-vibhaṅga)* states:[99]

> This is the bridle for undisciplined disciples.

As is implied above, the senses pursue improper objects and, like wild horses, lead you to engage in unsuitable actions. Just as a trainer tames a wild horse with a good bridle, so too teachers learn ethical discipline to control their senses and to turn toward suitable actions with great effort. Hence, teachers have "disciplined" their minds, which are like wild horses.

"Serene" refers to having accomplished the training of meditative concentration. Meditative concentration is a mental state in which the mind remains peacefully withdrawn. This is achieved by means of a reliance on mindfulness and vigilance in your ethical discipline, turning away from wrongdoing and engaging in good activities.

"Thoroughly pacified" refers to having accomplished the training of wisdom. This is done by specifically analyzing the meaning of reality in dependence on meditative serenity, wherein the mind becomes serviceable.

However, to have only the good qualities of knowledge that come from disciplining the mind with the three trainings is not sufficient. Teachers must also have the good qualities of scriptural learning. Therefore, "wealth of scriptural knowledge" refers to being erudite concerning the three scriptural collections and the like. Geshe Dromdön-ba (dGe-bshes ['Brom]-ston-pa) said that when the "gurus of the Mahāyāna" give an explanation, they must cause their students to have a deep understanding. When they are putting the teachings into practice, they must demonstrate what is helpful at a time when the teaching is on the wane, and what is useful in the situation at hand.

"Knowledge of reality" refers to a special training in wisdom—the knowledge of the selflessness of phenomena. In another way, it is said to be best if the teachers have a perception of reality; but, if they do not have it, it is acceptable for them to know reality through scripture and reasoning.

Although teachers are endowed with these good qualities of scriptural learning and knowledge, it is not enough for them to have good qualities that are equal to or lower than those of their students; instead, they need qualities that surpass those of their students. The *Verses about Friends (Mitra-varga)* says:[100]

> People degenerate by relying on those inferior to themselves;
> By relying on equals, they stay the same;
> By relying on those superior, they attain excellence; **[36]**
> Thus rely on those who are superior to yourself.
>
> If you rely on whomever is superior—thoroughly pacified
> And endowed with ethical discipline
> And exceeding wisdom—
> You will become superior even to those who are superior.

Pu-chung-wa (Phu-chung-ba) said, "When I hear the stories of excellent persons, I emulate them." Ta-shi (mTha'-bzhi) said, "I imitate the elders of the Ra-dreng (Ra-sgreng) monastic community."

Thus you must emulate those whose good qualities surpass your own.

These six qualities—being disciplined, serene, and thoroughly pacified, having good qualities that surpass those of the students, the wealth of knowledge from studying many scriptures, and thorough knowledge of reality—are the good qualities obtained for oneself. The remaining qualities—being energetic, having skill in instruction, possessing loving concern, and abandoning dispiritedness—are the good qualities for looking after others.

Further, it says:[101]

> Sages do not wash away sins with water,
> They do not clear away beings' suffering with their hands,
> They do not transfer their own knowledge to others;
> They liberate by teaching the truth of reality.

Thus, buddhas perform no action—such as "washing away others' sins with water"—other than looking after others by accurately showing them the path.

Among the four qualities of looking after others, "skill in instructing disciples" refers to being both skilled in the process of leading disciples and adept at causing them to understand. "Possessing loving concern" refers to having a pure motivation for giving the teachings. That is, the teacher teaches with a motivation of love and compassion and does not look for gain, respect, and so on. Bo-do-wa said to Jen-nga-wa (sPyan-snga-ba), "Son of Li-mo, however many teachings I have explained, I have never taken pleasure in even a single thanks. All beings are helpless." A teacher should be like this.

"Energetic" refers to constant delight in others' welfare. "Has abandoned dispiritedness" refers to never being tired of giving an explanation again and again—to bearing the hardships of explaining.

Bo-do-wa said:

> These five qualities—loving concern, knowledge of reality, and the three trainings—are foremost. My master Shang-tsün (Zhang-btsun) is not very learned with regard to all the scriptures and cannot withstand dispiriting circumstances. Therefore, he does not even thank those who help him. However, since he has these five qualities, he is helpful to whomever is in his presence. **[37]** Nyen-dön (gNyan-ston) does not have any skill in speech at all. Even when giving a single dedication of an offering, he can only think, "None of these people here understands what I am saying." But, as he has the five qualities, he is helpful to whomever enters his presence.

This being the case, those who achieve their own livelihood by praising or explaining the good qualities of the trainings, while not striving diligently to practice them, are not suitable to be teachers. That sort of meaningless praise is only words. It is similar to when someone who diligently seeks sandalwood asks one who makes a living by explaining the good qualities of sandalwood, "Do you have any sandalwood?" and that person replies, "No."

As the *King of Concentrations Sūtra* states:[102]

> In later times there will be
> Many monks without vows.
> Wanting to say, "I am learned,"
> They will praise ethical discipline,
> But will not strive diligently at their own ethical discipline.

Having also said this concerning concentration, wisdom, and liberation, the *King of Concentrations Sūtra* states:

> Some people express
> The good qualities of sandalwood
> Saying, "Sandalwood is like this:
> It is the pleasant aspect of incense."
> Then some other people
> Might ask them, "Do you possess
> A bit of that sandalwood
> Which you so praise?"
> They then reply, "I do not have
> The incense that I praise
> To gain my livelihood."
> Just so, in later times there will arise
> Monks who do not strive at yoga
> And make a living by praising ethical discipline.
> They will have no ethical discipline.

The sūtra states the same for the remaining three qualities—concentration, wisdom, and liberation.

The guru who helps you to achieve liberation is the foundation of your deepest aspiration. Therefore, you who wish to rely on a guru should understand these defining characteristics and strive to seek one who has them. Also, those who wish to have students should understand these characteristics and strive to possess them.

Question: **[38]** Because this is a degenerate time, it is difficult to find a teacher who has these good qualities in their entirety. Therefore, what should we do if we do not find such a teacher?

Reply: The *Tantra Requested by Subāhu (Subāhu-paripṛcchā-tantra)* states:[103]

> Just as a chariot with one wheel
> Will not go down the path even though it has a horse,
> So too, without assistants for meditation,
> People will not gain attainments.
> These assistants should have intelligence, a good appearance,
> great purity,
> Be of reputable lineage, and inclined toward the teachings.
> They should have great confidence, perseverance, and have
> disciplined the senses.
> They should speak pleasantly, be generous and compassionate,
> Forbear hunger, thirst, and the afflictions,
> And not worship other deities and brahmins.
> They should be focused, adept, grateful,
> And have faith in the three jewels.
> Since those who have all such good qualities
> Are very rare in this age of strife,
> Mantra practitioners should rely on an assistant who has
> One half, one quarter, or an eighth of these qualities.

Thus it says that assistants should have these defining characteristics in their entirety, or at least one eighth of these. It is explained in Döl-wa's arrangement of *Bo-do-wa's Method of Explaining* that the great Elder [Atisha] said, "It is also the same with respect to the guru." Therefore, accept as the defining characteristics of a guru a minimum of one eighth of all the defining characteristics set forth here, combining those that are easy to acquire with those that are difficult to acquire.

b. **The defining characteristics of the student who relies upon the teacher**

Āryadeva states in his *Four Hundred Stanzas (Catuḥ-śataka)*:[104]

> It is said that one who is nonpartisan, intelligent, and diligent
> Is a vessel for listening to the teachings.
> The good qualities of the instructor do not appear otherwise
> Nor do those of fellow listeners.

Āryadeva says that one who is endowed with the three qualities is suitable to listen to the teachings. He also says that if you have all these qualities, the good qualities of one who instructs you in the teachings will appear as good qualities, not as faults. In addition, he says that to such a fully qualified person the good qualities of fellow listeners will also appear as good qualities and not as faults. It is stated in Candrakīrti's commentary[105] that if you, the listener, do not have all these defining characteristics of a suitable recipient of the teachings, then the influence of your own faults will cause even an extremely pure teacher who instructs you in the teachings to appear to have faults. **[39]** Furthermore, you will consider the faults of the one who explains the teachings to be good qualities. Therefore, although you might find a teacher who has all the defining characteristics, it may be difficult to recognize their presence. Thus, it is necessary for the disciple to have these three characteristics in their entirety in order to recognize that the teacher has all the defining characteristics and in order then to rely on that teacher.

With respect to these three characteristics, "nonpartisan" means not to take sides. If you are partisan, you will be obstructed by your bias and will not recognize good qualities. Because of this, you will not discover the meaning of good teachings. As Bhāvaviveka states in his *Heart of the Middle Way (Madhyamaka-hṛdaya)*:[106]

> Through taking sides the mind is distressed,
> Whereby you will never know peace.

"Taking sides" is to have attachment for your own religious system and hostility toward others'. Look for it in your own mind and then discard it, for it says in the *Bodhisattva Vows of Liberation (Bodhisattva-prātimokṣa)*:[107]

> After giving up your own assertions, respect and abide in the texts of the abbot and master.

Question: Is just that one characteristic enough?

Reply: Though nonpartisan, if you do not have the mental force to distinguish between correct paths of good explanation and counterfeit paths of false explanation, you are not fit to listen to the teachings. Therefore, you must have the intelligence that understands both of these. By this account you will give up what is unproductive, and then adopt what is productive.

Question: Are just these two enough?

Reply: Though having both of these, if, like a drawing of a person who is listening to the teachings, you are inactive, you are not fit to listen to the teachings. Therefore, you must have great diligence.

Candrakīrti's commentary says,[108] "After adding the three qualities of the student to the two qualities of being focused and having respect for the teaching and its instructor, there are a total of five qualities."

Then, these five qualities can be reduced to four:

(1) striving very diligently at the teaching,
(2) focusing the mind well when listening to the teaching,
(3) having great respect for the teaching and its instructor, and
(4) discarding bad explanations and retaining good explanations.

Having intelligence is the favorable condition that gives rise to these four. Being nonpartisan gets rid of the unfavorable condition of taking sides.

Investigate whether these attributes that make you suitable to be led by a guru are complete; **[40]** if they are complete, cultivate delight. If they are incomplete, you must make an effort to obtain the causes that will complete them before your next life. Therefore, know the qualities of a listener. If you do not know their defining characteristics, you will not engage in an investigation to see whether they are complete, and will thereby ruin your great purpose.

c. **How the student relies upon the teacher**

One who has these qualifications of a suitable recipient of the teachings should investigate well whether a guru has the requisite characteristics as explained above. Then this student should receive the teaching's kind words from a qualified teacher. Even so, the biographies of Geshe Drom-dön-ba and Sung-pu-wa (gSung-phu-ba) are not in accord with each other. Sung-pu-wa had many gurus and listened to any correct explanation. Thus, when coming from Kham (Khams), he even listened to a lay practitioner explaining the teachings alongside the road. His disciples said that this was an inappropriate way to receive the teachings, to which he replied, "Do not say that. I have received two benefits."

Geshe Drom-dön-ba had few gurus—not more than five. Bo-do-wa and Gom-ba-rin-chen, themselves gurus, discussed which of these two ways was better. They agreed that Geshe Drom-dön-ba's way was better in these times when those with untrained minds still see faults in the teacher and lose faith. What they have said seems to be very true. Therefore, you should have few teachers.

In general, a teacher is someone from whom you have received the teaching's kind words; specifically, a teacher is someone who skillfully guides you with the instructions of all the paths in their entirety.

1) **How to rely in thought**

How to rely on the teacher in thought is explained in three parts:

1. A general indication of the attitudes needed to rely on the teacher
2. In particular, training in faith, the root
3. Remembering the teacher's kindness and being respectful

a) **A general indication of the attitudes needed to rely on the teacher**

The *Array of Stalks Sūtra (Gaṇḍa-vyūha-sūtra)*[109] states that you should respect and serve the teacher with nine attitudes. This includes the key points of all the attitudes that you should have in order to rely on the teacher. If these are further condensed, four attitudes remain. They are as follows: **[41]**

1) The attitude which is like the dutiful child. This means to give up your independence and submit to the guru's will. Dutiful children do not initiate an action on their own, but instead, looking at their parents' facial expressions, submit to their will and then do what they say. Look to the teacher in this way. The *Sūtra on the Concentration Which Perceives the Buddha of the Present Face to Face (Pratyutpanna-buddha-saṃmukhāvasthita-samādhi-sūtra)* states:[110]

> Students who rely properly on the teacher should always give up their self-assertiveness and instead act in accordance with the will of the teacher.

This refers to a fully qualified teacher; it is said that you should not let just anyone lead you around by the nose.

2) The attitude which is like a diamond. This means to make the relationship between teacher and student close and stable, not to be split apart by anyone—demons, bad friends, and the like. The same sūtra states:[111]

> And forsake fickleness in close relationships and changeability in facial expressions.

3) The attitude which is like the earth. This means to take on all the responsibilities of the guru's activities and not become dispirited by any of the responsibilities asked of you. It is as Bo-do-wa told Jen-nga-wa's monks,

> You have met with my *geshe* (*dge-bshes*) who is clearly a bodhisattva,[112] and have practiced in accordance with his words. You have great merit! Now let this be a privilege, not a burden.

4) How to assume responsibilities. This itself consists of six attitudes. The first, an attitude like the foothills, means that any suffering that might arise does not sway you. When Jen-nga-wa was staying in Ruk-ba (Rug-pa), Gom-ba-yön-den-bar's (sGom-pa-yon-ten-'bar) health declined due to the great cold. He then sought the advice of the venerable Shön-nu-drak (gZhon-nu-grags) as to whether he should leave. Shön-nu-drak replied, "We have stayed many times in Indra's palace, a comfortable residence with good material necessities. Only today do you have the experience of relying on a Mahāyāna teacher and listening to the teachings. Therefore, stay where you are, as is proper!"

The second, an attitude like a worldly servant, means to perform even the worst tasks in their entirety without wavering. For example, the scholar [Atisha] and all his translators had to stay in Tsang in an area of sewage and mud. Geshe Drom-dön-ba took off all his clothes and cleaned up the filth. **[42]** He covered the area with dry white earth, from where no one knows. He even built a [stone and earth] maṇḍala in front of the Elder Atisha.[113] Therefore, the Elder exclaimed, "*Ah-ray!*[114] I had one like you in India, too."

The third, an attitude like a sweeper, means to eliminate completely all pride and feelings of superiority, and consider yourself to be lower than your guru. As Geshe Drom-dön-ba said, "The water of good qualities does not collect on the heights of pride," and as Jen-nga-wa said, "In the planting time of spring, look at whether the green growth comes from the high mountain peaks or from the low valleys."

The fourth, an attitude like a foundation, means to take on even the heavy responsibilities of the most arduous activities of your guru with pleasure.

The fifth, an attitude like a dog, means not to get angry even when your guru despises or berates you. For example, each time that Dö-lung-ba (sTod-lung-pa) met with Geshe Lha-so (dGe-bshes lHa-bzo), Dö-lung-ba would berate him. Lha-so's disciple Nyak-mo-wa (Nyag-mo-ba) said, "This master hates us, both teacher and students!" To which Geshe Lha-so replied, "Do you think that he is berating me? To me it seems like I am being blessed by Heruka each time he does this." Also the *Perfection of Wisdom in Eight Thousand Lines (Aṣṭa-sāhasrikā)* says:[115]

> Even if the instructors of the teachings seem to despise and to ignore those who want their teachings, do not challenge them. Persist tirelessly and respectfully, and diligently seek the teachings.

The sixth, an attitude like a ferry, means not to tire of deeds for your guru's sake no matter how many times you engage in your guru's activities.

b) **In particular, training in faith, the root**

The *Formulae of the Three Jewels' Blaze (Ratnolka-dhāraṇī)* states:[116]

> Faith is the prerequisite of all good qualities—
> A procreator of them, like a mother
> Who then protects and increases them.
> It clears away doubts, frees you from the four rivers [ignorance, attachment, craving, and wrong views],
> And establishes you in the prosperous city of happiness and goodness.
>
> Faith cuts through gloom and clarifies the mind. **[43]**
> It eliminates pride and is the root of respect.
> It is a jewel and a treasure.
> Like hands, it is the basis of gathering virtue.
> It is the best of feet for going to liberation.

Also the *Ten Teaching Sūtra (Daśa-dharmaka-sūtra)* states:[117]

> Faith is the best of vehicles,
> Definitely delivering you into buddhahood.
> Therefore, persons of intelligence
> Rely on the guidance of faith.
>
> Virtues will not arise
> In people who have no faith,
> Just as green sprouts do not grow
> From seeds scorched by fire.

Thus, in light of what you gain when it is present and what you lose when it is not present, faith is the basis of all good qualities.

Geshe Drom-dön-ba said to Atisha, "In Tibet there are many who are meditating and practicing, yet they are not attaining any special good qualities." The Elder said, "All the significant and insignificant good qualities that pertain to the Mahāyāna arise from relying on a guru. You Tibetans only think of gurus as being common persons. How can good qualities arise?" Then again, when someone asked the Elder in a loud voice, "Atisha, please give an instruction," he laughed. "Ha, ha. My hearing is very good. For me to give personal instructions you need faith, faith, faith!" Thus, faith is extremely important.

In general, faith is of many types—faith in the three jewels, faith in karma and its effects, faith in the four noble truths. However, here we are speaking of faith in the guru. With regard to how disciples should view their gurus, the *Tantra Bestowing the Initiation of Vajrapāṇi (Vajrapāṇy-abhiṣeka-mahā-tantra)* says:[118]

> If you would ask, O Lord of Secrets, how disciples should view masters, then I would answer that they should view them just as they view the Bhagavan.
>
> If the disciples view their masters in this way,
> They will always cultivate virtues.
> They will become buddhas
> And benefit the entire world.

In the Mahāyāna sūtras as well it is taught that you must think of the guru as being the Teacher. The texts on discipline state this as well, and the meaning of their statements is as follows. When you recognize someone to be a buddha, you will not discern faults in that person, and you will pay attention to his or her good qualities. **[44]** Likewise, completely cast aside your conception of faults in the guru, and train yourself to discern the guru's good qualities. That is, do as it states in the tantra cited above, the *Tantra Bestowing the Initiation of Vajrapāṇi*:[119]

> Keep the masters' good qualities in mind
> Never seize upon their faults.
> Keeping their good qualities in mind, you will reach attainments.
> Seizing upon their faults, you will not.

Your guru might have good qualities for the most part, and have only slight faults. If you examine your guru for those faults, this will block your own attainments. Whereas, even in the case of a guru who mostly has faults, you will give rise to your own attainments if you train in faith by focusing on the good qualities while not looking for the faults.

Therefore, once someone is your guru, whether he or she has small or great faults, contemplate the disadvantages of examining for his or her faults. Repeatedly think about eliminating that tendency, and then stop it. Even when the influence of factors such as an overabundance of afflictions or a lack of conscientiousness leads you to conceive a fault in your guru, take pains to confess this and restrain yourself from ever doing it again. Once you have done this, the influence of that conception will gradually diminish.

Moreover, pay attention to the good qualities that the guru does have—such as ethical discipline, learnedness, and faith—

and reflect on these qualities. Once you have become conditioned to this, you may notice that your guru has a small number of faults. However, this does not impede your faith because you are focusing on the good qualities. For instance, although you see that there may be many good qualities in people whom you dislike, your strong perception of their faults overwhelms any perception of their good qualities. Likewise, you might notice many faults in yourself, yet, if the perception of your good qualities is very strong, it overwhelms any perception of your faults.

Thus, it is similar to the following example. The great Elder held the Mādhyamaka view and Ser-ling-ba held the view of a "true aspectarian" Cittamātrin. Therefore, Atisha's view was superior to that of Ser-ling-ba. Still, Atisha upheld Ser-ling-ba as the guru who was unrivaled amongst his gurus, because Atisha had obtained the spirit of enlightenment and a general presentation of the stages of the Mahāyāna path in dependence upon him. **[45]**

Reflect on your gurus' good qualities, and do not look for their faults. You must not discriminate among your gurus beginning with those from whom you have received one verse, even if they have such defects as faulty ethical discipline. For the *Cloud of Jewels Sūtra (Ratna-megha-sūtra)* states:[120]

> When you rely on the guru, your virtue increases and your nonvirtue decreases. Understanding this, develop the idea that your abbot is the Teacher whether he or she is greatly or slightly learned, is knowledgeable or not, or has kept ethical discipline or faulty discipline. Just as you have a liking for and faith in the Teacher, so too you should have a liking for and faith in the abbot. Develop reverence for your masters and serve them. Think that you will complete the collections that lead to enlightenment and eliminate the afflictions that you still have in dependence on this. Then you will obtain pleasure and joy. With respect to virtue act in accord with the gurus' words, but do not act in accord with the gurus' words with respect to nonvirtue.

Also the *Questions of Householder Ugra Sūtra (Gṛha-paty-ugra-paripṛcchā-sūtra)* says:[121]

> O householder, some bodhisattvas strive diligently at receiving oral transmissions of teachings and doing recitations. They might have masters from whom they have heard teachings, obtained oral transmission, or absorbed a verse of four lines that contains a teaching on generosity, ethical discipline, patience, joyous perseverance, meditative stabilization, and wisdom, or the accumulation of the

> collections of the bodhisattva path. They should respect them because of these teachings. The bodhisattvas might serve and venerate these masters without deceit. They might do so with all forms of gifts, respect, and worship for eons equal in number to the words, sentences, and letters in the verses that they were taught. Yet, still, O householder, they have not developed the respect for these masters that a master deserves. Since that is the case, what need is there to mention improper expressions of respect?

c) **Remembering the teacher's kindness and being respectful**

The *Ten Teaching Sūtra* says:[122] **[46]**

> Develop the following ideas with respect to your teachers. I have wandered for a long time through cyclic existence, and they search for me; I have been asleep, having been obscured by delusion for a long time, and they wake me; they pull me out of the depths of the ocean of existence; I have entered a bad path, and they reveal the good path to me; they release me from being bound in the prison of existence; I have been worn out by illness for a long time, and they are my doctors; they are the rain clouds that put out my blazing fire of attachment and the like.

Also the *Array of Stalks Sūtra* says:[123]

> Youthful Sudhana, the teachers are those who protect me from all miserable realms; they cause me to know the sameness of phenomena; they show me the paths that lead to happiness and those that lead to unhappiness; they instruct me in deeds always auspicious; they reveal to me the path to the city of omniscience; they guide me to the state of omniscience; they cause me to enter the ocean of reality's sphere; they show me the sea of past, present, and future phenomena; and they reveal to me the circle of the noble beings' assembly. The teachers increase all my virtues. Remembering this, you will weep.

Recollect your teacher's kindness in accordance with this statement. Personalize it by replacing "they" with "these teachers" in all of the phrases describing the teachers' kindness. Then picture before you your teachers. Saying the sūtra's words out loud, concentrate one-pointedly on their meaning. In this same way, substitute these words in the former sūtra [the *Ten Teaching Sūtra*], as well.

Furthermore, the *Array of Stalks Sūtra* says:[124]

> I, Sudhana, have come here
> Thinking one-pointedly, "These are my teachers, instructors in
> the teachings,

The ones who totally reveal the good qualities of all things,
And then fully teach the bodhisattva way of life."

"Because of giving birth to these qualities in me, they are like my mother.
Because of giving me the milk of good qualities, they are like my wet nurses.
They thoroughly train me in the branches of enlightenment.
These teachers turn away agents of harm; **[47]**
Like doctors, they free me from old age and death.
Like Indra, the chief of the deities, they let a rain of nectar fall;
Like the full moon, they fill me with the white teachings of virtue;
Showing the way toward peace, they are like the light of the sun;
With regard to friends and enemies, they are like mountains;
They have minds imperturbable as the ocean;
They wholly care for me and are like pilots of a ferry."
Thinking in this way, I have come here.

"These bodhisattvas have caused my mind to develop;
They have produced my enlightenment as a buddha's child;
Therefore these, my teachers, are praised by the buddhas."
With such virtuous thoughts, I have come here.

"As they protect the world, they are like heroes;
They are captains, protectors, and refuge.
They are an eye providing me with happiness."
With such thoughts, I respect and serve my teachers.

In accordance with this statement, you too should remember your teachers' kindness with these verses, using a melody and substituting yourself for Sudhana.

2) **How to rely in practice**

Aśvaghoṣa's *Fifty Verses on the Guru (Guru-pañcāśikā)* says:[125]

What need is there to say much here—
Do whatever pleases your gurus;
Eliminate all that displeases them.
Analyzing this, strive at it.

Once you have understood Vajradhara's statement,
"Attainments follow proper reliance on the master,"
Thoroughly please your gurus
In all things.

In brief, you must strive to achieve what pleases your gurus and eliminate what displeases them.

The three avenues to achieving what pleases your gurus are offering material gifts, respecting and serving with body and speech, and practicing in accordance with their words. This is also stated in Maitreya's *Ornament for the Mahāyāna Sūtras*:[126]

> Rely on the teacher by way of
> Respect, material things, service, and practice.

And also:

> A steadfast person who practices just as taught by the guru
> Pleases that guru properly.

1) Offering material gifts.

The *Fifty Verses on the Guru*:[127]

> If you always rely on your pledge master
> By giving things not normally given **[48]**—
> Your child, spouse, and your own life—
> What need to speak of ephemeral resources?

And also:

> Offering to your pledge master constitutes
> Continuous offering to all the buddhas.
> Offering to them is the collection of merit;
> From the collections of merit and sublime wisdom comes the supreme attainment.

Furthermore, Lak-sor-wa (Lag-sor-ba) said:

> If you offer what is bad while possessing what is good, you ruin your pledge. If the guru is pleased with this or you have nothing other than what is bad, then there is no fault.

This is similar to the *Fifty Verses on the Guru*, which says:[128]

> One who wishes for the inexhaustible
> Offers to the guru
> Whatever is slightly appealing, and
> Whatever is very special.

Furthermore, the students' perspective differs from the gurus' perspective. The students must do this offering, because the gurus are the supreme field through which the students accumulate the collections of merit and sublime wisdom. However, the gurus must not take the gifts into consideration. Sha-ra-wa (Sha-ra-ba) said:

> We use the word "guru" for whomever is pleased by practice and does not give even the slightest consideration to material gifts.

> One who does the opposite is not suitable to be a guru for those wishing to achieve liberation.

2) Respecting and serving with body and speech. This means such physical actions as bathing, massaging, cleaning dirt from the body, and nursing, as well as such vocal actions as pointing out the guru's good qualities.

3) *Practicing according to the guru's words.* This means to practice without contradicting what the guru instructs you to do. This is most important. For, as the *Garland of Birth Stories* says:[129]

> The worship that you should do in return for my help
> Is to practice in accordance with my instructions.

Question: We must practice in accordance with the gurus' words. Then what if we rely on the gurus and they lead us to an incorrect path or employ us in activities that are contrary to the three vows? Should we do what they say?

Reply: With respect to this, Gunaprabha's *Sūtra on the Discipline* states,[130] "If the abbot instructs you to do what is not in accord with the teachings, refuse." Also, the *Cloud of Jewels Sūtra* says,[131] "With respect to virtue act in accord with the gurus' words, but do not act in accord with the gurus' words with respect to nonvirtue." Therefore, you must not listen to nonvirtuous instructions. The twelfth birth story clearly gives the meaning of not engaging in what is improper.[132] **[49]**

However, it is improper to take the gurus' wrong actions as a reason for subsequent misbehavior such as disrespecting, reproaching, or despising the gurus. Rather, excuse yourself politely, and do not engage in what you were instructed to do. The *Fifty Verses on the Guru*:[133]

> If you cannot reasonably do as the guru has instructed,
> Excuse yourself with soothing words.

Furthermore, when you rely on your gurus in this way, acquire a portion of their teachings. As Maitreya's *Ornament for the Mahāyāna Sūtras* states:[134]

> By gaining a share of your gurus' teachings,
> You rely on the teachers in order to possess good qualities, not for material things.

Bo-do-wa said:

> When Ānanda was appointed as the Teacher's attendant, he thought of future followers of the teaching and then made the following vow, "I will serve and respect the Teacher under the conditions that I am not allowed to keep his unused robes or eat his leftover food, and that I am free to be with him at any time." We present-day followers do not value the teachings at all, but only value the guru's assigning status to us as demonstrated by each cup of tea that the guru gives to us. This is a sign of our deep corruption.

As for how long you should rely on a guru, Bo-do-wa said:

> With each student who comes to me, my burden increases. With each who leaves, it decreases. If you stay apart from the guru, it is not beneficial. Therefore, practice for a long time at a moderate distance.

d. **The benefits of relying on the teacher**

By relying on the teacher, you will come closer to buddhahood; you will please the conquerors; you will not be bereft of future teachers; you will not fall into miserable realms; neither bad karma nor afflictions will overpower you; through mindfulness of the bodhisattva deeds and by not contradicting them your collection of good qualities will continue to increase, and you will reach all of your provisional and final goals; after obtaining virtue through serving and respecting the teacher with thought and practice, you will accomplish others' welfare, as well as your own, and complete the collections of merit and sublime wisdom. **[50]**

In that vein the *Array of Stalks Sūtra* says:[135]

> Child of good lineage, bodhisattvas whom teachers properly support do not fall into miserable realms. Bodhisattvas whom teachers take into consideration do not contradict the bodhisattva training. Bodhisattvas for whom teachers care are elevated above the world. Bodhisattvas who have served and respected their teachers act without forgetting any of the bodhisattva deeds. Bodhisattvas whom teachers fully look after are not overcome by bad karma or afflictions.

And also:[136]

> Child of good lineage, the *bhagavan* buddhas are pleased with bodhisattvas who have engaged in what their teachers teach them. Bodhisattvas who are content not to contradict their teachers' words will come closer to becoming an omniscient one. Teachers

will be closer to one who has no doubt about their words. Bodhisattvas who bring to mind their teachers will fulfill all of their aims.

And also the *Sūtra of Showing the Tathāgata's Inconceivable Secret (Tathāgatācintya-guhya-nirdeśa-sūtra)* says:[137]

> Sons and daughters of good lineage, rely upon, become emotionally closer to, serve, and venerate the guru with great respect. If you do so, your thought will be virtuous through hearing virtuous teachings, whereby your practice as well will be virtuous. Then, through creating virtuous karma and becoming virtuous, you will please your virtuous friends. You also will not bring suffering upon others or yourself because you will not create nonvirtuous karma but will only cultivate virtue. As a result of guarding others and yourself, you will complete the path to unsurpassed enlightenment, and therefore will be able to work for the welfare of living beings who have entered wrong paths. **[51]** Thus, once bodhisattvas have relied on the guru, they will complete all their collections of good qualities.

Furthermore, by respecting and serving your teachers you exhaust karma whose effects you would otherwise experience in the miserable realms. Your action of serving the teacher expends these miserable effects and replaces them with only slight harm to your body and mind in this lifetime, either in actuality or in dreams. In addition, the benefits of respecting and serving your teachers are tremendous, such as a collection of virtue which surpasses even the roots of virtue that you derive from making offerings to limitless buddhas, and so forth. As the *Sūtra of Kṣitigarbha* says:[138]

> Those whom the teachers care for will purify the karma that would otherwise cause them to wander through the miserable realms for ten million limitless eons. They purify this karma with harm to their bodies and minds in this lifetime. This harm includes sickness such as an infectious disease with fever and calamities such as famine. They may purify their karma by merely undergoing something as little as a dream or a scolding. They produce more roots of virtue in one morning than those who give gifts to, worship, or observe precepts from limitless tens of millions of buddhas. Those who respect and serve their gurus are endowed with unimaginable good qualities.

And also:

> Notice that all of the buddhas' immeasurable good qualities of transforming others' minds arise from this proper reliance on the

> teacher. Therefore, rely on, become close to, serve, and venerate the guru, just as you would the buddhas.

Also, the *Garland of Birth Stories* states:[139]

> Any intelligent person should not be distant from excellent beings
> And should rely on these virtuous beings in a disciplined manner.
> Once you are close to them, particles of their good qualities
> Will stick to you automatically.

Bo-do-wa said:

> For the most part, we are in great danger of becoming like a worn animal skin. Just as when you drag a worn skin over the ground, debris sticks but gold coins do not, so it is that if you rely on teachers only occasionally their good qualities do not stick to you but each slight fault does. Therefore, to be successful, rely continuously on your teachers. **[52]**

e. **The faults of not relying on the teacher**

If you have taken someone as your teacher and then your method of reliance is wrong, not only will you be harmed by much madness and sickness in this lifetime, but in future lifetimes as well you will experience immeasurable suffering in miserable realms for an immeasurable period of time. The *Tantra Bestowing the Initiation of Vajrapāṇi* states:[140]

> "Bhagavan, what sort of fruition is there for those who reproach their masters?" The Bhagavan answered, "Vajrapāṇi, do not ask this question, for the answer will frighten the world, including the deities. However, Lord of Secrets, I will say something. O hero, listen carefully:
>
> As I have explained, any of the unbearable hells
> Resulting from such karma as the deeds of immediate retribution
> Are said to be the abode of those who reproach their teachers.
> They must stay there for limitless eons.
> Therefore, never reproach your master
> On any occasion."

Also the *Fifty Verses on the Guru* says:[141]

> You who despise the master—
> You greatly confused person—
> Will die by poison, demons, infectious disease,
> Leprosy, contagious fever, or other illnesses.

You will also go to a hell
After being killed by a king, or a fire,
Or by poisonous snakes, water, *ḍākās*,[142] thieves,
Demons, or deceptive spirits.

Never disturb in any way
The minds of the masters.
For, if you are confused and do so,
You will definitely roast in a hell.

It is explained that those who despise
Their masters will abide
In any of the frightful hells that have been explained—
Such as the Unrelenting.

Also, a citation from the *Commentary on the Difficult Points of the "Black Enemy of Yama" (Kṛṣṇa-yamāri-pañjikā)*, composed by the great adept Ratnākaraśānti, states:[143]

Someone who hears even a single verse
And does not conceive its speaker to be his or her guru
Will be reborn one hundred times as a dog
And then will take rebirth in a bad caste.

Furthermore, good qualities that have not yet developed will not develop, and those that have been developed will degenerate and then disappear. **[53]** The *Sūtra on the Concentration Which Perceives the Buddha of the Present Face to Face* states:[144]

If the students remain resentful, intractable, or hostile toward the guru, they have no way to obtain good qualities. It is also the same if they do not develop the idea that the teacher is indistinguishable from the Teacher. This is explained as follows: if you do not respect persons of the third vehicle[145] or monks who impart the teachings, or do not think of them as being the Teacher or as gurus, you have no way to obtain the good qualities that you have not yet obtained. Also, you will only waste those qualities that you have already obtained, for, as a result of not respecting these people, the teachings will disappear from your mind.

Moreover, if you rely on nonvirtuous teachers and bad friends, your good qualities will slowly diminish and all of your faults will increase. Then everything that is unwanted will develop. Therefore, always avoid them. The *Mindfulness of the Excellent Teaching (Saddharmānusmṛty-upasthāna)* states:[146]

The basis of all attachment, hostility, and ignorance is bad friends; they are like a poisonous tree trunk.

The *Great Final Nirvāṇa Sūtra (Mahā-parinirvāṇa-sūtra)* also says that bodhisattvas do not fear mad elephants and the like in the same way that they fear bad friends.[147] The former merely destroy the body, whereas the latter destroy both virtue and a pure mind. Moreover, it states that mad elephants and bad friends respectively destroy the body of flesh and the body of the teachings. Even more, the former cannot propel you into miserable realms, whereas the latter definitely can.

Also, the *Chapter of the Truth Speaker* states:[148]

> There are those whose minds are seized by bad friends, as if by poisonous snakes,
> But have forsaken the poison's antidote, the teacher.
> Alas, even if they listen to the precious and sublime teaching,
> They will fall into the great abyss of unrestraint.

Also, the *Verses about Friends* says:[149]

> The wise should not befriend
> Those who are without faith or who are stingy,
> Those who lie, or who speak divisively;
> They should not accompany sinful persons.
>
> Even those who do not sin
> Create the doubt that they might be doing so
> If they rely on those who do sin,
> Thereby increasing that which is unpleasant. **[54]**
>
> The person who relies on the unreliable
> Will have faults as a result,
> Just as unsmeared arrows are tainted
> When arrows smeared with poison are placed in the same quiver.

By relying on nonvirtuous teachers, your previously existent wrongdoing—deeds wrong by nature and deeds wrong by prohibition—does not diminish, and new wrongdoing increases. Geshe Drom-dön-ba said:

> The worst person, though keeping good company, does not become better than middling. The best, when keeping company with the worst, readily becomes part of the worst.

f. **A summary of the meaning of the previous five parts**

Thus, you must also understand as explained above the instruction that is renowned as "guru yoga."[150] Yet, you will get nowhere by training in an object of meditation for just a single session. When you practice a teaching from the heart, you must rely for a long time on an excellent teacher who guides you accurately. Moreover, it is as Chay-ga-wa (mChad-ka-ba) said, "When relying on the guru, there is the chance that you might give up your guru." So, if you rely without knowing how, you will not profit, but lose.

Therefore, these topics concerning reliance on the teacher are clearly the foundation of our deepest aspiration, which is more important than anything else. Consequently, I have taken citations from uncorrupted scriptures and their commentaries, which are easy to understand as well as inspiring, and I have given a general overview that is adorned with the sayings of excellent persons who are engaged in the meaning of the scriptures. Understand this in detail from other sources.

Our afflictions are extremely coarse. Some listen to the teachings given by many teachers. They do not know how to rely on the guru, and, even if they know how, they do not do it. Therefore, they will incur immeasurable misdeeds that are related to their improper reliance on the guru. Moreover, they will find it difficult to develop an awareness of practices such as confession of former wrongdoing and restraint from future wrongdoing.

Thus, after you have understood the benefits and faults as previously explained, reflect on them repeatedly. **[55]** Those whose practice of relying on the teacher was improper in previous lives should achieve an attitude of confession and restraint from the depths of their hearts.

Exert yourself in the practice of those teachings for which you are suited as a recipient, and repeatedly contemplate the complete qualifications of your teacher. Make many aspirational prayers and accumulate the collections of merit and sublime wisdom as causes for having such a teacher to look after you until you attain enlightenment. Once you have done this, you will quickly become like the conquerors' child Sadāprarudita, who had perfect courage, and the youthful Sudhana, who knew no limit in his search for teachers.[151]

5

THE MEDITATION SESSION

2. A brief indication of how to sustain the meditation
   a. The actual way of sustaining the meditation
      1) What to do during the actual meditation session
         a) Preparation
         b) Actual session
            i) How to sustain the meditation in general
            ii) How to sustain the meditation specifically
         c) What to do at the conclusion
      2) What to do in between meditation sessions
         a) Restraining the sensory faculties
         b) Acting with vigilance
            i) The foundations upon which you act
            ii) Acting vigilantly with respect to the foundations
         c) Appropriate diet
         d) How to practice diligently without sleeping at the wrong time and how to act properly at the time of sleep

2. A brief indication of how to sustain the meditation

How to sustain the meditation has two parts:

1. The actual way of sustaining the meditation (Chapter 5)
2. Refuting misconceptions about meditation (Chapter 6)

a. The actual way of sustaining the meditation

The actual way of sustaining the meditation is explained in two parts:

1. What to do during the actual meditation session
2. What to do in between meditation sessions

1) **What to do during the actual meditation session**

The actual meditation session is divided into three phases: (1) the preparation; (2) the actual session; and (3) the conclusion.

a) **Preparation**

The six aspects of preparation are the activities of Ser-ling-ba. Therefore, (1) clean well the place where you are staying, and neatly arrange the representations of the Buddha's body, speech, and mind. (2) Obtain offerings without deceit, and arrange them beautifully. (3) Sit up straight upon a comfortable seat in a suitable posture, your legs either in the full or half-lotus position, and then absorb yourself in the practices of going for refuge and developing the spirit of enlightenment. Asaṅga's *Śrāvaka Levels (Śrāvaka-bhūmi)*[152] says to sit in the full lotus posture upon a throne, low seat, or the like in order to clear away obscurations such as longing for desirable objects, and to walk back and forth in order to clear your mind of the obscurations of sleepiness and lethargy. (4) Imagine that seated in the space before you are the gurus of the vast and profound lineages, as well as immeasurable buddhas, noble bodhisattvas, *pratyekabuddhas*, *śrāvakas*, and those who abide in the Buddha's word.[153] Then visualize the field for accumulating the collections of merit and sublime wisdom.

(5) The cooperative conditions for the production of the path in your mind are *(1)* the accumulation of the collections, which are favorable conditions, and *(2)* the purification of your mind from obscurations, which are unfavorable conditions. **[56]** If you lack these cooperative conditions, it is extremely difficult to produce the path, even if you take pains to sustain the meditations that are the substantial causes of the path. Now you must purify your mind with the seven branches of worship, which comprise the crucial points for accumulating the collections and purifying the mind of obscurations.

With respect to the seven branches of worship, the first, the branch of obeisance, includes the combination of physical, verbal, and mental obeisance. It is expressed in the first verse of the *Prayer of Samantabhadra (Samantabhadra-caryā-praṇidhāna)*:[154]

> I bow down with a clear mind, body, and speech
> To all lions-among-humans,[155] leaving none out—
> Those who traverse the three times in the worlds
> Of the ten directions, however many there may be.

This verse is a sincere and respectful physical, verbal, and mental obeisance that does not simply conform to what others do. Do not take as your object of meditation the buddhas of a single direction in the universe or of a single time. Rather, take all the conquerors who reside in all ten directions as well as those who have already visited this world previously, will visit here in the future, and are appearing at present. The master Ye-shay-day (Ye-shes-sde) explains in his commentary,[156] "Even if you bow down to one buddha, the merit is immeasurable. What need is there to mention the merit of bowing down while imagining that vast number of buddhas?"

In regard to physical, verbal, and mental obeisance, physical obeisance is expressed by the second verse:

> I make obeisance to all the conquerors,
> With bowing bodies as numerous as the particles of those worlds,
> Perceiving all of the conquerors
> Through the strength of prayers that aspire to auspicious deeds.

Imagine all the conquerors abiding in all directions and times as if you are actually perceiving them as objects of your mind. Also, as you bow down, imagine duplicate images of your body emanating from your body in a number equal to the minute particles of the buddhas' realms. Moreover, you should have initially been motivated by the strength of deep faith in the auspicious deeds of the objects of your obeisance. The master Ye-shay-day explains,[157] "If even an obeisance with one body has great merit, one with a vast number of bodies has extremely great merit."

Mental obeisance is expressed by the next verse:

> Upon one particle there are buddhas as numerous as the particles of those worlds, and
> All are seated in the midst of their children.
> In this way, all are spheres of reality.
> I imagine conquerors filling all of those particles.

Buddhas are seated even upon each of the most minute particles and are equal in number to all of those particles. Each buddha is surrounded by bodhisattva disciples. Mental obeisance develops belief through recollecting the buddhas' good qualities.

Verbal obeisance is expressed by the next verse:

> In praise of all the *sugatas*,[158]
> I express the excellence of all the conquerors

With all the sound of an ocean of voices in song
And oceans of inexhaustible praise. **[57]**

First, in accordance with scripture, imagine that immeasurable heads emanate from each of your immeasurable bodies and that immeasurable tongues emanate from each head. Vocal obeisance is expressing with pleasant song the inexhaustible praises of the buddhas' good qualities. In this verse "song" means praise. The song's "voices" are its causes; that is, tongues. "Ocean" is a term for multiplicity.

With respect to the second branch of worship, offerings, there are both surpassable and unsurpassable offerings. The former is expressed by the next two verses:

I offer to the conquerors
Exquisite flowers, the best garlands,
Musical instruments, ointments, excellent umbrellas,
Superior lamps, and choice incenses.

I make offerings to the conquerors
With the best garments, superior perfumes,
Fragrant powders piled as high as Mount Meru—
All in the most excellent arrangements.

"Exquisite flowers" are wonderful, loose flowers such as those of the human and divine regions. "Garlands" are various flowers that are alternately strung together. Both of these terms include all types of real and imagined flowers. "Musical instruments" are stringed, wind, and percussion instruments. "Ointments" are ointments of fragrant incense for the body. "Excellent umbrellas" are the best umbrellas. "Lamps" includes luminous precious jewels as well as fragrant and luminous lamps such as butter lamps. "Burning incenses" are single-fragrance and mixed-fragrance incenses. "The best garments" are the best of every kind of apparel. "Superior perfumes" is said to be scented water given in offering bowls; it includes such water as that which is infused with a smell that spreads its odor into a universe of three billion world systems. "Fragrant powders" are equal in height and width to Mount Meru. They are also either alternating rows of colored sand for drawing a maṇḍala or fragrant incense powders suitable to be scattered or burned which have already been wrapped into parcels. "Arrangements" refers to all the above; they should be predominantly good, ornamental, and varied.

The next verse describes unsurpassable offerings:

I imagine all unsurpassable and vast offerings
For all the conquerors.
With the strength of my faith in auspicious deeds
I bow down and make offerings to all the conquerors.

Surpassable offerings are those of worldly persons. Therefore, unsurpassable offerings are completely good things created by those with power, such as bodhisattvas. The two final lines of this verse should be affixed to all of the above verses in which the sentiment of these two lines is not present. They indicate your motivation and the intended recipients of your obeisance and offering.

The next verse describes the third branch of worship, confession of sins:

Whatever sins I have done
With body, speech, or mind
Under the influence of attachment, hostility, or ignorance
I confess each and every one of them. **[58]**

The nature of sin is that the three mental poisons cause you to use your body, speech, or mind to actually engage in an activity—that is, to do it yourself—or to enjoin someone else to do it, or to rejoice in someone else's having done it. So as to broadly include all of this, the verse says, "Whatever." To confess sin is to recall the faults of your earlier sins and then to regret them. Confess them from the depths of your heart with an attitude of restraint toward future sin. When you do this, you prevent the growth of the sins you did before and discontinue committing them in the future.

The next verse expresses the fourth branch of worship, rejoicing:

I rejoice in all merit, whatever it may be,
Of all the conquerors of the ten directions, conqueror's children,
Pratyekabuddhas, those with more to learn,
Those with no more to learn, and all ordinary beings.

"Rejoicing" means to remember the benefits of the virtues of these five types of persons,[159] and then to cultivate delight in them as a poor person would with a discovered treasure.

The next verse expresses the fifth branch of worship, imploring to turn the wheel of the teaching:

I implore all the protectors,
Lights of the world in the ten directions
Who have reached buddhahood, which is without attachment,
To turn the peerless wheel of the teaching.

Imploring to turn the wheel of the teaching refers to first imagining that duplicate images of your body emanate from your body in a number equal to the buddhas of the ten directions. You then request them to give the teachings. These buddhas reside in the buddha-realms of the ten directions and do not wait long to teach after awakening into enlightenment and gaining the knowledge which is without attachment and without hindrance. The master Ye-shay-day cites[160] in his commentary the phrase "awakened into enlightenment" and explains it.

The next verse expresses the sixth branch of worship, supplication:

> I supplicate with palms joined in prayer
> Those wishing to demonstrate their final nirvāṇa—
> Please stay for eons equal in number to the particles of the universe
> In order to bring happiness and benefit to all beings.

Supplication involves imagining immeasurable duplicate images of your body. In front of you are the buddhas in the buddha-realms of the ten directions who are teaching how to pass into final nirvāṇa. You then request that they stay for eons equal to the number of minute particles within each of the buddha-realms in order to bring temporary happiness and ultimate benefit to living beings.

The next verse expresses the seventh branch of worship, dedication:

> Whatever merit I have accumulated, however slight,
> From obeisance, offering, confession,
> Rejoicing, imploring, and supplication—
> I dedicate it all to enlightenment.

Dedication refers to never exhausting any of the roots of virtue—which are illustrated by the above six branches of worship—because you have dedicated them with strong aspiration as causes of complete enlightenment for yourself and all living beings.

While understanding the meaning of the words of these verses in this way, slowly recite them as indicated without distraction. **[59]** Once you do this, you will have an immeasurable mass of merit.

You accumulate the collections of merit and sublime wisdom—the favorable conditions—through performing the five branches of obeisance, offering, rejoicing, imploring, and supplication. Through confession you clear away the obscurations, which are the unfavorable conditions. Cultivating delight in the virtue that you have done—which is part of rejoicing—will also increase your virtue. You may have few virtues as a result of accumulation, purification, and increase, but you will expand them enormously through dedication. Although virtuous effects may arise temporarily and then dissipate, through dedication they will never dissipate. To summarize, the seven branches of worship are included in the following three: accumulation, purification, and bringing about an expansion and a lack of dissipation.

(6)[161] Then, once you have pictured in your mind the objects of the maṇḍala and have offered the maṇḍala, make the following supplication many times with strong aspiration:[162]

> Please bless all living beings—my mothers—and myself so that we may quickly stop all flawed states of mind, beginning with not respecting the teacher and ending with conceiving signs of true existence in the two kinds of self.
>
> Please bless us so that we may easily produce all flawless states of mind, beginning with respecting the teacher and ending with knowing the reality of selflessness.
>
> Please bless us to quell all inner and outer obstacles.

b) **Actual session**

i) **How to sustain the meditation in general**

That which is known as "meditation" is the act of sustaining an object of meditation and specific subjective aspects[163] by repeatedly focusing your mind upon a virtuous object of meditation. The purpose of this is as follows. From beginningless time you have been under the control of your mind; your mind has not been under your control. Furthermore, your mind tended to be obscured by the afflictions and so forth. Thus, meditation aims to bring this mind, which gives rise to all faults and flaws, under control and then it aims to make it serviceable. Serviceability means that you can direct your mind as you wish toward a virtuous object of meditation.

You might try to sustain your meditation by jumping to this and that object of meditation. **[60]** You may consider setting up according to your wish a variety of virtuous objects of meditation in no specific order. Though you may do this, you will not be able to take up your object of meditation with this method. Consequently, you will greatly hinder your mind's ability to be directed as you wish toward a virtuous object of meditation. If you have made this a habit from the start, the virtuous practice of your whole lifetime will be flawed.

Therefore, from the beginning, firmly determine the definite order and enumeration of whatever objects of meditation you wish to sustain. Then, strengthen your will by repeatedly thinking, "I will not set up something that is different from what I have determined." Without exceeding or falling short of what you have determined, sustain your meditation with mindfulness and vigilance.

ii) **How to sustain the meditation specifically**

First reflect on the benefits of relying on the teacher, such as quickly attaining buddhahood, and the drawbacks of not relying on the teacher, such as giving rise to suffering in this and future lives. Then, think, many times and with an attitude of restraint, "I will never allow myself to conceive of faults in my guru." After considering any of your guru's good qualities that you know—such as ethical discipline, concentration, wisdom, and being learned—meditate on them until you produce a faith that has the aspect of mental clarity. Then, in accordance with the sūtras cited earlier, contemplate how your guru's kindness has been and will be helpful to you. Meditate on that until you develop respect from the depths of your heart.

c) **What to do at the conclusion**

By means of such prayers as the *Prayer of Samantabhadra* and *Aspiration in Seventy Verses (Praṇidhāna-saptati)*,[164] dedicate the virtue that you have accumulated. Do it with an aspiration so strong that it will be the cause of fulfilling your provisional and final aims. Meditate in this way during four sessions: predawn, morning, afternoon, and at nightfall.

Furthermore, if at first you meditate for a long time, you will be readily susceptible to laxity and excitement. If this becomes your habit, it will then be difficult to correct your awareness. Therefore, meditate in many short sessions. If you end your session while still wanting to meditate, you will be eager to reenter each future session. **[61]** Otherwise, it is said that you will feel nauseous when you see the cushion.

When your meditation has become somewhat stable, lengthen the session. In all the sessions make your practice free from the faults of being either too strict or excessively relaxed, and thereby sustain your meditation. In this way you will have few obstacles and will overcome problems such as overtiredness, laxity, and lethargy.

2) **What to do in between meditation sessions**[165]

In general there are many things to be done between meditation sessions, such as obeisance, circumambulation, and recitation [of prayers and scripture]. However, the principal thing to do in this context is as follows.

After you have made an effort to meditate in the actual session and are at the point of ending the session, you might not continue to rely on mindfulness and vigilance, and might instead completely let go of what should be sustained—the object of meditation and its subjective aspects. If you do so, your progress will be extremely small. Therefore, even in between sessions, look at teachings that reveal the meaning of your object of meditation, and recollect it again and again. Accumulate, by many means, the collections, which are favorable conditions for producing good qualities. Also, clear away, by many means, the obscurations, which are unfavorable conditions. By applying what you know, strive at whatever vow you have promised to observe, as this is the basis of everything. In addition, follow the instruction called "Consolidation" with regard to (1) training the mind in the object of meditation and its subjective aspects, (2) observing vows, and (3) accumulating the collections.

Furthermore, learn the four preconditions, which are causes that readily produce the paths of serenity and insight: (a) restraining the sensory faculties, (b) acting vigilantly, (c) appropriate diet, and (d) striving to practice without sleeping at the wrong time, and acting properly at the time of sleep.

a) **Restraining the sensory faculties**

There are five parts to this section, the first of which is *that with which you restrain* the sensory faculties. You restrain them with a constant maintenance of your mindfulness and a continuous persistence at mindfulness. With respect to these two, the first, maintaining your mindfulness, means that you practice your mindfulness repeatedly without forgetting the teachings about restraining the sensory faculties as well as the other three preconditions. The second, continuously persisting at mindfulness, means that you practice your mindfulness continuously and with respect. *What you are restraining* is the six sensory faculties. *What you are restraining them from* is the six attractive and six unattractive sensory objects.[166]

How to restrain the sensory faculties has two parts, and they are as follows:

> 1) *Guarding the sensory faculties:* **[62]** After the six consciousnesses arise based upon their sensory objects and faculties, the mental consciousness produces attachment for the six attractive sensory objects or hostility toward the six

unattractive ones. "Guarding the sensory faculties" means protecting your mind against such attachment and hostility, and making a great effort not to produce them.

2) *Practicing restraint with the six sensory faculties* is actually stopping the sensory faculties. For instance, you don't let them engage those sensory objects that will produce afflictions when, for instance, looked at.

Furthermore, "guarding the sensory faculties" means neither to take note of the six sensory objects nor to imagine them, and to achieve this through restraint, even when a sinful attitude such as attachment arises due to forgetfulness and an abundance of afflictions. "Take note of" refers to perceiving and paying attention to the intentional or unintentional appearance of sensory objects such as forms that you should not look at. "Imagining" can refer to the mental consciousness's apprehension of sensory objects that produce attachment, hostility, and ignorance, after the six consciousnesses have perceived them. It can also refer to hearing about these sensory objects from others and then imagining them despite never having perceived them.

Restraining means protecting the mind from being afflicted, and then setting it on something that is ethically neutral or virtuous. Here, the time for setting the mind on something that is "unobscured and ethically neutral" is not when the mind is apprehending a virtuous object of meditation, but at other times, such as during physical activities.

b) **Acting with vigilance**

i) **The foundations upon which you act**

This section has two parts: the five actions of movement, and the five actions of activity in a temple.

The five actions of movement are:

(1) *actions of the body*: going out to other places, like towns and temples, and returning from them;
(2) *actions of the eyes*: both slightly looking at various objects because you have seen them unintentionally, and fully viewing those objects you have intentionally looked at;
(3) *actions of the limbs, fingers, and toes*: stretching out and contracting the limbs, fingers, and toes;
(4) *actions of religious robes and alms bowls*: **[63]** handling and making use of the three kinds of religious robes and the alms bowl; and
(5) *actions related to alms*: eating, drinking, and so on.

The five actions of activity in a temple are:

(1) *actions of the body*: walking in a designated area; going to one who is in accord with the teaching; entering a passageway for the sake of receiving the teaching; standing in the presence of those whom you are going to see and who are in accord with the teaching—the abbot, master, guru, and the like; or sitting in the full lotus posture upon a seat, and so on;

(2) *actions of speech*: receiving the oral transmission of the twelve branches of scripture on which you have not previously received oral transmission; understanding all of these; reciting that which you have received; teaching them to others; and conversing with others in order to encourage their joyous perseverance;

(3) *actions of mind*: sleeping in the middle period of the night; retiring to a quiet place and then not speaking while you think over the meaning of what you have heard, practice concentration by means of the nine mental states, and strive for insight; and, when feeling fatigued during hot weather, doing something to dispel your desire to fall asleep at an improper time; and

(4) *actions of day* and (5) *actions of night*: both of these refer to not sleeping in the daytime or in the first and last periods of the night. These also refer to physical and verbal actions. Furthermore, the above statement "Sleeping in the middle period of the night" refers only to actions of night and actions of mind.

ii) **Acting vigilantly with respect to the foundations**

Acting vigilantly with respect to the above-mentioned ten foundations is as follows. When you begin either movement or activity, right from the outset act conscientiously and establish mindfulness with respect to that action. Imbued with both of these, analyze the elements of the situation and analyze how you should proceed; then think about and arrive at an understanding of the situation in light of what you have concluded.

In this regard, there are four elements:

1) *The element of basis*: With respect to any of the ten foundations—those of the actions of body, and so on—you should analyze what will be happening and how to proceed, and then consider the situation in light of what you have concluded.

[64] For example, with respect to actions of going out and returning, understand the manner of going and coming as it is taught in the texts on discipline. Then reflect while going and coming, "Now I am doing this and now this."

2) *The element of direction*: With regards to directions, you analyze to discover what will be happening and how to proceed, and then consider the situation in light of what you have concluded. For instance, when going out, do not go to the five places—one that sells liquor, and so on.[167] Having understood that you should go to places other than those, be vigilant with regard to this when you go out.

3) *The element of time*: With regards to any period of time, you analyze to discover what will be happening and how to proceed, and then consider the situation in light of what you have concluded. For example, once you have understood that it is proper to go to town in the morning but not in the afternoon, act accordingly and be vigilant at that time.

4) *The element of actions*: no matter how many actions you undertake, you analyze to discover what will be happening and how to proceed, and then consider the situation in light of what you have concluded. For example, when you go out, keep in mind any precepts there may be on going out, such as "Go to another domicile in a very restrained manner."

In short, be mindful of whatever behaviors may take place in the night or day. Then understand which are to be done and which not to be done. Whenever engaging in those which are to be done or turning away from those which are not to be done, be vigilant, and think, "Now I am engaging in or turning away from this, and now this." If you do this, it is said that you will not be tarnished by infractions in this lifetime; even after death, you will not fall into the miserable realms; and you will have the preconditions for attaining knowledge of the paths that you have not yet attained.

I have arranged both this section on acting vigilantly and the section on restraining the sensory faculties in accordance with the noble being Asaṅga's citations of sūtras and the subsequent commentaries on the meaning of those citations. Work on these practices, for it is said that if you do, you will have unusual success in all your virtuous practices; in particular, your ethical discipline will be completely pure; and you will easily attain the nondiscursive states of concentration that comprise meditative serenity and insight. **[65]**

c) **Appropriate diet**

An appropriate diet has four attributes:

1) *Not eating too little*: If you eat too little food, you will be hungry and will become weak, leaving no strength for virtuous activities. Therefore, "not eating too little" means that you must eat just the amount that will allow you not to be afflicted by hunger until tomorrow's meal.

2) *Not eating too much*: This is because if you eat too much, your body will be heavy, as if you were carrying a burden. It will be hard to breathe in and out. Sleepiness and lethargy will increase. You will be unfit for any action, so you will have no strength for eliminating the afflictions.

3) *Eating digestible and wholesome food*: With such food you eliminate old feelings of suffering related to food and you do not create new ones.

4) *Eating appropriate food which does not produce afflictions*: With such food you do not create misdeeds, and you stay happy.

Moreover, the remedy for craving food lies within meditating on the faults of food. There are three faults: (1) *The fault that arises from the causes of enjoyment*: Contemplate how any colorful, aromatic, and good-tasting food whatsoever appears like vomit once you have chewed it and moistened it with your saliva. (2) *The fault that arises from digesting food*: Contemplate how food produces such elements of the body as flesh and blood after it is digested in the middle or last period of the night. Contemplate how some food becomes feces and urine, and then remains in the lower part of the body; moreover, each day you have to excrete that. Think how many kinds of illnesses develop in connection with this food. (3) *The five faults that come from looking for food*: The five are as follows:

1) The fault of procurement: While being tormented by heat and cold, you must make great effort in order to procure food and assemble its causes. If you do not procure it, you suffer sorrow and the like. Even if you do procure the food, you fear that it will be stolen or wasted, and then suffer because of taking great pains to guard it.

2) The fault of ruining close relationships: Even close relatives, such as fathers and sons, will dispute and fight with one another for the sake of food. **[66]**

3) The fault of insatiability: Kings and the like will go to war with each other and experience much suffering when their craving for food intensifies.

4) The fault of the lack of independence: Those who eat others' food experience much suffering when they fight with opponents on behalf of their leader.

5) The fault that arises from wrongdoing: Having amassed sins of body, speech, and mind for the sake of food and its causes, you remember your sins when you are dying, and die with regret. Moreover, after death, you fall into a miserable realm.

Despite all of this, there is some benefit to food—after all, the body depends upon it. Eat your food after you think, "Since it is not correct to rely on food just for the sake of my body's maintenance, I will conduct myself in a pure manner in dependence on my body's maintenance. Benefactors and those who actually carry out acts of charity work so hard that their skin, flesh, and blood dry up! Then they make their gifts with a wish for a special result. I will ensure that their actions have great effects." Remember as well that Śāntideva's *Compendium of Trainings* says[168] to eat while reflecting that (1) you are benefiting the giver; (2) whereas now you are assembling micro-organisms in your body through the material gift of food, in the future you will gather these beings together through the teachings; and (3) you will accomplish the welfare of all living beings. Also Nāgārjuna's *Friendly Letter (Suhṛl-lekha)* states:[169]

> With an understanding that food is like medicine,
> Eat it without hostility or attachment;
> Not for haughtiness, might,
> Or robustness, but only to maintain your body.

d) **How to practice diligently without sleeping at the wrong time and how to act properly at the time of sleep**

The *Friendly Letter*:[170]

> O Reasonable One, after cultivating virtue all day
> And in the first and last periods of the night as well,
> Sleep between these periods with mindfulness,
> Not wasting even the time of sleep.

"All day" and "the first and last periods of the night" both refer to what should be done during and between meditation sessions. **[67]** Therefore, while sitting or standing, act purposefully, as I have explained before, by completely clearing your mind of the five obscurations.[171]

There are teachings both for meditation sessions and for between meditation sessions with regard to restraining the sensory faculties and acting vigilantly, as well as this section on making effort to practice instead of sleeping. Therefore, here I have singled out those teachings for between sessions. Your conduct during sleep takes place between sessions, so do not treat even that as having no purpose.

How should you sleep? During the day and in the first of the three portions of the night, spend your time doing virtuous activities; then sleep when the middle portion arrives. For, by sleeping you will enhance those elements of the body which are benefited by sleep. When you develop the body in that way, your body will be most serviceable for employment in both kinds of joyous perseverance[172] in the group of virtues, and this also will be helpful.

When you go to sleep, first come out from the meditation room, wash your feet, and then enter your own room. Then, lying on your right side, place your left leg upon the right, and sleep like a lion. As for sleeping like a lion, among all animals it is the lion who uses superior capacity, confidence, and fortitude to subdue its opponents. Likewise, one who joyously perseveres at practice instead of sleeping will use superior capacity, etc. to subdue opponents and will, at rest, sleep like a lion. This is unlike the sleep of hungry ghosts, deities, or those who are involved in desire, for they all have laziness, weak perseverance, and little capacity to subdue opponents.[173]

From another point of view sleeping on your right side like a lion means that your body naturally does not become limp. Even when you have fallen asleep, you do not lose your mindfulness. Your sleep does not become heavy. You do not have bad or sinful dreams. But if you should sleep in some other way, all the faults that are the opposite of these four will arise.

There are four kinds of thoughts with which to fall asleep: (1) *The idea of illumination*: First apprehend an image of light, and then sleep while imagining light. **[68]** Thereby, when you fall asleep, darkness will not arise in your mind. (2) *Mindfulness*: This arises from having heard, thought, and meditated on meaningful, virtuous teachings. Pursue this practice until you have fallen asleep. By this means, even when you are asleep, your mind will continue to engage the teachings, just as though you were not asleep. In short, you will sustain your virtuous practice even when you are asleep. (3) *Vigilance*: While you cultivate mindfulness in this way, any of the afflictions could arise. If any of them does, you notice it and eliminate it rather than acquiesce to it. (4) *The idea of rising*: This has three aspects. First, do not let the mind slip into a state of being completely overwhelmed by sleep. Instead, sleep very lightly like a deer, with a mind imbued with joyous perseverance. This will prevent heavy sleep, and you will be able to awaken without oversleeping. Second, think, "Ah, I will always practice staying awake[174] as the Buddha taught," and then with great effort develop an aspiration to this end. With this, your sleep will not deviate from the sleep of a lion, which the Buddha permitted. Third, think, "Just as I joyously persevered at cultivating virtue and not sleeping today, I will do the same tomorrow as well." This will prevent breaking the continuity of your aspiration to cultivate virtue. Even if you forget your aspiration, always work to make it stronger.

Conducting yourself in this way while eating and sleeping involves no misdeeds. Since acting purposefully in this manner will clearly stop you from wasting so much of your life, I have explained it as the noble Asaṅga, citing sūtra, determined it to be. Everything that I have said here about how to act before, during, after, and between sessions applies to all of the meditations described from here through and including the section on insight. **[69]** The only exceptions are the distinctive meditative procedures during the actual sessions. This concludes the explanation of what to do in between sessions.

6

Refuting Misconceptions About Meditation

There are persons who have not begun to recognize that the classic scriptures and their commentaries constitute personal instructions, and who, therefore, might have the following qualm.

Qualm: When you meditate on the path, you should do only stabilizing meditation rather than repeatedly analyzing your object of meditation, for repeated analysis with discerning wisdom is only for times of study and reflection. Moreover, repeated analysis will prevent you from future attainment of buddhahood because conceptual thought apprehends signs of true existence.

Reply: This is the nonsensical chatter of someone who is utterly ignorant of the crucial points of practice, for Maitreya's *Ornament for the Mahāyāna Sūtras* states:[175]

> Proper attention is based upon prior study. Sublime wisdom, which takes reality as its object, arises from your cultivation of proper attention.

Here Maitreya teaches that you should use the wisdom that comes from reflection to attend properly to the meaning of what you have studied. From this there will arise the wisdom that comes from meditation and perceives reality.

Therefore, first study with someone what you intend to practice, and come to know it secondhand. Next, use scripture and reasoning to properly reflect on the meaning of what you have studied, coming to know it firsthand. Once you determine the meaning of what you originally intended to practice with this kind of study and reflection and you have no doubts, then familiarize yourself with it repeatedly. We call this repeated familiarization "meditation." Thus, you need both repeated analytical meditation and nonanalytical stabilizing meditation, because meditation involves both nonanalytical stabilization on the meaning of what you originally intended to practice that was determined through study and reflection and the use of discerning wisdom to analyze this meaning. Therefore, to claim that all meditations are stabilizing meditations is like taking one grain of barley and saying, "This is all the barley grains there are." **[70]**

Moreover, just as study must precede the wisdom that comes from study, and reflection must precede the wisdom that comes from reflection, so too meditation must precede the wisdom that comes from meditation. As this is so, meditation means becoming familiar with what you have ascertained using the wisdom that comes from reflection. Therefore, it is said that the wisdom that comes from meditation is a product of the wisdom that comes from reflection.

Thus, the depth of the wisdom that comes from your studies is commensurate with your studies. The breadth of your reflection is commensurate with this wisdom, while the depth of the wisdom that comes from your reflections is proportionate to your reflections. The magnitude of your practice of meditation corresponds to the depth of your wisdom of reflection, while your ability to stop faults and achieve good qualities is commensurate with your practice of meditation. Therefore, the scriptures and their commentaries say that study and reflection are very important for the practice of meditation.

Objection: What is determined through study and reflection is not intended for meditation, but is merely for promoting superficial knowledge and eliminating others' misconceptions. Therefore, when you meditate, you must meditate on something unrelated to your study and reflection.

Response: This is incoherent, like showing a horse one racecourse and then racing it on another. This completely destroys the process of developing the three wisdoms[176] in succession, which is what the scriptures, as a whole, present. This also implies the nonsensical statement, "Much study is not needed to travel the true path."

One indication of a failure to recognize these critical points is in not distinguishing in the beginning between those who are well-trained in the sūtras or tantras and those who have no training at all, and then not assigning the appropriate amount of practice. Another such indication is that meditators are criticized if they study or do research. These mistaken customs persist in Tibet. **[71]**

While mere familiarization with knowledge acquired through the wisdom of study and reflection is indeed not a good quality that results from meditation, how could this contradict familiarization as simply being equivalent to meditation? If it did, then meditation would never be possible for an ordinary being who had not attained access to the first meditative stabilization.[177] For, the texts on knowledge often explain that the process of entering a higher level from the level of the desire realm creates a good quality that results from meditation, but there is no such result of meditation [creation of a good quality] associated with the desire realm itself.[178]

Therefore, understand "meditation" as it is explained in Dharmamitra's *Clear Words Commentary (Prasphuṭa-padā)*:[179]

> "Meditating" is making the mind take on the state or condition of the object of meditation.

For example, "meditating on compassion" and "meditating on faith" mean that the mind must be made to develop these qualities. Because of this, even the great translators sometimes use the term "path of meditation," and at other times use the term "conditioning," as in the phrase from Maitreya's *Ornament for Clear Knowledge*,[180] "the paths of seeing and conditioning." Conditioning and meditation are synonymous.

Furthermore, Venerable Maitreya says:[181]

> As for the branch of certain differentiation,[182]
> The path of seeing, and the path of meditation,
> It is repeated reflection, comprehension, and definite discernment
> That constitute the path of meditation.

Maitreya says that repeated reflection, comprehension, and definite discernment constitute the path of meditation for a Mahāyāna noble being. In light of this, it is ridiculous to claim that meditation and sustained analysis are contradictory.

Furthermore, there is no end to statements which explain that the purpose of sustained and repeated analysis is meditation. For instance, there are references to "meditating on faith," "meditating on the four immeasurables and the spirit of enlightenment," and "meditating on impermanence and suffering." Śāntideva in his *Engaging in the Bodhisattva Deeds* and *Compendium of Trainings* states,[183] "I compose this in order to condition my own mind." In this way, he says that all the stages of the path that he explains in these two texts are meditation. [72] Further, the *Compendium of Trainings* says,[184] "Therefore, meditate continuously on any distribution, protection, purification, or enhancement of your body, resources, or merit." This indicates that meditation includes any performance of the four practices of distributing, protecting, purifying, and enhancing with regard to your body, resources, or roots of virtue. With this in mind, do not take "meditation" to be very limited.

Moreover, to claim that all conceptual thought involves the apprehension of signs of true existence, and thus prevents enlightenment, is the worst possible misconception insofar as it disregards all discerning meditation. This is the system of the Chinese abbot Ha-shang. I explain its refutation in the section on serenity and insight. This misconception also interferes with the development of deep respect for the classic texts, because these texts are mainly concerned only with the need to use discerning analysis, whereas Ha-shang's system sees all analysis as unnecessary during practice. This is also a major cause of the teaching's decline, because those who have this misconception do not recognize the classic scriptures and their commentaries to be instructions and therefore belittle their value.

Question: If, as you say, there are two types of meditation—analytical meditation and nonanalytical stabilizing meditation—what kind of practice involves analytical meditation and what kind involves stabilizing meditation?

Reply: I will explain this. Analytical meditation is necessary for meditations such as those on faith in the teacher; the great importance and difficulty in obtaining leisure and opportunity; death and impermanence; karma and its effects; the faults of cyclic existence; and the spirit of enlightenment. This is because these meditations need an awareness that is long-lasting, very forceful, and capable of changing the mind. Without this, you will not be able to stop the forces that oppose these meditations, such as disrespect.

Furthermore, the development of such a powerful awareness solely depends upon repeated meditation with discerning analysis. [73] For example, when you mistakenly superimpose many attractive characteristics upon the object of your attachment, you produce intense attachment. Similarly, when you think often about the unattractive characteristics of your enemy, you produce intense hatred. It is the same in the case of any meditation on any of these types of practices [death and impermanence, karma and its effects, etc.], regardless of whether the image of the meditative object is clear. Therefore, practice analytical meditation, because your mind requires a long-lasting and very forceful way to apprehend its objects.

When you achieve stabilizing meditations such as meditative serenity, you create a serviceability that allows you to place your mind on one object of meditation according to your wish. If those whose minds cannot stay on one object of meditation analyze repeatedly while they are trying to achieve a stabilizing meditation, they will be unable to produce mental stability. Hence, in this case they should practice stabilizing meditation. I will explain this later in the section on meditative serenity and insight.

Not knowing this system, some even propound, "If you are a scholar, you only do analytical meditation. Adepts only do stabilizing meditation." This is not the case, because each must do both. The scholar must achieve stabilizing meditations such as meditative serenity, while the adept must pursue such practices as intense faith in the teacher. Furthermore, both the sūtra section of scripture and the tantra section of scripture very frequently say that you must use discernment for both of these methods of meditation. If you lack or are deficient in such analytical meditation, then you will not develop stainless wisdom, the precious life of the path. Even if you develop a little wisdom, it will not be increased greatly. Therefore, you will not quickly progress along the path, because the ultimate object that you achieve on the path is the wisdom that differentiates, comprehensively and without confusion, the real nature and diversity of phenomena. As the master Mātṛceṭa states, "...omniscience is best amongst wisdoms." Consequently, understand it as a definite sign of having taken the wrong path if no matter how much you cultivate the path, your mindfulness is dulled by obliviousness and you are slow-witted about what to eliminate and what to adopt.

Furthermore, by using discerning wisdom to conduct analytical meditation on the meaning of the scriptures, you understand the many attributes of the good qualities of the three jewels and the like, and you then greatly increase the faith associated with these attributes, etc. **[74]** Also, once you have used analytical meditation to comprehend the many faults of cyclic existence, you develop great disgust for and disenchantment with cyclic existence, and you then see the benefits of liberation from many perspectives. So you then diligently seek liberation. Using this meditation, you even fathom the spirit of enlightenment and the many wondrous activities of the six perfections and so forth. This greatly increases your irreversible faith, aspiration, and joyous perseverance. As all of this is based exclusively on the use of discerning wisdom in order to conduct analytical meditation on the meaning of the scriptures, the intelligent should in this manner bring about such certainty that others cannot sway them away from it.

Those with a very small understanding of how to meditate might say the following:

Qualm: If you do too much analysis with discernment and sustain that in meditation, you will hinder your concentration, which is one-pointed upon a single object of meditation. So you will not achieve firm concentration.

Reply: I will explain this. Concentration allows you to willfully fix your attention on any single object of meditation. If you have not already achieved such concentration, then this concentration will not develop if you attempt to achieve it for the first time while analyzing many objects. Therefore, simply do stabilizing meditation to achieve concentration until you attain it. If this is what you mean by your qualm, then I agree.

However, you might assert that if you do too much analytical meditation prior to achieving concentration, you hinder your concentration. If this is the case, then it is clear that you do not understand the way to achieve concentration as it is explained in the commentaries of the great trailblazers. For example, when a skilled smith repeatedly burns gold and silver in a fire and repeatedly washes them in water, they are purified of all their defilements and residues. The gold and the silver then become very soft and pliable. Hence, they are ready to be transformed into whatever ornaments you want, such as earrings. **[75]**

Likewise, you initially use your discerning wisdom to meditate repeatedly on faults, such as the afflictions, the secondary afflictions, karmic effects of wrongdoing, and the faults of cyclic existence, according to their order in scripture. This makes you completely displeased or disenchanted. By bringing this to mind, you turn away from the group of nonvirtuous things and clear away these defilements, like burning gold in fire. Next, you use your discerning wisdom to meditate repeatedly on good qualities, such as the good qualities of the teacher, the great importance of leisure and opportunity, good qualities of the three jewels, virtuous karma and its effects, and the benefits of the spirit of enlightenment, again according to their order in scripture. This causes the mind to become "moist"[185] or clear. Like washing gold in water, bringing this to mind directs the mind toward the virtuous group of phenomena, causes delight, and then moistens the mind with virtues. Once this happens, focus your mind on what you want to achieve—either meditative serenity or insight—and you will accomplish it without difficulty. Therefore, such analytical meditation is the superior method for achieving nondiscursive concentration.

In the same way, the noble being Asaṅga says:[186]

> For example, in order for smiths or their skilled apprentices to purify silver or gold of all defilements and impurities, they burn it in fire and wash it in water. By doing this, they understand that they can make it into this or that ornament by way of its serviceability and pliability. Then those who know the appropriate craft—the smiths and their skilled apprentices—use the smiths' tools to transform the metal into whatever kind of ornament they want. Likewise, yogis and yoginis become disenchanted by simply not turning their mind toward any impurities or defilements such as covetousness. They create delight simply by not turning toward the unhappiness of the afflicted mind and by being inclined toward joy in the group of virtues. **[76]** When they do this, their minds become linked to and calmly settled upon—without fluctuation or movement—any object to which they apply them within the scope of serenity or insight. They then can use their minds to properly attain whatever objective for which they aim.

Laxity and excitement are the two principal conditions that are unfavorable for attaining a concentration wherein the mind steadfastly stays upon one object of meditation. With respect to this, if you have a very forceful and long-lasting awareness of the good qualities of the three jewels and the like, you will easily eliminate laxity. Many authorities state that the remedy for laxity is uplifting the mind by means of seeing good qualities. Likewise, if you have a very forceful and long-lasting awareness of the faults of impermanence, suffering, and the like, you will easily eliminate excitement. Many scriptures say that disenchantment is praised as the remedy for excitement because excitement is a mental distraction involving attachment.

Therefore, you will easily attain the firm concentrations which please the learned to a degree commensurate with your cultivation of the trainings, beginning with faith in the teacher and ending with the engaged spirit of enlightenment. Not only must you sustain stabilizing meditations after you become free of both excitement and laxity, but you must also sustain analytical meditations. Because of this, the knowledgeable gurus of the lineage that handed down these personal instructions conveyed a clear understanding of whatever object of meditation they transmitted. In order to do this, they first thought over the meaning of the appropriate passages from both the sūtras and the commentaries in light of their guru's personal instructions. Enriching their presentation with the sayings of former gurus, they comprehensively explained the topic of meditation. They also said that success is more difficult for those who contemplate on their own than for those who transform their minds in a classroom, where those who know how to explain the teachings do so for those who know how to listen. This statement is excellent and true. [77] Therefore, it is improper to say, "Now is the time for meditation," and then solely do a little meditation, for the saying "a time for study and reflection and a time for practice" expresses the misconception that extensive explanation of the teachings is not compatible with the context of practice.

However, those who know how to bring all these explanations into practice seem barely to exist at all. Therefore, you should also create another concise presentation of what to sustain in meditation.

Whether you understand that all of the scriptures are personal instructions follows only from whether you know this meditative process. Even those who have trained for a long time in the classic texts of the sūtra and mantra vehicles may, when meditating on the path, interpret texts in which they have trained to support misconceptions such as the ones mentioned above. What need is there to mention those who have not trained in the scriptural collections? Therefore, there is a need to establish this in a more detailed manner. Nevertheless, fearing verbosity, I have not written more than just this. This concludes the explanation of the refutation of misconceptions concerning the method of sustaining meditation.

7

A Human Life of Leisure and Opportunity

B. The stages of how the students train their minds after they have relied on the teacher
   1. An exhortation to take full advantage of a life of leisure and opportunity
      a. The identification of leisure and opportunity
         1) Leisure
         2) Opportunity
            a) The five aspects of opportunity that pertain to yourself
            b) The five aspects of opportunity that pertain to others
      b. Contemplating the great importance of leisure and opportunity
      c. Contemplating the difficulty of attaining leisure and opportunity

Now it is necessary to show the stages through which the guru leads the disciple who properly relies on the teacher as previously explained.

B. The stages of how the students train their minds after they have relied on the teacher

The stages of how the students train their minds has two parts:

1. An exhortation to take full advantage of a life of leisure and opportunity (Chapter 7)
2. How to take full advantage of a life of leisure and opportunity (Chapters 8 and on)

1. **An exhortation to take full advantage of a life of leisure and opportunity**

Taking full advantage of a life of leisure and opportunity is explained in terms of three aspects: identifying leisure and opportunity; contemplating its great importance; and contemplating the difficulty of attaining it.

a. **The identification of leisure and opportunity**

1) **Leisure**

The *Verse Summary of the Perfection of Wisdom in Eight Thousand Lines* says:[187]

> Through ethical discipline you eliminate
> The eight conditions that lack leisure
> And many circumstances in a life as an animal.
> Through it, you always attain leisure.

According to this, leisure means freedom from a rebirth in any of the eight conditions that lack leisure. These eight conditions are stated in the *Friendly Letter*:[188]

> To be reborn with wrong views or without a conqueror's word,
> Or as an animal, a hungry ghost, a hell-being,
> An uncultured person in a border region,
> A stupid and mute person, or a deity of long life **[78]**
> Is to be afflicted by one of the eight faults that are conditions which lack leisure.
> After you have attained leisure, which is freedom from these,
> Strive to end birth.

With three of these eight you are unable to know what to adopt and what to cast aside: being reborn in a border region in which the four types of followers [fully ordained monks and nuns and novice monks and nuns] are not active; being mute, stupid, and having incomplete sensory faculties—which means incomplete limbs, ears, and so on; and lacking a conqueror's word, meaning born where a buddha has not arisen. If you have a wrong view which misconceives the three jewels, karma and its effects, and former and future lives as nonexistent, you do not believe in the sublime teachings. You will have great difficulty in developing a religious attitude if you are born in any of the three miserable realms, and, even if you do develop a little bit, you will be unable to practice because you will be tormented by suffering.

Mahāmati's *Clear Words: Explanation of the "Friendly Letter" (Vyakta-padā-suhṛl-lekha-ṭīkā)* explains[189] that a deity of long life is one who lacks discrimination and lives in the formless realm. Aśvaghoṣa's *A Talk on the Eight Conditions that Lack Leisure (Aṣṭākṣaṇa-kathā)* explains[190] that a deity of long life is one in the desire realm who is constantly distracted by activities of desire. Vasubandhu's *Treasury of Knowledge* states that the deities who lack discrimination exist in one area of Great Fruit—a land of the fourth meditative stabilization. This area is set off from the rest of Great Fruit in the way that a monastery is set off from a lay settlement.[191] Even more, these deities have inactive minds and mental processes, except for the time immediately following birth and during death. Finally, they live for many great eons. It is incorrect to say that a noble being who exists in the formless realm is in a condition that lacks leisure. Therefore, we say that ordinary beings who are born in the formless realm are in a condition that lacks leisure because they do not have the opportunity to achieve the path to liberation. The same can also be said for being reborn as a deity of the desire realm who is constantly distracted by sensual pleasures.[192]

Thus, with respect to calling these "conditions that lack leisure," the *Clear Words: Explanation of the "Friendly Letter"* states:[193]

> In these eight states there is no time for acts of virtue; therefore, they are called "conditions that lack leisure."

2) **Opportunity**

a) **The five aspects of opportunity that pertain to yourself**

According to the *Śrāvaka Levels* the five are:[194]

> Being human, being born in a central region, having complete sensory faculties,
> Having reversible karma, and having faith in the source. **[79]**

"Being born in a central region" means that you are born in an area wherein the four types of followers are active. "Having complete sensory faculties" means that you are not stupid or mute, and that you have your main limbs, secondary limbs, eyes, ears, and the like intact. "Having reversible karma" means that you have not done or caused others to commit the five deeds of immediate retribution.[195] "Faith in the source" means that you have faith in discipline, which is the root from which all mundane and supramundane virtues arise. Here, "discipline" refers to all three scriptural collections. These five are called "aspects of opportunity that pertain to yourself" because they are included in your mind-stream and are favorable conditions for practicing the teaching.

b) **The five aspects of opportunity that pertain to others**

The five are:[196]

> That a buddha has visited, that the sublime teaching is being taught,
> That the teaching remains, that there are those who follow it,
> That there is caring for others.

Among these, "that a buddha has visited," (or is appearing), means that a bodhisattva has accumulated the collections of merit and sublime wisdom for three countless eons, and has reached the heart of enlightenment; i.e., become a perfect buddha. "That the sublime teaching is being taught" means that a buddha or the disciples of that buddha are imparting the teaching. "That the teaching remains" means that it is not degenerating between the time of someone becoming a buddha and giving the teaching until this buddha passes into final nirvāṇa. Furthermore, this phrase refers to the teaching at the time its followers achieve it by knowing the ultimate sublime teachings. "That there are those who follow" this teaching means that there are some who understand that beings have the capacity to perceive the sublime teaching. They understand this through the very knowledge of the ultimate, sublime teachings mentioned above. These individuals then follow the teaching while teaching others according to their knowledge. "That there is caring for others" refers to benefactors and those who actually carry out acts of charity by giving religious robes and the like. Since these five conditions exist in the minds of others and are favorable conditions for the practice of the teachings, they are called "aspects of opportunity that pertain to others."

The first four aspects of opportunity that pertain to others (as presented here from the *Śrāvaka Levels*)[197] are at present incomplete for us. However, it is suitable to consider an approximation of three of these four—the sublime teaching being taught, the teachings given remaining, and there being followers of the teaching which abides—to be complete for us. **[80]**

b. **Contemplating the great importance of leisure and opportunity**

Until death, animals strive merely to avoid suffering and achieve happiness. Therefore, if you do this and do not practice the pure teachings for the sake of achieving lasting happiness, then you are like an animal despite being born in a happy realm. As Candragomin's *Letter to a Student (Śiṣya-lekha)* states:[198]

> Just as an elephant calf craves a few mouthfuls
> Of grass that grows at the edge of a deep pit and
> Falls into the chasm without obtaining any,
> So it is with those who desire the joys of this world.

Not just any life will suffice for the practice of such pure teachings in general or for the practice of the Mahāyāna path in particular. Consequently, you must attain such a life as was described earlier. The *Letter to a Student*:[199]

> With a human life you attain the spirit of enlightenment,
> Which is the basis for the path to the state of a *sugata*,
> Which brings great mental force, and which equips you to lead all beings.
> Neither *nāgas*, demigods, *vidyādharas*, *garudas*, *kinnaras*,[200] nor snakes attain this path.

Also the *Descent into the Womb Sūtra (Garbhāvakrānti-sūtra)* states:[201]

> Even though you have been born a human with such limitless suffering, you still have the best of situations. It is difficult to attain this even in ten million eons. Even when the deities die, the other deities say, "May you have a happy rebirth." By happy rebirth they mean a human rebirth.

Thus, even the deities hold human life as something toward which they aspire.

A life as a certain type of desire realm deity—one who has strong latent propensities due to previously having trained in the path as a human—can serve as a basis for initially seeing the truth. However, you cannot initially attain the path of a noble being during a life in the higher [deities'] realms.[202] Moreover, most desire realm deities are said to be in a condition that lacks leisure, as explained previously. Therefore, a human life is the supreme basis for initially achieving the path. Furthermore, since a human life on the Uttarakuru continent is not a suitable basis for vows, there is praise for a human life on the other three continents. Moreover, among these, there is praise for a human on Jambudvīpa.

Therefore, repeatedly meditate with thoughts such as this:

> Why would I waste this attainment of such a good life? When I act as though it were insignificant, I am deceiving myself. **[81]** What could be more foolish than this? Just this once I am free from continuously trekking the many narrow cliff-paths of leisureless conditions, such as miserable realms. If I waste this freedom and

return to those conditions, it would be similar to losing my mind, like someone dazed by a magic spell.

As Āryaśūra says:[203]

Human life plants the seed
For going beyond cyclic existence,
The supreme seed of glorious enlightenment.
Human life is a stream of good qualities
Better than a wish-granting jewel.
Who here would attain it and then waste it?

And also, *Engaging in the Bodhisattva Deeds* states:[204]

There is nothing more deluded
And nothing more confused
Than for me to have found such leisure
And yet not to cultivate virtue.

After I have recognized this,
If I remain idle through confusion,
Great sorrow will befall me
At the time of my death.

When my body roasts for a long time
In the intolerable fires of hell,
Blazing flames of unbearable regret
Will certainly ravage my mind.

This is a rare and helpful situation;
Somehow I found it by chance.
If despite my intelligence
I am drawn again to hell,

Then, like one bewildered by a magic spell,
I will have simply lost my wits.
What is it within me that causes this confusion?
I do not know even this.

Furthermore, Geshe Drom-dön-ba asked Jen-nga, "Are you mindful that you have a human life endowed with leisure and opportunity?" Jen-nga replied, "Each time I enter into meditation, I recite:

Now I have independence and favorable conditions.
If I do not take full advantage of this time,
I will plunge into the abyss and fall under the control of others.
Who will lift me out? **[82]**

Thus, every time he meditated, Jen-nga first recited this verse of teaching, which is from Candrakīrti's *Commentary on the "Middle Way" (Madhyamakāvatāra)*.[205] You should also do the same.

Contemplate the great importance of leisure and opportunity in this way with respect to your final goals. Also reflect on how important they are in terms of your temporary goals. That is, consider how you can easily achieve with this life qualities such as generosity, ethical discipline, and patience, which are the causes of resources, perfect attendants, and the body of a being in high status [rebirth amongst humans or deities]. Think as follows:

> In this way, this life is very important in terms of attaining high status and certain goodness [of either liberation or omniscience]. If I were to waste it and not strive day and night to create the causes of these two goals, it would be as if I were returning empty-handed from a land of jewels. Also, I will be bereft of happiness in the future and will not obtain a life of leisure. Without leisure, I will undergo continual suffering. Thus, what kind of self-deception is worse than this?

As Āryaśūra says:[206]

> Those who have obtained a human life rich in virtues
> Through a collection of merit over innumerable eons,
> And who then, due to confusion in this life,
> Fail to accumulate even the slightest treasury of merit
>
> Will in future lifetimes
> Enter the house of unbearable sorrow.
> Like the traders who go to a land of jewels
> And return home empty-handed,
>
> Without the karmic paths of the ten virtues
> You will not obtain a human life again.
> How can there be happiness without a human life?
> Without happiness, there is only suffering.
>
> Therefore, you have only deceived yourself before going to the next life.
> There is nothing more confused than this.

After thinking like this, develop a great desire to take full advantage of this life of leisure and opportunity. *Engaging in the Bodhisattva Deeds*:[207]

> Once you have given this body wages and bonuses,
> You must make it act for your welfare.
> Do not give it everything
> If it does not help you.

Also:

> Relying on the boat of a human body,
> Free yourself from the great river of suffering.

> Because this boat is difficult to obtain again,
> Do not sleep now, fool!

Furthermore, Bo-do-wa states in his *Jewel Heaps of Teachings Through Analogy (dPe chos rin chen spungs pa)*:

> An insect's obeisance, a ride upon a wild ass, the Tsang (rTsang) person's fish, and buttered balls of roasted barley flour.[208]

By thinking along these lines, develop the desire to take full advantage of a human life of leisure and opportunity. **[83]**

c. **Contemplating the difficulty of attaining leisure and opportunity**

Moreover, whether you start from a happy realm or a miserable realm, it is difficult to obtain such leisure and opportunity. For, the Buddha states in the *Bases of Discipline (Vinaya-vastu)*[209] that those who die in the miserable realms and are reborn there are similar in number to the dust particles on the great earth, whereas those who are reborn from there into happy realms are similar in number to the dust particles on the tip of a fingernail. Further, those who die in both types of happy realms [human and divine] and are reborn in the miserable realms are similar in number to the dust particles on the great earth, while those who die in the happy realms and are reborn there are similar in number to the dust particles on the tip of a fingernail.

Question: Why is a human life of leisure and opportunity so difficult to obtain?

Reply: It is because beings of the happy realms—humans and the like—are frequently involved in such ignoble activities as the ten nonvirtues. Because of this, they are reborn in the miserable realms. As Āryadeva's *Four Hundred Stanzas* states:[210]

> Humans for the most part
> Are involved in things ignoble.
> Therefore, most ordinary beings
> Will surely go to the miserable realms.

For instance, for even a single moment of anger toward a bodhisattva you must stay for an eon in the Unrelenting Hell. As this is so, it goes without saying that you will have to stay for many eons in the miserable realms on account of having in your mind-stream the imprints of many sins that you previously accumulated over many lifetimes. These imprints have not been erased by an antidote and have not yet issued effects. Still, if you completely clear away previously accumulated causes of miserable rebirths and restrain yourself from engaging in these causes again, you are assured of a happy rebirth. However, doing this is extremely rare. If you do not act this way, you will be reborn in a miserable realm. Once there, you will not cultivate virtue, but you will continually commit sins. You will not even hear the phrase "happy realms" for many eons! Therefore, a human life of leisure and opportunity is very difficult to obtain. *Engaging in the Bodhisattva Deeds*:[211]

> With behavior such as mine
> I will not attain a human body again.
> If I do not attain it,
> I will commit sin and never be virtuous. **[84]**
>
> If I do not cultivate virtue
> Even when I have the chance to do so,
> What virtue will I cultivate in a miserable realm,
> Completely confused and suffering?
>
> If I cultivate no virtue
> And accumulate sins,
> I will not hear even the name
> "Happy realms" for a billion eons.
>
> Thus the Bhagavan said
> That this human life is as difficult to obtain
> As it is for a sea turtle to put its neck
> Into a yoke tossing about on the vast ocean.
>
> If even a single moment's wrongdoing
> Causes you to abide in the Unrelenting Hell for an eon,
> It goes without saying that you will not enter a happy realm
> Due to sins heaped up since beginningless time.

Qualm: When I experience the suffering of the miserable realms, I will be extinguishing previous bad karma, and then I will be reborn in a happy realm. Hence, getting out of the miserable realms is not difficult.

Reply: While you are experiencing the suffering in the miserable realms, you are constantly accumulating sins. Therefore, although you may die in a miserable realm, you will continue to be reborn in miserable realms. Because of this, getting out of the miserable realms is difficult. *Engaging in the Bodhisattva Deeds*:[212]

> Experiencing only the effects of that karma,
> You will not get out—
> While experiencing the effects,
> You create other sins.

After you have reflected on the difficulty of obtaining a human life of leisure and opportunity in this way, develop the desire to take full advantage of such a life. Think, "If I use this life for wrongdoing, it is extremely wasteful. In light of this, I will spend my time practicing the sublime teaching."

Nāgārjuna's *Friendly Letter* states:[213]

> Since it is even more difficult to obtain a human life from an animal life
> Than for a sea turtle's head to enter
> The aperture of a yoke floating upon the great ocean,
> O King, lord of humankind, make this life fruitful by practicing the sublime teaching.
>
> One who is born as a human,
> And then becomes involved in wrongdoing
> Is even more foolish than one who fills
> A golden vessel adorned with jewels with vomit.

And Candragomin's *Letter to a Student* states:[214]

> After you have obtained a human life, so difficult to obtain,
> Resolutely achieve just that which you seek. **[85]**

Furthermore, the great yogi[215] said to Jen-nga, "Do it a little at a time." Jen-nga replied, "I understand this, but this leisure and opportunity are difficult to obtain." Bo-do-wa said:

> In the region of Pen-bo ('Pan [po]) there was a great fortress named May-cha-kar (rMa'i-phyva-mkhar). It was captured by an enemy, and could not be recaptured for a long time. Consequently, there was this old man who was tormented by the loss of this fortress. One time he heard someone cry, "The fortress has been taken back," whereupon he grabbed a spear, being unable to walk, and, dragging himself along with the help of the spear, exclaimed, "How nice it would be if recapture of the May-cha-kar fortress isn't a dream!" Similarly, you must find such delight in the attainment of leisure and opportunity, and you must practice the teachings.

Meditate until you attain the attitude indicated in these stories.

In order to develop this sort of fully qualified desire to take full advantage of a life of leisure, you must reflect on its four elements, as follows:

1) the need to practice the teachings, because all living beings only want happiness and do not want suffering, and because achieving happiness and alleviating suffering depend only on practicing the teachings;

2) the ability to practice, because you are endowed with the external condition, a teacher, and the internal conditions, leisure and opportunity;
3) the need to practice in this lifetime, because if you do not practice, it will be very difficult to obtain leisure and opportunity again for many lifetimes; and
4) the need to practice right now, because there is no certainty when you will die.

Among these, the third stops the laziness of giving up, which thinks, "I will practice the teaching in future lives." The fourth stops the laziness of disengagement, which thinks, "Although I should practice in this lifetime, it is enough to practice later on and not to practice in my early years, months, and days." Therefore, it is acceptable to create a list of three qualities by subsuming these two into one, "practicing quickly." In this case, mindfulness of death is indeed relevant here, but I will explain it later; otherwise this will become too wordy.

If you reflect on this human life of leisure and opportunity from many perspectives, you will greatly affect your mind. Therefore, contemplate as instructed above. **[86]** If you cannot do this, condense this material into three topics: what the nature of leisure and opportunity is, how it is important in terms of temporary and final goals, and how it is difficult to obtain in terms of its causes and effects. Then take from the above explanations whatever accords with your mind, and meditate on it.

With respect to how it is difficult to obtain a human life of leisure and opportunity in terms of the causes, consider the following. In general, even to obtain just a happy rebirth you must cultivate a single pure virtue, such as ethical discipline. In particular, to obtain complete leisure and opportunity requires many roots of virtue, such as having a foundation of pure ethical discipline, augmenting it with generosity and the like, and when dying making a connection with your next lifetime through stainless aspirational prayers. As this is so, it is obvious that very few achieve such causes. Therefore, once you have understood this, reflect on the difficulty of obtaining the general effect, a life in a happy realm, and the particular effect, a human life with leisure and opportunity.

The difficulty of obtaining a human life of leisure and opportunity in terms of the effects is explained as follows. Compared to the number of beings in the miserable realms—beings unlike us—even a mere rebirth in a happy realm seems almost nonexistent. Even compared to the number of beings in the happy realms—beings like us—a special life of leisure is very rare. Meditate on this.

Geshe Döl-wa greatly valued this teaching on the difficulty of obtaining leisure and opportunity. Thus, he said that the practice of all other teachings follows this one. Since this is so, strive at it.

8

THE THREE TYPES OF PERSONS

2. How to take full advantage of a life of leisure and opportunity
   a. How to develop certain knowledge of a general presentation of the path
      1) How all the scriptures are included within the paths of the three types of persons
      2) Why students are led in stages using the trainings of the three types of persons
         a) The purpose of leading students by means of the paths of the three types of persons
         b) Why one guides students through such stages
            i) The actual reason
            ii) The purpose

2. How to take full advantage of a life of leisure and opportunity

How to take full advantage of a life of leisure and opportunity is presented in two parts:

1. How to develop certain knowledge of a general presentation of the path (Chapter 8)
2. The actual way to take full advantage of a life of leisure and opportunity (Chapters 9 and on)

a. How to develop certain knowledge of a general presentation of the path

The way to develop certain knowledge of a general presentation of the path itself has two parts:

1. How all the scriptures are included within the paths of the three types of persons
2. Why students are led in stages using the trainings of the three types of persons

1) **How all the scriptures are included within the paths of the three types of persons**

In the beginning a person who is to become a buddha develops the spirit of enlightenment; in the middle, this person accumulates the collections of merit and sublime wisdom; and in the end, this person actualizes perfect buddhahood. All these actions are solely for the welfare of living beings. Therefore, all the teachings given by a buddha simply accomplish the welfare of living beings. This being the case, the welfare of living beings is what you should accomplish as well. **[87]** This welfare is twofold: the provisional goal of high status as a human or deity, and the final goal of the certain goodness of liberation or omniscience. Between these two, many of the Buddha's statements pertain to the attainment of the temporary goal of high status. All of these statements are included in the teachings for a person of genuine small capacity or the teachings shared with such a person, because persons of special small capacity do not work very much on behalf of this lifetime, but they diligently strive for the excellent high states of human or divine rebirth in future lifetimes by engaging in the cultivation of their causes. The *Lamp for the Path to Enlightenment*:[216]

> Know to be "least" those persons
> Who diligently strive to attain
> Solely the joys of cyclic existence
> By any means for their welfare alone.

There are two kinds of certain goodness: the liberation that is mere freedom from cyclic existence and the sublime state of omniscience. Many of the Buddha's statements pertain to the vehicle of the *pratyekabuddha* and the *śrāvaka*. All of these statements are included in the teachings for a person of actual medium capacity or the teachings shared with such a person, because persons of medium capacity develop disenchantment with all of cyclic existence, and then make their goal their own liberation from cyclic existence. They then enter the path of the three trainings, the method for attaining liberation. The *Lamp for the Path to Enlightenment*:[217]

> Those persons are called "medium"
> Who stop sinful actions,

Turn their backs on the joys of cyclic existence,
And diligently strive just for their own peace.

The Elder's [Atisha's] *Lamp for the Collection of Deeds (Caryā-saṃgraha-pradīpa)* states:[218]

Since the guru, the Buddha, said,
"Depend on the perfection and mantra vehicles
And attain enlightenment,"
Here I will write about the meaning of this.

According to this, the method of attaining omniscience is twofold: the Mahāyāna of the perfections and the Mahāyāna of mantra. These two are included in the teachings of a person of great capacity because persons of great capacity, under the influence of great compassion, make buddhahood their goal in order to extinguish all the sufferings of all living beings. They then train in the six perfections, the two stages, and the like. **[88]** The *Lamp for the Path to Enlightenment*:[219]

Those persons are called "superior"
Who sincerely want to extinguish
All the sufferings of others
By understanding their own suffering.

Below, I will explain how the method for these persons to attain enlightenment involves both the perfection and mantra vehicles.

With respect to the terms for the three types of persons, these statements in the *Lamp for the Path to Enlightenment* are similar in meaning to the statement in the *Compendium of Determinations (Viniścaya-samgrahaṇī)* of the *Levels of Yogic Deeds (Yoga-caryā-bhūmi)*:[220]

Furthermore, there are the three types of persons as follows. There are those who have correctly assumed the vow of ethical discipline of giving up the ten nonvirtues, which is not considered a vow and yet is similar to a vow. There are those who have correctly assumed the *śrāvaka*'s vow of ethical discipline. There are those who have correctly assumed the bodhisattva's vow of ethical discipline. Among these, the first are the least; the second, medium; and the third, superior.

Furthermore, the scriptures mention many ways of positing a least, a medium, and a superior person. Like Atisha's *Lamp for the Path to Enlightenment*, Vasubandhu's *Abhidharma-kośa Auto-commentary (Abhidharma-kośa-bhāṣya)* defines[221] the three types of persons. Among the persons of small capacity, there are indeed two types—

those who are intent on this lifetime and those who are intent on future lifetimes. However, here I am speaking of the latter, whom I will identify as those who engage in the unmistaken method for attaining high status.

2) **Why students are led in stages using the trainings of the three types of persons**

This explanation has two parts:

1. The purpose of leading students by means of the paths of the three types of persons
2. Why one guides students through such stages

a) **The purpose of leading students by means of the paths of the three types of persons**

I have given an explanation of the three types of persons. However, the stages of the path for the person of great capacity also include the paths for the other two types of persons in their entirety. Thus, these two paths are parts, or branches, of the Mahāyāna path. **[89]** As the master Aśvaghoṣa states in his *Cultivation of the Conventional Spirit of Enlightenment (Saṃvṛti-bodhicitta-bhāvanā)*:[222]

> Being harmless, truthful,
> And chaste; not stealing,
> And giving away all your possessions:
> These are deeds that give rise to happy rebirths.
>
> Once you have seen the suffering of cyclic existence,
> You cultivate the true path to abandon it,
> And you eliminate the two misdeeds;
> These are the deeds that give rise to peace.
>
> A person of great capacity should practice all these;
> They are the branches of the path of the supreme determination
> to be free.
> The knowledge that all phenomena are emptinesses
> Creates the stream of compassion for all beings.
>
> Limitless deeds of skill-in-means
> Are the activity of the supreme determination to be free.

Therefore, in this instance teachers lead you neither to the path for persons of small capacity, who make their goal the mere happiness of cyclic existence, nor to the path for persons of medium capacity, who make their goal the mere liberation from cyclic existence for their own sake. Rather, they take some of the paths that are common to these two types of persons and make them prerequisites for leading you to the path for persons of great capacity. Thus they make them components of the training in the path for persons of great capacity.

Therefore, once you have developed the desire to take full advantage of this human life of leisure and opportunity as explained before, you must know how to take full advantage of it. With respect to that, Bhāvaviveka's *Heart of the Middle Way* states:[223]

> These bodies are insubstantial,
> Like banana trees and bubbles.
> Who would not give them a substance that is like Mount Meru
> By making them conditions for helping others?
>
> These bodies are a basis for sickness, old age, and death.
> Those who have good character and compassion
> Make them in each moment
> A basis for promoting happiness in others.
>
> This life of leisure is free of the eight conditions of nonleisure.
> With the lamp of the sublime teaching
> Make good use of this leisure
> Through the deeds of a person of great capacity.

Thus, enter the Mahāyāna with the thought, "Day and night I will conduct myself as a person of great capacity, making good use of this body of mine, which is a home for illness, a basis for the sufferings of old age and the like, and which lacks an essence like a banana tree or a water bubble."

Question: From the outset one should guide students through the practices of a person of great capacity. **[90]** What is the use of training in paths which are shared with the persons of small and medium capacities?

Reply: Training in the paths that are shared with these two is a prerequisite for the development of the path of a person of great capacity. I will explain how this is so.

b) **Why one guides students through such stages**

Why one guides students through such stages is explained in terms of the actual reason and the purpose.

i) **The actual reason**

The entrance to the Mahāyāna is solely the spirit of supreme enlightenment. Once this is produced in your mind-stream, it is as Śāntideva states in his *Engaging in the Bodhisattva Deeds*:[224]

> The moment helpless beings, bound in the prison of cyclic existence,
> Develop this spirit of enlightenment
> They are called "children of the *sugatas*"...

Thus, these beings enter the Mahāyāna upon being named "conquerors' children" or "bodhisattvas." If they ruin their spirit of enlightenment, they expel themselves from the company of Mahāyāna practitioners.

Therefore, those who wish to enter the Mahāyāna must develop this spirit of enlightenment by making many forms of effort. The supreme texts that teach the stages of the bodhisattva path, Śāntideva's *Compendium of Trainings* and *Engaging in the Bodhisattva Deeds*, speak of how to develop it. They state that you first need to meditate on its benefits. Then you intensify your delight in these benefits from the depths of your heart. This must be accompanied with practicing the seven branches of worship along with the practice of refuge.

If you condense the benefits spoken of in this way, they are twofold: temporary and final. The first is again twofold: not falling into miserable realms and being reborn in happy realms. That is, once you have developed this spirit of enlightenment, you clear away many previously accumulated causes for miserable rebirths, and you end the continuous accumulation of them in the future. You also vastly increase your previously accumulated causes of happy rebirths since they are imbued with this spirit. Furthermore, because you are motivated by this spirit, the causes that you create anew will be inexhaustible. **[91]** Relying upon this spirit of enlightenment, you will easily achieve the final aims, liberation and omniscience.

From the outset you must have an uncontrived aspiration that seeks to attain these final and temporary benefits. If you do not have this, you might say, "I will strive to develop this spirit" on account of those benefits that arise from developing the spirit of enlightenment, but it will be mere words. The hollowness of this claim is very clear once you examine your mind.

Therefore, first you must train in the thought that is common to persons of small and medium capacities in order to develop a wish to attain the two benefits, high status [as a human or deity] and certain goodness [liberation or omniscience]. After you have developed such a wish, you engage in cultivating the spirit of enlightenment, the attitude that produces these benefits. As you do this, you must develop the great compassion and love that are the foundation of this attitude. In other words, when you contemplate how you wander through cyclic existence, bereft of happiness and tormented by suffering, your body hairs should stand on end. Without this experience, it would be impossible for you to become unable to tolerate other beings' torment while they suffer and are bereft of happiness as they wander through cyclic existence.

Engaging in the Bodhisattva Deeds:[225]

> These beings have yet to dream
> Of such an attitude
> Toward even their own welfare;
> How then could they produce it for other's welfare?

Consequently, in the context of the person of small capacity you reflect on how you are harmed by the suffering of the miserable realms. In the context of the person of medium capacity you contemplate on how, even in high status, there is suffering and there is no peaceful bliss. Then you foster the development of love and compassion by cultivating a sense of empathy for living beings, whom you hold as close to you. From this you develop the spirit of enlightenment. Therefore, training in the thought common to persons of small and medium capacities is the method for producing an uncontrived spirit of enlightenment; it is not some separate path along which your teacher leads you.

Accordingly, you work at many ways of purifying yourself of nonvirtue and accumulating virtue using the practices for developing both the attitude that is shared with persons of small capacity and the attitude that is shared with persons of medium capacity. These are practices such as going for refuge and thinking about karma and its effects. **[92]** Understand that these too help you to develop the spirit of enlightenment, because they correspond to either the seven branches of worship or the practice of refuge, which are methods of training that are prerequisites for the spirit of enlightenment in the context of the practices for the person of great capacity.

At this point the guru thoroughly expounds the ways in which the trainings of the persons of small and medium capacities serve as components for the development of the spirit of unsurpassed enlightenment. Moreover, you, the student, reach certain knowledge of this. Then, whenever you sustain a meditation, it is extremely important for you to keep this understanding in mind and train in these teachings as components for your development of the spirit of enlightenment. Otherwise, the path of the person of great capacity and the paths of the persons of small and medium capacities would be separate and unrelated. And since you do not attain any certain knowledge of the spirit of enlightenment until you reach the actual path of the person of great capacity, your lack of training in these topics as components of your development of the spirit of enlightenment would either prevent you from developing that spirit, or, while you lack this training, cause you to deviate from your great purpose of developing that spirit. Therefore, pay close attention to this point.

In this way, train in the paths of persons of small and medium capacities and train well in what is explained in the context of the person of great capacity. Then, to the best of your ability, develop an uncontrived spirit of enlightenment in your mind-stream. Next, in order to stabilize this spirit, make a special practice of refuge and then perform the rite of the aspirational spirit of enlightenment. After you have adopted this aspirational spirit through the rite, you must strive to learn its precepts. Then, develop a great yearning to learn the bodhisattva deeds, such as the six perfections and the four ways of gathering disciples. Once this yearning arises from the depths of your heart, decisively take up the pure vow of the engaged spirit of enlightenment. Then, at the risk of your life, avoid being polluted by the root infractions. Strive not to be soiled by even small and medium contaminations or by the creation of faults. Even if you are soiled, thoroughly purify yourself by repairing the infractions just as is taught in scripture.

Next, train broadly in the six perfections. In particular, train well in meditative stabilization—the heart of meditative serenity—in order to make your mind capable of being set on a virtuous object of meditation, according to your wish. **[93]** The Elder's *Lamp for the Path to Enlightenment* says[226] that you should develop meditative serenity for the sake of producing the superknowledges. He is simply giving an example. In other contexts he says that you should develop serenity for the sake of producing insight. Therefore, achieve serenity mainly for the purpose of insight. Then, in order to cut the bonds of the conception of the two selves, make a philosophical determination of the meaning of emptiness, which is selflessness. After sustaining an unmistaken method of meditation, achieve insight, the heart of wisdom.

Accordingly, Atisha's *Commentary on the Difficult Points of the "Lamp for the Path" (Bodhi-mārga-pradīpa-pañjikā)*[227] states that, except for the practices of serenity and insight, all the practices up to and including the training in the precepts of the vow of the engaged spirit of enlightenment constitute the training in ethical discipline. Serenity is the training in concentration or mind. Insight is the training in wisdom. Furthermore, all the practices up to and including meditative serenity constitute the factor of enlightenment called either method, the collection of merit, the paths that depend on conventional truths, or the stages of the vast path. The development of the three kinds of special wisdom constitutes the factor of enlightenment called wisdom, the collection of wisdom, that which depends on ultimate truths, or the stages of the profound path. Therefore, be very certain about their order, the fact that they are a comprehensive list, and the fact that you do not achieve enlightenment by either method or wisdom alone.

This is how the royal geese, the conquerors' children, who are on their way to the great ocean of a buddha's good qualities, spread their two wings and fly. One wing is conventional truths—all of the factors of method, the vast path. The other wing, which depends on ultimate truths, is knowing well both reality and selflessness. However, they do not take up only a single part of the path, or fly like a bird with a broken wing. As Candrakīrti's *Commentary on the "Middle Way"* states:[228]

> Spreading the broad, white wings of reality and conventionality,
> The royal geese, escorted by the flock of living beings,
> Fly on the winds of virtue to supremacy
> On the far shore of a buddha's ocean-like qualities. **[94]**

After you have trained your mind by means of the ordinary path, you must certainly enter the mantra path because, when you do, you will quickly complete the two collections. If you cannot practice more than just the ordinary path, or do not want to do it because your inclination inherited from former lives is too weak, then just improve on these very stages of the path.

It is taught in all the vehicles in general and in the mantra vehicle in particular that reliance on the teacher is very crucial. Consequently, once you enter the mantra path, you should follow the mantra explanations, and practice a method of relying on the teacher that is even more specialized than what I have explained before. Then, ripen your mind with initiations that come from pure tantric sources, and observe properly, at the risk of your life, all of the vows and pledges that you have received during your initiations. You can take the vow or pledge again if you are affected by a root infraction, but your mind will have been spoiled, and it will be very difficult to give rise to good qualities. Therefore, specifically strive never to be tainted by root infractions and not to be soiled by secondary infractions. Even if you are tainted by these, purify yourself of them with confession and restraint, since vows and pledges are the foundation of the path.

Then train in good instructions on either the yoga with signs (in the context of the lower tantras), or the yoga of the generation stage (in the context of highest yoga tantra). After this training has been made firm, train well in either the yoga without signs (in the context of the lower tantras), or the yoga of the completion stage (in the context of highest yoga tantra).

The *Lamp for the Path to Enlightenment* presents the body of such a path; these stages of the path also instruct you in this way. The Great Elder taught this in other texts, as well. His *Concise Method of Achieving the Mahāyāna Path (Mahāyāna-patha-sādhana-saṃgraha)* states:[229]

> If you wish to attain unsurpassed enlightenment,
> Which has inconceivable greatness,
> Be intent on practice and achieve its heart,
> For enlightenment depends upon practice. **[95]**
>
> As this body of perfect leisure and opportunity
> Was very difficult to obtain, and once obtained
> Will be very difficult to possess again,
> Make it meaningful by striving at practice.

And his *Concisely Written Method of Achieving the Mahāyāna Path (Mahāyāna-patha-sādhana-varṇa-saṃgraha)* says:[230]

> Just as, when a chance arises
> For prisoners to flee from prison,
> They flee from that place,
> As their goals are not the same as others',
>
> So too if an opportunity arises
> To cross over this great ocean of cyclic existence,
> You emerge from this household of existence,
> As your goals are not the same as others'.

Also:[231]

> Taking up the bodhisattva vow through abiding
> In the practice of refuge, higher ethical discipline,
> And the basis of the aspirational spirit of enlightenment,
> Practice properly, in stages, with what ability you have,
> All the deeds of the bodhisattvas—
> The six perfections and the like.

Also:[232]

> Cultivate the heart of wisdom and method—
> Insight, meditative serenity, and their unification.

Moreover, Bodhibhadra's *Chapter on the Collections of Concentration* (*Samādhi-sambhāra-parivarta*) states:[233]

> First, make firm your spirit of perfect enlightenment,
> Which has arisen from the strength of compassion.
> Do not be attached to enjoying the resources of cyclic existence,
> And turn your back on grasping.
> Endowed with perfect jewels such as faith,
> Respect your guru, who is equal to the Buddha.
>
> With the pledges that this guru taught,
> Joyously persevere in your meditations.
> Receive through your guru's kindness
> The bestowal of initiations, both vase and secret.
>
> Purifying body, speech, and mind,
> Such practitioners are fit for attainments.
> By completing the collections
> That arise from the branch of concentration,
> They will quickly achieve the supreme attainment.
> This is the way of mantra.

ii) **The purpose**

Question: If the teachings for the persons of small and medium capacities are prerequisites for the person of great capacity, they may as well be considered stages for the path of the person of great capacity. **[96]** Why use the expression, "stages of the path shared with the persons of small and medium capacities"?

Reply: There are two great purposes for differentiating three types of persons and guiding students accordingly: (1) it destroys the presumption of asserting that you are a person of great capacity despite not having developed the states of mind common to persons of small and medium capacities, and (2) it is of great benefit for those whose minds have the greatest, medium, and least capacity. How does it benefit them? Even the two persons of higher capacities must seek high status and liberation, so it is not wrong to teach students of medium and great capacities the practices that develop the attitudes of persons of small capacity and persons of medium capacity. They will develop good qualities.

Those persons of least capacity may train in higher practices, but this will lead to their giving up their lower perspective without rising to a higher perspective, and thus they would be left with nothing. Furthermore, there could be persons who have the fortune to have already produced the higher paths in past lives. If they are taught the paths shared with persons of lower capacity and they then train in them, they will quickly give rise either to those good qualities developed previously or to those not developed before. Consequently, as they have already developed lower paths, they can be led to successively higher paths, and thus their own path from practice in earlier lives will not be delayed.

The *Questions of the Royal Lord of Formulae (Dhāraṇīśvara-rāja-paripṛcchā)*[234] uses the example of a skillful jeweler gradually refining a jewel in order to illustrate the need to guide the student's mind in stages. Wary of being verbose, I have not cited it in full here. The protector Nāgārjuna also said to guide students in stages through the paths of high status and certain goodness:[235]

> Initially there are the teachings on high status;
> Then come the teachings on certain goodness.
> For, having obtained high status,
> You gradually reach certain goodness.

Also, the noble being Asaṅga states:[236]

> Further, bodhisattvas cause their disciples to accomplish the virtuous factor of enlightenment correctly and in stages. In order to do this, they initially give easy teachings to beings of childlike wisdom, having them practice easy instructions and explications. When they recognize that these beings have become endowed with average wisdom, they have them practice average teachings and instructions, and average explications. **[97]** When they recognize that these beings have become endowed with extensive wisdom, they have them practice profound teachings and instructions, and subtle explications. This is the graduated flow of activity for the welfare of these living beings.

Also, Āryadeva's *Lamp Which Is a Compendium of Deeds (Caryā-melāpaka-pradīpa)* describes how you first train in the thought of the perfection vehicle and then enter the mantra vehicle. It establishes that you must do so in stages. It then summarizes this point as follows:[237]

> The method by which beings who are beginners
> Engage in the ultimate purpose
> Was said by the perfect Buddha
> To be like the steps of a staircase.

Also, the *Four Hundred Stanzas*[238] states that the order of the path is definite:

> Initially, you stop the nonmeritorious.
> In the middle, you stop the misconception of self.
> Finally, you put an end to all bad views;
> One who knows this is an adept.

Also, the learned master Mātṛceṭa said:[239]

> It is like dyeing cloth that is free of stains:
> First they develop goodness in the students' minds
> Through discussions on generosity and the like,
> And then they have them meditate on the teaching.

Citing this passage, the great master Candrakīrti also held that the path has a definite order. Since the order we use in guiding others along the path clearly is very crucial for their practice, reach firm certainty about this method.

9

MINDFULNESS OF DEATH

b. The actual way to take full advantage of a life of leisure and opportunity
- 1) Training the mind in the stages of the path shared with persons of small capacity
  - a) The actual training of thought for a person of small capacity
    - i) Developing a state of mind that strives diligently for the sake of future lives
      - a′ Mindfulness of death, the contemplation that you will not remain long in this world
        - 1′ The faults of not cultivating mindfulness of death
        - 2′ The benefits of cultivating mindfulness of death
        - 3′ The kind of mindfulness of death you should develop
        - 4′ How to cultivate mindfulness of death
          - a″ The contemplation that death is certain
            - 1″ The contemplation that the Lord of Death will definitely come and therefore cannot be avoided
            - 2″ The contemplation that our lifetime cannot be extended and constantly diminishes
            - 3″ The contemplation of the certainty of death such that even while you are alive there is little time for religious practice
          - b″ The contemplation that the time of death is uncertain
            - 1″ The contemplation that the life span in this world is uncertain
            - 2″ The contemplation that the causes of death are very many and the causes of life few
            - 3″ The contemplation that the time of death is uncertain because the body is very fragile
          - c″ The contemplation that at the time of death nothing helps except religious practice
            - 1″ Friends will not help
            - 2″ Resources will not help
            - 3″ Your body will not help

b. **The actual way to take full advantage of a life of leisure and opportunity [98]**

The actual way to take full advantage of a life of leisure and opportunity is presented in three sections:

1. Training the mind in the stages of the path shared with persons of small capacity (Chapters 9-16)
2. Training the mind in the stages of the path shared with persons of medium capacity (Chapters 17-24)
3. Training the mind in the stages of the path for persons of great capacity.

1) **Training the mind in the stages of the path shared with persons of small capacity**

There are three divisions in this section:

1. The actual training of thought for a person of small capacity (Chapters 9-15)
2. The measure of the attitude of a person of small capacity (Chapter 16)
3. Clearing up misconceptions concerning the attitude of a person of small capacity (Chapter 16)

a) **The actual training of thought for a person of small capacity**

The actual training has two divisions:

1. Developing a state of mind that strives diligently for the sake of future lives (Chapters 9-10)
2. Relying on the means for achieving happiness in the next life (Chapters 11-15)

i) **Developing a state of mind that strives diligently for the sake of future lives**

This is explained in two parts:

1. Mindfulness of death, the contemplation that you will not remain long in this world (Chapter 9)
2. Contemplating what will occur in your future life: the happiness or suffering of the two types of beings (Chapter 10)

a′ **Mindfulness of death, the contemplation that you will not remain long in this world**

Mindfulness of death has four parts:

1. The faults of not cultivating mindfulness of death

2. The benefits of such cultivation
3. The kind of mindfulness of death you should develop
4. How to cultivate mindfulness of death

1′ **The faults of not cultivating mindfulness of death**

As previously mentioned, there are four errors that impede your taking full advantage of your life: [conceiving (1) the impure to be pure, (2) suffering to be happiness, (3) the impermanent to be permanent, and (4) the selfless to have a self]. Initially, it is merely the conception of the impermanent to be permanent that is the avenue of much injury. This conception is twofold: coarse and subtle. Of these two, in the case of your coarse impermanence, which is your death, the avenue of injury is the very thought, "I will not die." **[99]** Everyone has the idea that death will come later, at the end. However, with each passing day people think, "I will not die today; I will not die today," clinging to this thought until the moment of death. If you are obstructed by such an attitude and do not bring its remedy to mind, you will continue to think that you will remain in this life.

Then, as long as you have this attitude, you will continually think only of how to achieve happiness and evade suffering in this life alone, thinking, "I need this and that." You will not engage in religious practice because you do not think about things of great importance, such as future lives, liberation, and omniscience. Although you may perchance engage in study, reflection, meditation, and so forth, it will be only for the sake of this life, and whatever virtue you create will be of meager strength. Moreover, since your practice will be involved with wrongdoing, sins, and infractions, it would be rare for these virtuous activities not to be mixed with causes of miserable rebirths. Even if you try to engage in practices directed toward future lives, you will not be able to prevent the laziness of procrastination, thinking, "I will do it eventually." By passing time in distractions such as sleep, lethargy, senseless talk, and eating and drinking, you will not attain proper achievement, which comes through great effort.

If you are thus seduced by the hope that this body and life will last for a long time, you will create strong attachment to goods, services, and the like. As if swept away by the current of a river, you will be immersed in strong hostility toward what prevented you, or what you fear might prevent you, from having these objects of attachment; in delusion that is ignorant of their faults; and, as a consequence of these two, in afflictions such as pride and jealousy, as well as strong secondary afflictions. As a result of this, you will do more nonvirtuous actions each day such as the ten misdeeds of body, speech, and mind, the five deeds of immediate retribution, other misdeeds approaching these in gravity,[240] and the repudiation of the excellent teaching, all of which have the full power to induce strong suffering in places such as the miserable realms. **[100]** You will sap the life out of high status and certain goodness by increasingly distancing yourself from the remedies—the nectar of the well-spoken teachings. Then, death will overcome you and bad karma will lead you into a hot and unpleasant place among the strong and harsh sufferings of the miserable realms. What process could be worse than that?

The *Four Hundred Stanzas*:[241]

> What could be more dangerous
> Than to sleep as though at ease
> While subject to the Lord of Death,
> Ruler of the three worlds, himself without a master?

Also, *Engaging in the Bodhisattva Deeds*:[242]

> I will have to depart, leaving everything.
> But, not knowing this,
> I committed various sins
> For the sake of friends and foes.

2′ The benefits of cultivating mindfulness of death

When those who have a little understanding of the teaching conclude that they will die today or tomorrow, they see that friends and material possessions will not accompany them, and so they stop craving them. Naturally they then wish to take full advantage of their human birth through virtuous deeds such as giving gifts. Just so, if you create an authentic mindfulness of death, you will see that all toiling for worldly things such as goods, respect, and fame is as fruitless as winnowing chaff, and is a source of deception. Then you will turn away from wrongdoing. With constant and respectful effort you will accumulate good karma by doing such virtuous deeds as going for refuge and maintaining ethical discipline. You will thereby bring lasting significance to things, like the body, that would not have had such significance. You will ascend to a sublime state and will lead others there as well. What could be more meaningful?

For this reason, the scriptures use many examples to praise the mindfulness of death. The *Great Final Nirvāṇa Sūtra* says:[243]

> Among all reapings, the autumn harvest is supreme. Among all tracks, the track of the elephant is supreme. **[101]** Among all ideas, the idea of impermanence and death is supreme because with it you eliminate all the attachment, ignorance, and pride of the three realms.

Similarly, it is praised for being the hammer that instantly destroys all afflictions and wrongdoing, for being the gateway into the instantaneous achievement of all virtue and goodness, and so on. The *Collection of Indicative Verses*:[244]

> Understanding that the body is like a clay vessel and
> Similarly, that phenomena are like mirages,
> Here you destroy the demons' poisonous flower-tipped weapons
> And pass beyond the sight of the Lord of Death.

Also:[245]

> By seeing aging, the suffering of sickness,
> And dead bodies from which the mind is gone,
> The resolute abandon this prisonlike home,
> While ordinary worldlings can never eliminate attachment.

In brief, the only time to accomplish the aims of beings is now, when you have attained a special life of leisure and opportunity. The majority of us remain in the miserable realms; a few come to the happy realms, but the majority of these are in situations that lack leisure. Therefore, you do not get a chance to practice the teachings in these situations. Even when you have gained the circumstances allowing for practice, the reason that you do not practice the teachings properly is the thought, "I will not die yet."

Therefore, the thought that you will not die is the source of all deterioration, and the remedy for this is mindfulness of death, the source of all that is excellent. Consequently, you should not think that this is a practice for those who do not have some other profound teaching to cultivate in meditation. Nor should you think that although this is something worthy of meditation, you should cultivate it just a little at the beginning of the meditation session because it is not suitable for continuous practice. Rather, be certain from the depths of your heart that it is necessary in the beginning, middle, and end, and then cultivate it in meditation. **[102]**

3′ The kind of mindfulness of death you should develop

For those who have not practiced the path at all, the fear of death manifests itself as the worry that they will be separate from their relatives and so forth. This fear is caused by their strong attachment.

Therefore, do not develop this here. What, then, should you develop? Certainly nothing of your body, which you appropriated through karma and afflictions, shall survive death. This may frighten you, yet, for the time being, you cannot stop it. However, you should fear death if you have not secured your welfare in future lives by putting an end to the causes of the miserable realms and establishing the causes of high status and certain goodness. If you consider your fear about this, it is within your power not to be frightened at the moment of death because there are things you can do to secure your future welfare. If you do not act on these things, you will be tormented by regret at the time of death, in general fearing that you will not be liberated from cyclic existence and in particular fearing that you will fall into a miserable realm. The *Garland of Birth Stories*:[246]

> Though you hold fast, you cannot stay.
> What benefit is there
> In being frightened and scared
> Of what cannot be changed.
>
> Thus, when you analyze the nature of the world,
> Humans are regretful at death because they have sinned
> And have not brought forth virtuous actions.
> They worry about sufferings to come in future lives
> And the fear of dying clouds their minds.
>
> However, I do not know of anything I have done
> That would make me regretful,
> And I have made myself accustomed to virtuous actions.
> Why should anyone who abides in the teaching fear death?

The *Four Hundred Stanzas*:[247]

> Those who think with certainty,
> "I will die,"
> Give up fear. Therefore,
> How could they fear even the Lord of Death? **[103]**

Thus, when you contemplate impermanence again and again, you think, "I will undoubtedly separate from my body and resources soon," and you stop the craving that hopes not to leave them. Consequently, you will not fear death out of the distress of leaving.

4′ How to cultivate mindfulness of death

Cultivate this by way of the three roots, nine reasons, and three decisions. The three roots are:

(1) death is certain;
(2) the time of death is uncertain; and
(3) at the time of death nothing helps except religious practice.

a″ **The contemplation that death is certain**

Meditation on the certainty of death has three aspects:

(1) the Lord of Death will definitely come, and therefore cannot be avoided;
(2) our lifetime cannot be extended and constantly diminishes; and
(3) while you are alive, there is little time for religious practice.

1″ **The contemplation that the Lord of Death will definitely come, and therefore cannot be avoided**

No matter what kind of body you assume at birth, death comes. The *Collection of Indicative Verses*:[248]

> If all the buddhas, and their
> *Pratyekabuddha* and *śrāvaka* disciples
> Left their bodies,
> What can be said about ordinary beings?

No matter where you stay, death comes. The same text says:[249]

> Somewhere to live that is unharmed by death—
> Such a place does not exist.
> It does not exist in space, it does not exist in the sea,
> Nor if you stay in the midst of mountains.

Death's destruction of living beings is no different at any point in the past or future. The same text says:

> The wise know that all
> Who have come and will come perish,
> Leave this body, and go to the next life.
> Therefore, be sure to engage in pure behavior by abiding in the teaching.

You do not escape by fleeing from death, nor can you turn death away by such things as mantras. The *Advice to the King Sūtra* (*Rājāvavādaka*) says:[250]

> For example, four great mountains from the four directions—being hard, firm, solid-cored, indestructible, unsplittable, without fissures, extremely resilient, and massed into one—rise up into the sky and destroy the earth. **[104]** All the grasses, trees, trunks, branches, leaves, and all sentient beings, living beings,

> and creatures are crushed to dust. When these mountains come, it will not be easy to quickly run away, or to turn them away with force, wealth, magic substances, mantras, or medicine. Great King, in the same way, these four frights come, and it is not easy to quickly run away, or to turn them away with force, wealth, substances, mantras, or medicine. What are the four? They are aging, sickness, death, and decay. Great King, aging comes and destroys youth, sickness comes and destroys health, decay comes and destroys all that is excellent, and death comes and destroys life. It is not easy to quickly run away from them, or to turn them away with force or wealth, or to quell them with substances, mantras, or medicine.

Ga-ma-pa (Ka-ma-ba) said, "Now we should be frightened by death. At the time of death we should be fearless. But we are the opposite—we are not afraid now and at the moment of death we dig our fingernails into our chests."

2" **The contemplation that our lifetime cannot be extended and constantly diminishes**

The *Descent into the Womb Sūtra* says:[251]

> Currently, if we protect our bodies well in order to live comfortably, we will live, at the longest, one hundred years or a little more.

Thus, the maximum is no more than this. Even though it may be possible to live this long, the time until death passes very quickly. A year is consumed with the passage of months; months with the passage of days; and days with the passage of day and night, also with such periods of time as a morning, etc. Thus, few of us reach the expected life span of one hundred years, for much of our life span seems to be finished already, and what remains cannot be extended even for a moment. **[105]** Life diminishes day and night without a break. *Engaging in the Bodhisattva Deeds*:[252]

> This life is constantly lost
> Day and night without a pause,
> And there is nothing which can extend it.
> Why should death not come to someone like me?

Contemplate this with many examples. When weaving cloth, weavers use no more than one piece of thread on each pass, yet they quickly finish weaving the cloth. When animals such as sheep are led to slaughter, they move closer to death with every step they take. The water carried by the current of a strong river or the water in a waterfall on a steep mountain quickly disappears. Just as in these examples, your life is quickly spent and gone. Just as when herdsmen pick up their sticks, their livestock helplessly follow them home, so sickness and aging lead you helplessly into the presence of the Lord of Death. In this way, meditate on the certainty of death from many perspectives. The *Collection of Indicative Verses:*[253]

> For example, just as when weaving a cloth
> You reach the end
> By weaving individual courses,
> So too is human life.
>
> For example, just as those who are to be killed
> Come closer to the killing place
> With every step they take,
> So too is human life.
>
> Just as the strong downward current of a river
> Cannot be reversed,
> So too the movement of human life
> Is irreversible.
>
> Life is hard, brief,
> And full of suffering.
> It vanishes so quickly—
> Like that written on water with a stick.
>
> Just as livestock go home
> When the herdsmen raise their sticks,
> So sickness and aging lead humans
> To the Lord of Death.

Furthermore, it is said that the Great Elder went to the bank of a river and meditated, saying that the rippling flow of the water was good for meditation on impermanence. The *Extensive Sport Sūtra (Lalita-vistara-sūtra)*[254] also speaks of impermanence with many examples: **[106]**

> The three worlds are impermanent like an autumn cloud.
> The birth and death of beings is like watching a dance.
> The passage of life is like lightning in the sky;
> It moves quickly, like a waterfall.

Thus, once inward reflection yields some sense of certainty about impermanence, contemplate it by applying your understanding of it to many things, for it is said that everything around us teaches impermanence.

After you reflect on this again and again, you reach certain knowledge. It is not helpful to do just a little reflection and then say that nothing happened. As Ga-ma-pa said, "You say that nothing happened when you thought about it, but when did you reflect? If it was during the day, you were constantly distracted, and at night you slept. Do not lie!"

At the end of this life, the Lord of Death will destroy you and you will pass into the next world. Until then, there will never be a time when your life span does not diminish, whether you are going somewhere, walking around, or lying down. Thus, starting from the moment that you enter the womb, you do not remain for even an instant, but go headlong toward the next lifetime. Therefore, even your intervening life is exclusively consumed in a procession toward death led by the messengers, sickness and aging. Consequently, do not rejoice in the thought that while you are living you are stationary and not moving toward the next lifetime. For example, when falling from the top of a high cliff, the time of falling to earth through space is not enjoyable. As cited by Candrakīrti in his *Commentary on the "Four Hundred Stanzas" (Catuḥ-śataka-ṭīkā)*:[255]

> Hero of humans, beginning from the first night
> Of entering a womb in this world,
> One proceeds daily, without delay
> Into the presence of the Lord of Death.

In the *Story for Stopping the Four Errors (Catur-viparyaya-parihāra-kathā)* it says:[256]

> Do those who fall to earth from the peak of a high mountain
> Enjoy happiness in space as they are being destroyed?
> If they are constantly racing toward death from the time they
> are born, **[107]**
> How can living beings find happiness in the time in between?

These passages indicate that it is certain that your death will come quickly.

3" The contemplation of the certainty of death such that even while you are alive there is little time for religious practice

Even if you could live for the longest period explained above, it would be wrong to think that you have time. Much of your life has already been wasted. Half of what is left will be spent in sleep, and many of your waking hours will be wasted with other distractions. Further, as youth fades, the time of aging arrives. Your physical and mental strength deteriorate such that even if you want to practice religion, you lack the capacity to do so. Consequently, you have no more than a few chances to practice the teachings. The *Descent into the Womb Sūtra* says:[257]

> Moreover, half of the one-hundred-year life span is covered by sleep. Ten years are childhood. Twenty years are old age. Sorrow, lamentation, physical suffering, mental discomfort, and agitation take up time. Many hundreds of different physical illnesses also consume your time.

The *Story for Stopping the Four Errors* says:[258]

> In this time of one-hundred-year life spans even the longest of human lives is finished in only one hundred years. Of that, the beginning and end are made useless by youth and old age. Things like sleep and sickness destroy all hope for practice, leaving no time for it. How much remains to the life span of a being born among humans, who live in happiness?

Furthermore, Chay-ga-wa said that if you subtract from sixty years the time you lose to food and clothing, sleep, and sickness, not more than five years are left to devote to the teachings.

This being the case, the wonders of this life will be mere memories at the time of death, like waking up and remembering the pleasurable experiences in a single dream. Think, "If the enemy, death, is surely approaching and cannot be stopped, why should I delight in the delusions of this life?" **[108]** Then decide that you must practice the teaching and make many heartfelt pledges to do so.

The *Garland of Birth Stories:*[259]

> Alas, afflicted and worldly persons,
> I do not like unstable things.
> Even this glorious white water lily (*kumada*)
> Will become a memory.
>
> Alas, it is amazing that you beings are fearless,
> Placed in a realm like this.
> You are joyous and act unworried
> Though the Lord of Death blocks every path.
>
> As you have the powerful, dangerous, and unstoppable enemies
> Of sickness, aging, and death,
> You surely will go to a fearful place in the next life.
> I wonder what thoughtful person would delight in this?

Also, the *Letter to Kaniṣka (Mahā-rāja-kaniṣka-lekha)* says:[260]

> The ruthless Lord of Death

> Murders powerful beings without purpose.
> While such murder is sure to come,
> What wise person would be relaxed?
>
> Hence, as long as that great unforgiving warrior
> Has not fired the unstoppable arrow
> From which there is no escape,
> Strive for your own welfare.

Reflect in this way.

b″ The contemplation that the time of death is uncertain

It is certain that death will come sometime between today and one hundred years from now; it is uncertain on which day within that period death will come. Therefore, for instance, you cannot determine whether or not you will die today. However, you must assume that you will die and should think, "I will die today." For, if you assume that you will not die and think, "I will not die today," or, "I probably will not die today," you will continually make preparations to stay in this life and will not prepare for your next life. Meanwhile, you will be seized by the Lord of Death, and you will then die in sorrow. If you prepare for death every day, you will accomplish many goals for your next life. Hence, even if you do not die today, you will have done well. If you do die, it is even more meaningful in that you will have done what you needed to do. **[109]** For example, when it is certain that a great enemy is coming to do you severe harm sometime between now and some point in the future, but you do not know on which day the enemy will come, you must be cautious every day. It is like that.

If you think every day, "I will die today," or at least "I will probably die today," you will act for the benefit of whatever next life you will go to, and you will not make preparations to remain in this life. If you do not have this thought, you will see yourself as staying in this life, and you will make provisions for this life rather than act for the benefit of your next life. For example, when you plan to stay someplace for a long time, you make preparations to stay there. If you think that you are not going to stay there, but are going elsewhere, you make preparations for leaving. Hence, every day you must develop an awareness of the imminence of your death in the following way.

1″ The contemplation that the life span in this world (Jambudvīpa) is uncertain

In general, the life span on the Uttarakuru continent is definite. Even though on the other continents besides Uttarakuru and Jambudvīpa there is no certainty as to whether one will be able to complete one's own life span, for the most part there is a definite life span. The life span on Jambudvīpa is very indefinite, ranging from the initial life span that is vast beyond measure, to an eventual maximum length of ten years of age. Further, you can see that there is no certainty as to whether death will occur in youth, in old age, or in between. In the same vein, the *Treasury of Knowledge* says:[261]

> Here the life span is uncertain: at the end of the cycle,
> It is ten years; in the beginning, measureless.

The *Collection of Indicative Verses* says:[262]

> Among the many beings seen in the morning
> Some are not seen in the evening.
> Among the many beings seen in the evening
> Some are not seen in the morning.

Also:

> When many men and women
> And even youths die,
> How can the living be so confident to say,
> "This person is still too young to die"?
>
> Some die in the womb,
> Some at birth,
> Some when they can crawl,
> Some when they can run.
>
> Some are old, some are young,
> Some are young adults.
> Everyone goes gradually,
> Like ripe fruit falling. **[110]**

Bear in mind the cases you have seen or heard concerning the gurus and friends who reached the end of their life span but died without fulfilling their intentions, suddenly dying because of external and internal causes. Be aware of death, thinking over and over, "I too am subject to such a death."

2″ The contemplation that the causes of death are very many and the causes of life few

There are many sentient beings and insentient things that do harm to this life. Think in detail about the many forms of injury inflicted by humans and nonhuman demons; how many dangerous animals harm life and limb; and similarly how harm occurs due to internal diseases and external elements. Furthermore, your body must be created from the four elements—earth, water, fire, and wind—and even these are harmful to each other when they become imbalanced. When some are in excess and others are deficient, an illness develops, and you are robbed of your life. Hence, as these dangers are innately present within you, there is no security in body and life. In this vein, the *Great Final Nirvāṇa Sūtra* says:

> The idea of death is that hateful enemies constantly surround this life, ruining it at every moment. Nothing exists that extends your life.

Also, Nāgārjuna's *Precious Garland (Ratnāvalī)* says:[263]

> You dwell among the causes of death
> Like a butter lamp standing in a strong breeze.

In addition, his *Friendly Letter* says:[264]

> Life is more impermanent than a water bubble
> Battered by the winds of many perils.
> Thus, that you can inhale after exhaling,
> Or awaken from sleep—these things are fantastic.

The *Four Hundred Stanzas* says:[265]

> When the four elements are powerless to harm each other,
> They are called a balanced collection, and physical pleasure
> arises. **[111]**
> But it is totally unsuitable to call "pleasurable"
> A collection that is in opposition.

Because this is a time when the five impurities are rapidly spreading,[266] there are extremely few persons who accumulate the great power of virtuous deeds that enables a long life. Also, since the medicinal power of our food and such is weak, we have little resistance to disease. The provisions we do use are not easy to digest and thus have diminished power for enhancing the body's great elements. Further, since you have done little to amass the collection of merit and your wrongdoing is very potent, practices such as mantra recitation have little efficacy. All of this makes it extremely difficult to prolong your life.

Furthermore, there are no causes of staying alive that do not become causes of death. In other words, you seek such things as food and drink, shelter, and friends in order not to die, but even these can become causes of death. For instance, you may consume the wrong food and drink, or consume too much or too little. Your shelter could crumble, or your friends could deceive you. Thus, it is clear that there are no causes of staying alive that cannot become causes of death. Since life itself is headed toward death, the conditions for life would offer no security even if they were numerous. The *Precious Garland*:[267]

> The causes of death are many,
> Those of staying alive, few.
> These too become causes of death.
> Thus, always practice the teaching.

3″ The contemplation that the time of death is uncertain because the body is very fragile

Your body is very fragile, like a water bubble. Therefore, it does not take much damage to destroy it. Your life could be taken even by something that you only imagine to be harmful, like being pricked by a thorn. Hence, you can very easily be overcome by any of the causes of death. The *Friendly Letter* says:[268] **[112]**

> If not even ash will remain when the physical world—
> The earth, Mount Meru, and the seas—
> Is burned up by seven blazing suns,
> What need is there to mention humans, who are so very frail?

After you have reflected in this way, you should resolve that since there is no certainty as to when the Lord of Death will destroy your body and life, you will practice the teaching right now, without assuming that you still have time. Make this pledge many times from the depths of your heart. The *Letter to Kaniṣka* says:[269]

> The Lord of Death, a friend to no one,
> Descends suddenly. So do not wait,
> Saying, "I'll do it tomorrow."
> Practice the sublime teaching with urgency.
>
> It is not good for people to say,
> "I'll put it off until tomorrow and do this today."
> A tomorrow when you are gone
> Will undoubtedly come.

Furthermore, the lord of yogis, Śrī Jagan-mitrānanda,[270] says:

> Lord of the Earth, while this borrowed body
> Is still healthy, without sickness or deterioration,
> Take full advantage of it,
> Acting in order to end your fear of sickness, death, and deterioration.

> Once sickness, aging, deterioration, and the like occur,
> You might remember to practice, but what can you do then?

The contemplation of the uncertainty of the time of death is the most important of the three roots. This is the very thing that will redirect your mind, so work hard at it.

c″ **The contemplation that at the time of death nothing helps except religious practice**

1″ **Friends will not help**

When you see that you must go to your next life, no matter how many loving and very worried relatives and friends surround you at that time, you cannot take even one with you.

2″ **Resources will not help**

No matter how many piles of beautiful jewels you have, you cannot take even the slightest particle with you.

3″ **Your body will not help**

As you even have to discard the flesh and bones with which you were born, what need is there to mention anything else?

Consequently, think, "It will certainly come to pass that all the wonders of this world will leave me behind; I will leave them behind as well, and go to some other world. In fact, this will happen today!" **[113]** Contemplate how, at the time of death, only religious practice will serve as a refuge, a protection, a defense.

The *Letter to Kaniṣka* says:[271]

> When the past karma that caused
> This life is spent,
> And you are connected with new karma
> And led by the Lord of Death,
> Everyone turns back.
> Except for your virtue and sin,
> Nothing will follow you.
> Know this and act well.

Also, Śrī Jagan-mitrānanda says:[272]

> Divine One, no matter what fortune you have gained,
> When you depart to another life,
> As though conquered by an enemy in the desert,
> You are alone without children or queen,
>
> Without friends, without clothing,
> Without kingdom, and without palace.

> Though you have limitless power and armies,
> You will not see or hear them.
>
> Eventually not even one being or thing
> Will follow after you.
> In brief, if you lack even a name,
> What need is there to speak about anything else?

Try to achieve lasting happiness for your next life and beyond by being mindful of death in this way, reflecting on how leisure and opportunity are very important, are difficult to obtain, and are very easily lost despite being difficult to obtain. If instead you seek only to find happiness and to avoid suffering up until your death, then you are going to need a course of conduct which surpasses animal behavior, since animals are better than humans at temporal happiness. Otherwise, even though you have obtained a life in a happy realm, it will be just as though you had not. For, as *Engaging in the Bodhisattva Deeds* says:[273]

> Those who are tortured by bad karma
> Waste their wonderful leisure and opportunity, so hard to gain,
> In order to acquire some trifling thing
> Which is not so rare and which even animals may attain.

Therefore, although it is quite hard to produce this mindfulness of death, you must work at it because it is the foundation of the path. Bo-do-wa said:

> For me "appearance and exclusion" refers to my own meditation on impermanence.[274] **[114]** With it I exclude all the appearances of this life such as intimates, relatives, and possessions. Then, knowing that I must always go to the next life alone, without anything else, I think that I will do nothing except religious practice. Thereupon, a lack of attachment for this life begins. Until this arises in your mind, the paths of all the teachings remain blocked.

Also, Döl-wa said:

> Along the way, accumulate the collections and purify obscurations. Make supplications to the deity and the guru. Contemplate earnestly and with perseverance. If you do these, though you may think that knowledge will not arise in even one hundred years, it will arise anyway because nothing composite remains as it is.

When someone asked Ga-ma-pa about changing the object of meditation, he said to use the same one again. When someone asked him about what came next, he said, "There is nothing more."[275]

This being the case, if your mind is fit, meditate in accordance with what I have explained above.[276] If it is not fit, take up whatever is appropriate among the nine reasons and the three roots. Meditate again and again until you have turned your mind away from the activities of this life, which are like adorning yourself while being led to the execution ground.

No matter where the teachings of reliance on a teacher, leisure and opportunity, and impermanence may occur in the Buddha's word and its commentaries, recognize that they are meant to be practiced and sustain them in meditation. If you do so, you will easily find the intent of the Conqueror. Understand that you must proceed in this way in the context of the other teachings as well.

10

Reflecting on Your Future Life

b′ Contemplating what will occur in your future life: the happiness or suffering of the two types of beings
- 1′ Contemplating the suffering of hell denizens
  - a″ Contemplating the suffering of the great hells of living beings
  - b″ Contemplating the suffering of the adjoining hells
  - c″ Contemplating the suffering of the cold hells
  - d″ Contemplating the suffering of the occasional hells
- 2′ Contemplating the suffering of animals
- 3′ Contemplating the suffering of hungry ghosts
  - a″ Hungry ghosts who have external obstacles for obtaining food and drink
  - b″ Hungry ghosts who have internal obstacles for obtaining food and drink
  - c″ Hungry ghosts who have obstacles within the food and drink

b′ **Contemplating what will occur in your future life: the happiness or suffering of the two types of beings**

Since it is certain that you will die soon as previously mentioned, you cannot remain in this life. As you do not cease to exist after death, you will be reborn. Furthermore, you will be reborn in either a happy or a miserable realm, because there is no birthplace other than among these two types of beings. Since you are controlled by your karma and cannot choose where you will be born, you will be reborn in the manner in which your virtuous and nonvirtuous karma impel you to be reborn. **[115]** This being the case, contemplate the suffering of the miserable realms, thinking, "How would it be if I were born in a miserable realm?" As the protector Nāgārjuna says:

Reflect daily on the hells,
Both those extremely hot and cold.
Reflect also on the hungry ghosts
Emaciated by hunger and thirst.
Observe and reflect on the animals
Overcome by the suffering of stupidity.
Eliminate the causes of these and create the causes of happiness.

A human body in this world is difficult to obtain.
Once you have it, diligently stop
The causes of miserable rebirths.

It is extremely important to meditate in general on the sufferings of cyclic existence and, in particular, on the sufferings of the miserable realms, for if you contemplate how you have fallen into the ocean of suffering, you will then turn away from it, and thereby overcome your pride and arrogance. Seeing suffering as the result of nonvirtuous karma, you will be careful to avoid sins and infractions. Since you want happiness, not suffering, and understand that happiness is the result of virtue, you enjoy cultivating virtue. Once you have assessed your own condition, you develop compassion for others. After you have turned away from cyclic existence, you develop an aspiration for liberation. Frightened by suffering, you fervently go for refuge to the three jewels. Meditation on suffering is the great summary that includes these and many other key points of practice.

Similarly, *Engaging in the Bodhisattva Deeds* says:[277]

Since without suffering there is no determination to be free,
You, mind, stay fixed!

And also:

Furthermore, the good qualities of suffering are that you
Dispel arrogance with your disenchantment,
Develop compassion for the beings of cyclic existence,
Carefully avoid sin, and delight in virtue.

And further:

Overwhelmed by fear,
I offer myself to Samantabhadra.

Although *Engaging in the Bodhisattva Deeds* discusses these qualities of suffering from the viewpoint of suffering experienced in the past, the same qualities characterize future suffering as well. **[116]**

1′ Contemplating the suffering of hell denizens

a″ Contemplating the suffering of the great hells of living beings

[The *Levels of Yogic Deeds* says]:[278]

> There are eight great hells. The *Reviving Hell*, the first, lies thirty-two thousand leagues beneath us; the other seven are situated every four thousand leagues beneath that. The living beings of the Reviving Hell assemble and hack each other with various weapons that appear one by one through the force of karma, until they swoon and fall to the ground. Then a voice from the sky commands, "Revive!" and they rise up again, hack each other as before, and experience measureless suffering.
>
> In the *Black Line Hell*, the hell-guardians use black lines to mark [the bodies of] the living beings born there into quarters, eighths, and many other smaller divisions. The beings experience the pain of being split and chopped along these lines with weapons.
>
> When the living beings in the *Crushing Hell* gather and congregate, the hell guardians herd them all between two iron mountains shaped like goat heads and then squeeze them between the mountains, causing streams of blood to gush from all their orifices. They are also pressed between sheep-headed, horse-headed, elephant-headed, lion-headed, and tiger-headed mountains. When they gather together again, they are inserted into a great iron machine and pressed like sugarcane. Then they reassemble on an iron surface, where great iron boulders are hurled upon them, cutting, splitting, smashing, and flattening them, again causing torrents of blood to gush forth. **[117]**
>
> In the *Howling Hell* living beings who search for a home are herded into an iron house and incinerated by blazing fire and conflagration. The *Great Howling Hell* is similar to this, except that the beings are inside two iron houses, one within the other.
>
> In the *Hot Hell* the hell-guardians throw the living beings into a hot, blazing iron kettle many leagues across and boil them, deep-frying them like fish. Then they impale them through their anuses with blazing iron skewers, which emerge through the crowns of their heads; blazing flames leap forth from their mouths, eyes, noses, ears, and from all of their pores. Then they are placed either on their backs or face down on a blazing iron surface, where they are pounded flat with a hot, blazing iron hammer. In the *Extremely Hot Hell* the guardians force iron tridents into their victims' anuses, the left and right prongs coming out at their shoulders and the center prong at the crowns of their heads, causing blazing flames to shoot out from their mouths and other orifices. Their bodies are caught in a hot, blazing iron press; they are thrown head-first into a great blazing iron kettle full of boiling water and boiled, floating up, down, and all around, until their

> skin, flesh, and blood are destroyed and only their skeletons remain. Thereupon the guardians fish them out, spread them on the iron surface—where their skin, flesh, and blood regenerate—and then throw them back into the kettle. The remaining torments are similar to those of the Hot Hell.
>
> In the *Unrelenting Hell* the ground blazes for many hundreds of leagues from the east. As this blaze increases, it assumes the force of a conflagration. It then gradually incinerates the skin, flesh, intestines, and bones of the living beings, penetrating all the way to their marrow. **[118]** The beings' entire bodies are engulfed in blazing flames, as if they were the wicks of butter lamps. The same thing occurs from the other three directions. When the fires arrive from all four directions, they combine, and the beings experience uninterrupted suffering. You know them to be living beings only by the piteous wails they emit. On other occasions they are placed into blazing iron embers in an iron winnowing basket, and the basket is shaken violently. On other occasions they are forced to climb up great iron mountains, then fall from them onto an iron surface. On other occasions their tongues are pulled out of their mouths and stretched out with a hundred iron pegs, like ox hides, until they have no wrinkles or ridges. At other times, they are laid out on their backs on the iron surface, and their mouths are pried open with iron tongs, while blazing lumps of iron and boiling copper are forced in until their mouths, esophagi, and intestines are burned and the residue flows out below. The other torments are like those of the Extremely Hot Hell.

This is only a rough description of the torments, but there are many others as well. I have written about the locations and sufferings of these hells exactly as they are explained in the *Levels of Yogic Deeds*.

The duration of these sufferings is explained in the *Friendly Letter*:[279]

> Even though you experience
> Such horrible sufferings for a billion years,
> You do not die
> Until the nonvirtue is spent.

Thus, you must experience these sufferings until the force of your karma is exhausted. In reference to this it is said that fifty human years is a single day for the deities of the Heaven of the Four Great Kings [lowest of the six types of deities in the desire realm], thirty of these is a month, and twelve of these is a year. Five hundred such years is the life span of these deities. Taking all of that as a single day, thirty such days as a month, and twelve such months as a year, the life span of the hell denizens in the Reviving Hell is five hundred such years. **[119]** Similarly, one hundred, two hundred, four hundred, eight hundred, and sixteen hundred human years, respectively, equal single days for the deities from the Heaven of the Thirty-three through to those of the Heaven of Controlling Others' Emanations [the rest of the six types of desire realm deities]. Their life spans are one thousand, two thousand, four thousand, eight thousand, and sixteen thousand divine years. These periods make up single days respectively for the hell denizens from the Black Line through the Hot hells, who endure from one thousand up to sixteen thousand of their own years. The *Treasury of Knowledge* says:[280]

> Fifty human years
> Is a single day for the lower deities
> Of the desire realm;
> This is doubled for the higher deities.

And also:

> The life span of the desire realm deities is equal to a day
> In the six hells, the Reviving Hell and so forth, in sequence.
> Thus their life spans
> Are similar to those of the desire realm deities.
>
> The life span in the Extremely Hot Hell is half of an intermediate eon;
> In the Unrelenting Hell it is an intermediate eon.

The *Levels of Yogic Deeds* explains this in the same way.[281]

b″ **Contemplating the suffering of the adjoining hells**

Each of the eight hot hells has four walls and four doors and is encircled by an iron fence, which has four doors. At each of these doors there are four additional hells for living beings: the Pit of Embers, the Swamp of Putrid Corpses or the Swamp of Excrement that Stinks Like a Corpse, the Path of Razors and Such, and the River with No Ford.

The first of these contains embers in which the denizens sink up to their knees. When these beings go there in search of a home, they step into it, and their skin, flesh, and blood are completely destroyed, only to regenerate when they lift their feet out again.

Not far away lies the second hell, a swamp of excrement stinking like a corpse, into which living beings seeking a home attempt to cross but fall, sinking in over their shoulders. The swamp is inhabited by "sharp-beaked worms," which pierce the skin, flesh, intestines, and bones, boring down to the marrow. **[120]**

Nearby is the third hell where living beings who seek a home walk a path filled with razor teeth. With each step, the teeth lacerate their skin, flesh, and blood, but each time they lift their feet, their bodies regenerate. Nearby is the Sword-leafed Forest. When living beings who seek a home sit down to rest there in the shade, swords drop down from the trees, piercing and splitting their limbs, fingers, and toes. When they swoon, they are attacked by mongrel dogs, who carry them off by the scruffs of their necks and eat them. Nearby is the Forest of Iron Silk-cotton Trees. Living beings who seek a home come and climb these trees, which are covered with thorns that point downwards on the way up and upwards on the way down, so that the thorns pierce and split the beings' limbs, fingers, and toes. Iron-beaked crows sit on their shoulders or heads and pluck out and eat their eyeballs. Since all of these places subject their inhabitants to harm by means of weapons, they should be counted as one adjoining hell.

The fourth hell is nearby the silk-cotton trees. The River with No Ford is full of boiling water. Living beings who seek a home fall into it and are tossed about and cooked, as though they were peas thrown into a pot of water over a great blazing fire. On both banks of this river sit beings, armed with clubs, hooks, and nets, who keep the tormented from escaping, or who drag them out with the hooks and nets and lay them on their backs on the great blazing ground, demanding to know what they want. When they reply, "We do not understand at all and cannot see, but we are hungry and thirsty," they are fed blazing lumps of iron and boiling copper. **[121]**

I have presented these hells in accordance with the *Levels of Yogic Deeds* as well. It states that the life spans of living beings in the adjoining hells and occasional hells are not fixed, but they must suffer in these places for a long time, until the power of the karma for experiencing these sufferings is exhausted.

c″ Contemplating the suffering of the cold hells

Each of the eight great hells of living beings is ten thousand leagues in breadth, and the eight cold hells lie outside of these. The first, the Blistering Hell, is thirty-two thousand leagues below the earth. The other seven are situated every two thousand leagues beneath that.

In the *Blistering Hell* the denizens are blasted by a great wind that shrivels and then raises blisters all over their bodies. The *Popping Blisters Hell* is similar, except that the blisters pop as the body shrivels. The *Chattering-teeth*, *Weeping*, and *Moaning* hells are named after the sounds the denizens make. In the *Splitting Water-Lily Hell* the denizens are blasted by a great wind, which causes them to turn blue and split into five or six pieces. In the *Splitting-like-a-Lotus Hell*, the denizens turn from blue to red, and split into ten or more pieces, while in the *Great-Splitting-like-a-Lotus Hell*, the denizens' skin becomes very red and splits into a hundred or more pieces. I have presented the sequence, sizes, and sufferings of these hells in accordance with the *Levels of Yogic Deeds*.

The *Garland of Birth Stories* says that these hell denizens dwell in darkness as follows:[282]

> In the future life of a nihilist
> A cold wind will rise in that place of absolute darkness.
> Since it will make you so ill that even your bones will be destroyed,
> Who will want to enter there to help you?

Also, the *Letter to a Student* says:[283]

> An incomparable wind pierces your bones; **[122]**
> Your body shakes and freezes; you bend over and shrivel.
> Hundreds of blisters rise and pop.
> Creatures born from them eat and claw you; fat, lymph, and marrow ooze out.
>
> Exhausted, teeth clenched, all hair standing on end,
> You are tormented by wounds in your eyes, ears, and gullet.
> Mind and body stupefied by pain,
> You dwell in the cold hell and emit a pitiful wail.

You experience these sufferings until the bad karma [that causes them] is exhausted. The *Levels of Yogic Deeds* says:[284]

> Understand that the life span of living beings born in the cold hells is one-and-a-half times as long as that of the living beings born in the corresponding great hells of living beings.

Vasubandhu's *Treasury of Knowledge Auto-commentary* quotes a sūtra as follows:[285]

> For example, O monks: Fill a vessel full of sesame, heaping with eighty measures as it is measured here in Magadha. Then have someone cast out a single sesame seed every hundred years. O monks, in such a fashion this vessel becomes completely empty very quickly and much sooner than the complete life span of the living beings born in the Blistering Hell, but I cannot say what such a life span is. O monks, twenty life spans of the Blistering Hell make up a single life span in the Popping Hell.

And so on until,

> Also, O monks, twenty life spans of the Splitting-like-a-Lotus Hell make up a single life span in the Great-Splitting-like-a-Lotus Hell.

Thus, they live for such a period of time.

d″ **Contemplating the suffering of the occasional hells**

The occasional hells adjoin the hot hells and cold hells, and the *Levels of Yogic Deeds* says that they exist in the human regions as well. According to the *Bases of Discipline*,[286] they also exist near the shores of great lakes, as depicted in the *Edifying Tale of Saṃgharakṣita (Saṃgharakṣitāvadāna)*.[287] **[123]**

The *Treasury of Knowledge Auto-commentary* also says:[288]

> These sixteen hells for living beings are created by the force of the karma of all living beings. The occasional hells are created by the individual karma of one, two, or many living beings, and therefore are of many different types. They have no fixed location, since they exist in rivers, mountains, wastelands, below the earth, and in other places as well.

Thus, as explained below, the conditions for being born in any of these hells are very easy to create, and every single day you acquire more of them. Since you have already accumulated innumerable causes in the past, your complacence is inappropriate. Therefore, after reflecting on these hells, be frightened—nothing separates you from them after the mere cessation of your breath.

Engaging in the Bodhisattva Deeds says:[289]

> Having created the karma for hell,
> Why are you complacent like this?

And the *Friendly Letter:*[290]

> Sinners who hear of the boundless sufferings in the hells—
> Separated from them only until the mere termination of their breathing—
> And are not completely terrified,
> Have hearts as hard as diamonds.
>
> If you are frightened merely by seeing paintings of hell,
> By hearing of it, recalling it,
> Reading about it, and by representations of it,
> What need to mention experiencing the fierce actuality of it?

Among the sufferings of cyclic existence, those of the miserable realms are the most difficult to endure. Among these, the sufferings of the hells are the most unbearable, for the pain of being continually pierced by three hundred sharp spears for a full day is nothing compared to even the mildest of the hells' sufferings. Among the hells, the suffering of the Unrelenting Hell is by far the greatest. The *Friendly Letter*:[291]

> Just as among all kinds of happiness
> The cessation of craving is the king of happinesses, **[124]**
> So among all kinds of suffering
> The suffering of the Unrelenting Hell is most fierce.
>
> The suffering of being viciously pierced
> With three hundred lances for a full day
> Cannot compare, cannot even be mentioned,
> With the least sufferings of hell.

Know that the sole cause of such sufferings is your physical, verbal, and mental wrongdoing. Strive with whatever human skill you have not to be defiled by even the slightest wrongdoing. The same text says:

> The seed of these nonvirtuous results
> Is your physical, verbal, and mental wrongdoing.
> Strive with whatever skill you possess
> Not to have even a bit of it!

2′ Contemplating the suffering of animals

Powerful animals kill weaker ones. Deities and humans exploit animals. Since others control them, animals have no independence, and are harmed, beaten, and killed. The *Levels of Yogic Deeds* explains that since they dwell with deities and men, they have no other abode. The *Treasury of Knowledge Auto-commentary* says:[292]

> Animals range over the land, in the water, and in the sky. Their primary abode is the great ocean, and the others have spread from there.

Also, the *Friendly Letter*:[293]

> In rebirth as an animal there are various sufferings—
> Being killed, bound, beaten, and so forth.
> Those who have cast away the virtues of peace
> Horribly eat each other.
>
> Some die because of their pearls, fur,
> Bone, meat, or skin.
> Other powerless animals are put to work
> By being kicked, hit, whipped, jabbed with an iron hook, or prodded. **[125]**

The first verse teaches the general sufferings of animals and the second the specific sufferings. The words "and so forth" in "beaten, and so forth" include being put to work, having their noses pierced, and the like, and even refer to humans and nonhumans killing them, and so on. "Eat each other" refers to the harm common to all animals. "The virtues of peace" denotes the virtues that lead to nirvāṇa. Those who cast these away are indicated to be very stupid and unsuitable for the path. "Being kicked" through to being "prodded" refer to the five ways of putting animals to work—horses, buffaloes, donkeys, elephants, and oxen and the like, respectively. The foregoing comments are drawn from Mahāmati's *Clear Words: Explanation of the "Friendly Letter."*[294]

Some animals are born in darkness or in water, where they then age and die. Others are exhausted by heavy burdens. Some plow, are shorn, or are chased. Others are killed after being rendered helpless by various methods of slaughter. Some are tormented by hunger, thirst, sun, and wind. Others are harmed in different ways by hunters. Thus, they are constantly fearful. After reflecting on the ways in which they suffer, become disenchanted and repulsed.

As far as their life spans are concerned, the *Treasury of Knowledge* says,[295] "the longest, an eon." He explains that the most long-lived animals endure for about an eon, and that the life spans of short-lived animals are not fixed.

3′ Contemplating the suffering of hungry ghosts

Those who are exceedingly miserly are born as hungry ghosts. These beings are hungry and thirsty, and their skin, flesh, and blood are desiccated, giving them the appearance of burnt logs. Their faces are covered with hair, their mouths are extremely dry, and their tongues lick their lips constantly. There are three types of hungry ghosts:

a″ Hungry ghosts who have external obstacles for obtaining food and drink

When these hungry ghosts approach springs, lakes, and ponds, beings holding swords, long spears, and short spears block their way. **[126]** Or else the water appears to them as pus and blood, and they lose the desire to drink.

b″ Hungry ghosts who have internal obstacles for obtaining food and drink

These beings have goiters and great bellies, but their mouths, which spew flames, are as small as the eye of a needle. Though others do not prevent them, they are unable to ingest food or drink even when they obtain it.

c″ **Hungry ghosts who have obstacles within the food and drink**

Some of these hungry ghosts, unable to make use of clean and wholesome food and drink, cut their own flesh and eat it. Those called "Possessing a Garland of Flames" are burned because whatever they attempt to eat or drink bursts into flames. Those called "Filth-Eaters" can only ingest dirty, stinking, harmful, and despicable things, and so they eat feces and drink urine.

With respect to their abodes, the *Treasury of Knowledge Autocommentary* says:[296]

> The king of the hungry ghosts is called "Yama." Their primary abode is five hundred leagues beneath the city of Rājagṛha in Jambudvīpa. The others have spread from there.

Also, the *Friendly Letter* says:[297]

> Hungry ghosts never heal the suffering
> Of destitution due to desire.
> They are subject to very fierce suffering
> Produced by hunger, thirst, cold, heat, exhaustion, and fear.
>
> Some, with mouths the size of a mere needle's eye
> And stomachs as round as mountains,
> Are tormented by hunger, lacking the energy to search
> For even a bit of filthy garbage.
>
> Some have bodies of skin and bones, like a leafless tree,
> Like a palm tree without its top.
> Some, mouths on fire each night,
> Eat food that causes their mouths to blaze.
>
> Some wretched ones do not even find filth
> Such as pus, excrement, blood and the like;
> Hitting each others' faces, they drink the pus
> That oozes from the ripe goiters at their necks.
>
> For these hungry ghosts in summer
> The moon is hot, and in winter the sun cold. **[127]**
> For them fruit trees turn fruitless;
> Their mere glance dries up a stream.

The first verse teaches the general sufferings of the hungry ghosts, and the remaining verses teach the specific sufferings. "Exhaustion" refers to fatigue from running after food. "Fear" refers to the terror of seeing beings holding swords, clubs, and nooses. "Garbage" refers to unwanted trash. "At night" indicates that flames come out of their mouths nightly. "Causes their mouths to blaze" indicates that the food they eat causes their mouths to blaze. Some hungry ghosts' gazes will dry up even a sweet, cool stream, as though their eyes burned it with strong poison. The *Clear Words: Explanation of the "Friendly Letter"* explains[298] that for some hungry ghosts a stream appears as if it were filled with a mass of blazing embers; for others it seems to be a flowing stream of pus filled with various insects.

Also contemplate what Candragomin's *Letter to a Student* says:[299]

> Tormented by a terrible thirst, they see a pure stream
> From afar and desire to drink it. When they arrive,
> It changes into a river filled with a mixture of oyster shells,
> Strands of hair, and putrid pus, a cesspool of blood and excrement.
>
> If they go to the top of a cool hill with moist spring breezes
> And a grove of verdant sandalwood trees,
> It becomes for them a forest fire enveloped in leaping flames
> And heaped with falling, burning logs.
>
> When they go to a seashore covered
> With clear, glittering foam from crashing waves,
> It becomes for them a wasteland
> Blasted by hot sand, dark mist, and a searing wind.
>
> Dwelling in that place, they long for rain clouds to appear,
> Whereupon there issues from the clouds a rain of iron arrows,
> Smoking cinders, and sparkling, diamond-hard boulders,
> And, one after the other, gold and orange lightning bolts fall on their bodies like rain.
>
> For those afflicted by heat even a snowstorm is hot; **[128]**
> For those tormented by wind even fire is cold.
> This entire universe appears upside down to these hungry ghosts
> Confused by the fruition of terrible karma.
>
> Even if one afflicted with a mouth the size of a mere needle's eye
> And a stomach of many leagues drinks the water of the great ocean,
> The water cannot pass through the opening of its throat
> And its poisonous mouth evaporates every drop.

With regard to their life spans, the *Levels of Yogic Deeds*[300] and *Treasury of Knowledge*[301] say hungry ghosts endure for five hundred hungry ghost years, with each of their days being equivalent to a human month. The *Friendly Letter* says:[302]

Some living beings, enduring continuous suffering,
Bound tightly by the ropes
Of the karma of wrongdoing, do not die
For five thousand, or even ten thousand, years.

The *Clear Words: Explanation of the "Friendly Letter"*[303] explains that some hungry ghosts live five thousand and others ten thousand years. The *Levels of Yogic Deeds* says that the size of their bodies is not fixed in any of the three miserable realms—it varies in accordance with their nonvirtuous karma.

Thus, when you contemplate these sufferings of the miserable realms, think like this: "At present it is difficult to endure sitting for merely a single day with my hand stuck in burning coals, or to remain naked for that long in a cave of ice during the winter winds, or to go for a few days without food and drink, or for my body to be stung by a bee and the like. If even these are difficult to endure, how will I bear the sufferings of the hot hells, the cold hells, the hungry ghosts, or the animals devouring each other alive?" After you have assessed your current condition, meditate until your mind is filled with fear and dread. Simply knowing about this without conditioning your mind to it, or only meditating on it for a little while, will not accomplish anything. The *Bases of Discipline* says:[304] **[129]**

> The two sons of Ānanda's sister became monks and were made to learn to read. After reading for a few days, they became lazy and stopped. They were then entrusted to Maudgalyāyana, but acted as before, so Ānanda told Maudgalyāyana, "You must make them renounce!"
>
> Thus Maudgalyāyana took them on a walk, and miraculously revealed a hell of living beings. When they heard the sounds of cutting, hacking, and other such actions, the two nephews went to investigate and witnessed the sufferings of being cut, etc. Since there were two great boiling kettles there, they asked whether someone would not be placed in them as well. The hell-guardians replied, "Ānanda's two nephews have become monks and are wasting their time through their laziness; after they die, they will be reborn here." The two were terrified, and each thought, "If I am smart, I will make an effort right now!"
>
> They returned to where Maudgalyāyana was and reported what had happened. Then Maudgalyāyana said: "O novices, laziness gives rise to problems such as this and to others as well. You should have joyous perseverance!" Hence, the two began to persevere enthusiastically. If they recalled hell prior to eating, they were unable to eat. If they recalled it after eating, they vomited.

> Then Maudgalyāyana took them on a different walk, where they heard from another direction the music of the deities' magic lutes and the like. When they went to investigate, they saw heavenly palaces filled with goddesses, but no gods. When they asked why there were no gods, they were told, "Ānanda's nephews have become monks and are persevering joyously; when they die, they will be reborn here." The two were delighted, and told Maudgalyāyana, who said: "O novices, since this benefit, and others as well, arise from joyous perseverance, persevere joyously!"
>
> They did so, and when they were receiving an explanation of the scriptures, they were taught from the authoritative scriptures that you can be reborn from the happy realms into the miserable realms, as cited previously. **[130]** When they heard this, they asked Maudgalyāyana, "O noble being, must we also die as a deity or human, and then be reborn into the three miserable realms?" He replied, "O youths, until you stop your afflictions, you must move like a water wheel throughout cyclic existence in its five realms." The two, after they had renounced cyclic existence, said, "Henceforth, we will not indulge in the afflictions; thus, please explain the teachings to us!" Consequently, Maudgalyāyana gave them the teachings, and they became arhats.

Thus, meditation on suffering puts an end to laziness and generates joyous perseverance at accomplishing the path. It spurs you toward liberation and is the root of the cause for attaining it. Since it was praised for this even when the Teacher was alive, he had nothing superior to teach as a personal instruction for liberation. This passage shows clearly the progression of the contemplations for persons of small and medium capacities. As for the measure of the attitudes of these two types of persons, you must constantly strive to meditate on these points until you develop an attitude like that of Ānanda's nephews.

Neu-sur-ba (sNe'u-zur-pa) said:

> Examine whether or not you have previously created the conditions for being born in these miserable realms, whether or not you are currently creating them, whether or not you would consider creating them in the future. Since you will go there if you have created them, are creating them, or would consider creating them, think, "If I am born there, what will I do then; will I be able to do anything?" With your head pounding, or like a man struggling in the desert, consider that there will be absolutely nothing you can do, and develop as much fear and dread as possible.

This, clearly, is the key point. You currently have a good life for developing the path. Consequently, if you contemplate in this way, you will clear away previously accrued nonvirtuous karma and deter your future accumulations. Your prayers of fervent aspiration will redirect previously accrued virtues, causing them to increase. You will be able to enter many new avenues for engaging in virtuous actions. Therefore, you will make your leisure and opportunity meaningful every day. **[131]**

If you do not contemplate these things now, when you fall into a miserable realm, you will not find a refuge to protect you from these terrors even though you seek one. At that time, you will not have the intelligence to understand that which you should adopt and that which you should cast aside. As *Engaging in the Bodhisattva Deeds* says:[305]

> If I neglect to cultivate virtue
> Even when I have the good fortune to do so,
> What shall I do when I am confused
> By the sufferings of the miserable realms?

And also:

> Saying, "Who will protect me
> From this great terror?"
> I will stare, aghast,
> And search all around for a refuge.
>
> Seeing no refuge anywhere,
> I will be completely dejected.
> If there is no refuge there,
> What will I do?
>
> Thus, from today, I go for refuge
> To the Conqueror, protector of living beings,
> The one who strives to rescue living beings,
> The mighty one who dispels all fear.

The preceding discussion is a mere overview. You should by all means read the *Mindfulness of the Excellent Teaching*,[306] for it is explained more thoroughly there. Read it repeatedly, and reflect upon what you read.

11

Going for Refuge to the Three Jewels

ii) Relying on the means for achieving happiness in the next life
  a′ Training in going for refuge, the excellent door for entering the teaching
    1′ The causes of going for refuge
    2′ Based on that, the objects to which you go for refuge
      a″ Identifying the objects to which you go for refuge
      b″ The reasons why they are worthy to be a refuge
    3′ The way you go for refuge
      a″ Going for refuge by knowing the good qualities
        1″ The good qualities of the Buddha
          (a) The good qualities of the Buddha's body
          (b) The good qualities of the Buddha's speech
          (c) The good qualities of the Buddha's mind
            (i) The good qualities of knowledge
            (ii) The good qualities of caring
          (d) The good qualities of enlightened activities
        2″ The good qualities of the teaching
        3″ The good qualities of the community
      b″ Going for refuge by knowing the distinctions
        1″ The distinction based on their defining characteristics
        2″ The distinction based on their enlightened activities
        3″ The distinction based on devotion
        4″ The distinction based on practice
        5″ The distinction based on recollection
        6″ The distinction based on how they increase merit
      c″ Going for refuge through commitment
      d″ Going for refuge by refusing to acknowledge other refuges

ii) **Relying on the means for achieving happiness in the next life**

The means for achieving happiness in the next life are explained in two parts:

1. Training in going for refuge, the excellent door for entering the teaching (Chapters 11-12)
2. Developing the faith of conviction that is the root of all temporary happiness and certain goodness (Chapters 13-15)

a′ **Training in going for refuge, the excellent door for entering the teaching**

Going for refuge is explained in four parts:

1. The causes of going for refuge
2. Based on that, the objects to which you go for refuge
3. The way you go for refuge
4. Once you have gone for refuge, the stages of the precepts (Chapter 12)

1′ **The causes of going for refuge**

In general there are many causes. However, for our purposes, the following apply. As previously explained, you cannot remain in this life—you soon die—and, after death, you have no control over where you will be reborn, for you are under the control of your karma. With regard to karma, *Engaging in the Bodhisattva Deeds* says:[307]

> Just as a flash of lightning in a dark cloud
> Momentarily illuminates the darkness of a black night, **[132]**
> So too does there infrequently appear in the world, by a buddha's power,
> A few moments of intelligence to cultivate virtue.
>
> Thus virtue is always weak,
> And sin is fiercely powerful.

Since virtuous karma is weak and nonvirtuous karma is exceedingly powerful, if you contemplate how readily you fall into the miserable realms, you will be filled with fear and dread, and will resolve to seek a refuge. As Mahātma Dignāga says:[308]

> Adrift in the bottomless ocean of cyclic existence,
> Devoured by fierce sea monsters—
> Attachment and the like—
> To whom should I go for refuge today?

In brief, the causes of your going for refuge are twofold: your fear of the miserable realms and the like, and your conviction that the three jewels can protect you from them. Thus, you must strive to realize these two causes, because if they remain mere words, so will your refuge, but if they are strong and stable, your refuge will transform your mind.

2′ Based on that, the objects to which you go for refuge

a″ Identifying the objects to which you go for refuge

The *Praise in One Hundred and Fifty Verses* (*Śata-pañcāśatka-stotra*) says:[309]

> The one in whom no fault
> Can ever exist,
> The one in whom all good qualities
> Always exist—
>
> If you are sensible,
> It is correct to go for refuge to just such a person,
> To praise and honor him,
> And to abide in his teaching.

Thus, if you can distinguish a refuge from what is not a refuge, it is right to go for refuge to the Bhagavan Buddha, the true refuge. This citation applies to the teaching jewel and the community jewel as well. As Candrakīrti's *Seventy Verses on Refuge (Triśaraṇa-gamana-saptati)* says:[310]

> The Buddha, teaching, and community
> Are the refuge for those who desire liberation.

b″ The reasons why they are worthy to be a refuge [133]

There are four reasons why the Buddha is worthy to be a refuge. *First*, he has mastered himself and attained the sublime state of fearlessness. If he had not attained this, he would not be able to protect others from all fears, just as a person who has already fallen down cannot help up someone else who has fallen down. *Second*, he is in all ways skilled in the means of training disciples. If he were not so, he would not be able to fulfill your needs, even if you went to him for refuge. *Third*, he has great compassion. If he did not have it, he would not protect you even if you went to him for refuge. *Fourth*, he is pleased, not by material offerings, but by offerings of practice. If he were not, he would not act as a refuge for everyone, but would help only those who had previously helped him.

In brief, only one who is free of all fears, who is skilled in the means of freeing others from fear, who has great, impartial compassion for everyone, and who acts for everyone's welfare regardless of whether or not they have benefited him, is worthy of being a refuge. Since only the Buddha has these qualities, and the divine creator and so on do not, he alone is the refuge. Therefore, his teaching and the community of his disciples are also worthy of being a refuge.

Thus, after you have ascertained these things, which are taught in the *Compendium of Determinations*,[311] entrust yourself to the three jewels with a single-pointed focus. Develop this certainty from the depths of your heart, for, once you are able to do this, they cannot fail to protect you. This is so because there are two causes of your being protected: an external and an internal. The Teacher has already fully realized the external factor or cause, but you suffer because you have not yet developed the internal factor, entrusting yourself to the refuge.

Therefore, know that the Buddha, moved by his great compassion, assists you even if you do not request his help; that he is not lazy at this; and that he, the unrivaled and auspicious refuge, abides as your personal protector. **[134]** Recognizing this, go to him for refuge. The *Praise in Honor of One Worthy of Honor (Varṇārha-varṇa-stotra)* says:[312]

> He proclaims, "I am the friend
> Of you who have no protector."
> Out of his great compassion,
> He abides as if embracing the entire world.
>
> O Teacher, you are so compassionate
> And caring, and strive to act
> Lovingly without laziness—
> Who else is like you?
>
> You are the protector of all living beings,
> The benefactor of everyone.
> Beings sink down because
> They do not seek your protection.
>
> You are even able to assist the lowly
> If they have correctly adopted your teaching.
> Other than you
> No one knows these beneficial teachings.
>
> You have truly realized
> All the external factors, or powers.

Because they have not acquired the inner powers,
Ordinary persons remain subject to suffering.

3′ The way you go for refuge[313]

There are four aspects to going for refuge:

1. By knowing the good qualities
2. By knowing the distinctions
3. Through commitment
4. By refusing to acknowledge other refuges

a″ Going for refuge by knowing the good qualities

Since going for refuge by knowing the good qualities requires recalling the good qualities of the refuge, there are three subdivisions of this topic:

1. The good qualities of the Buddha
2. The good qualities of the teaching
3. The good qualities of the community

1″ The good qualities of the Buddha

These are explained in four parts:

1. The good qualities of the Buddha's body
2. The good qualities of the Buddha's speech
3. The good qualities of the Buddha's mind
4. The good qualities of enlightened activities

(a) The good qualities of the Buddha's body

This entails recollection of the Buddha's auspicious signs and exemplary features. Recall them as they are taught in the *Praise by Example (Upamā-stava)* [section of the *Praise in Honor of One Worthy of Honor*]:[314]

> Your body, adorned with the signs,
> Is beautiful, an elixir for the eye;
> It's like a cloudless autumn sky
> Decorated with clusters of stars.
>
> O golden Sage,
> Beautifully draped with religious robes—
> You are like a golden mountain peak
> Wrapped in the clouds of sunrise or sunset. **[135]**
>
> O protector, even the full moon
> Free of clouds cannot compare

With the radiant orb of your face
Free of the embellishment of jewelry.

Should a bee see
The lotus of your face
And a lotus opened by the sun,
It would wonder which was the real lotus.

Your white teeth beautify
Your golden face
Like pure moonbeams in autumn pouring through
The gaps between golden mountains.

O one so worthy of worship, your right hand,
Adorned with the sign of the wheel,
Makes the gesture of relief
To people terrified by cyclic existence.

O Sage, when you walk,
Your feet leave marks on this earth
Like splendid lotuses—
How can it be beautified by lotus gardens?

(b) **The good qualities of the Buddha's speech**

Reflect on the marvelous manner of the Buddha's speech. Even if every living being in the universe asks him a different question at the same time, he comprehends them all with one instant of his wisdom. Then he answers all the questions with a single word, which all beings understand in their own languages. The *Chapter of the Truth Speaker* says:[315]

It is like this: if all living beings simultaneously
Ask questions using many different expressions,
He understands them in a single moment,
And with a single utterance gives answers to each.

Therefore, know that in the world the Leader
Knows how to be eloquent.
He turns the wheel of teaching
That eradicates the suffering of deities and humans.

Furthermore, recall what is taught in the *Praise in One Hundred and Fifty Verses*:[316]

Your face is so captivating;
Listening to your pleasant speech
Is like seeing nectar
Flow from the moon. **[136]**

Your speech, like a rain cloud,
Settles the dust of attachment;
Like the *garuḍa*,
It expels the snake of hostility.

Again and again, it is like a sun
Dispelling the darkness of ignorance.
Since it razes the mountain of pride,
It is also like the *vajra*.

Because you see the truth, your speech never misleads;
Since it is faultless, it is correct;
Since it is well-composed, it is easy to understand.
Your words are well-spoken.

At first your speech
Captivates the listeners' minds;
Then if they give it thought,
It clears away attachment and delusion.

It relieves the destitute,
Protects the unruly,
And induces the reveler to renounce—
Your speech accords with everyone's needs.

It delights the learned,
Improves the minds of the middling,
And dispels the darkness of the lowly—
This speech is medicine for all living beings.

(c) **The good qualities of the Buddha's mind**

These are explained in terms of the good qualities of knowledge and the good qualities of caring.

(i) **The good qualities of knowledge**

Without obstruction the Buddha's knowledge contacts the real nature and diversity of all phenomena, as if they were a *dhātrī* fruit[317] placed in the palm of his hand. Thus, the Sage's knowledge comprehends all phenomena, whereas others' limited knowledge cannot comprehend the vast objects that are to be known. You should reflect on this knowledge as it is described in the *Praise in Honor of One Worthy of Honor*:[318]

Only your sublime wisdom
Comprehends all objects of knowledge;
For everyone other than you
There are objects yet to be known.

And also,

> O Bhagavan, the entire origination
> Of all types of phenomena throughout time
> Is within the range of your mind,
> Like an *ambalan* fruit in the palm of your hand.
>
> Like the wind moving across the sky,
> Your mind is unimpeded
> With respect to the single and the manifold
> Animate and inanimate phenomena. **[137]**

(ii) **The good qualities of caring**

In the same way that living beings are bound inescapably by the afflictions, so is the Sage bound by great compassion, which thus arises continuously as he beholds the suffering of living beings. You should reflect on this as set forth in the *Praise in One Hundred and Fifty Verses*:[319]

> The afflictions bind all
> These beings without exception.
> You, in order to release them from the afflictions,
> Are eternally bound by compassion.
>
> Should I first make obeisance to you,
> Or to the great compassion that causes you
> To dwell for so long in cyclic existence
> Despite knowing its faults?

Also, the *Chapter of the Truth Speaker* says:[320]

> The Supreme Sage feels great compassion
> When he sees beings whose minds
> Are constantly obscured by the dark gloom of ignorance,
> Locked in the prison of cyclic existence.

And also:

> The Conqueror feels great compassion when he sees beings
> Whose minds are overwhelmed by attachment,
> Who have great craving and always long for sensory objects,
> And who have fallen into the ocean of craving's attachment.
>
> The One Possessing the Ten Powers feels compassion
> Which seeks to dispel all suffering
> When he sees the afflictions of beings
> Harmed by a multitude of illnesses and miseries.
>
> The Sage's compassion arises constantly;
> It is impossible for it not to do so.

The Buddha is free of faults because he is concerned
With the needs of all living beings.

(d) **The good qualities of enlightened activities**

The enlightened activities of the Buddha's body, speech, and mind, being both spontaneous and everlasting, help all living beings. If disciples are open to his guidance, the Sage will give them that which is excellent, and lead them out of trouble. **[138]** Thus, the Buddha's activities are certain to do everything that needs to be done. You should reflect on this as set forth in the *Praise in One Hundred and Fifty Verses:*[321]

You explain the destruction of afflictions,
Reveal the deceitfulness of demons,
Proclaim the terrifying nature of cyclic existence,
And show the way to fearlessness.

O Compassionate One, wishing to help,
You act for the sake of living beings.
How could there be something helpful
Which you have not done?

And the *Praise in Honor of One Worthy of Honor* says:[322]

What trouble is there away from which
You cannot lead living beings?
What excellent thing is there
That you cannot bestow on the world?

The preceding briefly summarizes the way to reflect on the Buddha. If you reflect in a variety of ways, your faith will also arise in many ways. The more you reflect, the stronger and more enduring your faith will become. The same applies to the good qualities of the other two jewels.

When you have gained certainty by meditating in this way, you will understand that the scriptures and their commentaries are instructions, in that most of them teach the good qualities of the three refuges. People who reject analytical meditation as a practice, thinking that it is mere conceptualization, shut off many such ways of accumulating merit and clearing away obscuration. Therefore, be aware that such a rejection is a great obstacle to taking advantage of the boundless potential of a life of leisure and opportunity.

The more you practice these things, the more accustomed your mind will become to them, and the easier it will be to practice what you had initially found difficult to learn. You will develop the spirit of enlightenment, thinking, "I, too, should obtain buddhahood, like the Buddha whom I recollect." You will have visions of the Buddha day and night. **[139]** No matter how much you suffer at death, you will not lose your recollection of the Buddha. The *King of Concentrations Sūtra* says:[323]

> I instruct you
> And you should understand:
> Peoples' minds become absorbed in something
> To the degree that they reflect on it.
>
> Therefore, recollect the Master of the Sages as having a conqueror's
> Physical posture and limitless sublime wisdom.
> If you constantly familiarize yourself with such recollection,
> Your mind will become absorbed in it—
>
> You will desire the sublime wisdom of a holy being
> Whether you walk, sit, stand, or recline.
> Because you yourself will want to become a supreme conqueror in the world,
> You will also make prayers aspiring to enlightenment.

And also:

> Constantly give praise to the buddhas
> With your body, speech, and mind of clear faith.
> By conditioning your mind-stream in this way,
> You will see the Protector of the World day and night.
>
> Should you suffer the approach of death
> In sickness and sorrow,
> Your recollection of the Buddha will not be lost;
> It will not be erased by your suffering.

Bo-do-wa said:

> If you reflect on the Buddha's good qualities again and again, you will receive a blessing commensurate with the strength of your faith and the purity of your mind. Because you have gained certainty about them, you will go for refuge from the depths of your heart and train yourself in the precepts of refuge. Then everything you do will become a practice of the teaching.
>
> It is said that we value the Buddha's knowledge even less than that of an accurate diviner. If a reliable diviner says, "I know that this year you will not face any problems," we are relieved. If he says, "This year you will face problems—do this, and not that," we strive to follow his advice. If we do not, we think, "I did not follow his advice," and worry. But when the Buddha says, "You should give this up; you should practice this," do we commit

> ourselves to these injunctions? Do we worry if we do not follow them? **[140]** Or do we say, "Well, the teaching says that, but right now, under the circumstances, I can't follow it—I must do this instead," and completely forsaking the Buddha's teaching, proceed straightaway with disregard, according to our own ideas?

If you do not examine your mind, you will be pleased. If you are not misled by the superficial, look within your mind and reflect carefully, "This condition is despicable."

Thus, reflect again and again upon the good qualities of the Buddha, and strive to attain certainty from the depths of your heart. Once you gain this, you reach the very core of the practice of going for refuge, for you will gain certainty with respect to the teaching from which the Buddha arose, and the community that practices the teaching. Without this, there is no practice of going for refuge that transforms your mind, not to mention other paths.

2″ The good qualities of the teaching

Once you have made respect for the Buddha your primary cause, you should then recollect the teaching jewel as follows: "The Buddha possesses limitless good qualities, all of which arose from meditating on and realizing both the verbal teachings and the teachings as they are put into practice. That is, he actualized the true cessations, thereby eliminating faults, and meditated on the true paths, thereby giving rise to good qualities." The *Compendium of the Teachings (Dharma-saṃgīti)* says:[324]

> These *bhagavan* buddhas possess infinite and limitless good qualities. Such qualities are born from the teaching, from the proper practice of the teaching. The teaching creates and governs them. They arise from the teaching and are within the scope of the teaching. They depend upon the teaching, and the teaching produces them.

3″ The good qualities of the community

Chief among the members of the community are those persons who are noble beings. Think of them in light of their mindfulness of the good qualities of the teaching and their proper practice of it. The *Compendium of the Teachings*:[325]

> Think, "The community teaches the teaching, practices it, and reflects on it. It is the teaching's sphere. It upholds the teaching, entrusts itself to the teaching, worships the teaching, and conducts itself according to the teaching. **[141]** It has the teaching as its sphere of activity, and is the most excellent practitioner of the

> teaching. It is naturally honest and pure. It is endowed with the quality of compassion, and has [great] compassion. It always has solitude as its field of activity, is always absorbed in the teaching, and always practices virtue."

b" **Going for refuge by knowing the distinctions**

According to the *Compendium of Determinations*,[326] you go for refuge after understanding the distinctions among the three jewels.

1" **The distinction based on their defining characteristics**

The buddha jewel has the defining characteristic of full, perfect enlightenment. The teaching jewel has the defining characteristic of arising from the buddha jewel. The community jewel has the defining characteristic of correct practice by means of personal instruction.

2" **The distinction based on their enlightened activities**

Buddha has the enlightened activity of giving sermons. The teaching has the enlightened activity of focusing on the eradication of afflictions and suffering. The community has the enlightened activity of fostering enthusiasm.

3" **The distinction based on devotion**

You should appreciate the Buddha as the one to venerate and serve. You should appreciate the teaching as that which is to be realized. You should appreciate the community as those with whom you should associate because they have attributes that are similar to your own.

4" **The distinction based on practice**

You should worship and serve the Buddha. You should become familiar with the teaching by applying yourself to yoga. You should cultivate a relationship with the community through sharing the teaching and material goods.

5" **The distinction based on recollection**

You should recollect the good qualities of each of the three jewels by reciting "Thus, the Bhagavan...."[327]

6" **The distinction based on how they increase merit**

Supreme merit is increased through the influence of either persons or the teaching. The Buddha and the community are instances of the former. Also, you can increase merit in dependence on either a single person or many persons. The community is a case of the latter, because it requires four monks. **[142]**

c″ Going for refuge through commitment

According to Dharmamitra's *Commentary on the "Sūtra on the Discipline" (Vinaya-sūtra-ṭīkā)*,[328] going for refuge through commitment means upholding the Buddha as the teacher of refuge, the teaching—nirvāṇa—as the actual refuge, and the community as those who assist us to attain refuge.

d″ Going for refuge by refusing to acknowledge other refuges

Going for refuge by refusing to acknowledge other refuges means first of all understanding the differences in worth between Buddhist and non-Buddhist teachers, teachings, and disciples, for then you will uphold only the three jewels as your refuge, and refuse teachers, teachings, and disciples that do not accord with them. The distinctions between the Buddhist and non-Buddhist teachers, etc. are as follows.

The distinction of the teacher: The Buddha is without fault and has perfected good qualities, but the teachers of other religions are the opposite of this. Udbhaṭasiddhasvāmin's *Praise of the Exalted One (Viśeṣa-stava)* says:[329]

> Having forsaken other teachers,
> I go to you for refuge, O Bhagavan.
> If someone should ask why, it is because
> You have no faults and possess [all] good qualities.

And also:

> The more I reflect on
> Other, non-Buddhist, traditions,
> The greater becomes
> My faith, O Protector.
>
> Their minds are ruined by the faults of tenets
> Devised by those who are not omniscient.
> Those whose minds are ruined
> Cannot even see you, faultless Teacher.

The distinction of the teaching: The Conqueror's teaching allows you to attain its goal of bliss through a joyful path. It stops the stream of cyclic existence, clears away the afflictions, does not mislead those who desire liberation, is completely virtuous, and clears away faults. Non-Buddhist teachings are the opposite. The *Praise of the Exalted One*:[330]

> Your teaching causes one to attain
> Bliss through the joyful;
> Therefore, O Lion of Speakers,
> Intelligent beings have faith in your tradition. **[143]**

And the *Praise in Honor of One Worthy of Honor* also says:[331]

> The difference between your words, O Hero,
> And the words of others is
> That the former should be adopted, and the latter rejected;
> The former purifies and the latter defiles.
>
> The former is strictly reality,
> The latter only misleading teachings—
> What other difference do you need
> Between your words and those of others?
>
> The former is purely virtuous;
> The latter only creates obstacles—
> What greater difference could there be
> Between your words and those of others?
>
> The former purifies;
> The latter defiles and stains—
> This is the difference, O Protector,
> Between your words and those of others.

Through this citation you can also understand the distinction of the community.

12

The Precepts of Refuge

4′ Once you have gone for refuge, the stages of the precepts
  a″ How they appear in the *Compendium of Determinations*
    1″ The first set of subdivisions
      (a) Rely on excellent persons
      (b) Listen to the sublime teachings
      (c) Fix your attention properly on them
      (d) Cultivate a practice that conforms with the teachings
    2″ The second set of subdivisions
      (a) Do not excite your sensory faculties
      (b) Take up the precepts correctly
      (c) Be compassionate toward living beings
      (d) Strive to make periodic offerings to the three jewels
  b″ How they appear in the oral tradition
    1″ The special precepts
      (a) The proscriptive precepts
      (b) The prescriptive precepts
    2″ The general precepts
      (a) By recalling the distinctions and good qualities of the three jewels, go for refuge again and again
      (b) By recalling the great kindness of the three jewels, strive to worship them constantly and offer the first portion of your food and drink
      (c) Establish other living beings in this practice by considering them with compassion
      (d) Whatever activity you engage in, and whatever your purpose, make offerings and supplications to the three jewels, forsaking any other worldly methods
      (e) After you have understood the benefits, go for refuge three times in the day and three times at night
        (i) The benefits as they appear in the *Compendium of Determinations*
          (a′) The first set of four
            (1′) You will obtain vast merit
            (2′) You will obtain both joy and supreme joy

(3′) You will obtain concentration
(4′) You will attain purity
(b′) The second set of four
(1′) You will have great protection
(2′) You will reduce, extinguish, and totally annihilate all obscurations derived from incorrect belief
(3′) You are counted among excellent persons, who genuinely accomplish the sublime
(4′) You delight and receive the approval of your teachers and religious companions, and of the deities who take joy in the teaching
(ii) The benefits as they appear in personal instructions
(a′) You are included among Buddhists
(b′) You become worthy to uphold all vows
(c′) You reduce and eliminate previously accumulated karmic obstructions
(d′) You will accumulate vast merit
(e′) You will not fall into the miserable realms
(f′) You will not be thwarted by human or nonhuman hindrances
(g′) You will accomplish everything you wish
(h′) You will quickly achieve buddhahood
(f) Maintain your refuge and do not forsake the three jewels, even in jest or if it costs you your life

4′ Once you have gone for refuge, the stages of the precepts

The precepts are explained in two ways:

1. How they appear in the *Compendium of Determinations*
2. How they appear in the oral tradition

a″ How they appear in the *Compendium of Determinations*[332]

Here the precepts are explained in two sets of subdivisions.

1″ The first set of subdivisions

(a) Rely on excellent persons

As previously explained, you rely on excellent teachers when you see them as the source of all good qualities, for you have already gone to the Buddha for refuge and thereby uphold the teacher of the path as your refuge. The practice that conforms with this is actual reliance on the one who teaches the path to you.

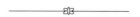

(b) **Listen to the sublime teachings, and** (c) **Fix your attention properly on them**

You should listen to whatever is appropriate among the sūtras and the like, teachings which are sublime because the Buddha and the Buddha's disciples explained them. In addition, fix your attention on whatever serves to dispel the afflictions, for you have already gone to the teaching for refuge and you have thus undertaken to actualize both the verbal teachings and the teachings as they are realized. The practice that conforms with this is listening to and fixing your attention properly on the sublime teachings.

(d) **Cultivate a practice that conforms with the teachings**

You should practice in accordance with the teachings on nirvāṇa. When you have gone to the community for refuge, you have thereby taken as companions persons who are on the path to nirvāṇa. **[144]** The practice that accords with this is training in the way of those who are intent upon liberation.

2″ **The second set of subdivisions**

(a) **Do not excite your sensory faculties**

When the sensory faculties draw the inattentive mind to objects, you should view this excitement with regard to sensory objects as a fault, and withdraw the mind from them.

(b) **Take up the precepts correctly**

You should take up the trainings set forth by the Buddha—as many as possible.

(c) **Be compassionate toward living beings**

The Conqueror's teaching is distinguished by compassion. Therefore, once you have gone to his teaching for refuge, you should also be compassionate toward living beings and forsake harming them.

(d) **Strive to make periodic offerings to the three jewels**

Each day you should make offerings to the three jewels.

b″ **How they appear in the oral tradition**

In the oral tradition, the precepts are divided into special precepts and general precepts.

1″ **The special precepts**

These are explained in terms of proscriptive and prescriptive precepts.

(a) **The proscriptive precepts**

The *Great Final Nirvāṇa Sūtra* states:[333]

> Those who go to the three jewels for refuge
> Come closer to the truly virtuous;
> They never go
> To other deities for refuge.
>
> Those who go to the sublime teaching for refuge
> Harbor no harmful, murderous thoughts.
> Those who go to the community for refuge
> Do not associate with non-Buddhist philosophers.

Thus, there are three proscriptive precepts: not going to other deities for refuge, abandoning harm and malice toward living beings, and not befriending non-Buddhist philosophers.

Not going to other deities for refuge is explained as follows: since you should not even hold worldly deities such as Rudra and Viṣṇu as your ultimate refuge, what need be said about *nāgas* and the local divinities who are hungry ghosts? While it is improper to entrust yourself to these beings without full belief in the three refuges, it is proper to merely seek these beings' help for some temporary religious purpose, just as, for example, you would seek the help of a benefactor in acquiring the means of livelihood, or consult a doctor for the cure of an illness. **[145]**

The second proscriptive precept entails refraining from doing harm or injury to living beings through thought or deed. This includes actions such as beating, binding, imprisoning, nose-piercing, and overburdening humans, animals, and so forth. The third proscriptive precept entails not agreeing with those who do not believe in the three jewels as a refuge and who repudiate them.

(b) **The prescriptive precepts**

There are three prescriptive precepts. The first is to treat images of the Buddha as objects of reverence—as though they were the Teacher himself—not pointing out their faults regardless of their quality, and not disrespecting them or treating them with contempt by putting them in dishonorable places, pawning them, etc. The *Friendly Letter*:[334]

> Just as the learned worship an image of the Sugata,
> Whatever it is made of, even wood...

The *Exegesis of the Discipline*[335] relates how Mānavakapila, who slandered the community of learners and those with no more to learn in eighteen different ways—saying, for example, "What do you know of the teaching or nonteaching, Elephant-head?"—was reborn as a monstrous fish with eighteen different heads, remaining an animal from the time of Teacher Kāśyapa until the time of the King of the Śākyas [the Buddha]. The *The Kṣudraka Bases of Discipline (Vinaya-kṣudraka-vastu)*[336] relates how, after the nirvāṇa of Teacher Krakucchanda, King Cārumat ordered that a great *stūpa* be built. A workman cursed it twice, exclaiming, "We'll never be able to complete a *stūpa* this huge!" Later, when it was nicely finished, he regretted his curses and used his wages to have a golden bell fashioned and placed on the *stūpa*. **[146]** As a result, he was reborn as Supriyavat ("Sweet Voice"), with an ugly complexion and tiny body, but a beautiful voice. Thus, you should never quibble over the quality of images, despise others for using fine materials for images and the like or for making them large, discourage their makers from finishing them, and the like.

It is said that the great yogi [Chang-chup-rin-chen] once gave a statue of Mañjughoṣa to the Elder for him to examine. He asked, "How good is this? If it is good, I will buy it with the four gold coins Rong-ba-gar-gay-wa (Rong-pa-mgar-dge-ba) gave me." The Elder replied, "Venerable Mañjughoṣa's body has no defects—the sculptor is middling," and placed it on his head. It is said that he did the same with respect to all finished images.

The second prescriptive precept is never to show disrespect for writings on the teachings, even those composed of as little as four words. Further, you should not pawn volumes of scriptures, treat them as merchandise, place them on the bare ground or in dishonorable places, carry them together with shoes, walk over them, etc. Treat them with respect, as though they were the teaching jewel itself. It is said that whenever Geshe Jen-nga-wa saw a scripture being carried, he would stand up with his hands joined together in front of him in a gesture of respect. In later life, when he was unable to rise, he would simply join his hands. Also, it is said that the Elder once encountered a mantra practitioner in Nga-ri who initially refused to listen to him teach. However, one day the Elder witnessed a scribe rubbing a page of the teaching with plaque from his teeth. Unable to bear this, he cried out, "Hey! Don't do that, don't do that!"—as a result of which the mantra practitioner gained faith in the Elder and received the teaching from him. Furthermore, Sha-ra-wa said: "We are playing around with the teaching in so many ways. Showing disrespect for the teaching and its teachers ruins our wisdom. We are stupid enough now—let's not create more stupidity! If we become even more stupid, what will we be able to do?"

The third prescriptive precept is never to revile or despise members of the community, renunciates, or those who merely possess the symbols of a practitioner of virtue [someone who is dressed as a monk or nun but has no vow]. Nor should you do this to the mere symbols [part of the robes] of these practitioners. Never in any way divide yourself and others into opposing factions and view the others as enemies. **[147]** Always treat members of the community with respect, as though they were the community jewel itself.

The *Exhortation to Wholehearted Resolve* says:[337]

> Those dwelling in the forest, desiring good qualities,
> Should not scrutinize others' faults.
> They should not think,
> "I am superior; I am the best"—
>
> Such arrogance is the root of all unruliness.
> Do not despise inferior monks,
> Or you will not achieve liberation for an eon.
> Such is the way of this teaching.

We should train ourselves to practice like the Precious Teacher [Drom-dön-ba] and Nal-jor-ba-chen-bo, who, if they saw a mere scrap of yellow cloth on the path, would not step on it, but would dust it off and carry it to a clean place. For, as much as we respect the three jewels, so will living beings respect us. The *King of Concentrations Sūtra*:[338]

> You will obtain a result similar
> To the kinds of karma you do.

2" The general precepts

There are six general precepts:

1. By recalling the distinctions and good qualities of the three jewels, go for refuge again and again
2. By recalling the great kindness of the three jewels, strive to worship them constantly and offer the first portion of your food and drink
3. Establish other living beings in this practice by considering them with compassion
4. Whatever activity you engage in, and whatever your purpose, make offerings and supplications to the three jewels, forsaking any other worldly methods

5. After you have understood the benefits, go for refuge three times in the day and three times at night
6. Maintain your refuge and do not forsake the three jewels, even in jest or if it costs you your life

(a) **By recalling the distinctions and good qualities of the three jewels, go for refuge again and again**

As previously explained, you should repeatedly keep in mind the differences between non-Buddhists and Buddhists, the distinctions among the three jewels, and the good qualities of the three jewels.

(b) **By recalling the great kindness of the three jewels, strive to worship them constantly and offer the first portion of your food and drink.**

The *King of Concentrations Sūtra*:[339]

> Though they obtain food due to the buddhas' merit,
> The childish do not repay their kindness.

Thus, knowing that all the temporary happiness and certain goodness that you experience, symbolized by food, are due to the kindness of the three jewels, you should make offerings with the intention of repaying their kindness.

With regard to offerings, there are (1) the actions of offering and (2) the attitudes. The first of these include the following ten types: **[148]**

1) *Offerings to the Buddha's body* means offerings to the actual Buddha's embodiment as form.

2) *Offerings to stūpas* means offerings to *stūpas* and the like for the sake of the Buddha.

3) *Offerings to a perceived object* means offerings to the above-mentioned two as they are manifest to your own sensory faculties.

4) *Offerings to a nonperceived object* refers to offerings made to a buddha or his *stūpas* that are not actually present, and made for the sake of all buddhas and *stūpas*. Offerings made for the sake of the Buddha to one or more images and *stūpas* after his nirvāṇa are also considered offerings to a nonperceived object. When you make offerings to either an unperceived buddha or his unperceived *stūpas*, you are also making offerings to both of the perceived objects, for the reality or emptiness of one of them is the reality of all of them. It is standard to make offerings, both to perceived and to nonperceived objects, with the

thought, "I make offerings to all the buddhas of the three times and to the *stūpas* of the ten directions of the limitless universe." It is said that making offerings to a percieved object produces a vast store of merit and making offerings to an unperceived object a greater store; making offerings to all the buddhas and *stūpas* produces a store far more vast than that. Thus, it is important that when you make offerings to a single buddha or his image, and the like, you recollect the indivisibility of reality and project the thought that you are making offerings to all of them.

5) *Offerings made by yourself* are offerings made manually by yourself. Do not have others make them for you out of your laziness, indifference, or carelessness.

6) *Offerings that you help others to make* refers to offerings that you, out of compassion, cause someone else to make. This occurs when you have some small things to offer and you think, "These suffering living beings, who have little merit and nothing to give, will gain happiness by making these offerings." Furthermore, the merit of offerings made both by yourself and by others you have helped to make offerings are shared by both of you, the difference in the size of the meritorious results of these three being similar to the above discussion in the fourth section. **[149]**

7) *Offerings of wealth and service* are offerings to a buddha or his *stūpa* consisting of gifts of clothing, food, bedding, seats, medicine, personal necessities, incense, aromatic powders and ointments, flower garlands, music, and various types of lamps. There is also offering respectful speech, prostrations, rising before the other, hands joined together respectfully, a variety of praises, obeisance with your limbs and head touching the ground, and clockwise circumambulation. Moreover, inexhaustible gifts such as fields can be given, as well as offerings of jewels, earrings, bracelets, and the like. At the least, there are offerings of bells, silver coins, or spools of thread.

8) *Vast offerings* means offerings of the above wealth and service over a long duration. Furthermore, they have seven qualities: being copious, excellent, both perceived and nonperceived, done by both oneself and others, and being offered with heartfelt delight, fervent aspiration, and with the merit being dedicated to perfect enlightenment.

9) *Offerings not contaminated with the afflictions* are offerings with six qualities: they are made (1) manually by yourself, not

making others do them out of contempt, carelessness, or laziness; (2) respectfully; (3) without distraction; (4) free of the afflictions in that they are not mixed with attachment and the like; (5) without expectation of receiving wealth and service from kings and so on who have faith in the Buddha; and (6) with proper material accompaniments. Proper material accompaniments include whatever is free of inappropriate things, as well as proper acts such as anointing something with *bala (ba-bla)* medicinal ointment, soaking something in clarified butter, burning a fragrant *gugul* resin, offering white *arka* flowers, and so forth. If you have neither prepared these offering materials yourself nor requested them from others, you should delight in all the appropriate offerings to the *tathāgatas* that exist throughout the universe, imagine them to be vast and pervasive, and rejoice in others offering them. **[150]** Having made this great, measureless offering, you will, with little difficulty, amass the accumulations necessary for attaining enlightenment. Strive constantly to do this with a contented, happy mind. As it says in the *Cloud of Jewels Sūtra* and the *Array of the Three Pledges (Tri-samaya-vyūha)*,[340] you can also give unowned flowers, fruit, trees, jewels, and the like.

10) *Offerings of practice* entail recollecting the four immeasurables, the fourfold condensation of the teaching [(1) all composite phenomena are impermanent, (2) all contaminated things are miserable, (3) all phenomena are selfless, and (4) nirvāṇa is bliss and peace], the three refuges, and the perfections; admiring profound emptiness and fixing on it without conceptualization; disciplining your mind through the vows of ethical discipline; and meditating on and striving for the factors of enlightenment, the perfections, and the four ways to gather disciples, all for at least as long as it takes to milk a cow [ten to fifteen minutes].

To make these ten types of offerings to the three jewels is to make a complete offering.

The second aspect of offerings, the attitudes, is as follows. When you make these ten types of offerings, there are six attitudes that will render immeasurable the result of even a small offering to any of the three jewels. You should make offerings with the thoughts that

(1) there is no higher field of good qualities;
(2) there is no higher benefactor;
(3) he is the best of all living beings;

(4) he is extremely rare, like an *udumvara* flower;[341]
(5) since only one buddha appears in a universe of three billion world systems, he is the only one; and
(6) he is the foundation of all mundane and supramundane good.

I have written about these ten types of offerings and six attitudes as they appear in the *Bodhisattva Levels*.[342]

You should always make the best offering you can. Make especially good offerings on auspicious occasions and holidays, to the best of your ability. Furthermore, since you constantly have to eat and drink, always offer the first portion of your food and drink. **[151]** If you do this without fail, you will easily amass a large accumulation of merit. Thus, from the depths of your heart, always offer the first portion of whatever you consume, even water.

Further, Sha-ra-wa stated:

> Do not offer things such as moldy sweet cheese and yellowed leaves, but use what you have that is good. Offering the first portion of tea will not be beneficial if it is done like the clearing away of some dust.

A sutra says:

> For example, it will not work just to put seeds on a fertile field without actually planting them in season. So it is appropriate continuously to plant the seeds of temporary happiness and certain goodness throughout the four seasons in the fertile field that gives rise to all temporary happiness and certain goodness in this and future lives—but you till this field with the plow of faith.

If you do not do this, you will be extremely poor in merit.

Hence, as the *Praise in Honor of One Worthy of Honor* says:[343]

> No field of merit like you
> Exists in the three worlds—
> You are the supreme recipient of gifts,
> The pure one who makes a row of monks pure.
>
> Just as the height and breadth
> Of the firmament have no limit,
> There is no limit to the fruition
> Of helping or harming you.

Since our practice is such that we cannot even think of a supreme field of merit as we would an ordinary field, we should always strive to make offerings to the three jewels. By doing so our mind's power with respect to the stages of the path will increase as a result of the strength of the roots of virtue grown in this excellent field of merit. Therefore, when our mind's power is so weak that we cannot retain the words when we study, understand the meaning when we reflect, or gain knowledge when we meditate, we should rely on the power of the field of merit. This is a personal instruction. In this vein, Śrī Mātṛceṭa also says:[344]

By depending on you, [Bhagavan,]
My mind, though weak, has broadened
Like a river in the rainy season,
Attaining great skill in composing poetry. **[152]**

It is taught that offerings are not determined by the material objects offered, but by your faith. Thus, if you do not have material possessions to offer, then offerings of maṇḍalas and water, or of things not held as property and the like, will suffice if you have faith. Some have possessions but are unable to give them up, quoting the verse,[345] "As I have no merit, I am very poor; I have no other wealth for offerings." This is, as Bo-do-wa said, like a blind person trying to fool a sighted person by dropping a bit of sod incense into a smelly conch cup and saying, "This is water scented with sandalwood and camphor."

Pu-chung-wa said, "First I gave sod incense with a sharp odor. Next I obtained sweet-smelling, long sticks of incense made from four substances to give. Now I give aromatic *akaru*, *turuṣka*, and the like." Thus, if you despise small offerings and do not give them, your entire life will pass in that way. However, if you make earnest effort in stages, beginning with small things, conditions will improve. You should practice as Pu-chung-wa did. It is said that on one occasion he made a preparation of incense worth twenty-two gold coins.

Great beings who have gained control over material things emanate many hundreds of thousands of bodies, each of which in turn emanates hundreds of thousands of hands. Visiting all the buddha-realms, they make offerings to the Conquerors for many eons. They can do all this, while others settle for small achievements that look good, and say, "I do not expect enlightenment through making offerings." This is the nonsense of those who have little exposure to the teaching. Thus, we should do as it says in the *Cloud of Jewels Sūtra*:[346]

> Study any of the vast offerings and acts of service in the sūtras such as these. With supreme wholehearted resolve, sincerely dedicate these offerings and acts of service before the buddhas and bodhisattvas.

(c) **Establish other living beings in this practice by considering them with compassion [153]**

This means that you should use all available means to caringly establish other living beings in the practice of going for refuge.

(d) **Whatever activity you engage in, and whatever your purpose, make offerings and supplications to the three jewels, forsaking any other worldly methods**

Whatever activity you engage in, and whatever your purpose, rely on and do that which accords with the three jewels, such as making offerings to them. But never do that which does not accord with the three jewels, such as relying on the Bön (Bon) religion. Always entrust yourself to the three jewels.

(e) **After you have understood the benefits, go for refuge three times in the day and three times at night**

The benefits of going for refuge are explained first according to the *Compendium of Determinations* and then according to the personal instructions.

(i) **The benefits as they appear in the *Compendium of Determinations***

These are explained in two sets of four.

(a′) **The first set of four**

(1′) **You will obtain vast merit**

As the *Immortal Drumbeat Dhāraṇī* (*'Chi med rnga sgra'i gzungs*) says:[347]

> The Bhagavan Buddha is inconceivable.
> The sublime teaching is also inconceivable.
> The noble community is inconceivable.
> For those having faith in the inconceivable
> The fruition is also inconceivable.

Also, Āryaśūra's *Compendium of the Perfections* (*Pāramitā-samāsa*) states:[348]

> If the merit of going for refuge took form,
> Even these three realms would be too small to contain it—
> A cupped hand cannot measure
> The great ocean, the storehouse of water.

(2′) **You will obtain both joy and supreme joy**

The *Collection of Indicative Verses* states:[349]

Those who, recalling the Buddha
During the day and at night,
Go for refuge to him,
Gain the advantage of being human.

You should apply this to the other two jewels as well. Thus, the one who relies on these three refuges grows more joyful with the thought, "I have really gotten something worth getting!"

(3′) **You will obtain concentration and** (4′) **You will attain purity [154]**

You will be liberated through training in concentration and wisdom.

(b′) **The second set of four**

(1′) **You will have great protection**

This will be explained later.

(2′) **You will reduce, extinguish, and totally annihilate all obscurations derived from incorrect belief**

You will reduce and clear away bad karma accumulated on account of your believing in bad teachers, teachings, and friends and upholding them as refuges.

(3′) **You are counted among excellent persons, who genuinely accomplish the sublime**

You are included among excellent persons.

(4′) **You delight and receive the approval of your teachers and religious companions, and of the deities who take joy in the teaching**

You please your teachers and religious companions. How are the deities delighted? They sing praises of such people, joyfully thinking, "The person named such and such, who, like us, has gone for refuge, will die and be reborn here. Because he or she has gone for refuge and has become stable in it, he or she will be our companion."

(ii) **The benefits as they appear in personal instructions**

As explained in the personal instructions, the benefits of going for refuge are eight in number.

(a′) **You are included among Buddhists**

In general, there are a number of ways to distinguish Buddhists from non-Buddhists. However, since it is widely acknowledged that the Elder and Śāntipa distinguish them according to the refuges they seek, you should count as Buddhists those who have obtained and not forsaken their refuge. Thus, to initially be included among Buddhists you must uphold the three jewels as your teacher and so forth from the depths of your heart. Without this you are not included among Buddhists, no matter what virtue you have cultivated.

(b′) **You become worthy to uphold all vows**

The *Treasury of Knowledge Auto-commentary* says:[350]

> Those who go for refuge enter the door leading to the taking of all vows.

Also, Candrakīrti's *Seventy Verses on Refuge* says:[351]

> O lay practitioners, going for refuge to the three jewels is the basis for the eight vows.[352] **[155]**

The intended meaning of these passages is that you make your aspiration for nirvāṇa firm by going for refuge, and that your vows arise from this.

(c′) **You reduce and eliminate previously accumulated karmic obstructions**

In the section where it teaches that going for refuge clears away sins, the *Compendium of Trainings* says:[353]

> Here you should take the edifying tale of the pig as an example.

Thus, just as the god who was about to be reborn as a pig avoided such a birth by going for refuge, so too do you eliminate the condition for rebirth in a miserable realm by going for refuge. Consequently, it is said:

> Those who go for refuge to the Buddha
> Do not go to miserable realms.
> After giving up human form,
> They assume the bodies of deities.

The same teaching applies to taking refuge in the teaching and the community: some previously accumulated sins are reduced, and some are eliminated.

(d′) **You will accumulate vast merit**

This has been explained previously.

(e′) **You will not fall into the miserable realms**

You should understand this from the earlier explanation.

(f′) You will not be thwarted by human or nonhuman hindrances

As it says in a sūtra:[354]

> People who are terrified
> Mostly go for refuge to deities of the
> Mountains, forests, temples,
> And the trees of sacred places.
>
> Such refuges are not the foremost;
> Such refuges are not supreme.
> If you rely on such a refuge,
> You will not be freed from all suffering.
>
> When you go for refuge to the Buddha,
> The teaching, and the community,
> You will see with wisdom
> The four noble truths—
>
> Suffering, the origin of suffering,
> Correctly overcoming suffering,
> And the happy eightfold noble path
> Leading to nirvāṇa.
>
> This is the foremost refuge;
> This is the supreme refuge.
> If you rely on such a refuge,
> You will be freed from all suffering.

Here you should use as examples the stories about the non-Buddhist who mastered the magic rope, and so forth.[355] **[156]**

(g′) You will accomplish everything you wish

If, before undertaking a religious activity, you make offerings to the three jewels, go for refuge, and then pray to succeed, you will easily accomplish it.

(h′) You will quickly achieve buddhahood

The *Sūtra Requested by a Lion (Siṃha-paripṛcchā-sūtra)* says:[356]

> Through faith you overcome a lack of leisure.

Thus, one who obtains a special kind of leisure, encounters the refuge, and trains in the special path will achieve buddhahood without delay.

Each day, recall the benefits in the above manner. Then go for refuge three times during the day and three times during the night.

(f) Maintain your refuge and do not forsake the three jewels, even in jest or if it costs you your life

Inevitably you will lose your body, life, and resources. But, if you forsake the three jewels for the sake of these, you will suffer continually throughout many lives. Thus, you should repeatedly vow that whatever happens you will not forsake your refuge—not even mouthing the words in jest.

Former teachers have said that there is a precept that you should practice going for refuge to the *tathāgata* of whichever direction you are going in. I have not seen a source for this.

I have presented the six general precepts in accordance with how they appear in Atisha's *Commentary on the Difficult Points of the "Lamp for the Path to Enlightenment."* The first three of the special precepts are explained in the sūtras, the other three in Vimalamitra's *Six Aspects of Going for Refuge (Saḍ-aṅga-śaraṇa-gamana)*:[357]

> An image, verse, or
> Discarded scrap of yellow cloth:
> Out of faith and belief, consider it to be the Teacher;
> Do not mistakenly deny anything he has said,
> Rather place it on the crown of your head;
> View pure and impure persons
> As though they were noble. **[157]**

With respect to the precepts drawn from the *Compendium of Determinations*,[358] the sayings of Ga-ma-pa state, "Neu-sur-ba did not teach these [precepts of going for refuge], but he and I received them together from Gön-ba-wa." They appear in the presentation of the stages of the path transmitted from Gön-ba-wa through Lum-ba-wa (Lum-pa-ba).

How contravening these precepts causes weakening and forsaking of your refuge is explained as follows. Some assert that if you violate six of the precepts—the first three special precepts, plus the precepts of constantly going for refuge, not forsaking refuge even for the sake of your life, and making offerings to the three jewels—you have given up your refuge. Others include the last three special precepts and assert that contravention of nine precepts constitutes forsaking refuge. Contravention of the remaining precepts weakens your refuge.

However, an actual forsaking of refuge means that you have contravened the precept not to forsake refuge even for the sake of your life. Similarly, even if you do not forsake the three jewels, if you follow both them and a teacher, teaching, and community that are contrary to them, you contravene the precept not to acknowledge other refuges. Since you are not fully entrusting yourself to the refuge, you have forsaken it. I think that if these two do not occur, other contraventions of the precepts are just contraventions, but not causes of forsaking refuge.

This being the case, going for refuge is the main door to the Buddha's teaching. If you go for refuge in a way that transcends mere words, you will not be defeated by outer and inner obstacles, for you are relying upon the highest power. Since good qualities develop easily and deteriorate with difficulty, they can only continue to increase. Therefore, it is extremely important, as previously explained, to uphold the refuges by means of fearing suffering, recalling the good qualities of the refuges, and so forth, and to make an effort not to transgress the precepts.

Question: Thus when you generate fear through mindfulness of death and the thought that, after death, you will be reborn in a miserable realm, the refuge that protects you from this is the three jewels. You uphold them as your refuge and do not contravene their precepts. Nonetheless, how do the refuges protect you?

Reply: The *Collection of Indicative Verses* states:[359]

> I, the Tathāgata, the Teacher,
> Reveal to you
> The path that stops the pains of existence;
> You must follow it. **[158]**

Thus, the Buddha is the one who teaches refuge, and the community assists you in accomplishing refuge, but the real refuge is the jewel of the teaching, because once you have attained it, you are liberated from fear. With regard to this, the ultimate teaching jewel is defined as being the special fulfillment of the gradual increase of two things—the beginning practitioner's elimination of a mere portion of faults, and his or her knowledge that brings about a mere portion of good qualities. This is not something that appears adventitiously.

13

The General Characteristics of Karma

b′ Developing the faith of conviction that is the root of all temporary happiness and certain goodness
   1′ Reflecting on karma and its effects in general
      a″ The actual way in which to reflect in general
         1″ The certainty of karma
         2″ The magnification of karma
         3″ Not experiencing the effects of actions that you did not do
         4″ The actions you have done do not perish

At this point master the classifications of virtue and nonvirtue, as well as their effects. You must then make it your practice to properly cast aside nonvirtues and adopt virtues. For, unless you reflect at length on the two kinds of karma[360] and their effects, and then properly cast aside the nonvirtuous and adopt the virtuous, you will not stop the causes of miserable rebirths. Thus, you may fear the miserable realms and yet not be able to escape what you fear.

Consequently, in order to be protected from the miserable realms at the time when you must experience the effects, you have to restrain the mind from engaging in nonvirtue at the time when you are creating the causes. This, in turn, is contingent upon attaining conviction about karma and its effects.

b′ Developing the faith of conviction that is the root of all temporary happiness and certain goodness[361]

The second part of the explanation of how to achieve happiness in the next life—developing the faith of conviction in karma and its effects—consists of reflecting on karma and its effects in general (Chapters 13–14) and in detail (Chapter 14).

1′ Reflecting on karma and its effects in general

This explanation is divided into:

1. The actual way in which to reflect in general (Chapter 13)
2. Reflecting on the distinctions among the varieties of karma (Chapter 14)

a″ The actual way in which to reflect in general

In general, the actual way to reflect on karma and its effects entails four points:

1. The certainty of karma
2. The magnification of karma
3. Not experiencing the effects of actions that you did not do
4. That the actions you have done do not perish

1″ The certainty of karma

All happiness in the sense of feelings of ease—whether of ordinary or noble beings, including even the slightest pleasures such as the rising of a cool breeze for a being born in a hell—arises from previously accumulated virtuous karma. It is impossible for happiness to arise from nonvirtuous karma.

All sufferings in the sense of painful feelings—including even the slightest suffering occurring in an arhat's mind-stream—arise from previously accumulated nonvirtuous karma. **[159]** It is impossible for suffering to arise from virtuous karma. The *Precious Garland*:[362]

> From nonvirtues come all sufferings
> And likewise, all miserable realms.
> From virtues come all happy realms
> And the joys in all rebirths.

Consequently, happiness and suffering do not occur in the absence of causes, nor do they arise from incompatible causes such as a divine creator or a primal essence.[363] Rather, happiness and suffering, in general, come from virtuous and nonvirtuous karma, and the various particular happinesses and sufferings arise individually, without even the slightest confusion, from various particular instances of these two kinds of karma. Attaining certain knowledge of the definiteness, or nondeceptiveness, of karma and its effects is called the correct viewpoint for all Buddhists and is praised as the foundation of all virtue.

2″ **The magnification of karma**

An effect of immense happiness may arise from even a small virtuous karma. An effect of immense suffering may arise from even a tiny nonvirtuous karma. Hence, internal [karmic] causation seems to involve a magnification that is not found in external causation. Moreover, it is said in the *Collection of Indicative Verses*:[364]

> Like a poison that has been ingested,
> The commission of even a small sin
> Creates in your lives hereafter
> Great fear and a terrible downfall.
>
> As when grain ripens into a bounty,
> Even the creation of small merit
> Leads in lives hereafter to great happiness
> And will be immensely meaningful as well.

Become certain about how great effects may arise from small actions by studying the narratives of past events presented in texts such as the *Bases of Discipline*, the *Sūtra of the Wise and the Foolish (Dama-mūrkha-sūtra)*,[365] and the *Hundred Actions Sūtra (Karma-śataka-sūtra)*. For example, there are the stories from the *Bases of Discipline*[366] about the herdsman Nanda and the frog beaten by his staff, the goose, the fish, the five hundred tortoises, the five hundred hungry ghosts, the farmer, and the five hundred bulls, and, from the *Sūtra of the Wise and the Foolish*, the accounts of Suvarṇadevatā, Suvarṇavasu, and Hastipāla. **[160]**

Furthermore, there are those who have partially lapsed in these four things—ethical discipline, rituals, livelihood, and philosophical view. That is, they have not at all lapsed in the latter, but have not completely accomplished pure forms of the former three. The Buddha said that such people will be born as *nāgas*. The *Questions of the Nāga Kings of the Ocean (Sāgara-nāga-rāja-paripṛcchā)* says:[367]

> "Bhagavan, in the beginning of the eon I lived in the great ocean and the *tathāgata* Krakucchanda was in the world. At that time, the *nāgas* and their sons and daughters within the great ocean had become few and even I had a reduced retinue. Now, Bhagavan,

> the *nāgas* and their sons and daughters within the great ocean are immeasurable and their numbers know no limit. O Bhagavan, what are the causes and conditions for this?"
>
> And the Bhagavan said: "O Lord of *Nāgas*, there have been those who renounced the world and went forth into the discipline—the well-spoken teaching—but who did not completely perfect the pure ethical discipline. They were not completely perfect in that their rituals had deteriorated, their livelihood had deteriorated, and their ethical discipline had deteriorated. Still, their view was straight. They were not born among the living beings of the hells. They were, upon their death, reborn in the places where *nāgas* are born.

Further, it is said that during the continuation of the teaching of Teacher Krakucchanda, nine hundred and eighty million householders and renunciates were born as *nāgas* on account of their lapsed rituals, livelihood, and ethical discipline. During the continuation of the teaching of Teacher Kanakamuni, there were six hundred and forty million. During the continuation of the teaching of Teacher Kāśyapa, there were eight hundred million. During the continuation of the teaching of our own Teacher, nine hundred and ninety million have been or will be reborn as *nāgas*. Even since our own teacher passed into nirvāṇa, those of the four types of followers who commit sins and whose ethical discipline lapses are reborn as *nāgas*. **[161]**

Nonetheless, it is said that, although their practice is not pure, upon their death as *nāgas* and transference to a new life they are reborn as deities or humans through the power of their unlapsed conviction in the teaching. Except for those who entered the Mahāyāna, all of them will pass into nirvāṇa during the teachings of those who will become buddhas in this auspicious eon.

Therefore, solidify the certainty that even the subtlest of virtuous and nonvirtuous actions follow you like shadows and produce both great happiness and great suffering. Then, strive to cultivate even the subtlest of virtues and to eliminate even the subtlest of sins and infractions. The *Collection of Indicative Verses:*[368]

> Just as the shadows of birds who dwell
> In the sky move along with them,
> Beings are followed by
> What right and what wrong they have done.
>
> Just as when those with few provisions
> Set out on the road and travel in suffering,

Living beings who have not cultivated good karma
Travel to the miserable realms.

Just as when those who have prepared many provisions
Set out on the road and travel in happiness,
Living beings who have cultivated good karma
Travel to the happy realms.

And also:

Do not scorn even the tiniest sin,
Thinking that it will do no harm;
It is through the accumulation of drops of water
That a great vessel gradually fills.

And further:

Do not think that the commission
Of even a tiny sin will not pursue you.
Just as a large vessel is filled
By falling drops of water,
So too is a fool filled up with sins
Accumulated a little at a time.

Do not think that the cultivation
Of even a tiny virtue will not pursue you.
Just as a large pot is filled
By falling drops of water,
So too are the steadfast filled up
By virtues accumulated a little at a time.

Again, the *Garland of Birth Stories*:[369]

By accustoming themselves to virtuous and nonvirtuous karma
Humans become habituated to these actions.
Though you may ignore such matters,
In other lives you will experience their effects, like a dream. **[162]**

Those who do not train in generosity, ethical discipline, and the like
May have good family lineages, good bodies, and health,
And may have great power or enormous wealth,
But they will not find happiness in future lives.

As for those whose family lineage and such are inferior but who are not attached to sin
And who have qualities such as generosity and ethical discipline,
Their happiness in future lifetimes will grow

As surely as the monsoons of summer fill up the ocean.

Once you have become certain that virtuous and nonvirtuous karma
Give rise to happiness and suffering in lives beyond,
Eliminate sins and make effort at virtuous actions.
You without faith, do as you will.

3″ **Not experiencing the effects of actions that you did not do**

If you have not accumulated the karma that is the cause for an experience of happiness or suffering, you will in no way experience the happiness or suffering that is its effect. Those who enjoy the fruits of the innumerable collections amassed by the Teacher need not have accumulated all of the causes of these effects, but they do need to accumulate a portion.

4″ **The actions you have done do not perish**

Those who have done virtuous and nonvirtuous actions create pleasant and unpleasant effects. As Udbhaṭasiddhasvāmin's *Praise of the Exalted One* says:[370]

The brahmins say that virtue and sin
May transfer to others—like giving and receiving a gift.
You [O Buddha] taught that what one has done does not perish
And that one does not meet with the effects of what one has not done.

Furthermore, the *King of Concentrations Sūtra* states:[371]

Further, once you have committed an action, you will experience its effect;
And you will not experience the effects of what others have done.

Moreover, the *Bases of Discipline* says:[372]

Even in one hundred eons
Karma does not perish.
When the circumstances and the time arrive
Beings surely feel its effects.

14

The Varieties of Karma

b″ Reflecting on the distinctions among the varieties of karma
- 1″ The principal teaching of the ten paths of action
- 2″ The determination of the effects of actions
  - (a) Nonvirtuous actions and their effects
    - (i) The actual paths of nonvirtuous actions
    - (ii) Distinctions of weight
      - (a′) The weights of the ten paths of nonvirtuous action
      - (b′) A brief discussion of the criteria for powerful actions
        - (1′) Strength in terms of recipient
        - (2′) Strength in terms of support
        - (3′) Strength in terms of objects
        - (4′) Strength in terms of attitude
    - (iii) An exposition of the effects
      - (a′) Fruitional effects
      - (b′) Causally concordant effects
      - (c′) Environmental effects
  - (b) Virtuous actions and their effects
    - (i) Virtuous actions
    - (ii) The effects of virtuous actions
  - (c) A presentation of other classifications of karma
    - (i) The distinction between projecting and completing karma
    - (ii) Karma whose result you will definitely or only possibly experience

2′ Reflecting on karma and its effects in detail
- a″ The attributes of the fruitions
- b″ The effects of the fruitions
- c″ The causes of the fruitions

b″ Reflecting on the distinctions among the varieties of karma

The presentation of the distinctions among the varieties of karma has two parts:

1. The principal teaching of the ten paths of action
2. The determination of the effects of actions

1″ The principal teaching of the ten paths of action

Question: **[163]** Given that I have ascertained the causality of happiness and suffering as explained previously, have understood that karma increases, that I will not meet with the results of actions that I have not done, and that actions I have done will not perish—about what sorts of karma and effects should I initially develop certainty? Which should I adopt and which should I cast aside?

Reply: In general, you can conclude that there are three ways to engage in good and bad conduct—physically, verbally, and mentally. Although not all the virtues and nonvirtues of these three ways are included within the ten paths of action, still the Buddha, the Bhagavan, summarizing the key points, taught the most obvious, or coarse, among the virtues and nonvirtues as being the ten paths of virtuous and nonvirtuous actions. He taught that the extremely great foundations for a misdeed are the ten paths of nonvirtuous action. He saw that when you give up these ten, you adopt virtuous actions and that the most important points of these virtuous actions are also ten in number. Therefore he taught ten paths of virtuous action. The *Treasury of Knowledge*:[373]

> Systematizing the most obvious among them,
> The Buddha said that the paths of action—
> Virtuous or nonvirtuous—are ten.

And the *Exegesis of the Discipline* says:[374]

> If you practice these three paths of action—
> Guarding your speech, being restrained mentally,
> And not committing physical nonvirtues—
> You will achieve the path taught by the Sage.

Knowing the ten paths of nonvirtuous actions and their effects, restrain yourself from even being motivated to commit them. Then practice the paths of action of the ten virtues in which your body, speech, and mind are not at all mixed with the paths of nonvirtuous action. This practice is indispensable as the basis for all three vehicles as well as for the accomplishment of the two aims of beings. Hence, the Conqueror repeatedly praised it from many perspectives.

The *Questions of the Nāga Kings of the Ocean* states:[375]

> What I have called virtues are the taproots of the perfections of all deities and humans. They are the taproots of the enlightenment of *śrāvakas* and *pratyekabuddhas*. They are the taproots of the unexcelled, perfect enlightenment. And what are these taproots? They are the ten virtuous actions. **[164]**

And also:

> For example, O Lord of *Nāgas*, all villages, cities, municipalities, districts, countries, and kings' palaces; all grass, bushes, medicinal herbs, and trees; all fruits of labor, all stocks of seeds, the growth of all harvests, their plowing, harrowing, and production—everything rests on the earth. Their source is the earth. Likewise, O Lord of *Nāgas*, these paths of the ten virtuous actions are the sources of divine or human birth, of attaining the goal of the virtuous practices of learners and those with no more to learn, of the enlightenment of a *pratyekabuddha*, of all the bodhisattva deeds, and of all the qualities of a buddha.

Therefore Candrakīrti, in the *Commentary on the "Middle Way,"* summarized the significance of the Buddha's praise in the *Sutra on the Ten Levels (Daśabhūmika-sūtra)* for the ethical discipline in which you eliminate the ten nonvirtues:[376]

> For ordinary beings, those born from the Buddha's speech,
> Those whose natures are certain as self-enlightened, or conquerors' children,
> There are no causes of certain goodness
> Or high status, apart from ethical discipline.

Repeatedly guard your ethical discipline by maintaining a sense of restraint. There are some who have no such restraint even with regard to a single practice of ethical discipline, yet still say, "I am a practitioner of the Mahāyāna." This is very dishonorable. The *Sutra of Kṣitigarbha* states:[377]

> By means of these ten paths of virtue you will become a buddha. However, there are those who, for as long as they live, do not even minimally maintain even a single path of virtuous action, but who say such things as, "I am a Mahāyāna practitioner; I seek unexcelled, perfect enlightenment." Such people are great hypocrites and liars. They deceive the world in the presence of all the *bhagavan* buddhas, and they preach nihilism. When they die, they seem confused and they fall back. **[165]**

You should understand "falling back" to be a synonym for taking a completely miserable rebirth.

2″ The determination of the effects of actions

There are three parts to the determination of the effects of actions:

1. Nonvirtuous actions and their effects
2. Virtuous actions and their effects
3. A presentation of other classifications of karma

(a) Nonvirtuous actions and their effects

These are explained in three parts:

1. The actual paths of nonvirtuous actions
2. Distinctions of weight
3. An exposition of the effects

(i) The actual paths of nonvirtuous actions

The ten paths of nonvirtuous actions are as follows:

1. Killing

What is killing? The *Compendium of Determinations* teaches this in five categories—basis, perception, attitude, affliction, and conclusion. However, you can condense the middle three into the category of attitude and add the category of performance to give a condensed presentation of each of the paths of action in four categories—basis, attitude, performance, and culmination.[378] Such a presentation is easy to understand, and there is no contradiction between it and the intention in Asaṅga's teaching.

Among these, the basis of killing is a being who is alive. Moreover, the *Levels of Yogic Deeds*[379] adds the qualification "other," as in "another living being." This is in consideration of cases of suicide, and when there is a sin of commission that lacks culmination.[380]

Concerning the three aspects of attitude—perception, motivation, and affliction—perception has four types:

(1) perceiving a living being (the basis) to be a living being;
(2) perceiving a living being not to be a living being;
(3) perceiving what is not a living being not to be a living being;
(4) perceiving what is not a living being to be a living being.

The first and third perceptions are accurate, whereas the second and fourth are mistaken.

In some cases, there may be a specific motivation. For example, someone may plan to kill only someone called Devadatta, and he or she then commits murder. However, if this person mistakes

Yajñadatta for Devadatta and kills him instead, there is no actual sin.[381] Hence, such an action of killing requires an accurate perception. If at the time of performance the killer has a general motivation, thinking that no matter what happens he or she will kill, an accurate perception is not necessary. Know this to be the case for any of the remaining nine nonvirtuous actions.

The affliction is any of the three mental poisons, and the motivation is the desire to kill. **[166]** As for the performance, it makes no difference whether the performers do it themselves or cause someone else to do it. The nature of the performance is killing by way of a weapon, poison, a spell, or the like.

The culmination is the death of another on account of the performance, either at that point in time or at another point in time. Further, the *Treasury of Knowledge* says:[382]

> If the killer dies prior to or at the same time as the victim
> There is no actual infraction, since the killer has then assumed another life.

I concur.

2. Stealing

The basis of stealing is anything owned by another.

Among the three aspects of attitude, the perception and the affliction are the same as above. The motivation is the desire to take the thing from another person even though he or she has not given it to you.

As for the performance, the performer is as before. The nature of the performance in the act of stealing is either robbing by force or theft by subterfuge—they are equivalent. Further, whether people engage in deceit about debts and trusts, or take what is not given by other deceitful means, and whether they act for the sake of their own interests or others' interests, or to harm another—these are all equally considered stealing.

As for the culmination, the *Compendium of Determinations* says,[383] "moving it to another location." While there are many cases that are incompatible with the meaning of this passage, moving the thing from its original place to another is merely an illustration. In the case of things such as fields, moving it is not possible, yet you must be able to posit a culmination. Therefore, in such a case the culmination is thinking that you have acquired it. Further, if you cause another to rob or cause them to steal, it is enough that the other person has that thought. This is like the case in which someone is killed without your knowledge, but by some person whom you have sent. When the victim dies, the one who caused the murderer to kill incurs an actual sin.

3. Sexual Misconduct

There are four possible bases of sexual misconduct: a person with whom you should not have intercourse, inappropriate body parts, inappropriate places, and inappropriate times. *Those with whom one should not have intercourse* in the case of men are women with whom you should not copulate, all men, and eunuchs. The *Compendium of Determinations* refers to the first:[384] **[167]**

> Those indicated in the sūtras—such as your mother and those protected by mothers—are "those with whom you should not have intercourse."

The meaning of this is as the scholar Aśvaghoṣa said:[385]

> "Those with whom you should not copulate"
> Are those held by another, those having a religious insignia,
> Those under the protection of family or king,
> A prostitute who has been taken by another,
> And those related to you—
> These are the ones with whom you should not copulate.

"Those held by another" are others' wives. "Those who have a religious insignia" are renunciate women. "Those protected by family" are those who have not yet become brides and are protected by kinsfolk such as their fathers, who are protected by a father-in-law or a mother-in-law, who are protected by a guard, or who—in the absence of these—are protected even by themselves. "Those protected by a king" or his representative are those concerning whom a punitive law has been laid down. The line stating that sex with a prostitute for whom another has paid is sexual misconduct shows that there is no sexual misconduct in hiring a prostitute yourself. The Great Elder also taught this in a similar way.

"Men," the second in the list of those with whom you should not have intercourse, refers both to oneself and to others.

Inappropriate body parts are body parts other than the vagina. The master Aśvaghoṣa says:

> What are inappropriate body parts?
> The mouth, the anus, the calves or
> Thighs pressed together, and the hand in motion.

This accords with what the Great Elder says:[386]

> The "inappropriate body parts" are the mouth, the anus, the front or rear orifices of a boy or girl, and your own hand.

Inappropriate places are areas such as the vicinity of gurus, for instance; a place where there is a *stūpa;* in the presence of many people; and on uneven or hard places that are harmful to the person with whom you are having intercourse. The Master Aśvaghoṣa says:[387]

> In this case, inappropriate places
> Are ones that are locations of the sublime teaching,
> *Stūpas*, images, and the like, and bodhisattvas;
> And the vicinity of an abbot, a preceptor, or one's parents.
> Do not have intercourse in these inappropriate places. **[168]**

The Great Elder also taught this.

Inappropriate times are when the woman is menstruating, when she is at the end of a term of pregnancy, when she has an infant who is nursing, when she is observing a one-day vow, and when she has an illness which makes sexual intercourse inappropriate. Sexual intercourse is also inappropriate in excess of a proper amount. A proper amount is having intercourse up to five times a night. The master Aśvaghoṣa says:[388]

> In that case, inappropriate times are when
> A woman is menstruating, pregnant,
> Has an infant, is unwilling,
> Is in pain or is unhappy and the like,
> Or is maintaining the eight-part one-day vow.

Again, the Great Elder is similar to Aśvaghoṣa with the difference that he says that daytime is an inappropriate time.

Given that the three bases—sexual intercourse using inappropriate body parts, in an inappropriate place, or at an inappropriate time—become sexual misconduct even in regard to your own wife, it is certainly the case that they become sexual misconduct in regard to others.

Of the three aspects of the category of attitude—perception, motivation, and affliction—perception is spoken of in the *Compendium of Determinations* and in the texts on discipline. The *Compendium of Determinations*[389] says that the "perception of this as that" must be accurate. However, the Buddha says in the texts on discipline that in the case of the cardinal transgression of unchastity, it is the same whether the perception is mistaken or accurate.

The *Treasury of Knowledge Auto-commentary*[390] explains that if you have approached another's wife with the perception that she is your own wife, then this does not become an actual path of nonvirtuous action. Vasubandhu presents two systems in regard to when intercourse under the perception that another person's wife is the wife of a third person—one in which intercourse becomes a path of nonvirtuous action and one in which it does not.

The affliction is any of the three mental poisons. The motivation is the desire, due to unchastity, to copulate. As for the performance, the *Compendium of Determinations*[391] states that even in terms of causing others to commit sexual misconduct, the instigator of such an action incurs the misdeed of sexual misconduct as well. However, the *Treasury of Knowledge Auto-commentary*[392] explains that such instigation is not an actual path of action. You should examine whether Asaṅga's explanation may mean that such instigation is a fault which is not an actual path of action.

The culmination is the sexual union of the two parts.

4. Lying **[169]**

The eight bases of lying are that seen, that heard, that distinguished, and that cognized, as well as the four opposites of these [that not seen, etc.]. Lying is when someone else—the recipient of the lie—comprehends the meaning of the lie.

Of the three aspects of the category of attitude—perception, affliction, and motivation—perception includes misrepresenting a perception, such as what you have seen, as something you have not seen, or misrepresenting what you have not seen as something you have seen. The afflictions are the three mental poisons. The motivation is your desire to misrepresent your perception.

The performance is indicating something through speaking, through choosing not to speak, or through gesture. Further, in terms of the purpose, it is said to be the same whether you speak for your own purposes or for the sake of others. In this case it is said that even causing others to engage in the three types of speech—lying, divisive speech, or offensive speech—is the same as doing it yourself. Vasubandhu's *Treasury of Knowledge* and *Auto-commentary*[393] explain that all four vocal nonvirtues constitute paths of action when you cause others to do them. The texts on discipline say that you yourself must speak in order to incur a full infraction.

The culmination of a lie is someone else's comprehension. The *Treasury of Knowledge Auto-commentary* explains that if no one comprehends the words, then speaking them is simply the nonvirtuous action of senseless speech. Divisive speech and offensive speech are similar in this respect.

5. Divisive Speech

The bases of divisive speech are living beings who are compatible or incompatible. Of the three aspects of the category of attitude, the perception and the affliction are as before. The motivation is the desire that living beings who are compatible be separated or the desire that living beings who are incompatible remain so.

The performance is the expression of subject matter that may be either pleasant or unpleasant, and may be either true or false. You may speak of these matters either for your own or for another's purpose.

The culmination is the other's understanding of the divisive words that have been spoken. As the *Compendium of Determinations* says,[394] "The end of this path of action is when those who are to be divided understand the divisive words."

6. Offensive Speech

The basis of offensive speech is a living being in whom you can engender hostility. Of the three aspects of the category of attitude, the perception and the afflictions are as before. The motivation is the desire to speak in an offensive manner. **[170]**

The performance is saying something unpleasant, which may be either true or false, about the deficiencies of someone else's family lineage, body, ethical discipline, or behavior.

As for the culmination, the *Compendium of Determinations* says,[395] "The end is speaking in an offensive manner to that person." The *Treasury of Knowledge Auto-commentary* explains the meaning of this to be that the person to whom the offensive speech is spoken must understand it.

7. Senseless Speech

The basis of senseless speech is speech about a topic that is not meaningful. Of the three aspects of the attitude, the perception is as follows. Although Asaṅga says nothing more than "a perception of that as that," here senseless speech means that you yourself perceive the topic about which you wish to speak and then speak. It does not have to involve someone else who understands it.

The affliction is any of the three. The motivation is the desire to make arbitrary, unconnected remarks. The performance is to undertake the speaking of senseless speech. The culmination is having finished an utterance of senseless speech.

Furthermore, senseless speech has seven bases:

(1) speaking of fighting, faultfinding, disputes, and divisions;

(2) speech such as transmitting and reciting texts with a mind that delights in the treatises of non-Buddhists or in the mantra vehicle of brahmins;
(3) expressions of helplessness, such as wailing;
(4) speaking of laughter, play, entertainment, or enjoyment;
(5) talking about news of commotion, such as news of kings, ministers, nations, and thieves;
(6) speaking like a drunkard or a lunatic;
(7) the talk of one who maintains a wrong livelihood.

Disjointed, irreligious, and senseless speech is speech that is jumbled, reveals the afflictions, or is uttered while laughing, singing, or viewing actors and the like.

There are two systems with regard to the first three vocal faults—one asserts that they are senseless speech and one that they are not. However, what I have stated here is in line with the former.

8. Covetousness

The bases of covetousness are the wealth or possessions of another. Of the three aspects of the attitude, the perception is perceiving the basis to be what it is. **[171]** The affliction is any among the three. The motivation is the desire to make the wealth or property your own.

The performance is striving at that contemplated purpose. The culmination is thinking "May it become mine," about wealth and the like. Asaṅga describes this as "the determination that it will become yours." For this to be full-fledged covetousness, five qualities are required:

(1) having a mind that is exceedingly attached to your own resources;
(2) having a mind of attachment that wants to accumulate resources;
(3) having a mind of longing due to comprehending or experiencing the good things of others—their wealth and so forth;
(4) having an envious mind, thinking that whatever is another's should be your own;
(5) having a mind that is overcome, due to covetousness, by shamelessness and an obliviousness about the determination to be free from the faults of covetousness.

If any one of these five minds is not present, there is no actual covetousness. The *Levels of Yogic Deeds* says to apply these five to all ten nonvirtues.

As for the manner in which an action might constitute covetousness that is not full-fledged, it is such covetousness when you give rise to the following desires:

(1) the thought, "Oh, how nice it would be if the master of the house were to become my servant and things could be however I would wish them";
(2) also such a thought with regard to his wife and children, etc. and his physical possessions such as food and so forth;
(3) the thought, "Oh, how nice it would be if others knew me to have such good qualities as being dispassionate, retiring, persevering, learned, and generous";
(4) the thought, "How nice it would be if kings and ministers and the four types of followers of the Buddha were to respect me and if I were to obtain such necessities as food and clothing";
(5) developing desire, thinking, "Oh, may I be reborn in the future as a deity and enjoy the deities' five sensory objects, and may I be reborn from the worlds of the fierce ones and Viṣṇu, as a deity in the Heaven of Controlling Others' Emanations [the highest of the six divine regions of the desire realm]"; **[172]**
(6) developing desire for the possessions of parents, children, servants and the like, or the possessions of your fellow religious practitioners.

9. Malice

The basis, perception, and afflictions are the same as in the case of offensive speech. The motivation is the desire to do such things as strike others, thinking such thoughts as, "How nice it would be if they were killed, or bound, or their resources were ruined, either naturally or by another person."

The performance is having that thought. The culmination is a determination or decision to do things such as beating. Moreover, it is complete if the following five attitudes are present, and incomplete if they are not. The five are:

(1) an attitude of hostility driven by a reifying apprehension of the characteristics of the causes of harm and the phenomena related to them;
(2) an impatient attitude by way of not being patient with those doing the harm to you;

(3) a resentful attitude based on repeated, improper attention to and mindfulness of the causes of your anger;
(4) an envious attitude which thinks, "How nice if my enemy were beaten or killed";
(5) an attitude that is dominated by a lack of shame about your malice and obliviousness about the determination to be free of its faults.

Attitudes of simple malice are as follows. To the extent that you reflect, "Someone has harmed me or is harming me," and think about how to bring harm to whoever is doing or did the harm—all this is malice. Other examples of simple malice are the wish that someone else's relatives, resources, or virtue, etc. might deteriorate in this lifetime and the wish that someone else might go to a miserable realm in a future lifetime.

10. Wrong Views

The bases of wrong views are existent objects. Of the three aspects of the attitude, the perception is perceiving to be true the meaning of a mistaken denial of the existence of an existent object. The affliction is any of the three mental poisons. The motivation is the desire to deny the existence of an existent object.

The performance is the initiation of that attitude. **[173]** Moreover, there are four types of such performance: mistaken denial of causes, effects, activities, and existent entities. Mistaken denial of causes is thinking that right or wrong behavior do not exist, and so forth. Mistaken denial of effects is thinking that the fruitions of these sorts of behavior do not exist.

Mistaken denial of activity is of three types :

(1) Mistaken denial of the activities of planting and retaining seeds is thinking that there are no fathers and mothers.
(2) Mistaken denial of the activities of going and coming is thinking that there are no former and future lives.
(3) Mistaken denial of the activity of birth is thinking that living beings cannot have spontaneous birth.

The fourth type of performance of wrong view, mistaken denial of existent entities, is thinking that arhats and such do not exist.

The culmination is the certainty that you have denied something. A full-fledged wrong view is associated with these five attitudes:

(1) an attitude of confusion due to not knowing objects of knowledge exactly;
(2) a violent attitude, due to delighting in sins;

(3) an attitude that continuously operates in the wrong way because of pondering improper teachings;
(4) an attitude that is impaired because of a mistaken denial that thinks that such things as gifts, religious offerings, burnt offerings, and right behavior do not exist;
(5) an attitude that is dominated, due to these wrong views, by shamelessness and obliviousness about the determination to be free of its faults.

If these five are not present, a wrong view is not full-fledged.

Although it is certainly the case that there are other wrong views, only this is called "wrong view," for it is the greatest of all wrong views in that it is through this wrong view that you sever all your roots of virtue. Further, it is this wrong view that is conducive to your doing whatever sins you want.

With respect to these ten nonvirtues, you may undertake killing, offensive speech, and malice with any of the three mental poisons, but you bring them to culmination with hostility. You may undertake stealing, sexual misconduct, and covetousness with any of the three mental poisons, but you bring them to culmination only with attachment. As for lying, divisive speech, and senseless speech, you may both undertake them and bring them to culmination with any of the three mental poisons. You may undertake wrong view with any of the three mental poisons, but you bring it to culmination only with delusion. **[174]**

Among these ten, intentions are actions (Skt. *karma*), yet they are not paths of action (Skt. *karma-patha*). The seven nonvirtuous actions of body and speech are not only actions but are also paths of action because body and speech are the bases of the intended operation. The three mental nonvirtues—covetousness and so on—are paths of action but are not actions.

(ii) **Distinctions of weight**

Distinctions of weight are explained in two parts:

1. The weights of the ten paths of nonvirtuous action
2. The criteria for powerful actions

(a′) **The weights of the ten paths of nonvirtuous action**

There are five causes that make an action weighty. As exemplified by killing, they are as follows. Actions of killing that are *weighty due to attitude* are those done with intense forms of the three mental poisons.

Killing that is *weighty due to performance* includes:

(1) killing with a mind delighting in and being glad about having taken life, taking life, or taking life in the future;
(2) engaging in the action yourself, causing others to take it up, and praising it;
(3) doing it with a mind that is pleased when such a thing is seen, and doing it after prolonged premeditation and preparation;
(4) doing it constantly and diligently, and each time killing a great deal;
(5) killing your victim by torture;
(6) killing after frightening your victim into performing inappropriate actions;
(7) killing while your victim is weak, suffering, or impoverished, or while the victim is moaning, or piteously reciting laments.

A killing that is *weighty due to the absence of an antidote* is one that is done:

(1) while not taking any precepts on a daily basis;
(2) while not doing such things as observing one-day vows on the new moon, or on the eighth, fourteenth, or fifteenth days of the month; while not occasionally being generous, collecting merit, speaking about the teaching, making obeisance, rising when a respected person enters your presence, pressing your palms together in respect, or having an attitude of veneration;
(3) while not from time to time becoming ashamed, embarrassed, or having a preponderance of contrition;
(4) while not having reached either a state of freedom from worldly attachment or clear knowledge of the teaching.

Killing that is *weighty due to clinging to the perverse* is that done in reliance on any sort of wrong view. [175] For example, there are those who kill out of a desire to be religious, relying on the views of those who make animal sacrifices. They think that there is no fault in slaughtering livestock because the Lord of All Beings created them to be used.

Killing that is *weighty due to its basis* is taking the life of a large animal, a human, a fetus, your parents, your aunt or uncle, someone such as a guru, a close friend, a learner, a bodhisattva, an arhat, or a *pratyekabuddha*. Also, it is killing which is weighty due to its basis when you know that a *tathāgata* cannot be killed, and you bring forth blood from a buddha with an intention to harm.

Killing that is done with the opposite of these five causes is a light killing. You should understand that the weight of the remaining nine nonvirtuous actions is similar to killing, except for the bases, which are as follows. Stealing is weighty due to its basis if it involves taking a great deal, or taking good things; or is stealing after deceiving those who trust you; or stealing from the lowly, the impoverished, renunciates, or other Buddhist practitioners; or involves stealing what is highly valued; or stealing the property of learners, arhats, *pratyekabuddhas*, the community, or *stūpas*.

Sexual misconduct that is weighty due to its basis is sleeping with those whom you should not have intercourse with—your mother, those who are her relatives, the wives of men who are close friends, nuns, probationary nuns, or female novices. In terms of an inappropriate body part, sexual misconduct that is weighty due to its basis is oral intercourse. In terms of improper time, it is intercourse with one observing a one-day vow, a pregnant woman at the end of term, or one who is ill. In terms of an inappropriate place, it is intercourse in the vicinity of a *stūpa* or within the compound of the community.

Lying that is weighty due to its basis is, through desiring to delude and deceive, telling lies with many purposes; telling lies to those who have helped you—from parents through the buddhas, to good persons, and to friends; and telling a lie that gives rise to one or more of the three weighty actions—killing, stealing, and sexual misconduct. Telling a lie in order to split apart the community is the weightiest among all of these. **[176]**

Divisive speech that is weighty due to its basis is speech that splits apart those who have been friends for a long time, teachers, parents, parents and their children, or the community; and divisive speech that gives rise to weighty actions—the three physical actions.

Offensive speech that is weighty due to its basis is speaking offensive words to parents and the like, or to someone like a guru; speaking offensive words with untrue and inaccurate lies; and directly scolding, criticizing, or reproaching.

Senseless speech that is weighty due to its basis is as follows. The weight of the senseless speech of the three other nonvirtuous vocal actions—lying, and so forth—is as above. Other actions of senseless speech that are weighty due to their bases include senseless words based on fighting, faultfinding, disputes, and divisions; such activities as reading the treatises of non-Buddhists with an attitude of attachment; and ridiculing, taunting, or speaking inappropriately toward parents, kinspeople, and someone like a guru.

Covetousness that is weighty due to its basis includes desiring the offerings made to the community and *stūpas*; and with arrogance about your own good qualities, desiring to receive, from kings and the like or from learned religious companions, profit and services for your knowledge.

Malice that is weighty due to its basis includes malice directed toward parents, kinspeople, gurus, those without fault, the poor, the suffering, the pitiful, and those who have done something wrong to you but confess this to you from the depths of their hearts.

Wrong views that are weighty due to their bases are the rejection of all the fundamental religious tenets (this is weightier even than other wrong views) and also the view that in the world there are neither arhats, those who have reached reality, nor those who have entered reality. Understand wrong views that are the opposite of these to be light.

The *Levels of Yogic Deeds* speaks of six ways in which actions are weighty:[396]

> (1) conditioning—actions motivated by intense forms of the three mental poisons or by their absence;
> (2) habituation—frequently doing or becoming used to and deeply involved in either virtuous or nonvirtuous actions for a long time; **[177]**
> (3) nature—in that among the three physical and four vocal actions the former ones are weightier than the ones after them, and among the three mental actions the latter are weightier than the former;
> (4) basis—actions that help or harm those like the Buddha, the teaching, the community, and gurus;
> (5) fixation on incompatible factors—for as long as you live you completely take up nonvirtuous actions and do not cultivate virtue even once;
> (6) eradication of unfavorable factors—having eliminated the group of nonvirtues, you become free from attachment and cultivate virtuous actions.

The *Friendly Letter* says:[397]

> The five types of virtuous and nonvirtuous actions
> Arising out of persistence, obsession, a lack of remedy,
> And the principal foundations of virtue
> Are huge; among them, strive to cultivate virtue.

That is, there are five types because the "principal foundations of virtue" are divided into foundations that have virtues—such as the three jewels—and foundations who provide assistance, such as your parents.

(b′) **A brief discussion of the criteria for powerful actions**

The strength of actions is explained in terms of four aspects: recipient, support, objects, and attitude.

(1′) **Strength in terms of recipient**

There is strength in actions directed toward the three jewels, gurus, those who are like gurus, parents, and the like, for, though you direct no intense thoughts toward them and do them only small harm or help, the ensuing misdeed and merit is great. Further, the *Mindfulness of the Excellent Teaching* states:[398]

> Even if you take something small from the Buddha, the teaching, or the community, the fault will be large. However, if you offer some similar substance that is greater than what you stole from them, you will clear away the karma of stealing from the Buddha and the teaching. However, there is no clearing away the karma of stealing from the community without experiencing the result, because of the weightiness of the recipient.
>
> If you have stolen something that is the means for sustenance of the community, you will fall to rebirth as a living being in a great hell. **[178]** If you have stolen something that is not the means for their sustenance, you will be reborn within that region, in a hell surrounding the Unrelenting Hell such as the Hell of Great Black Darkness.

In particular, if those who do not care about their ethical discipline were to use material of the community—merely a leaf, flower, or piece of fruit—they would be reborn as a living being in a great hell. After a long time, they would be free of this hell. However, they would then be reborn in a dry and barren wilderness as animals with no hands or legs, or as blind hungry ghosts without hands or legs. They would then experience suffering for many years. The *Sun Essence Sūtra (Sūrya-garbha-sūtra)* mentions great dangers such as these.

Moreover, the Buddha said that you cannot even use something such as a flower dedicated to the community or to a monk. Further, you may not give it to a householder, and for a householder to use it is unsuitable. Also, the misdeed is very great. The *Sun Essence Sūtra* states:[399]

Do not give to householders
What has been dedicated to the spiritual communities—
It would be better to cut off your own limbs
With sharp razors.

Those outside of the community
Should not use things from within it—
It would be better to eat a lump of iron
Like a blazing tongue of fire.

Those who are householders
Are not to use things of the community—
It would be better to take up and eat
A fire akin to the size of Mount Meru.

Those who are householders
Should not use the community's things—
It would be better to be disemboweled
And hoisted upon a stake.

Householders should not spend a night
In a dwelling of the community—
It would be better to enter
A house full of burning embers.

Within the community, persons who are bodhisattvas are extremely powerful recipients in terms of activities that are either virtuous or nonvirtuous. The *Seal of Engaging in Developing the Power of Faith Sūtra (Śraddhā-balādhānāvatāra-mudrā-sūtra)*[400] says that it is an immeasurably greater sin for someone to become angry and turn his or her back on a bodhisattva, saying, "I will not look upon this evil person," than for someone to become angry and put all the living beings in the ten directions into a gloomy prison. **[179]** Further, it states[401] that if someone were to despise any bodhisattva, it would be a sin immeasurably greater than that of someone stealing all the belongings of all the living beings in Jambudvīpa. Again, it says that if someone were to have malice or anger for a bodhisattva, who delights in the Mahāyāna, and speak disagreeably to such a bodhisattva, it would be a sin immeasurably greater than that of someone who demolishes or burns as many *stūpas* as there are grains of sand in the Ganges River.

Further, the *Seal of Engaging in Certain and Uncertain Destinies Sūtra (Niyatāniyata-mudrāvatāra-sūtra)* speaks[402] of someone who looks with faith upon a bodhisattva (who delights in the Mahāyāna) and who, wanting to look with clear faith upon such a bodhisattva, speaks praises of him or her. This person would accumulate merit that is immeasurably greater than that of someone who lovingly gives eyes to all the living beings of the ten directions after they all have lost their eyes, and frees such living beings from incarceration, establishing them in the bliss of a universal monarch or Brahmā.

Again, the *Sūtra on the Magic of Final Peace (Praśānta-viniścaya-prātihārya-sūtra)*[403] speaks of someone who does as little as obstruct a bodhisattva's virtuous action of giving a single closed handful of food to an animal. Such a person commits a sin immeasurably greater than someone who kills all the living beings in Jambudvīpa, or steals all of their belongings. Therefore, take this subject very seriously.

(2′) **Strength in terms of support**

Although even a small lump of iron sinks to the bottom of a body of water, the same substance made into a vessel, even a large one, floats on top. Likewise, the Buddha said, sins committed by those who are not knowledgeable and those who are knowledgeable are heavy and light as well. The *Great Final Nirvāṇa Sūtra* states the reason for this:[404]

> Just as a fly that is stuck to nasal mucus cannot extricate itself, so the ignorant cannot extricate themselves from even small shortcomings. Further, they cannot do virtuous actions, because they are without regret. Even though they have previous virtuous actions, they defile them with sins, because they hide their faults. The causes of experiencing a fruition of a nonvirtue in the present lifetime are therefore transformed into causes of great suffering and become causes for experiencing a very severe hell. **[180]**
>
> This is similar to the way in which if a handful of salt is put in a little water, the water becomes hard to drink, or to the way in which a person who borrows a gold coin from another but cannot repay it falls deeply in debt and suffers.
>
> Further, in five ways even light causes of fruitions in the present will ripen in a hell: being ignorant, having small roots of virtue, having weighty sins, not having been regretful and performed a purification, and not initially cultivating virtue.

Therefore, the Buddha said that nonvirtues are light for the knowledgeable who regret their former nonvirtuous actions, restrain themselves from future nonvirtuous actions, do not conceal their sins, and do virtuous actions as remedies for those nonvirtuous actions. However, nonvirtues are weighty for those who make a pretense of being knowledgeable and do not do these actions but belittle them and engage consciously in nonvirtuous action.

The *Heap of Jewels Sūtra (Ratna-rāśi-sūtra)*[405] speaks of a bodhisattva who has renounced the householder's life holding a lamp wick coated with a trifling amount of butter in front of a *stūpa*. The merit accumulated from this is then compared to all the living beings in the universe of three billion world systems having entered the Mahāyāna, possessing the kingdom of a universal monarch, and then each making offerings to a *stūpa* of the Buddha with butter lamps whose vessels were the size of an ocean and whose wicks were the size of Mount Meru. It states that even this would not match even a hundredth of the former's merit. This is a case in which the attitude—the spirit of enlightenment—and the recipient—the *stūpa*—are not different, but there is a pronounced difference in the object offered. However, this is clearly a case exemplifying strength in terms of the support [vow]. Following the line of reasoning in this passage, it is evident that, regarding cultivation of the path by someone without the support of a vow, someone having a vow, and, within having a vow, the support of possessing one, two, or three vows, the latter will have quicker progress than the former. It is clear as well that when people such as householders practice such things as generosity, there can be a great difference in the strength of the roots of virtue produced. This difference comes from whether they act within having a vow such as a one-day vow or whether they act without a vow. **[181]**

The *Sūtra on Overcoming Faulty Ethical Discipline (Duḥśīla-nigraha-sūtra)*[406] speaks of a monk who does not observe ethical discipline but who drapes himself in the flag of a sage [monk's robe].[407] The nonvirtue that such a monk incurs when he enjoys for a single day what a donor has given with faith is far greater than the sins a human being possessing the ten nonvirtues would accumulate continuously over a hundred years. The Buddha is saying that this is a case of the strength of sin from the viewpoint of the support.

Also, the *Exegesis of the Discipline* speaks of both those who have faulty ethical discipline and those who have slackened from their precepts:[408]

> For those who have faulty ethical discipline
> Or who are not correctly restrained
> It is far better to eat iron lumps blazing with flames
> Than to eat the alms of their region.

One of the sayings of the Precious Teacher Drom-dön-ba states that compared to sins that are related to the teaching, the sins of the ten nonvirtues are insignificant. This appears to be the case.

(3′) **Strength in terms of objects**

Among the giving of gifts to living beings, the gift of the teaching is vastly superior to the gift of material things. Among offerings to the buddhas, the offering of practice is vastly superior to the offering of material things. Following these examples, understand the others.

(4′) **Strength in terms of attitude**

The *Heap of Jewels Sūtra*[409] mentions all of the living beings in the universe of three billion world systems each making a *stūpa* of the Buddha as large as Mount Meru, and each paying reverence to it in all their actions for ten million eons. It says that far greater than the merit from that is the merit in a bodhisattva's throwing just a single flower toward a *stūpa* with an attitude that is imbued with a desire to attain omniscience. Understand that, in the same manner, there are variations in the amount of merit you accumulate from the perspective of differences in attitude such as focusing on superior or inferior goals, or focusing on your own or others' interests. The amount varies as well from the perspective of the strength or weakness of your attitude, whether it is brief or long-lasting, and so on.

With regard to wrongdoing, afflicted attitudes that are strong and long-lasting have greater strength and, among these, hatred is very powerful. *Engaging in the Bodhisattva Deeds*:[410]

> All the good behavior—
> Generosity, offering to the *sugatas* and the like—
> Amassed for a thousand eons **[182]**
> Is destroyed by a single moment of hatred.

Anger, moreover, toward spiritual companions and, even more, toward conquerors' children is very weighty. The *King of Concentrations Sūtra*:[411]

> When people have malice toward each other,
> Learning and ethical discipline cannot protect them from its fruition,
> Concentration does not protect them, nor can living in solitude;
> Generosity does not protect them, nor does offering to the buddhas.

Engaging in the Bodhisattva Deeds:[412]

> Were you to harbor harmful thoughts
> Toward such a conqueror's child, a benefactor,
> You would remain in hell for eons as numerous
> As those thoughts—thus the Sage has said.

(iii) **An exposition of the effects**

(a′) **Fruitional effects**

Each of the ten paths of action depends upon a basis of the three mental poisons that occur in three strengths: small, medium, and great. Therefore, there are three fruitional effects for each action. In the *Levels of Yogic Deeds*[413] it says that through each of the great forms of the ten nonvirtues—killing and so forth—you will be reborn in the hells, through each of the ten medium forms you will be reborn as a hungry ghost, and through each of the ten small forms you will be reborn as an animal. The *Sutra on the Ten Levels*, however, speaks of the effects for the small and medium forms in reverse.

(b′) **Causally concordant effects**

Even when you are reborn from the miserable realms as a human, [you still experience the effects of nonvirtuous actions] as follows:

> [as a causally concordant effect of killing,] a short lifetime;
> [as an effect of stealing,] a lack of resources;
> [from sexual misconduct,] an unruly spouse;
> [from lying,] much slander;
> [from divisive speech,] loss of friendships;
> [from offensive speech,] hearing unpleasant words;
> [from senseless speech,] others not listening to your words;
> and [from covetousness, malice, and wrong views] respectively, predominance of attachment, hostility, and confusion.

The *Chapter of the Truth Speaker*[414] and *Sutra on the Ten Levels* both state that each of the nonvirtuous actions has two effects. They say that even if you are born a human, still:

> [as a result of killing] you would have a short life span and many illnesses;
> [as a result of stealing] you would have few resources and the resources you do have would be shared with others;
> [as a result of sexual misconduct] your helpers would be disorderly or untrustworthy, and you would have a contentious spouse;
> [as a result of lying] others would slander you a great deal, and they would deceive you;
> [as a result of divisive speech] your helpers would not get along and would misbehave;
> [as a result of offensive speech] you would hear unpleasant and quarrelsome speech; **[183]**

> [as a result of senseless speech] your words would not be respected or understandable, and your confidence would not be unshakable;
> [as a result of covetousness] you would have great attachment and no contentment;
> [as a result of malice] you would seek the unbeneficial or not seek the beneficial, and you would harm others or others would harm you;
> [as a result of wrong views] you would have bad views and would be deceitful.

The former gurus assert that liking to kill and so on even once you have been born a human are causally concordant behavioral effects, and the above-mentioned effects are causally concordant experiential effects.

(c′) **Environmental effects**

From the nonvirtuous action of killing, such things in the external environment as food and drink, medicine, and fruits will have little strength, be ineffective, have little potency and power, or, being difficult to digest, will induce illness. Hence, most living beings will die without living out their expected life spans. The environmental effects of stealing are that you will have few fruits, the fruits will not be perfect, will change, or will be partially spoiled. There will be severe droughts or torrential downpours. The fruits will dry up or disappear. The environmental effects of sexual misconduct are living where there is excrement and urine, mud, filth, unclean things, many evil smells, misery, and discomfort.

The environmental effects of lying are that any work that you do in fields or on boats will not flourish; there will be no harmony among your workers, and for the most part they will be deceitful; and you will be fearful and have many causes to be afraid. The environmental effects of divisive speech are that you will be in a place that is bumpy, craggy, uneven, and difficult to traverse; and you will be fearful and have many causes to be afraid. The environmental effects of offensive speech are that you will be in a place that is full of logs, thorns, large rocks, sharp stones, and many broken bricks; that lacks waterfalls, lakes, or ponds; is rough, drab, arid, salty, barren, vile, and is a place of dangerous animals; **[184]** and you will have many causes to be afraid. The environmental effects of senseless speech are that you will be in a place where fruit trees do not bear fruit, bear fruit at the wrong time, or bear no fruit at the proper time; the unripened appear to be ripe; the roots are not strong;

the tree does not last long; there are not many comforts such as parks, groves, and pools; and you will have many reasons to be afraid.

The environmental effects of covetousness are that all excellent things will deteriorate and diminish every year, every season, month, and even each day, and will not increase. The environmental effects of malice are that you will be where there are epidemics, injury, and infectious diseases; quarrels, and many disputes with opponents' armies; lions, tigers, and the like; poisonous snakes, scorpions, and many fireflies; and harmful *yakṣas*, robbers, and the like. The environmental effects of wrong views are that you will be in an environment where the best and principal sources of resources will disappear; where unclean things will appear to be most pure, and misery will appear to be bliss; and where you will have no home, protector, or refuge.

(b) **Virtuous actions and their effects**

(i) **Virtuous actions**

The *Levels of Yogic Deeds* says that virtuous actions include the physical actions of those who reflect on the faults of killing, stealing, and sexual misconduct and have a virtuous attitude. They have also carried out the performance of correctly restraining themselves from these nonvirtuous actions and have brought this restraint to culmination. It states that the same can be said for the four vocal actions and the three mental actions, the difference being to substitute "vocal actions" and "mental actions" for "physical actions."

Therefore, apply to each of the ten actions the four aspects of basis, attitude, performance, and culmination. This is illustrated in the following example of the path of action of giving up killing. **[185]** The basis of giving up killing is another living being. The attitude is seeing killing's faults and desiring to give it up. The performance is the activity of having correctly restrained yourself from the killing. The culmination is the physical action of completing the correct restraint. Understand the others in this way as well.

(ii) **The effects of virtuous actions**

There are three types of effects—fruitional, causally concordant, and environmental. The fruitional effect is that you are born as a human, a deity of the desire realm, or a deity in one of the two upper realms through small, medium, and great virtuous actions, respectively. You should take the causally concordant and environmental effects to be the opposite of those of the nonvirtuous actions.

The *Sutra on the Ten Levels* says[415] that those who have cultivated these ten through fear of cyclic existence and without [great] compassion, but following the words of others, will achieve the fruit of a *śrāvaka*. There are those who are without [great] compassion or dependency on others, and who wish to become buddhas themselves. When they have practiced the ten virtuous actions through understanding dependent-arising, they will achieve the state of a *pratyekabuddha*. When those with an expansive attitude cultivate these ten through [great] compassion, skillful means, great aspirational prayers, in no way abandoning any living being, and focusing on the extremely vast and sublime wisdom of a buddha, they will achieve the level of a bodhisattva and all the perfections. Through practicing these activities a great deal on all occasions they will achieve all the qualities of a buddha.

Thus, I have explained the two sets of ten paths of action along with their effects. I have explained everything that is unclear in other texts in accordance with the intended meaning of the *Levels of Yogic Deeds* and the *Compendium of Determinations*.

(c) **A presentation of other classifications of karma**

Other classifications of karma are presented in two parts:

1. The distinction between projecting and completing karma
2. Karma whose result you will definitely or only possibly experience

(i) **The distinction between projecting and completing karma**

Although the karma that projects a rebirth into a happy realm is virtuous and the karma that projects a rebirth into a miserable realm is nonvirtuous, there is no such certainty with regard to completing karma. **[186]** Nonvirtuous actions create even in the happy realms such effects as not having complete limbs, fingers, or sensory organs; and having an unpleasant color, a short life span, many illnesses, and poverty. Further, virtuous actions create consummate wealth even for animals and hungry ghosts.

This being the case, there are four sides to the relationship between being projected and being completed. Among lives that are the result of virtuous projecting karma there are both results from virtuous completing karma and from nonvirtuous completing karma. Among lives that are the result of nonvirtuous projecting karma there are both results from nonvirtuous completing karma and from virtuous completing karma. Asaṅga's *Compendium of Knowledge (Abhidharma-samuccaya)* says:[416]

> Understand that virtuous and nonvirtuous actions project and bring to completion birth in the happy realms and the miserable realms. Projecting karma projects a fruition. Completing karma is that by which, in a rebirth, you experience the wanted and unwanted.

The *Treasury of Knowledge* explains that a single action projects a single rebirth and does not project many rebirths. There are many completing actions, but many projecting actions do not project a single body. The *Treasury of Knowledge*:[417]

> One projects one rebirth;
> Those that bring about completion are many.

The *Compendium of Knowledge*:[418]

> There is karma where a single action projects one body. There is karma where a single action projects many bodies. There is karma where many actions project a single body. There is karma where many actions project many bodies.

The commentary explains Asaṅga's four types of karma, respectively, as a single instant of an action nourishing a seed of only a single lifetime's fruition; that action nourishing a seed of many lifetimes' fruitions; many instants of an action again and again nourishing a seed for just a single body; and many mutually dependent actions repeatedly nourishing seeds for the many bodies of a succession of lifetimes.

(ii) **Karma whose result you will definitely or only possibly experience**

The *Levels of Yogic Deeds*:[419]

> Karma whose result you will definitely experience is that consciously done and accumulated. Karma whose result you are not certain to experience is that consciously done but not accumulated. **[187]**

The same text sets forth the distinction between having done karma and having accumulated karma:[420]

> What is karma that you have done? An action that you have thought about or that you have consciously set into motion either physically or vocally.

It continues:

> Karma that you have accumulated is that not included among the following ten types of actions: actions done in dreams; those done unknowingly; those done unconsciously; those done without intensity or not continuously; those done in error; those done forgetfully; those done without wanting to; those naturally ethically neutral; those eradicated through regret; and those eradicated with a remedy.
>
> Karma that you have accumulated is the remaining actions, the ones not included in these ten types of action. Karma that you have not accumulated is just the ten types of actions indicated above.

The *Compendium of Determinations*[421] presents four permutations between karma done and karma accumulated. Killing that is karma which you have done but not accumulated is seen in the following cases: that done unknowingly, that done in a dream, that not done intentionally, that which another person forced you to do against your will, that done only once and then regretted, that much lessened upon assuming a vow to give up killing after overcoming the desire to kill by means of a deep understanding of its faults, that whose seed you weaken before its fruition can start by means of separating from worldly attachment, and that whose seed you have actually destroyed with a supramundane path of elimination.

Killing that is karma that you have accumulated but have not done is seen in the following case: you investigate and analyze for a long time in order to kill a living being, but you do not kill it. Killing that is karma that you have done and accumulated is seen in all the killing not included in the previous two permutations. Killing that is karma that you have neither done nor accumulated is whatever is not included in the above three.

Also understand in the same way, as appropriate, the nonvirtuous actions from stealing through senseless speech. The three mental nonvirtuous actions do not have the second permutation. **[188]** Within the first permutation, there are no mental actions that are not intentionally done nor are there any that you are forced by another to commit.

From the viewpoint of the time at which you experience a result, there are three types of certainty of experiencing results of karma: experiencing it here and now; experiencing it after taking rebirth; and experiencing it at another time.

Karma that you experience here and now is the effect of actions which ripen in the very lifetime in which you do the actions. There are eight such types of karma mentioned in the *Levels of Yogic Deeds*:

(1) nonvirtuous actions [that you have done] with a predominant [attached] attitude of looking after your body, resources, and existence;
(2) virtuous actions [that you have cultivated] with a predominant attitude of not looking after these;
(3) in the same way, [nonvirtuous actions that you have done with an attitude of] strong malice toward living beings;
(4) [virtuous actions that you have cultivated with an attitude of] deep compassion and helpfulness;
(5) [nonvirtuous actions that you have done with] great animosity toward the three jewels, gurus, and the like;
(6) [virtuous actions that you have cultivated with] an attitude of deep faith and belief in these;
(7) nonvirtuous actions [that you have done] with an attitude of enmity toward those who have helped you such as parents and gurus, and an attitude of not repaying them for what they have done;
(8) virtuous actions [that you have cultivated] with a strong attitude of wishing to repay those who have helped you.

Karma that you will experience after you have been reborn is the effect of actions which you will experience in the second [next] lifetime. *Karma that you will experience at other times* is the effect of actions which will ripen in or after the third lifetime.

The way in which the many virtuous and nonvirtuous karmas that exist in your mind-stream ripen is as follows:

(1) Whichever karma is weightiest will ripen first.
(2) If weights are equal, whatever karma is manifest at the time of death will ripen first.
(3) If this also is the same, whatever karma you have predominantly become habituated to will ripen first.
(4) If this also is the same, whatever karma you have done first will ripen earliest.

As cited in the *Treasury of Knowledge Auto-commentary*:[422]

> As to the actions that give rise to cyclic existence,
> There are those that are weighty, those that are near,
> Those to which you are habituated, and those you did earliest.
> Among these, the former will ripen first.

2′ Reflecting on karma and its effects in detail

It is certainly the case that you will acquire a good body and mind through giving up the ten nonvirtuous actions. Nonetheless, if you were to bring about a body and mind that are fully qualified, this would accelerate your cultivation of the path as nothing else would. **[189]** Therefore, seek such a life.

a″ **The attributes of the fruitions**

There are eight fruitions: consummate life span, consummate color, consummate lineage, consummate power, trustworthy words, renown as a great power, being a male, and having strength. *Consummate life span* is when a virtuous projecting karma from a previous lifetime projects a long life span and you live for the long time that was projected. *Consummate color* is having an excellent body by way of its good color and shape; being pleasant to look at because you do not have incomplete sensory faculties;[423] and being beautiful due to being well-proportioned. *Consummate lineage* is having been born with the good lineage that is esteemed and famed in the world. *Consummate power* is great resources, an abundance of close associates such as relatives, and many helpers. *Trustworthy words* are words that living beings will accept because you are suitable to be trusted not to delude others physically or vocally, and are an authoritative witness in all disputes. *Renown as a great power* is to be honored by a great multitude of beings because of your fame and wide acclaim due to your confident generosity and possession of good qualities such as perseverance. *Being a male* is to have a male organ. *Having strength* is, by the power of previous karma, naturally experiencing little injury, no illness, and great enthusiasm arising from this life's circumstances.

Moreover, the first, consummate life span, is living in a happy realm. The second, consummate color, is the body. The third, consummate lineage, is birth. The fourth, consummate power, is resources and helpers. The fifth, trustworthy words, is being an authority in the world. The sixth, renown as a great power, is fame about such power. The seventh, being a male, is having the capacity for all good qualities. The eighth, strength, is having power in your activities.

b″ **The effects of the fruitions**

There are eight effects of the fruitions:

1) The effect of consummate life span is that you accumulate much virtuous karma for a long time in terms of working for the welfare of both yourself and others. **[190]**

2) The effect of consummate color is that merely through seeing you, disciples are pleased and gather around you. They then listen to your words and want to carry out your instructions.

3) The effect of consummate lineage is that people carry out your instructions without disregard.

4) The effect of consummate power is that through giving you gather living beings and then mature them.

5) The effect of trustworthy words is that through kind speech, purposeful behavior, and being one whose aims are the same as the disciples', you gather living beings and mature them.

6) The effect of renown as a great power is that, because you have helped and assisted others in all activities, they repay your kindness and listen immediately to your instructions.

7) The effect of being a male is that you will have the capacity for all good qualities, a capacity for all skilled actions by way of aspiration and endeavor, and a capacity for broad wisdom, the discrimination of objects of knowledge. Moreover, you will be unafraid in assemblies and will have no reversals or obstacles whether accompanying all living beings, speaking to them, enjoying resources with them, or dwelling in isolation.

8) The effect of strength is that, because you are not disillusioned about either your own or others' welfare and are steady in your great enthusiasm for them, you will obtain the power of discernment, and then quickly have the superknowledges.[424]

c" **The causes of the fruitions**

There are eight causes of the fruitions:

1) The cause of consummate life span is not harming living beings and the application of a nonviolent attitude. Further, it is said that:

> By rescuing those approaching a place where they will be killed,
> And likewise giving life to others,
> And turning harm away from living beings,
> You will acquire a long life span.
>
> Through caring for the sick,
> Through a doctor's giving medicine to the sick,
> And through not harming living beings with sticks,
> Clumps of earth, and the like, you will be without illness.

2) The cause of consummate color is giving light, such as butter lamps, and new clothing. Further, it is said that:

By relying on kindness
And giving jewelry, you will have a good physical form.
The result of being without jealousy
Is said to be good fortune.

3) The cause of consummate lineage is first overcoming pride and then making obeisance and so forth to gurus and the like, and respecting others as if you were their servant. **[191]**

4) The cause of consummate power is giving food, clothing, and so forth to those who request them; even when they are not requested, giving such assistance; and giving to those who suffer and to recipients who have good qualities but no possessions.

5) The cause of trustworthy words is habituation to giving up the four vocal nonvirtues.

6) The cause of renown as a great power is making aspirational prayers to acquire various good qualities in the future, making offerings to the three jewels, and making offerings to parents, *śrāvakas*, *pratyekabuddhas*, abbots, masters, and gurus.

7) The cause of being a male is delight in the attributes of a male, lack of delight in female things and seeing their disadvantages, stopping the yearnings of those who want to be reborn in women's bodies, and rescuing those whose male organs will be cut off.

8) The cause of strength is accomplishing what cannot at all be done by others, assisting in what can be done with your collaboration, and giving food and drink.

If these eight causes are endowed with three causes—[pure attitude, pure application, and pure recipient]—their fruitions will be outstanding. Among the three causes, there are two types of pure attitude—self-directed and other-directed. The two self-directed pure attitudes are:

(1) not hoping for fruition, which is dedicating the virtues from your creation of the causes for unexcelled enlightenment;
(2) intense power, which is achieving the causes from the depths of your heart.

The two other-directed pure attitudes are:

(1) abandoning jealousy, competitiveness, and contempt when you see fellow practitioners of the teaching who are better, equal, or less than yourself, and admiring them;

(2) even if you are unable to do the above, discerning many times every day that you must do it.

There are two types of pure application—self-directed and other-directed. The self-directed pure application is applying yourself to cultivating virtue for a long time, without interruption, and with great intensity. The other-directed pure application is causing those who have not adopted vows and other commitments to do so, praising those who have made such commitments so that they may delight in them, making them continue, and making them not abandon them. Pure field is so called because those two—attitude and application—are similar to a field in that they give effects that are numerous and good. **[192]**

I have explained these three by way of a commentary that supplements what Asaṅga says in the *Bodhisattva Levels*.

15

Cultivating Ethical Behavior

3′ How you engage in virtue and turn away from nonvirtue after you have reflected on karma and its effects in general and in detail
  a″ A general explanation
  b″ In particular, the way of purification through the four powers
    1″ The power of eradication
    2″ The power of applying remedies
    3″ The power of turning away from faults
    4″ The power of the foundation

3′ How you engage in virtue and turn away from nonvirtue after you have reflected on karma and its effects in general and in detail

a″ A general explanation

Engaging in the Bodhisattva Deeds:[425]

> "From nonvirtue comes suffering;
> How can I truly be free of this?"
> It is fitting that at all times, day and night,
> I think only of this.

And also:

> For the Sage has said that conviction
> Is the root of all virtues,
> And to constantly meditate on fruitional effects
> Is the root of this conviction.

Thus, having understood virtuous and nonvirtuous karma and their effects, do not leave it at just an understanding but meditate on it over and over, because this is a very obscure subject and it is difficult to acquire certainty about it. Further, the *King of Concentrations Sūtra* says:[426]

> Were the moon and the stars to fall from their place
> And the earth with its mountains and cities to perish
> Or the realm of the sky to completely transform,
> You [Buddha] still would not speak a word of untruth.

Thus, have conviction in the teachings of the Tathāgata, and then sustain your meditation on them. If you do not have uncontrived certainty about this quality of truth in the Buddha's teachings, then you will not gain the certainty that will please the Conqueror with regard to any of the teachings.

Some, who claim that they have acquired certain knowledge of emptiness, are uncertain about karma and its effects and do not value it. This is a mistaken understanding of emptiness. For, once you understand emptiness, you will see that it is the meaning of dependent-arising, and it will assist you in becoming certain about karma and its effects.

The same sūtra says:[427]

> Like illusions, bubbles, mirages, and lightning,
> All phenomena are like the moon [reflected] in water.
> It is not the case that living beings—who die
> And go on to their next lives—are offspring of Manu [the first human at the beginning of the eon].
>
> Yet the karma that you possess does not disappear;
> The virtuous and nonvirtuous give rise to their effects accordingly;
> This logical approach is sound; though subtle and difficult to see, **[193]**
> It is within the scope of the Conqueror.

Therefore, develop certain knowledge of dependent-arising together with the causality of the two kinds of karma, and examine your physical, verbal, and mental actions all day and all night. By this means, you will put an end to miserable rebirths. However, if at the outset you are not versed in the classifications of cause and effect, understanding only a fragment of their depth and having a lax attitude with your physical, verbal, and mental actions, then you are merely throwing open the door to the miserable realms. For, as the *Questions of the Nāga Kings of the Ocean* states:[428]

> Lord of *Nāgas*, a single practice of the bodhisattvas correctly puts a stop to rebirth in the miserable realms. What is this single

practice? It the discernment of what is virtuous. You must think, "Am I being true? How am I spending the day and the night?"

When the former gurus in this lineage had examined their minds in that way, they said:

> On this occasion of training in karma and its effects, when we compare our actions of body, speech, and mind to what is taught in the teaching, they will not be in conformity. In this we are deficient. Therefore, we are not at all liberated. We must see whether we are in conformity or not by comparing ourselves to the laws of karma and its effects. When we examine our mind in light of the teachings, we are wise if we sincerely recognize nonconformity or a complete lack of conformity. The *Collection of Indicative Verses:*[429]
>
> > Those who are childish and know themselves
> > To be childish are wise in this regard.
>
> When we are comparing ourselves with the teachings, it can be like carrying a corpse[430]—we are at odds with the teachings. When you hope to be the best of religious persons and revered scholars, you are being the worst of the childish. The *Collection of Indicative Verses:*[431]
>
> > Those who are childish but consider themselves
> > To be wise—they are called childish.
>
> At the very least, understand what is being said with regard to the teachings and examine yourself accordingly.

Also, Bo-do-wa, who quotes this teaching as seen in the *Garland of Birth Stories,* asserts that you must examine your mind. As it says in the *Garland of Birth Stories:*[432]

> From the sky to the earth is a long way.
> From the distant shore of the ocean to the closest edge is also a long way.
> From the mountains of the east to the mountains of the west is an even longer way.
> But from the ordinary [person] to the sublime teaching is longer yet than that. **[194]**

This verse says that a great gulf exists between us, ordinary people, and the teaching. This verse is a teaching that the gift-bearing brahmin Subhāṣita explained to the bodhisattva prince Candra after the prince had offered one thousand gold coins to him.

Moreover, Dö-lung-ba said:

> If someone who knew how to examine our mind-stream were to do so, that person would soon find something that had gone quite

> far from the teaching—like sending a ball of thread down a steep incline.

Furthermore, how you turn away from wrongdoing once you have reflected in this way is stated in the *Chapter of the Truth Speaker*:[433]

> O King, do not kill.
> Life is very dear to all beings.
> Hence, they want to maintain their lives for a long time.
> So think not of killing, even in the depths of your mind.

Apply this attitude of restraint toward the ten nonvirtuous actions as well as the misdeeds previously explained. Do so without even giving rise to the motivating thoughts. Become accustomed to this attitude, and use it frequently.

If you do not reject wrongdoing in this way, you will experience suffering. No matter where you go, you will not be free from it. Therefore, it is not sensible to engage in actions that seem to bring happiness in the short term, yet have effects you must endure with tears covering your face. On the other hand, it is sensible to engage in actions that give you faultless happiness and delight when you experience the ripening of their effects. The *Collection of Indicative Verses*:[434]

> If you fear suffering
> And do not enjoy it,
> Do not commit sinful actions
> Either in public or in private.
>
> Whether you have committed sinful actions
> Or are committing them,
> You will not escape suffering
> Even if you tried to run away.
>
> No matter where you stay, there is no place
> That karma has not created,
> Neither in the sky nor in the ocean,
> Nor even a place in the mountains. **[195]**

And also:

> The childish, who have little wisdom,
> Act as enemies to themselves;
> Through this, they perform sinful actions
> The effects of which will become intense.
>
> You were good not to engage in such actions
> That give rise to torment,

Whose effects you endure one by one,
Weeping, your face covered with tears.

You were good to engage in such actions
That do not give rise to torment,
Whose fruitions you undergo one by one
Happily and with a joyful mind.

Because you desire happiness
You were wild and have been sinful;
You will cry while experiencing
The fruitions of such sins.

And also:

Although sins will not necessarily
Cut you immediately like a weapon,
Rebirths taken through sinful actions
Will be evident in your future lives.

Sinful actions will bring about
Lifetimes in the future
Where the fruitions of these actions
Will be of various intensities.

Just as rust emerges from iron
And feeds on that very iron,
So too do those who have committed actions without examination
Travel to the miserable realms through their own actions.

Kam-lung-ba (Kham-lung-ba) said to Pu-chung-wa, "Our teacher Geshe Drom-dön-ba says that only karma and its effects are of importance, but contemporary scholars do not value it as something to explain, listen to, or meditate on. I wonder, is it the only practice that is difficult?" Pu-chung-wa replied, "It is just so."

Geshe Drom-dön-ba said, "O followers of the Elder, great pretension is inappropriate; this dependent-arising is subtle." Pu-chung-wa said, "As I grow old, I have turned my attention to the *Sūtra of the Wise and the Foolish.*" Sha-ra-wa said, "The Buddha said that any faults and shortcomings that occur are not due to some bad area or the building of a new house but are only the arising of such and such from having done such and such an action."

b" **In particular, the way of purification through the four powers**

Though you make great effort not to be defiled by wrongdoing, faults may arise due to such things as carelessness and a preponderance of afflictions. **[196]** If this happens, it is inappropriate to disregard them without caring, so you must try to apply the remedy about which the compassionate Teacher spoke.

Now, in regard to how to remedy any infractions, do as it is explained in the context of the three vows. However, you should remedy sins through the four powers. The *Sūtra Giving the Four Teachings (Catur-dharma-nirdeśa-sūtra)* says:[435]

> Maitreya, if bodhisattvas, the great heroes, possess these four teachings, then they will overcome any sins that they have committed and accumulated. What are the four? They are the power of eradication; the power of applying remedies; the power of turning away from faults; and the power of the foundation.

You will definitely experience the result of karma that you have done and accumulated. Since the four powers can destroy this kind of karma before it starts to take effect, it goes without saying that the four powers can destroy karma whose result is indefinite. The four powers are as follows.

1″ The power of eradication

The first power is great contrition for having done nonvirtuous actions since beginningless time. In order to feel this, it is necessary to meditate on the way in which you produce the three effects of actions—fruitional and so forth. At the time of putting this into practice, do so by way of the two methods—the confession of sins in the *Sūtra of the Golden Light (Suvarṇa-prabhāsa-sūtra)*[436] and the confession of sins by way of the thirty-five buddhas.[437]

2″ The power of applying remedies

The second power has six sections:

1) "Dependence on the profound sūtras" includes such activities as receiving the oral transmission of sūtras such as the *Prajñāpāramitā*, retaining their meaning, and reading them.

2) "Interest in emptiness" means to comprehend the reality in which there is no self and which is luminously clear, and to have conviction that the mind is primordially pure.

3) "Dependence on recitation" means to recite, according to the rituals, the special formulae such as the hundred-syllable [mantra of Vajrasattva]. The *Tantra Requested by Subāhu* states:[438]

> The flames from fires that spread in spring forests
> Are out of control, burning up all the thickets;

Likewise, the winds of ethical discipline fan the fires of recitation
And the flames of great perseverance burn up sins.

Just as when the sun's rays destabilize snow
It melts in the unbearable brilliance,
So too do the snows of sins disappear
When destabilized by the sunbeams of recitation and ethical discipline. **[197]**

Lighting a butter lamp in a dark gloom
Entirely clears away the darkness;
Likewise, the darkness of sins accumulated for a thousand lifetimes
Is quickly dispelled by the butter lamp of recitation.

Further, repeat the recitations until you see signs that you have cleared away your sins. The *Formula of Exhortation (sKul byed kyi gzungs)* states that the signs are dreaming the following: vomiting bad food; consuming such foods as yogurt and milk; vomiting; seeing the sun and the moon; moving through the air; blazing fires; subduing water buffalo and persons in dark clothing; seeing the community of monks or nuns; seeing a tree that gives out a milky substance; riding upon an elephant or a bull; climbing upon a lion throne; climbing up a mansion or a mountain; and listening to the teaching.

4) "Dependence upon images" means to make images of the Buddha once you have acquired faith in him.

5) "Dependence on worship" means to make a variety of offerings to an image of the Buddha or to a *stūpa*.

6) "Dependence on names" means to hear the recitation of and retain the names of buddhas and great conquerors' children.

These six types of remedies are only those that occur in Śāntideva's *Compendium of Trainings*. There are many others.

3″ The power of turning away from faults

The third power is actually restraining yourself from the ten nonvirtuous actions. In the *Sun Essence Sūtra*, the Buddha said that this restraint destroys all karma, afflictions, and obscurations of the teaching created physically, verbally, or mentally by way of killing and the like. The third power eliminates bad actions that you have previously created yourself, caused others to create, or have rejoiced in others creating. Confession that lacks an attitude of wholehearted restraint becomes merely words. Dharmamitra's *Commentary on the*

"Sūtra on the Discipline" explains that the Buddha was thinking of this fact when he said in scripture, "Is there subsequent restraint?" Therefore, it is very important to have an attitude of restraint within which you have conviction not to commit that action again. Moreover the development of this attitude depends on the first power.

4″ The power of the foundation

The fourth power is going for refuge to the three jewels and cultivating the spirit of enlightenment. **[198]** With regard to this, the Conqueror spoke in general about a variety of means through which beginners could remove their sins. However, a complete remedy requires all four powers to be present.

The sins are removed in several ways. One way is when small sufferings occur instead of the great sufferings of rebirth in the miserable realms. Another is that, even if you are born in a miserable realm, you do not experience its sufferings. Still another is that a mere headache in the present life serves to remove the sin. Likewise, the sins whose effects you must experience for a long time may become ones whose effects you experience for only a short time or that you need not experience at all. There is no certainty about how sins are removed, because it depends on whether the purifier is of great or little strength, whether the remedy is one in which the four powers are complete or incomplete, intense or not intense, of long or short duration, and so forth.

The statement in both sūtra and texts on discipline that "karma does not perish even in one hundred eons" is made with regard to the karma for which you have not cultivated a remedy with the four powers. However, if you purify yourself with a remedy having the aforementioned four powers, it is said that you will even remove karma that you are bound to experience. Haribhadra's *Long Explanation of the Perfection of Wisdom Sūtra in Eight Thousand Lines* (*Abhisamayālaṃkārālokā*) states:[439]

> Thus, with powerful remedies you can completely eliminate the unfavorable factors, which diminish when you possess the group of remedies. This, for example, is like the tarnish on gold. Because all such things as obstructions to the sublime teaching will necessarily diminish as just explained, you will completely eliminate infractions which originate from arrogance.
>
> You should understand that the statement, "Any karma at all, even for a hundred eons…," is qualified by, "If you have not cultivated the group of remedies." Were this not the case, there

> would be a contradiction with reason and a contradiction with many sūtras.
>
> You can also understand the Buddha's expression, "karma whose effects you will definitely experience," with the qualification that you have not cultivated the group of remedies. Understand that the Buddha's expression, "karma whose effects you will not definitely experience," refers to effects that occur only sometimes, even though you may not have cultivated the group of remedies. **[199]**

In this way, confession, restraint, and so forth weaken the capacity of karma to bear fruit. Such karma will not bear fruit even when it comes in contact with other conditions. Likewise, it is said that anger and the production of wrong views weaken the ability of roots of virtue to give effects. Bhāvaviveka's *Blaze of Reasons (Tarka-jvālā)* says:[440]

> Wrong views and malice weaken virtuous karma. Remedies such as repudiation, restraint, and confession weaken bad karma. Whenever any of these attitudes are present, they reduce the potency of the seeds deposited by the virtuous and nonvirtuous karma, even though the combination of conditions for the karma to take effect are already in place. So where would an effect come from, and what would it be like? Because there is no combination of conditions for maintaining the potency of the seeds deposited by karma, the time for being maintained has changed. Because of this, there is a thorough eradication of the karma. As it has been said, "Moreover, by upholding the sublime teaching you will experience in this life the effects of a sin whose consequence you are certain to experience." And, "Furthermore, with this remedy, karma for rebirth in the miserable realms transforms into a mere headache."
>
> *Qualm*: If karma that would otherwise result in rebirth in a miserable realm can be weakened and have the effect of becoming merely a headache, how can this be considered a complete removal?
>
> *Reply*: The culminating effect of your sinful karma will be the experience of suffering in the hells. With this remedy, though, you do not experience even tiny sufferings in the hells. How can this not be considered a very complete removal? Yet, how could these results of headaches and the like be examples of karma not having any effects?

You have not found a remedy that destroys the seeds of the afflictions. Yet, you have weakened the karma with a contrary condition. Consequently, even though other conditions do assemble, the karma does not fructify. You can see many such situations among external and internal causes and effects.

Therefore, although you strive at the accumulation of much virtuous karma, if you do not guard against the causes that destroy virtuous karma such as anger, the virtuous karma will not give its effect, as stated above. Hence, you must strive to guard against causes that destroy virtuous karma and make an effort to remedy nonvirtuous karma. **[200]**

Qualm: If you can totally remove even very powerful karma, how is it that the sūtras say, "Except for the fruitions of former karma"?

Reply: There is no fault with this reasoning. The Buddha spoke in this way with the following intention: when fruitions such as blindness already exist, it is difficult to remove them with a remedy. However, it is easy to stop the effects from arising at the time of the cause, i.e., when the effect has not already taken place. The *Blaze of Reasons* says:[441]

> *Qualm*: If it is the case that a sin will be completely eliminated, why did the Buddha teach, "Except for the fruitions of former karma"?
>
> *Reply*: The Buddha taught this while having in mind the case of the karma of blindness, having one eye, being lame, crippled, dumb, deaf, and the like, where there is no ability to eliminate the effects of karma that has already come to fruition.
>
> The intention that is in the form of a cause comes to an end when you acquire a different motivation. This is demonstrated by the cases of people [who committed murder but later repented] such as Angulimāla, Ajataśatru, Aśoka, Svaka, and those who killed their fathers.[442]
>
> *Qualm*: [Upon their deaths] Ajataśatru and the killers of their mothers had developed other virtuous attitudes. Why then were they reborn in the Unrelenting Hell? Did they fail to eliminate their karma?
>
> *Reply*: It was taught that they were reborn in such places as the Unrelenting Hell in order to develop conviction in their karma and its effects. It is not the case that they failed to completely eliminate their remaining karma. Like a silk ball that falls and bounces up, they were born in a hell and were then freed. They were also untouched by the fiery garlands of hell and so forth. This being so, it is proven both that you can completely eradicate sins and that karma certainly has effects.

It is not definite that some particular persons can eliminate their karma. The Buddha spoke of this in the *King of Concentrations Sūtra*. King Śūradatta killed Supuṣpacandra and felt contrite about it.[443]

[201] He built a *stūpa* and made very extensive offerings. Three times each day he would confess his sins. He did this for nine hundred and fifty billion years. Even though he maintained his ethical discipline correctly in that way, upon his death he was reborn in Unrelenting Hell. For ten or twenty billion eons he experienced limitless sufferings—having his eyes squeezed out and so forth.

Nonetheless, confession is not senseless. For if you do not confess sins, you will experience sufferings that are greater and of longer duration than if you had confessed them.

Through confession and restraint you can purify yourself of sins without any remainder. However, there is a vast difference between the purity of having never been tarnished by a fault from the beginning and the purity attained through confession of that fault. For example, the *Bodhisattva Levels* says:[444]

> You can redress the occurrence of a root infraction through adopting the bodhisattva vow. However, it will be impossible to attain the first bodhisattva level in this lifetime.

Further, the *Sūtra Gathering All the Threads*[445] states that even though you clear away sins, you will need at least ten eons to attain the level of forbearance [second of the four levels of the path of preparation]:

> The youthful Mañjuśri asked, "O Bhagavan, if someone, under the influence of a sinful companion, were to do such a thing as abandon the teaching, how, Bhagavan, would this person be freed from that in this lifetime?"
>
> The Bhagavan replied, "Mañjuśri, if you were to confess your fault three times a day for seven years, you would clear it away. Subsequent to this you would attain the level of forbearance in ten eons, at the least."

Therefore, complete purification means to completely purify yourself of the arising of unpleasant effects. However, since you greatly extend the time needed to attain such things as knowledge of the path, strive not to be tarnished by faults from the start. **[202]** The Buddha said that for this reason noble beings do not consciously engage in even the subtlest of sins or infractions, even for the sake of their own lives. If it was the case that purity through confession was similar to faults that have never taken place, then there would be no need to act in this way.

This is also evident in the world. Although an injured hand, foot, and so on may heal, they are different from the ones that have never had an injury.

Through striving in that way, you should do as the *Collection of Indicative Verses* says:[446]

> A person of sinful conduct—
> Who has committed sins and not gained merit,
> Who has parted from the teaching and attained its opposite—
> Will fear death, like a weak boat breaking apart in a great river.
>
> A person who has gained merit and has not committed sins,
> And who has practiced the teaching of the holy ones' system,
> Will never fear death,
> Like a sturdy boat going across a river.

Do not act like the person of the first verse but do whatever you can to act like the person of the second verse.

Further, there is little sense in saying many reasonable words but acting in an unruly way. Even if you only know a little, there is great benefit in practicing whatever teaching you know by casting aside what is wrong and adopting what is right. The *Collection of Indicative Verses* says:[447]

> The unruly may speak at length on what is reasonable,
> Yet they do not act accordingly.
> Like herdsmen counting others' livestock,
> They do not attain the fortune of virtuous practice.
>
> Those who practice the teaching in accordance with their instructions
> And eradicate attachment, hostility, and ignorance
> Attain the fortune of virtuous practice,
> Though they may speak little of what is reasonable.
>
> Through delighting in conscientiousness
> And fearing unruliness,
> Monks pull themselves from the miserable realms,
> Like elephants pull themselves from the mud.
>
> Through delighting in conscientiousness
> And fearing unruliness,
> Monks shake off all sins
> Like the wind shakes leaves from the trees.

This being so, the proper view of dependent-arising and the causality of the two types of karma is the indispensable foundation for the practices of all the vehicles and the aims of all beings. As Nāgārjuna's *Friendly Letter* says:[448]

> If you actually desire high status [as a human or deity] and liberation,

You must familiarize yourself with the correct view. **[203]**
With wrong views even a person who acts well
Will have terrible fruitions in all lives.

Hence, using what has been explained as illustrations, you should look at the *Mindfulness of the Excellent Teaching*, the *Sūtra of the Wise and the Foolish*, the *Hundred Actions Sūtra*, the *Hundred Bodhisattva Stories (Bodhisattvāvadāna-kalpalatā)*, the prefaces in the discipline,[449] and other scriptures as well to develop an intense and enduring certainty. Take this to be a goal of crucial importance.

16

The Attitude of a Person of Small Capacity

b) The measure of the attitude of a person of small capacity
c) Clearing up misconceptions concerning the attitude of a person of small capacity

b) **The measure of the attitude of a person of small capacity**

Previously you have had an uncontrived interest in this life, while your interest in future lives has merely been an understanding that follows what others say. You have generated the attitude of a person of small capacity when these interests change places, and your interest in the future has become paramount, while your interest in this life has become merely incidental. However, you must make this attitude stable. Thus, once it has occurred, cultivate it diligently.

c) **Clearing up misconceptions concerning the attitude of a person of small capacity**

Misconception: In the scriptures it says that you must turn your mind away from all the excellent things of cyclic existence. Someone could misinterpret this and think that is improper to develop an interest in high status [as a human or deity] in which body, resources, and the like are excellent, because it is within cyclic existence.

Response: There are two kinds of objects of interest: those which you diligently seek temporarily and those which you diligently seek ultimately. Even persons who strive for liberation must diligently but temporarily seek excellent bodies, etc., in cyclic existence. For, they will ultimately attain certain goodness through a succession of lives in high status. **[204]**

Further, not everything within high status—excellent body, resources, and attendants—is included within cyclic existence. The most excellent body is a buddha's embodiment as form; the most excellent resources are the riches of this embodiment's realm; and the most excellent attendants are this embodiment's retinue. Intending this, Maitreya says in the *Ornament for the Mahāyāna Sūtras*[450] that you achieve high status as a human or deity by means of the first four perfections:

> Excellent resources and body
> And excellent retinue—high status.

Again, it is said in many texts that you achieve a buddha's embodiment as form by means of the first four perfections.

Therefore, those who achieve omniscience accomplish a great amount of exceptional ethical discipline, generosity, patience, and the like for a long time. Consequently, they diligently seek the effects of these as well—exceptional high status with its body and so forth.

The achievement of the final goal, certain goodness, is spoken of in *Engaging in the Bodhisattva Deeds*:[451]

> Relying on the boat of the human body,
> Free yourself from the great river of suffering.

As Śāntideva says, you must rely on a life in a happy realm—exemplified in the verse by the human body—and cross the ocean of existence, reaching omniscience. Moreover, you must pass successively through many lifetimes. Consequently, ethical discipline—the preeminent cause of achieving a body in a happy realm—is the root of the path.

Moreover, you need a body in a happy realm that is fully qualified, for even if you have achieved the path, you will make little progress with a body that is not completely qualified and only possesses good qualities to some extent. For this, it is not enough to partially observe the fundamental trainings of novice monks and the like. You must strive to maintain the fundamental trainings of monks and so on in their entirety.

Misconception: Some say that if maintaining ethical discipline is for the purpose of achieving a rebirth in a happy realm, you can achieve this even by a one-day vow. So, why become a monk, which is a difficult life with little purpose? Others say that if the purpose of vows of individual liberation is to become an arhat, why become a monk and lead a life which is difficult and of little purpose? Rather, we should value a life as a lay practitioner, for you can also become an arhat in such a life, and, besides, you cannot become a monk until you reach the age of twenty. **[205]**

Reply: Understand these claims to be great nonsense from persons who do not understand the key points of the teaching. Rather, strive to maintain the fundamental trainings completely, gradually assuming the higher vows while using the lower ones as supports.

This concludes the explanation of training the mind in the stages of the path that are shared with persons of small capacity.

17

The Eight Types of Suffering

2) Training the mind in the stages of the path shared with persons of medium capacity
   a) The mental training
      i) Identifying the mind intent on liberation
      ii) The method for developing the mind intent on liberation
         a′ Reflection on suffering and its origin
            1′ Reflection on the truth of suffering—the faults of cyclic existence
               a″ Showing the significance of the Buddha's asserting the truth of suffering as the first of the four truths
               b″ The actual meditation on suffering
                  1″ Reflection on the universal suffering of cyclic existence
                     (a) Reflection on the eight types of suffering
                        (i) The suffering of birth
                        (ii) The suffering of old age
                        (iii) The suffering of illness
                        (iv) The suffering of death
                        (v) The suffering of encountering what is unpleasant
                        (vi) The suffering of separation from what is pleasant
                        (vii) The suffering of not getting what you want
                        (viii) The suffering of the five appropriated aggregates

2) Training the mind in the stages of the path shared with persons of medium capacity [206]

I bow with respect to the revered teachers who have great compassion.

Be mindful of death and reflect on how you will fall into a miserable realm after you die. Turn your mind away from this world and diligently seek a happy, future rebirth. If you strive to reject sin and to cultivate virtue through the standard practice of going for refuge and through reflection upon virtuous and nonvirtuous karma and the certainty of their results, you will achieve a happy rebirth. However, do not be satisfied with this alone: after you have developed the attitude that is shared with persons of small capacity, develop the attitude that is shared with persons of medium capacity—namely, disgust with all of cyclic existence. On this basis, you may aspire to become a person of great capacity by developing the spirit of supreme enlightenment.

Consequently, you must train in the attitude of a person of medium capacity. Why? Because even were you to reach the level of a deity or a human, you would be mistaken if you believed this to be pleasurable by nature, since you would still not have escaped the suffering of conditionality.[452] Therefore, in reality, you would have no happiness whatsoever—your life would still come to a bad end, for you would surely fall into a miserable realm again. A human or divine lifetime is like resting on a precipice just before falling into the abyss. *Engaging in the Bodhisattva Deeds*:[453]

> After repeatedly coming to happy rebirths,
> And experiencing much joy there,
> You die and fall into the protracted
> And unbearable suffering of the miserable realms.

Candragomin's *Letter to a Student*:[454] **[207]**

> You who whirl constantly in cyclic existence,
> Yet who enter a happy realm mistaking mere calm for happiness,
> Will certainly wander helplessly
> Through hundreds of like and unlike realms.

Consequently, you have to become as thoroughly disenchanted with the happy realms as you were with the miserable realms. As Āryadeva's *Four Hundred Stanzas* says:[455]

> High states frighten the wise
> As much as hell.
> Rare is the state of existence
> That does not terrify them.

Also, the *Verse Summary of the Perfection of Wisdom in Eight Thousand Lines* says:[456]

> Those whose minds are attached to cyclic existence will continue to wander there constantly.

The *Letter to a Student:*[457]

> The more you conceive all beings as happy,
> The more dense the darkness of your delusion becomes.
> The more you conceive all beings as suffering,
> The more the darkness of your delusion lessens.
> The more you contemplate what is pleasant,
> The more the flames of attachment spread.
> The more you contemplate what is unpleasant,
> The more the flames of attachment abate.

From beginningless time you have been conditioned to believe that the wonders of cyclic existence are sources of happiness, and you have habitually projected upon them a false image of beauty. But if, as a remedy, you train yourself to meditate on suffering and unpleasantness, you will put an end to these wrong ideas. Candragomin says that if you neglect to meditate on these, ignorance and attachment will increase, and you will continue to fuel the process of cyclic existence. Hence, it is vitally important to meditate on the faults of cyclic existence.

The faults of cyclic existence are explained in three parts:

1. The mental training (Chapters 17–21)
2. The measure of the determination to be free (Chapter 22)
3. Dispelling misconceptions (Chapter 22)

a) **The mental training**

This is explained in two parts:

1. Identifying the mind intent on liberation
2. The method for developing the mind intent on liberation

i) **Identifying the mind intent on liberation [208]**

Liberation means freedom from bondage, and what binds you to cyclic existence is karma and the afflictions. Under their power, the aggregates are reborn in a threefold manner: in terms of the three realms they are reborn in the desire realm, and so forth; in terms of kinds of beings, they are reborn as the five [deities, humans, animals, hungry ghosts and hell-beings] or six kinds of beings [the five plus demi-gods]; and in terms of the type of birth, they are reborn in four ways—by birth from a womb, birth from eggs, birth from heat and moisture, and spontaneous birth. Since this is the nature of bondage, freedom from rebirth impelled by karma and the afflictions is liberation, and the desire to obtain that freedom is the mind intent on liberation.

Moment by moment the compositional activity of karma and the afflictions arises and is destroyed, but this destruction is not liberation. Though things that have been produced do not abide for a second moment, this destruction is not contingent upon conditions for liberation, such as the cultivation of a remedy [knowledge of selflessness]. If this were liberation, it would follow that everyone would be liberated without effort, and that is absurd. Consequently, if you fail to cultivate the remedy, you will be reborn in the future, since you only stop rebirth by cultivating the remedy.

ii) **The method for developing the mind intent on liberation**

The desire to relieve the suffering of thirst is based on seeing that you do not want to be tormented by thirst. Likewise, the desire to attain liberation—which relieves the suffering of the aggregates appropriated by karma and the afflictions—is based upon seeing that the appropriated aggregates are flawed insofar as they have suffering as their nature. Unless you develop a determination to reject cyclic existence through meditating on its faults, you will not seek relief from the suffering of the appropriated aggregates. The *Four Hundred Stanzas*:[458]

> How can one who is not disenchanted
> With this world appreciate peace?
> Cyclic existence, like home,
> Is difficult to leave behind.

Developing the mind intent on liberation has two parts:

1. Reflection on suffering and its origin (Chapters 17–20)
2. Reflection from the viewpoint of the twelve dependent-arisings (Chapter 21)

a′ **Reflection on suffering and its origin**

This is explained in two parts:

1. Reflection on the truth of suffering—the faults of cyclic existence (Chapters 17–19)
2. Reflection on the process of cyclic existence in terms of its origin (Chapter 20)

1′ **Reflection on the truth of suffering—the faults of cyclic existence**

Reflection on the truth of suffering is explained in terms of:

1. Showing the significance of the Buddha's asserting the truth of suffering as the first of the four truths
2. The actual meditation on suffering

a″ **Showing the significance of the Buddha's asserting the truth of suffering as the first of the four truths**

Qualm: **[209]** The true origins are the causes and true sufferings are their effects. Why, then, did the Bhagavan reverse that order, if the origins precede sufferings, and say: "Monks, this is the noble truth of suffering; this is the noble truth of the origin"?

Reply: In this case, the Teacher reversed the sequence of cause and effect, not out of error, but because this reversal is vital for practice. Why? If his disciples failed to develop a proper determination to liberate themselves from cyclic existence first, they would sever the very root of liberation. How then could he lead them to liberation? Thus, in the beginning, the darkness of ignorance enshrouded his students; they mistook the wonders of cyclic existence—which are in fact suffering—for happiness. As the *Four Hundred Stanzas* says:[459]

> Fool! If there is no end whatsoever
> To this ocean of suffering,
> Why are you,
> Who are caught up in it, not afraid?

By saying "In fact this [cyclic existence] is not happiness but suffering," the Buddha explained many forms of suffering, and led his disciples to become disenchanted with cyclic existence and recognize it as suffering. As this is a necessary precondition, the Buddha spoke first about the truth of suffering.

Once you recognize suffering, you see yourself as submerged in an ocean of suffering, and realize that, if you want to be liberated from suffering, you must counteract it. Moreover, you recognize that you cannot stop suffering unless you counteract its cause. By investigating the cause of suffering, you come to understand its true origin. Consequently, the Buddha spoke next about the truth of the origin. **[210]**

Next you develop an understanding of the truth of the origin, an understanding that contaminated karma produces the suffering of cyclic existence, that afflictions produce karma and that the conception of self is the root of the afflictions. When you see that you can eliminate the conception of self, you will vow to realize its cessation, which is also the cessation of suffering. Thus, the Buddha spoke next about the truth of cessation.

Qualm: If teaching the truth of suffering promotes the desire for liberation, should not the Buddha have taught the truth of cessation immediately after teaching the truth of suffering?

Reply: There is no mistake. Why? At this point, after you recognize the truth of suffering, you have a desire for liberation, and think, "If only I could attain a cessation that relieves this suffering!" But if you have not identified the cause of suffering, and have not seen that you can eliminate that cause, you do not yet regard liberation as something attainable and thus do not think, "I will realize a cessation."

In this way, when you do think, "I shall realize a cessation that is liberation," you become interested in the truth of the path, wondering about the path that leads to this cessation. For this reason, the Buddha spoke about the truth of the path last.

In the same way, the *Sublime Continuum* says:[460]

> Recognize that you are ill; eliminate the cause of the illness;
> Attain health; rely on a remedy.
> Likewise, you should recognize, eliminate, attain, and rely upon
> Suffering, its cause, its cessation, and the path, respectively.

This being the case, the four truths are taught repeatedly throughout the Mahāyāna and the Hīnayāna. Since the Sugata has included in the four truths the vital points concerning the process of cyclic existence and its cessation, this teaching is crucial for achieving freedom. Since this synoptic outline of practice is important, it must be taught to students in just this order. Why? Unless you reflect on the truth of suffering to the point of actually becoming revolted by cyclic existence, your desire to attain liberation will be mere words, and whatever you do will lead to origins of further suffering. Unless you reflect on the origin of suffering until you have a good understanding of the root of cyclic existence, which is karma and the afflictions, you will be like an archer who does not see the target—you will miss the essential points of the path. You will mistake what is not a path to freedom from cyclic existence for the path and exhaust yourself without result. Finally, if you fail to understand the need to eliminate suffering and its origin, you will also fail to recognize the liberation that provides relief from suffering and its origin; **[211]** hence your interest in liberation will be a mere conceit.

b″ **The actual meditation on suffering**

The actual meditation on suffering is explained in two parts:

1. Reflection on the universal suffering of cyclic existence (Chapters 17–19)
2. Reflection on specific sufferings (Chapter 19)

1″ **Reflection on the universal suffering of cyclic existence**

This is divided into three:

1. Reflection on the eight types of suffering
2. Reflection on the six types of suffering (Chapter 18)
3. Meditation on the three types of suffering (Chapter 19)

(a) **Reflection on the eight types of suffering**

Meditate in accordance with what is said in Nāgārjuna's *Friendly Letter:*[461]

> Your Highness,[462] be disenchanted with cyclic existence,
> Which is the origin of many sufferings—
> Being deprived of what you want, death, illness, old age, and so on.

Here, cultivating a sense of disenchantment with cyclic existence means reflecting on it as the origin of many sufferings. The eight types of suffering include the four that Nāgārjuna states explicitly—being deprived of what one wants, and so forth—as well as the four that are indicated by the words "and so on."[463] The Bhagavan taught these eight in many discourses when he identified the truth of suffering.

During every session in which you meditate on the teachings shared with persons of medium capacity, take up as well the shared teachings that I explained in the section on the practices appropriate to persons of small capacity. As for the teachings that are not shared with persons of small capacity, if your mind is strong, sustain them in meditation in exactly the way that I have written them here; if it is weak, then leave out the scriptural citations, and only meditate on the meaning of the points I have outlined.

Though these are analytical meditations, you should nonetheless arrest excitement and so forth[464] with regard to your mental object, not taking up any object—virtuous, nonvirtuous, or ethically neutral—other than that which you are meditating upon. Without letting your mind fall under the influence of sleep, lethargy, or laxity, meditate continually in a state of consciousness that is very clear and pure. For, as *Engaging in the Bodhisattva Deeds* says, there will be little result from any virtuous practice if the mind is distracted:[465]

> The One Who Knows Reality[466] has said that
> Prayers, austerities, and such—
> Even if practiced for a long time—
> Are pointless if done with a distracted mind. **[212]**

Also, the *Sūtra of Cultivating Faith in the Mahāyāna (Mahāyāna-prasāda-prabhāvanā-sūtra)* says:[467]

> O child of a good family, from this enumeration you should know that faith in the Mahāyāna of the bodhisattvas, and all that emerges out of the Mahāyāna, comes from properly contemplating the meaning and the teaching with a mind that is not distracted.

Here, a "mind that is not distracted" means a mind that does not wander to objects that are other than the virtuous object of meditation; "the meaning and the teaching" refers to the meaning and the words; and "properly contemplating" means analyzing and reflecting with discernment. This shows that any achievement of a virtuous quality requires both undistracted focus and analytical discernment. Therefore, the Buddha says that any achievement of a virtuous quality in the three vehicles requires a state of mind that is both (1) an actual meditative serenity, or a similitude of it, which rests one-pointedly on its virtuous object of meditation without wandering from it; and (2) an actual insight, or a similitude of it, which carefully analyzes a virtuous object of meditation and distinguishes both the real nature and the diversity of phenomena. Similarly, the *Sūtra Unravelling the Intended Meaning (Saṃdhi-nirmocana-sūtra)* says:[468]

> Maitreya, you should know that all the virtuous qualities, mundane or supramundane, of the *śrāvakas*, the bodhisattvas or the *tathāgatas* result from meditative serenity and insight.

Construe "meditative serenity" and "insight" here as including both actual serenity and insight and states of mind that are similar to them. For it is not certain that all of the good qualities of the three vehicles develop as a result of *actual* serenity and insight.

(i) **The suffering of birth**

There are five points to contemplate:

1) *Birth is suffering because it is associated with pain*: **[213]** birth is accompanied by many intense feelings of pain for the following four types of living beings: those born as hell-beings,

hungry ghosts who invariably suffer, beings born from a womb, and beings born from an egg.

2) *Birth is suffering because it is associated with dysfunctional tendencies*:[469] all of the compositional factors of the three realms, because they are associated with dysfunctional tendencies that are in harmony with the class of the afflictions, are ill-suited [to the service of virtue] and uncontrollable. Moreover, once you possess the compositional factors of a living being within the three realms, you too are bound to dysfunctional tendencies that are in harmony with the class of afflictions. In short, because the compositional factors are associated with seeds that generate, sustain, and increase the afflictions, they are ill-suited to the service of virtue; furthermore, you cannot control them as you would wish.

3) *Birth is suffering because it is the origin of suffering*: you take birth in the three realms and on that basis suffer old age, illness, and death.

4) *Birth is suffering because it is the origin of the afflictions*: when you are born in cyclic existence, the three mental poisons arise for objects of attachment, hostility, and ignorance, and as a result, body and mind are disturbed and in pain, and you cannot be happy. The afflictions torment your body and mind in numerous ways.

5) *Birth is suffering because it is an unwanted separation*: all births end in death, which is undesirable, and causes you to experience only suffering.

Thus, at birth you are bound to pain and endowed with dysfunctional tendencies. Birth leads to illness, aging, and so forth, as well as to the afflictions and death. Consider how these give rise to suffering as well.

In particular, the suffering you undergo in the womb is as described in Candragomin's *Letter to a Student*:[470] **[214]**

> After you have entered the womb, which is like hell,
> You are hemmed in by foul-smelling filth
> And trapped in pitch-dark gloom.
> Your body cramped, you must undergo enormous sufferings.

The *Descent into the Womb Sūtra* explains the meaning of these words:[471]

> Filthy with quantities of urine, brain-like substances, thick saliva, and marrow, the fetus dwells above the intestines and below the stomach, in a space which is filled with many kinds of filth and is

> home to a myriad of bacteria, with two very foul-smelling openings and hollows and apertures in the bone. Its front faces the vertebrae and its back, the stomach wall. It is nourished every month by its mother's uterine blood. The bits of food its mother has eaten are ground by her two rows of teeth and swallowed. As it is swallowed, the food is moistened from below by saliva and the oozing of mouth sores, while it is polluted from above by thick saliva. The remains of that vomit-like food enter from above through the umbilical cord's opening and generate growth. Through the thickening, quivering, elongated, and globular stages, the embryo is completely transformed into a fetus with arms and legs. The placenta encloses its arms, legs, and cheeks. Reeking like an old rag used for mucus, the stench is unbearable. Enshrouded in pitch darkness, it moves up and down. The bitter, sour, pungent, salty, spicy, and astringent tastes of food affect it like hot coals. Like an intestinal worm, it feeds on filthy fluids; it finds itself in a swamp that oozes rotting filth. Its life-force is unstable. The heat of its mother's body torments, heats, and overheats it all in three degrees: slightly, moderately, and greatly. It experiences distressing, intense, violent, and unbearable agony. Whenever its mother moves a little, moderately, or greatly, it also moves in the same way, constrained by five bonds.[472] **[215]** It experiences agony that is distressing, intense, violent, unbearable, and almost inconceivable, as though it had been thrust into a pit of burning cinders.

Similarly, it is said that the fetus is harmed in the womb when the mother eats too much or too little; eats food that is too oily, pungent, cold, hot, salty, sour, sweet, bitter, spicy, or astringent; indulges her sexual desires; runs too much or too fast; jumps or swims; or sits or squats in front of the fire. It is also said that the fetus is confined by the stomach and held firm by the intestines, as though it were bound by five bonds or impaled on a stake.

There is even further suffering when the infant emerges from the womb and is born into the outside. Candragomin's *Letter to a Student* says:[473]

> It is crushed slowly, like sesame seeds in an oil press,
> And then somehow it is born.
> Nonetheless, those who do not lose their lives immediately
> Must settle for pain.
>
> The body that dwelt and grew in that filth
> Is smeared with the womb's slime and has an unbearably foul smell.
> Memory is lost upon being inflicted with such torment,

> Which is like having an inflamed boil burst or being on the verge of vomiting.

The *Descent into the Womb Sūtra* explains the meaning of these words:[474]

> Thus, when all its major and minor limbs have developed, the fetus stirs in a frightful, pitch-dark place of urine that oozes rot, has an unbearable stench, is contaminated by excrement and urine, and continually dripping with foul-smelling filth, blood, and putrid fluids. Energy arising from the maturation of previous karma makes its feet turn up and its head turn down toward the opening. With both arms drawn in, it is slightly, moderately, and utterly smashed between two machines of bone. **[216]** The distressing, intense, violent, and unbearable agonies cause all the limbs of the body—painful as fresh wounds—to turn blue. All of the body's organs become hot. Since the uterine slime is now much reduced, the surface of the body dries out, and so the lips, throat, and heart become parched. Confined and full of insufferable dread, it emerges—however difficult this may be—when drawn out by the influence of causes and conditions, by energies arising from the maturation of previous karma. Once outside, the air burns like caustic liquid on a wound; the mere touch of a hand or a cloth feels like the cut of a sword. It experiences distressing, intense, violent, and unbearable agony.

It is said that when taken up onto someone's lap and the like, or touched with hot or cold objects, the newborn baby experiences distressing, intense, violent, and unbearable agony, like a flayed cow being eaten by vermin or a leper whose lesions are struck with a whip.

Among the eight types of sufferings, regard this first type, along with the eighth type [the suffering of the five appropriated aggregates], as the most crucial and meditate upon both of them. Therefore, as explained before, you should repeatedly investigate them with discerning wisdom and meditate on them.

(ii) **The suffering of old age**

There are five points to contemplate:

1) *A handsome body deteriorates*: your back bends down like a bow; your head is white like the *dra-wa* (*spra-ba*) grass flower; wrinkles cover your forehead like the lines of a cutting board. In ways such as these, youth breaks down and you become unattractive.

2) *Physical strength and vigor deteriorate*: for example, when you sit down, you drop like a sack of dirt cut from a rope; when you rise up, it is like uprooting a tree; when you speak, you are incoherent; and when you walk, you stumble. **[217]**

3) *The senses deteriorate*: your eyes cannot see forms clearly, and so forth; and the power of memory and the other faculties wanes due to extreme forgetfulness, and so on.

4) *Enjoyment of sense objects fades*: you have difficulty digesting food and drink, and cannot enjoy desirable objects.

5) *The deterioration of life is painful*: as your life nears exhaustion, you head rapidly toward death.

Think about these points again and again. As the *Extensive Sport Sūtra* says:[475]

> As aging progresses and we pass a certain point,
> We are like a tree struck by lightning,
> Withered by old age like a terrible, decrepit house.
> O Sage, speak quickly about an escape from old age.
>
> Age enfeebles the masses of men and women
> As a windstorm strips vines from a grove of *sal* trees.
> Age steals our vigor, skill, and strength—
> It is as though we are stuck in mud.
>
> Age makes attractive bodies unattractive.
> Age steals our glory and our strength.
> Age steals our happiness and subjects us to insults.
> Age takes our vigor; age begets death.

Jen-nga-wa said: "The pain of death is horrible but brief; how horrible is aging!" Ga-ma-pa said: "It is well that aging happens little by little. If it happened all at once, it would be intolerable."

(iii) **The suffering of illness**

Here there are also five points [to contemplate]:

1) *Illness changes the nature of the body*: the flesh wastes away, the skin dries out, and so forth.

2) *Pain and anguish increase and are seldom absent*: the elements of the body—water, earth, air, and fire—are not in equilibrium and fluctuate chaotically, causing physical torment, which in turn produces mental anguish. You spend night and day in this state.

3) *There is no desire for attractive things*: as you are told that desirable things harm those who are sick, you cannot indulge

in them freely; **[218]** and you do not have the range of movements and postures that you would wish.

4) *You must have recourse, however unwillingly, to unpleasant objects*: the sick are forced to take unpalatable medicine, food, drink, and the like; and have to rely on harsh therapies that involve such things as being burned with fire or being penetrated with instruments.

5) *You lose your vital energy*: it is painful to realize that your illness is terminal.

Reflect with care upon these points. As the *Extensive Sport Sūtra* says:[476]

> Hundreds of illnesses and the pain of rampant disease
> Afflict us, just as humans oppress wild animals.
> Regard the beings overwhelmed by old age and disease
> And quickly speak about escape from suffering.
>
> In deep winter, wind and great blizzards
> Take the vigor from the grasses, shrubs, trees, and herbs.
> In the same way, disease takes the vigor out of living beings;
> It breaks down their faculties, physical appearance, and strength.
>
> It will drain a great fortune in wealth and grain to the last.
> Disease constantly humiliates living beings;
> It harms them and is contemptuous of beauty.
> It torments them, like the sun beating down from the sky.

(iv) **The suffering of death**

Again, there are five points to contemplate:

1) You are separated from objects that are fine and attractive.

2) You are separated from close relatives who are fine and attractive.

3) You are separated from companions who are fine and attractive.

4) You are deprived of a body that is fine and attractive.

5) As you die, you experience terrible pain and anguish.

Reflect on these repeatedly, until you become disenchanted.

How do the first four of these constitute suffering? You suffer upon seeing that you are losing these four excellent things. The *Extensive Sport Sūtra*:[477]

> You die and pass on to another life, and in so doing
> You are forever separated from people who are beautiful and beloved. **[219]**

> Like a leaf fallen from a tree, or the current of a river,
> You will never return and meet them again.
>
> Death makes the powerful weak.
> Death takes you away, as a river carries away a log.
> People go alone, unaccompanied, with no companion—
> Powerless because their karma has its effects.
>
> Death seizes myriad living beings,
> As sea-monsters seize swarms of creatures,
> As an eagle seizes a snake, or a lion an elephant,
> As fire takes hold of grass, trees, and swarming creatures.

(v) **The suffering of encountering what is unpleasant**

Here there are also five points to contemplate:

1) Merely encountering your enemies, for example, causes pain and anguish.
2) You dwell in fear of being punished by them.
3) You fear they will speak maliciously, without kind words.
4) You dread death.
5) You worry that you will go to a miserable realm after death for having acted in ways contrary to the teaching.

Reflect on these.

(vi) **The suffering of separation from what is pleasant**

Again, there are five points to contemplate. When you are separated from a very dear relative, for example:

1) In your mind, sorrow arises.
2) In your speech, you lament.
3) You bring harm to your own body.
4) You are saddened, recalling and missing the good qualities of what you have lost.
5) Recourse is no longer available for what you have lost.

Reflect on these.

(vii) **The suffering of not getting what you want**

Again, there are five points, similar to separation from what is pleasant. Seeking but not getting what you want means, for example, farming a field but reaping no harvest, or engaging in business but receiving no profits. The pain of disappointment comes from working hard to get something that you long for, and then not getting it.

(viii) **The suffering of the five appropriated aggregates**

The Buddha said, "In brief, the five appropriated aggregates are suffering."[478] Reflection on the meaning of this teaching again takes in five points. It is the nature of the five aggregates appropriated by karma and the afflictions to be:

(1) vessels for future suffering;
(2) vessels for suffering based on what presently exists; **[220]**
(3) vessels for the suffering of pain;
(4) vessels for the suffering of change; and
(5) vessels for the suffering of conditionality.

Reflect on these again and again.

Here, with regard to the first point, you induce suffering in future lives by taking up these appropriated aggregates. As for the second, the appropriated aggregates form the basis for states, such as illness and old age, that are grounded in the already existing aggregates. The third and the fourth both come about because the appropriated aggregates are linked with dysfunctional tendencies toward these two types of suffering. As regards the fifth, the very existence of the appropriated aggregates constitutes the nature of the suffering of conditionality, because all of the compositional factors which depend on previous karma and afflictions are the suffering of conditionality. This will be explained in detail in the section on the three sufferings.[479]

If you do not cultivate a genuine sense of disenchantment with cyclic existence—the nature of which is the appropriated aggregates—you will have no chance to develop a genuine mind intent on liberation, and there will be no way for you to develop great compassion for living beings wandering through cyclic existence. Hence this reflection is extremely important, regardless of which vehicle—Mahāyāna or Hīnayāna—you enter. Even when you have developed a sense of disenchantment with cyclic existence, follow flawless scriptures and authoritative commentaries and seek an exact understanding of them. Then, use prolonged and discerning analytical meditation to bring about a powerful transformation of your mind.

Thus, I have followed the well-founded presentation of the noble Asaṅga in explaining the Bhagavan's purpose in teaching the eight types of suffering as a way to understand the truth of suffering, the faults of cyclic existence.

Bo-do-wa said:

> As soon as we are born as any one of the six types of beings, we are faced with the sufferings of sickness, death, and so forth. When the cause of sickness is present, we are sick; when the cause of death is present, we die. This is neither inappropriate nor accidental; it is the character or nature of cyclic existence. While we are in cyclic existence there is no escaping it. If we are disgusted by it, then we must eliminate the process of birth. **[221]** To do this, we must eliminate its cause.

Reflect in this way on the arising of the sufferings explained above—the sufferings of birth, old age, illness, death, and so forth.

18

The Six Types of Suffering

(b) Reflection on the six types of suffering
(i) The fault of uncertainty
(ii) The fault of insatiability
(iii) The fault of casting off bodies repeatedly
(iv) The fault of repeated rebirth
(v) The fault of repeatedly descending from high to low
(vi) The fault of having no companions

(b) **Reflection on the six types of suffering**

[Mahāmati's] *Clear Words: Explanation of the "Friendly Letter"* says that there are seven types of suffering, but since the last merely restates each of the faults, you should contemplate six types here.

(i) **The fault of uncertainty**

As you pass through cyclic existence, close relatives such as your father and mother become enemies in other lifetimes, while enemies become close relatives. Similarly, your father becomes your son and your son your father; and your mother becomes your wife and your wife your mother. Since there is nothing but a succession of such transformations, there is nothing that you can count on. The *Friendly Letter*:[480]

> For those in cyclic existence there are no certainties
> Because fathers become sons, mothers become wives,
> Enemies become friends,
> And the converse happens as well.

Even in this life, enemies become friends and vice versa. The *Tantra Requested by Subāhu* says:[481]

> Within a short space of time, an enemy can become a friend
> And a friend can become an enemy.
> Likewise, either one may become indifferent,
> While those who were indifferent may become enemies
> Or intimate friends.
> Knowing this, the wise never form attachments.
> They give up the thought of delighting in friends
> And are content to focus on virtue.

By meditating on this, you should check the arising of the attachment and hostility that come from discriminating between friends and enemies. Be aware that among the phenomena of cyclic existence, absolutely nothing can be trusted. Become disenchanted.

(ii) **The fault of insatiability**

The *Friendly Letter*:[482]

> Each of us has drunk more milk
> Than would fill the four oceans; yet
> Those in cyclic existence who act as ordinary beings[483] **[222]**
> Are intent on drinking still more than that.

Think about it: each living being has drunk so much mother's milk in the past, and yet—without training on a path to liberation—will drink that much again in the future. This is just an example. When you reflect on how you have no lack of experience with the wonders and sufferings of cyclic existence, you should become disenchanted. You indulge in pleasures in pursuit of satisfaction, yet, with worldly pleasures, you are never satisfied no matter how much you enjoy them. Hence, time after time your craving grows, and on that account you wander for ages through cyclic existence. For an immeasurably long period of time you will experience intolerable suffering, which those pleasures will not ameliorate in the least. The *Friendly Letter*:[484]

> Just as a leper tormented by maggots
> Turns to fire for relief
> But finds no peace, so should you understand
> Attachment to sensual pleasures.

Also in the *Compendium of the Perfections* it is said:[485]

> You get what you want,
> Use it up, then acquire more,

And still you are not satisfied,
What could be sicker than this?

And Candragomin's *Letter to a Student* says:[486]

What being has not come into the world hundreds of times?
What pleasure has not already been experienced countless times?
What luxury, such as splendid white yak-tail fans, have they not owned?
Yet, even when they possess something, their attachment continues to grow.

There is no suffering they have not experienced many times.
The things they desire do not satisfy them.
There is no living being that has not slept in their bellies.
So why do they not rid themselves of attachment to cyclic existence?

Think about this.

Furthermore, you will become very disenchanted [with cyclic existence] if you reflect on what the *Alleviating Sorrow (Śoka-vinodana)* says:[487]

Again and again in hells
You drank boiling liquid copper—
So much that even the water in the ocean
Does not compare. **[223]**

The filth you have eaten
As a dog and as a pig
Would make a pile far more vast
Than Meru, the king of mountains.

On account of losing loved ones and friends
You have shed so many tears
In the realms of cyclic existence
That the ocean could not contain them.

The heads that have been severed
From fighting one another,
If piled up, would
Reach beyond Brahmā's heaven.

You have been a worm
And, having been ravenous, you ate so much sludge
That if it were poured into the great ocean
It would fill it completely.

Thus, the *Array of Stalks Sūtra* states:[488]

Remember the infinite bodies which, in the past,
You wasted senselessly on account of desire;
Now in this life truly seek enlightenment;
Take up disciplined conduct and thereby destroy desire.

Remember the infinite bodies which, in the past,
You wasted senselessly on account of desire.
As many times as there are grains of sand in the Ganges
You failed to please the buddhas and ignored their teachings
such as this.

Even if you gained the vast wonders of cyclic existence, they would be illusory. Bear in mind the countless bodies you have wasted in the past, experiencing limitless and pointless suffering. Consider that it will continue this way unless you make an effort to put an end to it. Develop a sense of disenchantment. Jen-nga-wa said:

> Honorable teachers, how many bodies have you taken from beginningless time? Now, since you never practiced Mahāyāna teachings, you must apply yourselves assiduously.

Sang-pu-wa (gSang-phu-ba) said:

> In this cyclic existence there are many turns of fortune for better and for worse; do not stake your hopes on them.

Reflect until you give rise to this kind of thinking; after you have developed it, you must continually sustain it in meditation.

(iii) **The fault of casting off bodies repeatedly**

The *Friendly Letter*:[489]

Each of us has left a pile of bones
That would dwarf Mount Meru. **[224]**

For each living being, if the bones discarded upon taking up new bodies did not disappear, they would tower over even Mount Meru.

(iv) **The fault of repeated rebirth**

The *Friendly Letter*:[490]

If you looked for the limit of mothers by counting with earthen
pellets
The size of juniper berries, the earth would not suffice.

Earlier scholars took this to mean that each pellet represents a living being who has been your mother, but this is incorrect. The *Clear Words: Explanation of the "Friendly Letter"*[491] cites a sūtra which indicates that it refers to the line of matrilineal predecessors, from one's own mother to her mother, and so forth:

> For example, O monks, if someone took from this vast earth pellets the size of juniper berries and set them aside, saying, "This is my mother, and this is my mother's mother," then, monks, the clay of this vast earth would be exhausted, yet the line of matrilineal predecessors would not.

Again, the reading of those former scholars is wrong because Nāgārjuna's text says "the limit of mothers."

You should understand how this causes you to be disenchanted as follows. The *Four Hundred Stanzas* says:[492]

> You cannot see the initial cause
> Of even a single effect;
> Seeing how vast the causes of even one effect are,
> Who would not be frightened?

Candrakīrti's commentary on this says:[493]

> It is right to cultivate a constant sense of disenchantment, and a corresponding mode of conduct, in the face of this vast wilderness—cyclic existence—where movement is difficult on account of the dense forest of ignorance whose reaches cannot be measured.

(v) **The fault of repeatedly descending from high to low**

The *Friendly Letter*:[494]

> Having become Indra, worthy of the world's honor, you will still fall
> Once again to the earth because of the force of past karma.
> Even having become a universal monarch,
> You will once again become a slave for other beings in cyclic existence.
>
> Though you have long experienced the pleasures
> Of caressing the breasts and waists of divine women,
> You will once again encounter the unbearable sensations **[225]**
> Of the grinding, cutting, and flesh-tearing hell-devices.
>
> Having dwelled long on the peak of Mount Meru,
> Enjoying the pleasant touch of soft ground on your feet,
> Imagine undergoing the unbearable pain
> Of walking once again over hot coals and rotting corpses in hell.
>
> Having frolicked in beautiful groves
> And enjoyed the embraces of divine women,

> You will arrive once again in the forests of hell, where the
> leaves
> Are swords that slice off ears, nose, hands, and legs.
>
> Though you have entered the Gently Flowing River
> With beautiful goddesses and golden lotuses,
> You will plunge once more in hell into scalding water—
> The unbearable waters of the Impassable River.
>
> Having gained the great pleasures of a deity
> In the realm of desire, or the detached happiness of Brahmā,[495]
> You will once again become fuel for the fires
> Of the Unrelenting Hell, suffering pain without respite.
>
> Having been a deity of the sun or the moon,
> Illuminating all the world with the light of your body,
> You will return once more to dense, black darkness,
> Where you cannot see even your own outstretched hand.

The three devices for grinding, cutting, and tearing flesh are those of the Crushing, Black Line, and Extremely Hot Hells, respectively. To be attended by divine women means to be served by goddesses. The "pleasures of deities in the desire realm" refers to the deities in the desire realm from the Heaven of the Thirty-three and above. Here, the light of the sun and the moon is described in terms that are familiar to ordinary people, without distinguishing between the support—the palace of the deity—and what is supported—the deity; if you do distinguish them, then the light is the light of the palaces of the sun and moon.

Considering all the ways that you can fall from high to low places—as illustrated by these examples—you should be disenchanted with cyclic existence, because all of its wonders will collapse in the end. As the *Bases of Discipline* states:[496]

> The end of accumulated things is depletion.
> The end of things that are high is a fall. **[226]**
> The end of meetings is separation.
> The end of life is death.

(vi) **The fault of having no companions**

The *Friendly Letter*:[497]

> In this way, you will come to grief.
> Therefore take light from the lamp of the three types of merit;
> Otherwise, you will go alone into endless darkness
> That neither sun nor moon can penetrate.

"You will come to grief" means "Know that you must die as I have indicated before, and take the light of merit." "The three types of merit" refers either to physical, verbal, and mental virtue, or to the three foundations from which merit arises—generosity and so on. "Endless darkness" refers to the darkness of ignorance.

In regard to having no companions, *Engaging in the Bodhisattva Deeds* says:[498]

> This body comes forth whole, yet
> The bones and flesh that accompany it
> Will break apart and disperse. As this is so,
> Why mention others, such as loved ones?
>
> You are born alone.
> Also you die alone.
> As others cannot share your suffering,
> Of what use is the hindrance of loved ones?

Thus, these six faults comprise three types:

1) In cyclic existence, there is no secure basis that you can count on.
2) However much you may indulge in its pleasures, they will not bring satisfaction in the end.
3) You have been caught in cyclic existence from beginningless time.

The first of these has four parts:

1) There is no security in obtaining a body, for you discard bodies repeatedly.
2) There is no security in agents of help or harm, for they are not certain.
3) There is no security in attaining a wonderful condition, for what is high becomes low.
4) There is no security in companions, for at death you go without companions.

The third of these four refers to being reborn again and again; there is no limit to the stream of rebirths. Reflect on suffering under this threefold arrangement as well.

19

Further Meditations on Suffering

(c) **Meditation on the three types of suffering**[499]

(i) **The suffering of change [227]**

Pleasant feelings experienced by beings in cyclic existence are like the pleasure felt when cool water is applied to an inflamed boil or carbuncle: as the temporary feeling fades, the pain reasserts itself. This is called *the suffering of change* and includes not only the feeling itself, but also the main mind and other mental processes that are similar to it,[500] as well as the contaminated objects which, when perceived, give rise to that feeling.

(ii) **The suffering of pain**

When a painfully inflamed boil makes contact with an irritant such as salt water, it is agonizing. This is how you recognize the feeling of pain. Painful feelings like this constitute *the suffering of pain*, because as soon as they arise the body and the mind are tormented, as in the case of kidney pain. Also, as explained above, the suffering of pain is not just the feeling.

(iii) **The suffering of conditionality**

Contaminated neutral feelings are like an inflamed boil which is in contact with neither soothing nor irritating substances. Because these feelings coexist with dysfunctional tendencies, they constitute the *suffering of conditionality*, which, as explained above, does not refer to the feelings alone. Insofar as the suffering of conditionality is affected by previous karma, as well as the afflictions, and coexists with seeds that will produce future suffering and affliction, it coexists with persistent dysfunctional tendencies.

Thus, attachment increases when a pleasant feeling arises, and hostility increases when pain arises. Ignorance increases when you misapprehend the body—which is part of a dysfunctional situation that is neither pleasant nor painful—as permanent, when it is in fact impermanent. Attachment gives rise to suffering such as future rebirth in the five realms [the realms of the hell-beings, hungry ghosts, animals, humans, and deities]; hostility brings about suffering such as sorrow in this life, as well as the future suffering of miserable realms; while ignorance acts in such a way as to maintain in existence the sufferings produced by the other two [attachment and hostility]. Therefore, attachment ceases when you see pleasant feelings as suffering. **[228]** In the case of painful feelings, hostility ceases when you consider that since these aggregates [of body and mind] are a collection of causes for suffering, painful feelings arise from them just as physical affliction does. In the case of neutral feelings, ignorance ceases when you see that they are impermanent, exhaustible, and perishable in nature. In this way, you prevent the three feelings from giving rise to the three mental poisons. I have explained these points in accordance with *Compendium of Determinations* and the *Levels of Yogic Deeds*.

In the same way that someone bearing a heavy burden cannot be happy so long as the burden must be borne, you too will suffer so long as you carry the burden of the appropriated aggregates. Though you have occasional moments when painful feeling is absent, because the aggregates are firmly embedded in the dysfunctional tendencies of suffering and the afflictions, the suffering of conditionality is still present, and therefore myriad sufferings are just on the verge of arising in countless ways. Therefore, since the suffering of conditionality pervades all suffering and is the root of the other two types of suffering, meditate on it often in order to become disenchanted with it.

Moreover, your current pleasant feelings—which cause attachment to grow—mostly arise only upon the relief of suffering; pleasure does not exist naturally, independently of the removal of suffering. For example, if you suffer because of too much walking, a pleasant state of mind arises when you sit down. Then, as the earlier intense suffering fades, pleasure appears to arise gradually. Yet sitting is not naturally pleasant, because if you sit too long, suffering arises again, just as before. Suppose that sitting and other postures were causes of pleasure by their very nature. Just as suffering increases in proportion to your involvement with causes of suffering, so should pleasure increase the longer you walk, sit, lie down, drink or eat, or stand in the sun or shade. However, it is clear that if you do any of these for too long, suffering is all that results. **[229]** For, as the *Descent into the Womb Sūtra* says in the same vein:[501]

> Nanda, the physical activities of walking, sitting, standing, or lying down must each be understood as suffering. If meditators analyze the nature of these physical activities, they will see that if they spend the day walking and do not rest, sit down, or lie down, they will experience walking exclusively as suffering and will experience intense, sharp, unbearable and unpleasant feelings. The notion that walking is pleasant will not arise.

After discussing the other three physical activities in the same way, the text continues:

> Nevertheless, Nanda, because they break the continuity of suffering in one or the other of the physical activities, some other, new suffering arises; and this they take to be pleasure. Nanda, when this contaminated feeling of pleasure arises, it is only suffering that is arising; when it ends, it is only this nature of suffering that ends. When it arises yet again, it is only compositional activity that arises; when it ends, it is only compositional activity that ends.

Also, as Āryadeva's *Four Hundred Stanzas* says:[502]

Pleasure, when it increases,
Is seen to change into pain;
Pain, when it increases,
Does not likewise change into pleasure.

2″ **Reflection on specific sufferings**

Of the six kinds of specific sufferings, I have already explained above the sufferings of the three miserable realms.

(a) **The suffering of human beings**

From what has been explained above, you should understand that the suffering of human beings consists of the pain of hunger and thirst, unpleasant sensations of heat and cold, and the suffering of searching for sustenance[503] and becoming fatigued. It is also birth, old age, illness, death, and so on—the seven that I have already explained before.[504] Furthermore, you should understand human suffering according to the following two citations. Vasubandhu's *Discussion of the Requisite Collections* (*Sambhāra-parikathā*) says:[505]

It is apparent that humans also have
All the sufferings of the miserable realms—
Tormented by pain, they are like hell-beings;
Deprived, they are like those in the Lord of Death's world [the hungry ghosts].

Humans also have the suffering of animals **[230]**
In that the powerful use force
To hurt and oppress the weak—
These sufferings are just like a river.

Some suffer from poverty;
For others, suffering arises from discontent.
The suffering of yearning is unbearable.
All of them quarrel and can be killed.

The *Four Hundred Stanzas*:[506]

For the privileged, pain is mental;
For common people, it is physical.
Day after day both types of pain
Afflict this world.

(b) **The suffering of the demigods**

The *Friendly Letter*:[507]

Also, the demigods, by their very nature, experience great mental suffering

> Because of their hatred of the splendor of the deities.
> Though they are intelligent, they do not see the truth
> Because of the mental obscurations characteristic of this realm of rebirth.

In other words, they are tortured by their unbearable envy of the deities' wealth. Because of this, they fight with the deities and endure many sufferings, such as having their bodies cut and split apart. They are intelligent, but they have mental obscurations, fruitions of past karma, which make it impossible for them to see the truth from within their situation. The *Mindfulness of the Excellent Teaching* states that they are animals, but the *Levels of Yogic Deeds* places them in the realm of the deities.

(c) **Reflection on the suffering of the deities**

This is explained with regard to (1) the deities of the desire realm and (2) the deities of the form and formless realms.

(i) **The deities of the desire realm**

The sufferings of the desire realm deities are considered in three parts:

1. The sufferings of dying and falling
2. The sufferings of anxiety
3. The sufferings of being cut, gashed, killed, and banished

(a′) **The sufferings of dying and falling**

(1′) **The suffering of dying**

The *Friendly Letter*:[508]

> Although the deities have great pleasure in heaven,
> The suffering of dying there is even greater than that.
> The wise who understand this cease to create
> Attachments for the perishable heavens. **[231]**

Deities derive pleasure from indulging their sensual desires, yet greater than this is the tremendous suffering they experience while dying, when they become aware of the five signs of death, about which the same text says:[509]

> Their bodies turn an unattractive color,
> Their cushions become uncomfortable,
> Their flower garlands wilt, and their clothing smells;
> An unaccustomed sweat breaks out over their bodies.
>
> The five signs that signal the deities in heaven,
> Foretelling their death and departure therefrom,

Are similar to the signs
That foretell death for humans on earth.

(2′) **The suffering of falling to lower realms**

The *Friendly Letter:*[510]

They must take leave of the divine worlds.
If their merit has run out,
Then, powerless, they will become
Animals, hungry ghosts, or denizens of hell.

(b′) **The suffering of anxiety**

Deities with vast stores of merit gain the most desirable objects. Upon seeing them, deities of lesser merit become anxious and experience great anguish and pain on this account.

(c′) **The sufferings of being cut, gashed, killed, and banished**

When deities fight with demigods, they undergo the pain of having their limbs and minor extremities cut off, having their bodies split apart, and being killed. When their heads are cut off, they die, but their other limbs regenerate after being cut off or gashed, and they survive. As regards banishment, when there is a battle, the more powerful deities expel the weaker deities from their homes. Moreover, as Vasubandhu's *Discussion of the Requisite Collections* says:[511]

Deities who indulge in sensual pleasures
Are not happy in mind—
They are burned by an inner fire
Sparked by the infection of sensual desire.

How can there be happiness
For those whose minds are distracted?
Since their minds are not under control **[232]**
And undistracted even for a moment,

They are by nature disturbed and agitated.
They will never be calm—
Like a fire that has wood for fuel
And that rages, whipped by the wind.

And also:

They are like invalids, not long recovered
From an illness, who eat improperly and get sick again.

(ii) **The deities of the form and formless realms**

The deities of the highest realms—the form and the formless—though they escape these sufferings, nevertheless die in possession of afflictions and obscurations. Because they have no control over their future dwelling place, even they suffer on account of dysfunctional tendencies. Moreover, as the *Discussion of the Requisite Collections* says:[512]

> Those in the form or formless realms
> Are beyond the suffering of pain and the suffering of change.
> By nature they have the bliss of meditative concentration;
> They remain motionless for an eon.
>
> But even this is most assuredly not liberation;
> After they have counted on it, they will again fall.
> Though it may seem as though they have transcended
> The turbulence of the miserable realms,
>
> Yet, like birds soaring in the sky,
> They cannot stay forever, though they try—
> Like an arrow shot with the strength of a child,
> They will fall back down in the end.
>
> Just as butter lamps that burn for a long time
> Are in fact perishing in every moment,
> They are afflicted by the changes of
> The suffering of conditionality.

Reflect in this way on the general and specific sufferings of the five or six types of beings. Then, when you have become disgusted with cyclic existence, you will wonder about its causes. What causes cyclic existence?

20

THE ORIGIN OF SUFFERING

2′ Reflection on the process of cyclic existence in terms of its origin
- a″ How the afflictions arise
  - 1″ Identifying the afflictions
  - 2″ The order in which the afflictions arise
  - 3″ The causes of the afflictions
  - 4″ The faults of the afflictions
- b″ How you thereby accumulate karma
  - 1″ Identifying the karma that you accumulate
    - (a) Karma that is intention
    - (b) Karma that is the intended action
  - 2″ How you accumulate karma
    - (a) Accumulating karma for pleasant feelings
      - (i) Accumulating karma for the pleasure that comes from enjoying desirable objects—sights, sounds, and the like
      - (ii) Accumulating karma for gaining bliss in meditative concentration, after you have rejected attachment to external sensual pleasures
    - (b) Accumulating karma for neutral feelings
- c″ How you die and are reborn
  - 1″ Causes of death
  - 2″ The mind at death
    - (a) Dying with a virtuous mind
    - (b) Dying with a nonvirtuous mind
    - (c) Dying with an ethically neutral mind
  - 3″ Where heat gathers
  - 4″ How you reach the intermediate state after death
  - 5″ How you then take rebirth

2′ Reflection on the process of cyclic existence in terms of its origin

The origin of cyclic existence is explained in three parts:

1. How the afflictions arise
2. How you thereby accumulate karma
3. How you die and are reborn

a″ How the afflictions arise

Karma and the afflictions are both necessary as causes for the creation of cyclic existence, but the afflictions are primary. **[233]** For, just as a seed without moisture, soil, etc. will not produce a sprout, so in the absence of afflictions—even though you have accumulated immeasurable karma in the past—there will be no sprout of suffering because the karma lacks the necessary cooperating conditions. A further reason afflictions are primary is because—even without previously accumulated karma—if afflictions are present, you immediately accumulate new karma, and will thereby appropriate aggregates in the future. Similarly, Dharmakīrti's *Commentary on the "Compendium of Valid Cognition"* says:[513]

> The karma of one who has transcended craving for existence
> Lacks the potency to project another birth
> Because its cooperating conditions are gone.

and also:

> Because the aggregates will arise again, if you have craving.

Consequently, it is very important to rely on a remedy for the afflictions. Moreover, since this requires understanding the afflictions, you should become knowledgeable about the afflictions. There are four parts to this:

1. Identifying the afflictions
2. The order in which they arise
3. The causes of the afflictions
4. The faults of the afflictions

1″ Identifying the afflictions

Asaṅga's *Compendium of Knowledge* gives a general definition of an affliction:[514]

> An affliction is defined as a phenomenon that, when it arises, is disturbing in character and that, through arising, disturbs the mind-stream.

Thus, when it is produced, it disturbs the mind-stream.

The specific definitions of the ten afflictions are as follows:

1) *Attachment* means noticing a pleasant or attractive external or internal object and desiring it. When attachment clings to its object and grows stronger, it is hard to tear yourself away from the object, just as it is difficult to remove oil which has soaked into a cloth.

2) *Hostility* means observing origins of suffering—such as living beings, pain, weapons, or thorns—and giving rise to a harsh, tormented mind that contemplates harming these objects. **[234]**

3) *Pride* means observing—either internally or externally—qualities that are high, low, good, or bad, and, based on the reifying view of the perishing aggregates, allowing your mind to become inflated; you assume an aspect of superiority.

4) *Ignorance* means possessing the affliction of misunderstanding on account of a mind that is unclear about the nature of the four truths, karma and its effects, and the three jewels.

5) *Doubt* means considering those three—the four truths, karma and its effects, and the three jewels—and being uncertain whether they exist or are real.

6) *The reifying view of the perishing aggregates* is an afflictive intelligence that observes the appropriated aggregates and regards them as "I" or "mine," that is, as the self or that which belongs to the self. Here, since "perishing" means impermanent and "aggregates" is plural,[515] the terms indicate that what are apprehended are simply impermanent and multiple phenomena; there is no permanent and unitary person. This is why it is called "the view of the perishing aggregates."

7) *An extremist view* is an afflictive intelligence that observes the self as apprehended by the view of the perishing aggregates and regards that self either as permanent and eternal, or as subject to annihilation in such a way that there will be no rebirth from this life into a future life.

8) *A belief in the supremacy of wrong views* is an afflictive intelligence that observes one of the three views—the view of the perishing aggregates, an extremist view, and a wrong view—along with a view-holder's aggregates on the basis of which such a view occurs, and regards such a view as supreme.

9) *A belief in the supremacy of ethics and religious discipline* is an afflictive intelligence which observes an ethical discipline that renounces faulty ethical discipline, or a religious discipline which requires certain forms of dress, manner, speech, and physical behavior, as well as the mental and physical aggregates

on the basis of which these forms of ethics and asceticism occur, and regards them as cleansing you of sin, freeing you from afflictions, and removing you from cyclic existence.

10) *Wrong view* is an afflictive intelligence that denies the existence of things such as past and future lives or karma and its effects, or that believes that the cause of living beings is a divine creator or a primal essence, etc.[516]

I have explained these ten afflictions in accordance with the *Compendium of Knowledge* and *Levels of Yogic Deeds* and with Vasubandhu's *Explanation of the Five Aggregates (Pañca-skandha-prakaraṇa)*.[517] **[235]**

2″ The order in which the afflictions arise

One way to look at this is to consider ignorance as distinct from the view of the perishing aggregates. For example, when twilight falls on a coiled rope, its status as a rope will be unclear and someone may imagine that it is a snake. Similarly, according to this view, the misapprehension of the aggregates as a self arises due to the darkness of ignorance, which prevents clarity about how the aggregates exist. The other afflictions then develop from this misapprehension. On the other hand, if you hold that ignorance and the view of the perishing aggregates are identical, then the view of the perishing aggregates is itself the root of the afflictions.

When the view of the perishing aggregates apprehends a self, discrimination arises between self and other. Once you have made that distinction, you become attached to what is associated with yourself and hostile toward that which pertains to others. As you observe the self, your mind also becomes inflated. You develop a belief that this very self is either eternal or subject to annihilation. You come to believe in the supremacy of a view of the self and the like, and you also come to believe in the supremacy of the detrimental practices associated with such views. Similarly, you develop the wrong view that denies the existence of things such as the Teacher who taught selflessness and that which he taught—karma and its effects, the four truths, the three jewels, and so forth; or else you become doubtful as to whether such things exist or are real. Dharmakīrti's *Commentary on the "Compendium of Valid Cognition"*:[518]

> Once there is a self, there is an idea of an other.
> On behalf of self and other, there is attachment and hostility.
> All of the faults come about
> In association with these.

3″ The causes of the afflictions

These are sixfold as presented in the *Bodhisattva Levels:*

1) *Basis* refers to the latent proclivity for afflictions.

2) *Object* refers to the appearance of objects conducive to the arising of an affliction.

3) *Social context* refers to the influence of bad friends and foolish people.

4) *Explanation* refers to listening to wrong teachings.

5) *Habituation* refers to the process of becoming accustomed to past afflictions.

6) *Attention* refers to incorrect attention that projects "pleasantness" onto what has an unpleasant character, conceives an impermanent thing to be permanent, and the like [the four erroneous conceptions that mistakenly consider things that are actually impermanent, painful, impure and lacking a self to be permanent, pleasant, pure and possessed of a self]. **[236]**

4″ The faults of the afflictions

When an affliction arises, at first it completely afflicts your mind, causing you to err with regard to what you are observing, reinforcing your latent proclivities, and causing the same sort of affliction to recur. It may harm you, others, or both; it leads to misdeeds in this life, in future lives, or in both. It creates experiences of pain and anguish, as well as the sufferings of birth, and the like. It takes you far from nirvāṇa, your virtue is destroyed and your resources are depleted. In society you feel apprehensive, joyless, and devoid of confidence, while your notoriety spreads in all directions, and excellent persons such as teachers and protectors rebuke you. You die with regret, your aims unfulfilled, and after death you are reborn into a miserable realm.

Furthermore, as the *Ornament for the Mahāyāna Sūtras* says:[519]

> Through afflictions, you destroy yourself, destroy other beings,
> and destroy your ethical discipline.
> After you have ruined your joy, you are shunned; your protectors and teachers rebuke you.
> Disreputable, you will be reborn in a leisureless condition.
> You suffer great anguish in losing the virtue you had or have
> yet to attain.

Further, you should be aware of the faults as described in *Engaging in the Bodhisattva Deeds:*[520]

> Enemies such as hatred and craving
> Have neither feet nor hands,
> And are neither brave nor intelligent.
> How, then, have they enslaved me?
>
> While they dwell within my mind,
> They are pleased to do me harm.
> They are not to be endured without anger—
> Tolerance of them is ridiculous!
>
> Even if all the deities and demigods
> Should rise up as my enemies,
> They cannot lead me or force me
> Into the fires of the Unrelenting Hell.
>
> But this powerful enemy, the afflictions, **[237]**
> Casts me in an instant into fires
> So hot that if they met even Mount Meru
> Not even ashes would remain.
>
> The enemy that is my afflictions
> Has lasted a long time, without beginning or end.
> No other enemy has the power
> To last for such a long time.
>
> Given appropriate service and attention
> Everyone helps you and makes you happy,
> But if you serve your afflictions
> They only inflict further suffering.

You must have an understanding that accords with what Gön-ba-wa said:

> To eliminate afflictions, you must know the afflictions' faults, their characteristics, their remedies, and the causes for their arising. After you have recognized their faults, regard them as defective and consider them enemies. If you do not recognize their faults, you will not understand that they are enemies. Therefore, it is said that you should reflect on this, following what is said in the *Ornament for the Mahāyāna Sūtras* and *Engaging in the Bodhisattva Deeds.*

And also:

> Study Vasubandhu and Asaṅga's texts on knowledge as well in order to understand the characteristics of the afflictions. At the least, study Vasubandhu's *Explanation of the Five Aggregates*. Once you know the root and secondary afflictions, then when any attachment, hostility, or such arises in your mind-stream, you can

identify it—thinking, "This is that; now it has arisen"—and fight the affliction.

b″ **How you thereby accumulate karma**

1. Identifying the karma that you accumulate
2. How you accumulate karma

1″ **Identifying the karma that you accumulate**

(a) **Karma that is intention**

The *Compendium of Knowledge:*[521]

> What is intention? It is mental karma that involves the mind; it acts to engage the mind in virtuous, nonvirtuous, and ethically neutral activities.

Thus, intention is mental karma, a mental process that moves and urges the mind with which it is associated toward objects.

(b) **Karma that is the intended action**

This is the physical and verbal action motivated by intention. **[238]** The *Treasury of Knowledge:*[522]

> Karma is both intention and what intention produces.
> Intention is mental karma;
> What it produces are physical and verbal karma.

The Vaibhāṣikas divide physical and verbal karma into two types, the perceptible and the imperceptible, and hold that both types always have form. Vasubandhu refutes this, asserting that physical and verbal karma are intentions that work along with perceptible physical and verbal behavior; thus, both forms of karma [intention and intended] are actually intentions.[523]

In general, karma is of three types: virtuous, nonvirtuous and ethically neutral, but here we are concerned only with the first two. Virtuous karma is of two types, contaminated and uncontaminated. I will only discuss contaminated virtuous karma, of which there are two types: that present in a noble being's mind and that present in an ordinary person's mind. Only the latter need concern us here.

Nonvirtuous karma is karma that is nonmeritorious. Meritorious karma is virtuous karma in the minds of beings of the desire realm. Invariable karma is contaminated virtuous karma in the minds of beings of the form or formless realms. Similarly, the *Treasury of Knowledge* says:[524]

> Merit is the virtuous karma of the desire realm.
> Invariable karma produces the higher [deities'] realms.

Why is it called invariable karma? In the desire realm, karma that should bear fruit while you are a deity may instead bear fruit while you are a human, an animal, or a hungry ghost; thus, its effect is variable. In the higher [deities'] realms, karma that should bear fruit at a certain level does not mature at levels other than that; thus, it is invariable. Thus, the *Treasury of Knowledge*:[525]

> Why? Because the fruition of karma
> On these levels is not variable.

2″ **How you accumulate karma**

In general, noble beings create and accumulate only virtuous karma, yet stream-enterers and once-returners [noble beings on lower levels] may accumulate nonvirtuous karma. However, such noble beings do not accumulate karma that would impel them into a cyclic existence of either happy or miserable realms. For, as Nāgārjuna's *Fundamental Treatise on the Middle Way (Mūla-madhyamaka-kārikā*) says:[526] **[239]**

> As the root of cyclic existence is compositional activity,
> The wise do not create activity that impels rebirth.
> Unwise are those who do.
> The wise do not because they see reality.

Also, the master Vasubandhu says:[527]

> When you have seen the truth, you are not impelled to rebirth.

Consequently, as long as you operate under the influence of the conception of a self, you will accumulate karma that will impel you into cyclic rebirth. Once you have perceived reality—that is, selflessness—you may still be reborn in cyclic existence by the power of former karma and afflictions, but you will not accumulate any new karma that can impel such rebirth. As Asaṅga's *Levels of Yogic Deeds* states, stream-enterers and once-returners do not assent to the conception of a self, but rather reject it—in the same way the strong overpower the weak. Hence every ordinary person—from the highest level of the supreme stage of the Mahāyāna path of preparation on down—accumulates karma that impels rebirth in cyclic existence. Accordingly, when those who are under the influence of afflicted ignorance and the view of the perishing aggregates become physically, verbally, or mentally involved in nonvirtue—

killing, for example—they accumulate nonmeritorious karma. Those who perform virtuous acts within the desire realm—such as practicing generosity or maintaining ethical discipline—accumulate meritorious karma. Those who cultivate meditative states—such as meditative serenity—at the level of the meditative stabilizations of the form realm or the formless absorptions accumulate invariable karma.

Qualm: Consider someone who has seen the faults of all worldly wonders and is motivated by an aspiration for liberation. Does not this person create much virtuous karma? Moreover, consider the virtuous karma that is an intention similar to a wisdom consciousness accurately analyzing the meaning of selflessness. Is this a true origin, a cause of cyclic existence?

Reply: In general, those who are on the paths of accumulation and preparation do accumulate ordinary karma that impels rebirth. **[240]** However, motivations based on thoughts such as those you describe, as well as virtuous karma similar to the wisdom that analyzes selflessness, constitute the group of remedies for the craving for future existence. Further, in both their objective and subjective aspects, they operate in a manner contrary to the conception of self, the root of cyclic existence. Thus, they are not actual or usual true origins that impel rebirth. However, because they approximate actual true origins leading to a future rebirth, they are included among true origins. Similarly, the *Compendium of Determinations* says:[528]

> *Question:* Why are those mundane phenomena which eradicate the craving for rebirth, and which produce the supramundane path that is not directed toward rebirth, included under the truth of the origin?
>
> *Reply:* By nature, they are not directed toward rebirth in cyclic existence. However, they approximate the physical, mental, and verbal good conduct which leads to rebirth. Consequently, you should understand that on this account they are included under the truth of the origin.

Asaṅga says that after careful reflection on the faults of cyclic existence, you give rise to a sense of disgust that can motivate virtuous karma which generates a supramundane path; yet this karma approximates an origin of suffering in cyclic existence. Therefore you must strive to develop this sense of disgust, as well as the wisdom that knows selflessness.

This being the case, you might not have acquired, through extensive meditative analysis of the faults of cyclic existence, the remedy that eradicates the craving for the wonders of cyclic existence. Also you might not have used discerning wisdom to properly analyze the meaning of selflessness, and might not have become familiar with the two spirits of enlightenment [conventional and ultimate]. Under such circumstances, your virtuous activities—with some exceptions on account of the field's power—would constitute typical origins of suffering, and hence would fuel the process of cyclic existence.

How you accumulate karma is explained in two parts:

1. Accumulating karma for pleasant feelings
2. Accumulating karma for neutral feelings

(a) **Accumulating karma for pleasant feelings**

(i) **Accumulating karma for the pleasure that comes from enjoying desirable objects—sights, sounds, and the like [241]**

This has two subtypes: if your concern is mainly for the pleasures of this lifetime, prior to death, then you accumulate nonmeritorious action; if your concern is primarily for the sensual pleasures of future lives, you accumulate meritorious action.

(ii) **Accumulating karma for gaining bliss in meditative concentration, after you have rejected attachment to external sensual pleasures**

If you focus on a meditative object primarily for the sake of the blissful feelings that arise from concentration, you will accumulate invariable karma leading to rebirth at the level of the first, second, or third meditative stabilizations in the form realm.

(b) **Accumulating karma for neutral feelings**

You might have stopped attachment to sensual pleasure, become weary even of meditative bliss, and created karma to have neutral feelings. If so, you will accumulate invariable karma leading to rebirth in the fourth meditative stabilization of the form realm or in a higher level, up to and including the peak of cyclic existence [the highest level of the formless realm].

This schema of subdivisions is what Vasubandhu intended to convey in the *Treasury of Knowledge*. By his reasoning, when you stop clinging to all of cyclic existence, and then engage in physical, verbal, and mental virtue for the sake of liberation, you leave cyclic existence further behind and come closer to liberation.

c″ **How you die and are reborn**

This is explained in five parts:

1. Causes of death
2. The mind at death
3. Where heat gathers
4. How you reach the intermediate state after death
5. How you then take rebirth

1″ **Causes of death**

Death from the exhaustion of your life span means dying after you have used up all of the life span that was projected by your previous karma; as the time has come, you die. Death from exhaustion of your merit means, for example, dying deprived of the necessities of life. There is also death from failure to avoid danger, in regard to which the sūtras list nine causes and conditions for premature death: **[242]** overeating, eating something indigestible, eating without having digested the previous meal, failing to expel undigested food that has accumulated in the stomach, intestinal obstruction, not relying on specific medicines for specific illnesses, failing to understand the distinction between accustomed and unaccustomed activities, untimely death [i.e., accidental death], and engaging in sexual intercourse.

2″ **The mind at death**

(a) **Dying with a virtuous mind**

Those who die with virtuous minds, whether through remembering on their own or through being reminded by others, turn their minds to virtues, such as faith, for as long as coarse discrimination [ordinary types of consciousness] remains. In the case of death for those who have cultivated either virtue or nonvirtue unequally, they either remember on their own, or are reminded by others, what they have become accustomed to do repeatedly in the past, and this becomes extremely powerful. Their minds then become absorbed in this and forget all else. If they are equally familiar with both virtue and nonvirtue, then they cannot stop remembering what they remember first, and cannot engage their minds in anything else.

Those who have cultivated virtue seem to pass from darkness into light; as they die various pleasant and attractive images appear, as though in a dream. They die comfortably, and, at the point of death, intense feelings of suffering do not arise in their bodies. For those who are currently doing what is right, the final agony of death is minimal.

(b) **Dying with a nonvirtuous mind**

Those who die with nonvirtuous minds, whether through remembering on their own or through being reminded by others, remember nonvirtue, such as attachment, for as long as coarse discrimination remains. At the point of death, they experience intense physical pain. When those who are currently cultivating nonvirtue die, they experience signs foretelling the effects of the nonvirtue they have engaged in. As if in a nightmare, many unpleasant images appear to them. They seem to pass from light to darkness. **[243]** When those who have committed serious nonvirtuous actions observe these unpleasant signs, they experience physical pain and their hair stands on end. They shake their hands and feet, void urine and excrement, reach up toward the sky, roll their eyes back, drool, and more. If they have been moderate in their nonvirtue, then not all of these things will happen—some will and some will not. Wrongdoers suffer terrible agony at the moment of death; such agony is found everywhere that beings are born, except among deities and hell-beings.

At the time of death, whereupon discrimination will become unclear, beings are attached to the self with which they have long been familiar. After that, through the influence of attachment to the self, they think, "I am ceasing to exist," and they crave embodiment. This causes the intermediate state. Attachment to the self also occurs among stream-enterers and once-returners, but as they investigate it with wisdom they reject it rather than assent to it, the way a powerful person dominates a weak person. Attachment to self does not occur among nonreturners.

(c) **Dying with an ethically neutral mind**

Those who are currently cultivating neither virtue nor nonvirtue, or who have done neither, do not remember virtue and nonvirtue, either on their own or at the urging of others. At death they have neither pain nor pleasure.

When you die with a virtuous mind, it lasts as long as there is coarse discrimination, but once subtle discrimination is activated, the virtuous mind stops and becomes an ethically neutral mind. At this point you cannot retrieve the virtue with which you had become familiar, nor can others remind you. As the same holds true for nonvirtuous minds, all minds of death are ethically neutral after the onset of subtle discrimination. **[244]** Vasubandhu's *Treasury of Knowledge Auto-commentary*[529] says that both virtuous minds and nonvirtuous minds are clear, and thus incompatible with the cessation of coarse consciousness at death.

3″ **Where heat gathers**

Among those who are currently cultivating nonvirtue, consciousness leaves the body coming down from the upper parts, which become cold first. When it reaches the heart, it leaves the body. The consciousness of someone who is currently cultivating virtue leaves coming up from the lower parts and the body becomes cold from the lower parts. In both cases consciousness leaves from the heart. The point at which consciousness first enters the fertilized ovum becomes the body's heart; consciousness finally leaves the body from where it first entered.

Given that, at first the heat of the body either descends from the upper parts and gathers in the heart or ascends from the lower parts and gathers in the heart. After that, though Vasubandhu and Asaṅga do not say so, you should understand that in both cases the remaining heat in the body gathers into the heart from the other end of the body.

4″ **How you reach the intermediate state after death**

As the consciousness leaves from that spot, as just explained, you die and reach the intermediate state immediately, just as one arm of a balancing scale tips up when the other arm tips down. As to its causes, the intermediate state is contingent upon (1) having become attached to your body and being filled with delight in your previous worldly activities, and (2) karma—whether virtuous or nonvirtuous. Furthermore, the being of the intermediate state possesses a complete set of sensory faculties—such as eyes—as well as the form of the body it will have in the realm into which it will be reborn. Until it takes rebirth, its vision is unimpeded, like divine vision [a type of superknowledge], and its body as well is unimpeded, as though it had miraculous powers.

The *Treasury of Knowledge:*[530]

> It has the form which it will have in the "prior time,"
> Which is the time prior to death in the next life,
> Beginning with the moment of birth in the next life.
> Others of the same type or those with pure divine vision see it.
> It has miraculous karmic power

> And all sensory faculties; it is unimpeded.
> It does not change; it feeds on odors.

Vasubandhu means that the being of the intermediate state can be seen by beings there who are of its own type and by persons who have used meditation to attain the impeccable divine vision. **[245]** He also claims that once you reach the intermediate state for a certain rebirth, you will not change to the intermediate form of any other rebirth. However, the *Compendium of Knowledge* holds that such changes do occur.

As for the term "prior time," the *Treasury of Knowledge* refers to four states: (1) from death until taking birth is the intermediate state; (2) the first moment of taking birth is the birth state; (3) from the second moment of life up to the last moment of death is the state of the prior time; and (4) the last moment of death is the death state. The state of the prior time is "prior" in relation to the death state in the next rebirth of the being of the intermediate state.

Some claim mistakenly that the being of the intermediate state has the shape of the body from its previous life. There are also those who claim—in view of Asaṅga's explanation of this being's physical shape in its next life—that it is in the image of the body from its former life for three-and-one-half days and in the image of the body it will possess in its next life for three-and-one-half days. In the absence of any accurate sources, such assertions are simply fabrications. The *Levels of Yogic Deeds* says that the being of the intermediate state does not desire its former body since its consciousness does not remain there. Hence the assertion that it becomes disturbed upon seeing its former body is also a fabrication.

The intermediate state appears to those who have cultivated nonvirtue as like a black blanket or the pitch-black darkness of night, while to those who have cultivated virtue it is like a white cloth or a moonlit night. You see beings of the intermediate state who are the same type as yourself, as well as the place where each of you will be reborn. The *Descent into the Womb Sūtra* describes the color differences in the intermediate state:[531]

> For someone who is to be reborn a hell-being, the intermediate state is like a charred log; for one to be reborn an animal it is like smoke; for one to be reborn a hungry ghost, it is like water; for one to be reborn a deity of the desire realm and a human, it is like gold; for one to be reborn a deity of the form realm, it is white.

There is an intermediate state when you are born into the two lower realms [the desire and form realms] from the formless realm, but when you are born into the formless realm from the two lower realms, you attain the aggregates of a formless being immediately upon dying; there is no intermediate state. **[246]** In the classic texts that are reliable sources there is no description of any other special cases where there is no intermediate state. Consequently, with respect to the assertion that there is a direct transition upward [to a heaven] or downward [to a hell], it is wrong to claim that there is no intermediate state.

The *Descent into the Womb Sūtra* says that beings of the intermediate state who are to be reborn as deities ascend; those to be reborn as humans move straight forward; and those to be reborn as wrongdoers move with their heads lowered and their eyes cast downward. It seems that this last part is meant to describe the intermediate states for the three miserable realms. The *Treasury of Knowledge Auto-commentary:*[532]

> The three—humans, hungry ghosts, and animals—each move in their own way.

With regards to life span, if a being of the intermediate state has not found the conditions for rebirth, it may remain for any length of time up to seven days. Once it has found such conditions, its life span is not definitely seven days. If it does not find the conditions for rebirth within seven days, it assumes another body within the intermediate state. It may stay in the intermediate state from one to seven weeks; however, as it certainly will have found the conditions for rebirth within that time, it stays no longer than that. Since the texts that are reliable sources do not describe a longer life span than this, the claim that the being of the intermediate state may stay longer is incorrect.

A being of the intermediate state that is to be reborn as a deity, for instance, may die after seven days and either again reach the intermediate state of a deity or else reach the intermediate state of a human or some other form. This is possible because a change in its karma can transform the seeds for its intermediate state. The same holds for other beings of the intermediate state as well.

5″ How you then take rebirth

If a being of the intermediate state is to be born in a womb, it observes beings of the same type as itself at its future birthplace. It then wishes to gaze at them, play with them, and so forth, and desires to reach this place. It misperceives its father's semen and its mother's blood as its parents lying together—its parents are not actually lying together at this time, yet, as if in an illusion, it sees them lying together—and becomes attached. If it is to be born female, it turns away from the woman and desires the man, wanting to lie with him. If it is to be born male, it turns away from the man and desires the woman, wanting to lie with her. **[247]** In this way, as the *Levels of Yogic Deeds* explains, it does not see its actual parents—it sees them lying together through misperceiving the semen and blood.

Having conceived such a desire, the being of the intermediate state draws closer and closer to the man and woman, eventually arriving at a point where it cannot see any part of their bodies except for their genitals. Angry at this sight, it dies and is reborn.

Moreover, the mother and the father generate desire, which becomes intense for a period, at the end of which a gelatinous semen is emitted. Then drops of semen and blood invariably issue forth from the two of them, mixing within the mother's reproductive tract, then congealing like the skin on the top of boiled milk that has been allowed to cool.

At this point, the intermediate state of the being who is to be reborn ends, and this being's fundamental consciousness enters the congealed mass. The force of this consciousness brings together a developed combination of blood and semen that is conducive to producing the sensory faculties, as well as a mixture of the former congealed blood and semen and subtle traces of the four great elements that are the causes of the five sensory faculties. These traces are something that is other than the congealed blood and semen. Something that has sensory faculties and that is other than what was formerly there arises. After the consciousness has entered, at this point it is called "rebirth." Those who do not accept that a fundamental consciousness exists assert that the mental consciousness takes rebirth.

If the being of the intermediate state has accumulated little merit, it is born into a low class. As it dies and enters the womb, it hears a loud clamor and sees itself entering a marsh, a thick forest, or some other such place. If it is currently cultivating virtue, it is born into an elite class. It hears peaceful and pleasant sounds, and sees itself entering a mansion, palace, or the like. This being then remains in the womb for thirty-eight weeks and there develops all of the limbs and extremities. Four days later, it is born. According to the *Descent into the Womb Sūtra*:[533]

> The fetus is fully developed after nine months or more have passed; at eight months it is almost fully developed. **[248]** At six or seven months it is not fully developed, as its limbs are not complete.

Study the *Descent into the Womb Sūtra* for details on these stages of development.

If the being of the intermediate state does not have a desire to go to a birthplace, it will not migrate there, and having not done so, will not be reborn there. Take, for example, the case of those who have committed and accumulated karma for rebirth in a hell, like those who have no vow against activities such as butchering sheep or poultry or marketing hogs. In these peoples' intermediate state they see, as if in a dream, sheep and such at their future birthplace, and rush there, driven by their delight in their former habits. Then anger is aroused at the forms which attracted them to the birthplace, at which point their intermediate state ends, and they are reborn. Hungry ghosts with goiters, and others who are similar to hell-beings, take rebirth in a like manner.

If the being of the intermediate state is to be reborn as an animal, hungry ghost, human, desire-realm deity, or form-realm deity, it observes at its birthplace delightful beings similar to itself. Then, conceiving a liking and a desire for that place, it migrates there and becomes angry upon seeing the birthplace, at which time its intermediate state ends, and it is reborn.

This is according to the *Levels of Yogic Deeds*. Rebirth in hell for those who are not people like those mentioned above—persons who have no vow, such as poultry butchers and hog sellers—occurs in a similar fashion.

The *Treasury of Knowledge* says:[534]

> You desire smells, places, or other things.

In his commentary on this Vasubandhu explains[535] that if the being of the intermediate state is to be reborn from heat and moisture, it craves smells, while if it is to be reborn spontaneously, it desires a place and is subsequently reborn there. It further explains that if this being is to be reborn in a hot hell, it craves warmth, while if it is to be born in a cold hell, it longs to be cool. Egg-birth is explained similarly to womb-birth. I have followed the *Levels of Yogic Deeds* in explaining how you die and are reborn in unexceptional cases.[536]

21

THE TWELVE FACTORS OF DEPENDENT-ARISING

b′ Reflection from the viewpoint of the twelve dependent-arisings
1′ The division into twelve factors
2′ Abbreviated classification of the factors
3′ The number of lifetimes required to complete all twelve factors
4′ How their significance is summarized

b′ **Reflection from the viewpoint of the twelve dependent-arisings**

The second part of the method for developing the mind intent on liberation is to reflect on the twelve aspects of dependent-arising. This topic has four parts:

1. The division into twelve factors
2. Abbreviated classification of the factors
3. The number of lifetimes required to complete all twelve factors
4. How their significance is summarized

1′ **The division into twelve factors [249]**

The twelve factors of dependent-arising are:

(1) Ignorance

The *Treasury of Knowledge*:[537]

> Ignorance is like animosity and falsehood.

Animosity and falsehood refer neither to the absence of friendship and truth, nor to what is different from these two, but rather to the classes of phenomena that are directly antithetical to and incompatible with friendship and truth. Likewise, ignorance also refers neither to the absence of that cognition which is the remedy for ignorance nor to what is other than this, but to the classes of phenomena that are directly antithetical to and incompatible with cognition.

Regarding this, the great scholar Dharmakīrti asserts that "Here, the remedy—cognition—is the cognition of the real, the meaning of the selflessness of persons. Therefore, its antithesis is the reifying view of the perishing aggregates, the conception of a self in persons." Along with this interpretation, which sees ignorance as a misapprehension of the meaning of reality, there is a second view, held by the scholar Asaṅga and his brother Vasubandhu, who assert that ignorance is merely confusion about the meaning of reality. In brief, they say that ignorance is a mind that does not know its object, but also that it is not a misconception. However, Dharmakīrti on the one hand, and Asaṅga and Vasubandhu on the other, are alike in asserting that the wisdom that knows selflessness is the principal remedy for ignorance.

Asaṅga's *Compendium of Knowledge* states that there are two types of confusion: confusion about karma and its effects, and confusion about the meaning of reality. Through the first you accumulate compositional activities for rebirth in miserable realms; through the second you accumulate the compositional activities for rebirth in happy realms.

(2) Compositional activity

Compositional activity is karma. There are two kinds of karma: nonmeritorious karma, which impels miserable rebirths, and meritorious karma, which impels happy rebirths. The latter is further divided into two types: meritorious karma, which impels happy rebirths into the desire realm, and invariable karma, which impels happy rebirths into the higher [deities'] realms.

(3) Consciousness

In the sūtras the Buddha speaks about the six types of consciousness. **[250]** Nonetheless, here the principal consciousness is the fundamental consciousness, according to those who assert that such a consciousness exists, or the mental consciousness, according to those who do not assert this.

Further, you become entangled in and accumulate nonvirtuous karma through your ignorance of the fact that the suffering of pain arises from nonvirtue. These latent karmic propensities infuse your consciousness. The consciousness of the lifetime in which this happens is "the consciousness of the causal period," while that which enters the birthplace in a miserable realm, in the future and in dependence on the causal period consciousness, is the "consciousness of the effect period."

Likewise, due to the power of your confusion about the reality of selflessness, you perceive happy realms to be happy, not understanding that they are actually miserable. Through such misperceptions, you accumulate meritorious and invariable karma. The consciousness of the lifetime in which you accumulate such karma is the "consciousness of the causal period," while that which, in dependence on this, enters a happy rebirth in either the desire realm or the higher [deities'] realms is "the consciousness of the effect period."

(4) Name-and-form

"Name" is the four [of the five] aggregates that are nonphysical: feeling, discrimination, compositional factors, and consciousness. As for the fifth aggregate, form, if you are reborn in a formless realm, you have no actual form, only the seed of form. Thus, the "form" in the term "name-and-form" applies to any form, such as the fertilized ovum, that is appropriate to any situation other than the formless realm.

(5) Six sources

If you are born from a womb, four sources—the eyes, ears, nose, and tongue—are formed through the further development of "name," [that is, consciousness] and the oblong mass of the fertilized ovum into which consciousness initially enters. The physical and mental sources, however, exist from the time of the fertilized ovum—the time of name-and-form.

If you are born spontaneously, there are no such stages, since your sources form simultaneously with your entering rebirth. However, for those born from eggs or for those born from moisture, the explanation is similar to the explanation of those born from a womb, with the exception of the word "womb." This is explained in the *Levels of Yogic Deeds*.

This being the case, once name-and-form are established, you have an actual body. **[251]** When the six sources are established, the experiencer has been created, because the particulars of the body have formed. The five physical sources do not exist in the formless realm.

(6) Contact

When sensory object, sensory faculty, and consciousness come together, you distinguish three types of objects—attractive, unattractive, and neutral. The passage where a sūtra says "caused by the six sources"[538] refers to sensory objects as well as consciousnesses.

(7) Feeling

Corresponding to contact's discrimination of three types of objects, there occur three sorts of feelings—pleasant, painful, and neutral.

(8) Craving

This means both craving not to be separated from pleasant feelings and craving a separation from painful feelings. The statement in a sūtra that "craving is caused by feeling"[539] means that feelings accompanied by ignorance cause craving. Where there is no ignorance, craving does not occur, even if feelings are present.

This being the case, contact is the experiencing of the object and feeling is the experiencing of birth or the fruition of karma. Hence, when these two are complete, experience is complete. There are three types of craving, one for each of the three realms.

(9) Grasping

Grasping refers to yearning after and attachment to four types of objects:

(1) holding onto what you want: yearning after and attaching to the sensuous, forms and sounds, for example; to bad views (excluding the reifying view of the perishing aggregates); to ethical discipline associated with bad views and bad conduct; and to the view of the perishing aggregates;
(2) holding onto views;
(3) holding onto ethical discipline and conduct; and
(4) holding onto assertions that there is a self.

(10) Potential existence

In the past, compositional activity infused your consciousness with a latent propensity, that, when nurtured by craving and grasping, became empowered to bring forth a subsequent existence.

"Existence" is a case of calling a cause [an activated propensity] by the name of its effect [the subsequent rebirth].

(11) Birth

Birth refers to consciousness initially entering one or another of the four types of rebirth.

(12) Aging-and-death

Aging is the maturation and transformation of the [mental and physical] aggregates. Death is the casting aside of the aggregates' continuum.

2′ **Abbreviated classification of the factors [252]**

The *Compendium of Knowledge:*[540]

> What sort of categories do you obtain by abbreviating the factors? There are four types: the projecting factors, the projected factors, the actualizing factors, and the actualized factors.
>
> What are the projecting factors? Ignorance, compositional activity, and consciousness. What are the projected factors? Name-and-form, the six sources, contact, and feeling. What are the actualizing factors? Craving, grasping, and existence. What are the actualized factors? Birth, aging, and death.

Qualm: Well then, do the two types of causality—one with respect to projection and the other with respect to actualization—demonstrate one instance of causality wherein one person takes rebirth or do they demonstrate two instances? If the former, it would be incorrect to claim that the actualizing factors, craving and so on, occur after the establishment of the group of factors beginning with resultant period consciousness and ending with feeling [the projected factors]. If the latter, there would be no ignorance, compositional activity, or causal period consciousness [projecting factors] in the latter cycle of causality [the ordering of projection], and no craving, grasping, or existence [actualizing factors] in the former cycle of causality [the ordering of actualization].

Reply: There is no such fault, because, whatever is projected by the projecting causes [ignorance, compositional activity, and consciousness] must be created by the actualizing causes [craving, grasping, and existence]. When what is projected [name-and-form, the six sources, contact, and feeling] has been actualized, it is that very thing, the projected, that is designated as being born, aging, and dying.

Qualm: Well then, what is the point of presenting two cycles of causality?

Reply: Such a presentation demonstrates that the characteristics of the true sufferings that are the effects of projection differ from those that are the effects of actualization. The former [consciousness of the effect period, name-and-form, the six sources, contact, and feeling] are dormant at the time of projection. Since they have not actually been established, they will only become suffering in the future. However, the latter [birth, aging, and death] are situations in which the suffering has been actualized, and hence are suffering in this lifetime. Moreover, the two cycles of cause and effect were presented for the sake of demonstrating that the effect—taking rebirth—has two causes: projecting causes and causes that actualize what has been projected [by the projecting causes]. **[253]** The *Levels of Yogic Deeds* states the reason for this:[541]

> Given that the factors of birth and aging-and-death and the group of factors beginning with resultant period consciousness and ending with feeling are phenomena with shared characteristics, why have they been taught to be of two types? This is done (1) in order to demonstrate the different characteristics of things that bring suffering and (2) in order to demonstrate the distinction between projection and actualization.

And also:

> Among the factors, how many are both included within true sufferings and become sufferings in this lifetime? There are two: birth and aging-and-death.
>
> How many are just included within true sufferings and will only become sufferings in the future? The ones that are dormant—the group of factors beginning with [resultant period] consciousness and ending with feeling.

Therefore, the two factors of (1) craving, which is an actualizing factor, and (2) feeling, which gives rise to this craving, are not in the same sequence of dependent-arising. The feeling that gives rise to craving is an effect of some other sequence of dependent-arising.

Projecting and being projected should be understood by way of four considerations:

1) What has been projected? The four-and-a-half factors beginning with resultant period consciousness and ending with feeling have been projected.

2) What has done the projecting? Compositional activity, which is dependent on ignorance, has done the projecting.

3) How has a projection occurred? Projection has occurred by means of latent karmic propensities being infused in the causal period consciousness.

4) "Projected" means having created the effects [resultant period consciousness, name-and-form, sources, contact, and feeling] conducive to actualization once the actualizers, such as craving, are present.

The actualizers and the actualized should be understood by way of three considerations:

1) What does the actualizing? It is done by grasping, which is caused by craving.

2) What is actualized? Birth and aging-and-death are actualized.

3) How does actualization occur? Actualization occurs by means of the empowerment of the latent karmic propensities that were infused in consciousness by compositional activity.

Vasubandhu, in his *Explanation of the Divisions of Dependent-Arising* (*Pratītya-samutpādādi-vibhaṅga-nirdeśa*),[542] took the factor of birth as the only actualized factor and then taught aging-and-death to be the faults of these factors of projection and actualization. **[254]**

This being the case, actualization should be understood as follows: nonvirtuous compositional activity that is motivated by ignorance about karma and its effects deposits latent propensities of bad karma in the consciousness. This makes ready for actualization the group of factors of a miserable rebirth that begins with the resultant period consciousness and ends with feeling. Through repeated nurturing by craving and grasping, these latent propensities are empowered, and birth, aging, and so forth will be actualized in subsequent miserable rebirths.

Alternatively, motivated by ignorance about the meaning of selflessness, meritorious compositional activity—such as ethical discipline within the desire realm—or invariable compositional activity—such as the cultivation of meditative serenity within the higher [deities'] realms—deposits latent propensities of good karma in the consciousness. This makes ready for actualization the group of factors beginning with resultant period consciousness and ending with feeling for, respectively, a happy rebirth in the desire realm or a rebirth as a deity in the higher realms. Through repeated nurturing by craving and grasping, these latent propensities are empowered, and subsequently birth and so forth will be actualized in those happy rebirths.

The twelve factors, moreover, are subsumed under three paths—those of afflictions, karma, and sufferings. As the wise Nāgārjuna said:[543]

> The first, the eighth, and the ninth are afflictions.
> The second and the tenth are karma.
> The remaining seven are sufferings.

The *Rice Seedling Sūtra* (*Śāli-stamba-sūtra*) mentions four causes which subsume the twelve factors of dependent-arising.[544] It explains that when the seeds of consciousness sown in the field of karma by ignorance are subsequently moistened by the water of craving, they give rise to the sprout of name-and-form in the mother's womb.

3′ **The number of lifetimes required to complete all twelve factors**

While it is possible for countless eons to go by between the projecting and the projected factors, it is also possible for the projected factors to be actualized in the very next lifetime, with no intervening lifetime. Since the actualizing factors [craving, grasping, and existence] and the actualized factors [birth and aging-and-death] occur without an intervening lifetime, it is possible, at the shortest, to complete all twelve factors in two lifetimes. **[255]** You might, for example, in a lifetime such as this one first accumulate karma that results in rebirth as a deity as well as the subsequent experience of a deity's life and resources. When this occurs, two-and-a-half factors—ignorance, compositional activity, and consciousness of the causal period—as well as craving, grasping, and existence (up to the point of death) are completed in this lifetime. In the subsequent lifetime, the four-and-a-half projected factors [consciousness of the resultant period, name-and-form, the six sources, contact, and feeling] and the two actualized factors [birth and aging-and-death] will be completed.

Even at the longest, completion of all twelve factors will be delayed no longer than three lifetimes, for the actualizers [craving, grasping, and existence], the two actualized factors [birth and aging-and-death], and the three projecting factors [ignorance, compositional activity, and consciousness] all require their own lifetimes, while the projected factors [name-and-form, the six sources, contact, and feeling] are included in the lifetime of the actualized factors. Furthermore, though many lifetimes may intervene between the projectors and the actualizers, they are not lifetimes of their own particular cycle of dependent-arising, but are rather lifetimes of other cycles of dependent-arising. Among these calculations of two or three lifetimes, the lifetimes of the intermediate state have not been reckoned separately.

Thus, even during the lifetime in which the resultant factors have been actualized, there is no self that is the person who accumulates karma or experiences its results. Rather, as previously explained, there are resultant factors, which are themselves merely phenomena, arising from causal factors, which are themselves merely phenomena. Not understanding this process of cyclic existence and being confused about it, you posit a self. Desiring your "self" to be happy, you physically, verbally, and mentally engage in virtue and nonvirtue for that purpose, whereby you again fuel the process of cyclic existence. Therefore, the two karmic factors [compositional activity and existence] arise from the three afflictive factors [ignorance, craving, and grasping], and from them, the seven suffering factors [consciousness, name-and-form, sources, contact, feeling, birth, and aging-and-death] arise. Afflictions arise again out of the seven sufferings, and—as before—you pass through cyclic existence. Thus, the wheel of existence turns without interruption. The master Nāgārjuna says in his *Heart of Dependent-Arising*:

> From the three arise the two;
> From the two arise the seven, and again from the seven
> Arise the three. The wheel of existence
> Itself repeatedly turns.

When you reflect on your wandering in such a way through cyclic existence, the twelve factors of dependent-arising are the best method for generating disenchantment with cyclic existence. Contemplate your projecting karma, the virtuous and nonvirtuous karma that you have accumulated over countless eons, that has neither issued forth fruitions nor been eradicated by antidotes. **[256]** When craving and grasping in the present lifetime nurture them, you wander through happy or miserable realms under their control. Arhats have immeasurable projecting karma accumulated when they were ordinary beings, but are free of cyclic existence because they have no afflictions. Once you have reached a firm conviction about this, you will hold the afflictions to be enemies and will make an effort to eradicate them.

With regard to this, the great spiritual friend Pu-chung-wa engaged in mental training based solely on the twelve factors of dependent-arising and made the stages of the path simply a reflection on the progression through and cessation of these factors. That is, he explained that reflection on the progression through and cessation of the twelve factors of miserable realms is the teaching for persons of small capacity and then reflection on the progression through and cessation of the twelve factors of the two happy realms is the teaching for persons of medium capacity. The teaching for persons of great capacity is to assess their own situation according to these two practices [of persons of small and medium capacities]. They then develop love and compassion for living beings, who have been their mothers and have wandered through cyclic existence by way of the twelve factors, train themselves in the wish to become a buddha for the sake of these beings, and learn the path to this end.

4′ How their significance is summarized

You should understand well, as explained above, how cyclic existence—the aggregates of suffering—is formed through the power of its origin—karma and the afflictions—and, in particular, how the wheel of existence turns in the context of the twelve factors. Understanding this and becoming familiar with it destroys the unbearable gloom of confusion—the root of all problems. It eradicates all mistaken views holding external and internal compositional activities to arise causelessly or from incompatible causes. It increases the precious wealth of the treasury of the Conqueror's teachings, and it is what motivates you toward the path to liberation through exact knowledge of the characteristics of cyclic existence and intense disenchantment with them. **[257]** It is the best means for activating the latent propensities by which you will attain the sublime state of a noble being.

Thus, the *Tantra Requested by Subāhu* says:[545]

> The path of dependent-arising destroys ignorance.

The *Rice Seedling Sūtra* states that when you understand dependent-arising well, you put an end to all bad views that take as their object the beginning, the end, or the present. Master Nāgārjuna said:[546]

> This dependent-arising is the profound
> Treasure in the storehouse of the Conqueror's speech.

The *Bases of Discipline*[547] states that it was the custom of the excellent pair Śāriputra and Maudgalyāyana occasionally to travel among the five kinds of beings. After they had traveled there, they would return to Jambudvīpa and recount the sufferings of these beings to the four types of the Buddha's followers.

Some among the followers lived either with or near some persons who disdained pure conduct. The followers brought them before the excellent pair, who instructed them in these accounts of the sufferings of other realms. As a result of this instruction, they came to delight in pure conduct and were brought to a higher understanding as well.

The Teacher, seeing this, questioned Ānanda, who informed him of the reasons, whereupon the Buddha said, "Because there will not always be teachers like this excellent pair, make a painting in the gate house of a five-part wheel of cyclic existence, around the circumference of which are the twelve dependent-arisings in both forward and reverse progressions." The wheel of existence was then drawn.

On another occasion, a painting of the Buddha was to be sent to King Udrāyaṇa. Before it was sent, the twelve dependent-arisings in forward and reverse progressions were written in verse at the bottom. The king memorized this, and then, at dawn, sitting with legs crossed and body straight, concentrated his attention upon virtue. By focusing upon the two processes of dependent-arising, he achieved the sublime state of a noble being.

22

The Attitude of a Person of Medium Capacity

b) The measure of the determination to be free
c) Dispelling misconceptions

b) The measure of the determination to be free

You must understand in detail the characteristics of cyclic existence, both by way of suffering and its origin and by way of the twelve factors of dependent-arising. **[258]** Once you understand these characteristics, you will develop a desire to abandon and to quell suffering and its origin. At this point, although you may have a simple determination to be free, you should not be satisfied merely with this. Hence, Candrakīrti's *Commentary on the "Sixty Stanzas of Reasoning"* (*Yukti-ṣaṣṭikā-vṛtti*) says:

> Once we are certain that living in the three levels of cyclic existence—impermanence's blazing fire—is like entering a burning house, we want to escape it.

And, as cited previously:[548]

> Just as, when a chance arises
> For prisoners to flee from prison…

Develop an attitude about cyclic existence like those who feel aversion for their confinement in a blazing house or a prison, and want to escape. Then progressively increase this feeling of aversion and desire to escape.

Sha-ra-wa described a superficial determination to be free as being like when you pour powder into inferior beer; the powder forms just a thin layer on the surface. If your ability to see the undesirability of true origins—the causes of cyclic existence—is superficial like this, then your search for liberation, the cessation of suffering and its origin, will be the same. Likewise, your desire to attain the path to liberation will be mere words. Thus, you will not be able to develop either the compassion that cannot bear to see the sufferings of living beings in cyclic existence or the uncontrived spirit of unsurpassed enlightenment that instills you with strength. Hence, your understanding of the Mahāyāna will also be merely intellectual. Therefore, you must practice these teachings for the person of medium capacity and regard them as crucial instructions.

c) **Dispelling misconceptions**

Qualm: Although it is appropriate in the Hīnayāna to cultivate disenchantment with cyclic existence, it is inappropriate for bodhisattvas, for, if bodhisattvas were to cultivate intense disgust and disenchantment with cyclic existence, they would be like the *śrāvakas* and fall into an extreme of peace, having become displeased with their involvement in cyclic existence. **[259]** As the *Sūtra of Showing the Tathāgata's Inconceivable Secret* states:[549]

> Bodhisattvas, thinking of the maturation of living beings, view cyclic existence as beneficial. Accordingly, they do not view great nirvāṇa [liberation] as beneficial to the maturation of beings.

And further:

> Were bodhisattvas to fear involvement in cyclic existence, they would fall to a destitute place.

And also:

> Bhagavan, whereas the *śrāvakas* fear involvement in cyclic existence, bodhisattvas voluntarily take innumerable rebirths in cyclic existence.

Response: This is a great error that misconstrues the sūtra's meaning. For, the sūtra passage that says, "Thus, bodhisattvas should not become disenchanted with cyclic existence," does not teach bodhisattvas not to be disgusted with the sufferings of birth, aging, illness, death, and so on—the result of our wandering through cyclic existence under the influence of our karma and afflictions. Rather, this sūtra teaches joyous perseverance. In order to train in the bodhisattvas' activities for the sake of others until the end of cyclic existence, bodhisattvas must put on armor [courage]. Once they do this, even if all the sufferings of all beings were collected and the bodhisattvas constantly experienced them mentally and physically, they would still persevere joyously, delighting in the magnificent deeds that help others, without becoming disenchanted with or frightened by sufferings. Thus, the Buddha said that bodhisattvas must not be disenchanted with cyclic existence.

The master Candrakīrti says:

> Bodhisattvas, who take on the sufferings of all beings moment by moment until the end of cyclic existence, do not fear harm to their bodies or minds. Bodhisattvas, who take on the sufferings of all beings simultaneously until the end of cyclic existence, delight in this activity. Each instant of such joyous perseverance acts as the cause whose effect produces boundless collections of wealth, bringing omniscience to all beings. Once bodhisattvas understand this, it is appropriate for them to take hundreds of rebirths.

In order to emphasize this point, Candrakīrti then cites the aforementioned sūtra passages from the *Sūtra of Showing the Tathāgata's Inconceivable Secret*. **[260]**

This same sūtra states that cyclic existence should be viewed as beneficial because bodhisattvas gain happiness proportionate to the effort they make when they strive for the welfare of living beings. Hence, the Buddha says that not being disenchanted with cyclic existence means not being disenchanted with accomplishing the good of living beings in cyclic existence, as well as enjoying this activity.

When you wander through cyclic existence by the power of karma and afflictions, you are tormented by many sufferings. If you are unable to accomplish even your own aims, what need is there to mention that you cannot accomplish those of others? Since such wandering is the door to all problems, bodhisattvas must be even more disenchanted with cyclic existence than Hīnayāna practitioners and must stop their own wandering caused by karma and the afflictions. Nevertheless, bodhisattvas must enjoy being reborn in cyclic existence through their aspirational prayers and compassion. These two ways of being reborn are not the same.

Failing to make this distinction leads to qualms like that above. The *Bodhisattva Levels* says that if the proponents of such a position have taken the vows of a bodhisattva then they have committed a misdeed permeated with afflictions. However, fearing too many words, I will not quote the passage in full.

Hence, it is amazing that bodhisattvas see the defects of cyclic existence and are thoroughly disgusted, yet do not give up their vow because they are motivated by great compassion. If those who see the wonders of cyclic existence as like a celestial mansion—without reducing their craving even in the slightest—claim to be serving others, how could their unwillingness to abandon cyclic existence please the wise? As Bhāvaviveka's *Heart of the Middle Way* says:[550]

> Since bodhisattvas see the faults of cyclic existence, they do not remain here.
> Because they care for others, they do not remain in nirvāṇa.
> In order to fulfill the needs of others, they resolve
> To remain in cyclic existence.

Once you see the limitless sufferings of all living beings—such as the one hundred and ten sufferings explained in the *Bodhisattva Levels*—you allow this to be the cause for great compassion. At this time, when you cultivate a heart that has a forceful and enduring inability to withstand the sight of others' sufferings, it would be contradictory to be not even slightly disenchanted with cyclic existence. **[261]**

The theme of Āryadeva's *Four Hundred Stanzas* is the stages of the path upon which bodhisattvas develop great revulsion for cyclic existence and then, seeing living beings as their close relatives, enter the ocean of cyclic existence for their sake. In his commentary on that work, the great master Candrakīrti clarified this:[551]

> Due to the Buddha's explanation of the faults of cyclic existence, his disciples learned to fear it and desire freedom from it. The Bhagavan said the following so that they would develop a strong connection to the Mahāyāna: "O monks, among all who have passed through cyclic existence for a long time, there is not one being among all the various types of living beings who has not been like a father, mother, son, daughter, relative, or step-relation to you."

And further:

> By understanding the words of the Bhagavan, bodhisattvas are able to leap into the ocean of cyclic existence. They do this so that all beings who have been their close relatives—like father and mother—throughout beginningless time and who are now bereft and without a protector may be freed by the boat of the Mahāyāna.

The unsurpassed mantra vehicle also requires this method. For, as Āryadeva says in his *Lamp Which Is a Compendium of Deeds*:[552]

> Through these stages, you should engage in these activities wholly free of elaborations. The stages for doing this are as follows: in the very beginning, you should recall the beginningless sufferings of cyclic existence, and then desire the bliss of nirvāṇa. Therefore, you should completely give up all agitation, and even cultivate the idea that the rulers of kingdoms suffer.

23

ASCERTAINING THE NATURE OF THE PATH LEADING TO LIBERATION

d) Ascertaining the nature of the path leading to liberation
   i) The kind of life through which you halt cyclic existence
   ii) The kind of path you cultivate to halt cyclic existence
      a′ The certainty of the enumeration of the three trainings
         1′ The stages of disciplining the mind
         2′ Their results
         3′ The objects that they eliminate
      b′ The determination of the order of the three trainings

Exhort yourself and meditate on the faults of cyclic existence. As Śrī Jagan-mitrānanda says:[553]

> Although we have sunk into the midst of cyclic existence,
> An ocean of suffering with neither bottom nor shore, **[262]**
> We are not disenchanted; we have no fear; we are pleased and excited.
> What is going on in our minds?
>
> Although we have entered a fire constantly blazing
> With problems, poverty, hardship in acquiring food and shelter,
> Effort in keeping and finally loss, as well as separation, illness, and aging,
> We boast of happiness. This seems insane.

And:

Alas, the worldly have eyes yet are blind;
Although you see the obvious,
You do not think about it at all.
Has your mind become hardened?

Consequently, as Guhyadatta's *Edifying Tale of the Seven Maidens (Sapta-kumārikāvadāna)* states:[554]

We see the things of the world as wavering images of the moon in water.
We see attachments as shadows of the hoods and coils of angry snakes.
We see these beings to be ablaze with the flames of suffering.
We therefore go to the cremation grounds, O King, delighting in the determination to be free.

Thus, when you see that cyclic existence—environments and beings—is like a moon in water that is stirred by the wind—impermanent, disintegrating, not resting even for an instant; that sensory objects—like shadows of the bodies of poisonous snakes—hold little value but great danger; and that the five types of beings are scorched by the blazing fires of the three sufferings; then you give rise to a disposition like that of northern children, a disposition that has completely turned away from attachment to cyclic existence. When this happens, there occurs the determination to be free—a longing that delights in liberation.

The expression "northern children" is to be understood as follows: in the north, roasted barley flour is scarce, and consequently the inhabitants eat small amounts of turnips. Once, there were some children there who, being hungry and wishing to eat roasted barley flour, asked their mother for food. Since she had no roasted barley flour, she offered them fresh turnip, which they refused. Then she offered them dried turnip, but they did not want that either, so she then gave them cooked turnip. But they turned this down as well. Finally she offered them frozen cooked turnip, whereupon they turned away with a great feeling of nausea, exclaiming, "Everything is turnips!" **[263]** Likewise, with respect to whatever worldly happiness is seen, heard of, or remembered, you must, as the Kadampa (bKa'-gdams-pa) teachers have said, generate the same feeling, thinking, "This is the world," "This also is the world," "Everything is suffering," and "I want nothing to do with it."

In this way, by contemplating your previous beginningless wanderings through cyclic existence, you become disenchanted and revolted, and by contemplating the necessity of continuing to wander here indefinitely, you give rise to fear and anxiety. With a determination that transcends mere words, you must, as Nāgārjuna's *Friendly Letter* says, stop your birth in cyclic existence, the root of all harm:[555]

> Cyclic existence is like that; birth—
> Whether in the lands of deities and humans, hell-beings,
> Hungry ghosts, or animals—is not auspicious.
> Understand that birth is a vessel of much harm.

What is more, you must eliminate both causes of birth in cyclic existence: karma and afflictions. Still, between these two, if you have no afflictions, you will not take birth, no matter how much karma you have. Hence, you should destroy the afflictions, by cultivating a path that is complete and without error, because, once you have afflictions, even if it were possible to eradicate previously accumulated karma, you would immediately accumulate new karma.

Ascertaining the nature of the path leading to liberation has two parts:

1. The kind of life through which you halt cyclic existence
2. The kind of path you cultivate to halt cyclic existence

i) **The kind of life through which you halt cyclic existence**

The *Friendly Letter*:[556]

> To be reborn with wrong views or without a conqueror's word,
> Or as an animal, a hungry ghost, a hell-being,
> An uncultured person in a border region,
> A stupid and mute person, or a deity of long life
> Is to be afflicted by one of the eight faults that are conditions
> which lack leisure.
> After you have attained leisure, which is freedom from these
> rebirths,
> Strive to end birth.

It is not possible to stop birth in cyclic existence if you have no time. Therefore, once you have obtained a life of leisure and opportunity, you *must* stop it. **[264]** I have already explained this.

The great yogi Chang-chup-rin-chen said:

> Now is the time to make ourselves different from domestic animals.

Also, Bo-do-wa said:

> For as long as we have wandered through cyclic existence in the past it has not stopped by itself. Given this, it will not stop by

> itself now either. Hence, we must put a stop to it, and the time to do so is today, when we have obtained leisure and opportunity.

For those who have attained a life of leisure and opportunity, dwelling in a household presents many obstacles to the practice of religion and has numerous shortcomings. However, the life of a renunciate, being the opposite of that, is the very best for stopping cyclic existence. The wise, therefore, should delight in such a life.

Repeated reflection on the faults of householders and the virtues of renunciates will lead those who have already become renunciates to have a firm attitude, while leading those who have not yet become renunciates to develop good inclinations [to become renunciates and the like] and then act on them. I will explain how this is so.

Householders, if they are wealthy, suffer in their efforts to protect that wealth, and, if poor, suffer from exhaustion brought about by seeking wealth. In this way they lead confused lives that have no pleasure, and they imagine these lives to be pleasurable. Understand that this misconception is the result of bad karma. The *Garland of Birth Stories:*[557]

> Never consider as pleasurable
> The household, which is like a prison.
> Whether they are rich or poor,
> Those who dwell in households are greatly ailing.
>
> One undergoes afflictions by guarding wealth,
> While the other becomes exhausted by seeking it.
> Whether they are rich or poor,
> They have no happiness.
>
> The confusion that delights in this householder's existence
> Is merely the consequence of sin.

Therefore, keeping many possessions and discontentedly seeking more is not the business of renunciates. If it were, they would not differ from householders.

Furthermore, since living in a household is at odds with religion, it is difficult to practice religion there. The same text states:[558]

> If you do the business of the household, **[265]**
> It is unfeasible to refrain from speaking falsely,
> And it is unfeasible not to punish
> Others who do wrong.
>
> If you practice religion, householder pursuits suffer;
> If you attend to the household, how can you practice religion?
> Religious activity is peaceful;
> A householder's aims are achieved through ruthlessness.

Therefore, because of the flaw of being at odds with religion,
Who, desiring to help themselves, would live in a household?

And also:

A household is a nest of vipers such as
Arrogance, pride, and delusion.
It destroys tranquillity and the bliss of happiness,
And is a place of many unbearable sufferings.
Who would stay in a place so similar to a snakepit?

Contemplate again and again the defects of dwelling in a household, and aspire to the life of a renunciate. In reference to this, renunciates are content with alms, simple religious robes, and alms bowls. In solitude, they remove their afflictions and aspire to become objects of others' veneration. As it says in Guhyadatta's *Edifying Tale of the Seven Maidens*:[559]

When will we thus come
To shave our hair,
Don clothes from the garbage
And seek solitude?

Gazing ahead only a yoke's length,
When will we, blameless,
Take in our hands earthen alms bowls,
And, from household to household, partake of alms?

Attached to neither material gain nor veneration,
Cleaning up the bramble swamps of the afflictions,
When will we become
Recipients of the townspeople's donations?

Renunciates are content with meager food and drink, and with clothes heavy with frost from sleeping without a roof over their heads in bedding made of grass. They aspire to sleep in their place on soft grass in front of a tree, nurtured by the happiness and joy of the teaching. As is said in the *Edifying Tale of the Seven Maidens*:[560]

When will I become unattached to my body,
Rising from a pile of grass,
Clothing heavy with frost,
And taking only humble food and drink? **[266]**

When will I, clothed in soft grass—
Green like the parrot—
Lie down in front of a tree
With a banquet of the blissful things of this life?

Bo-do-wa said:

> The very night after snow fell on the roof of the house, I became happy because something like this occurred in the *Edifying Tale of the Seven Maidens*. I want nothing other than to practice in this way.

Renunciates aspire to dwell in a meadow or on the bank of a river, reflecting on the similarity between their own bodies and lives and the arising and disintegration of waves. They aspire to stop, by means of discerning wisdom, the conception of self—root of cyclic existence and creator of all bad views. They aspire to overcome their obsession with the pleasures of cyclic existence, and to reflect on the animate and inanimate world as being like a magician's illusions. As is said in the *Edifying Tale of the Seven Maidens*:[561]

> When, dwelling on a river bank or in a meadow,
> Will we come to see again and again
> That the rising and falling of waves
> And the world of this life are similar?
>
> When will we rid ourselves
> Of the view of the perishing aggregates—
> The mother of all bad views—
> And not crave the enjoyments of cyclic existence?
>
> When will we come to know
> That the animate and inanimate worlds
> Are like dreams, hallucinations, a magician's illusions, clouds,
> Or a city of the *gandharvas*?

All of these persons lived as renunciates, while at the same time aspiring to these higher achievements. As Chay-ga-wa said:

> If there is someone living as a sage in the Valley of the Ascetics, then the father has fundamentally raised his child well.

Sha-ra-wa said:

> When householders are very busy, you, monks, should dress nicely and visit them. They will then think, "The life of a renunciate is wonderful!" This establishes in them a latent predisposition for a future life as a renunciate.

Also, the *Questions of Householder Ugra Sūtra* says[562] that bodhisattvas who dwell in households should aspire in this way: **[267]**

> Householder bodhisattvas should think, "When will I leave the household, an origin of suffering, and experience the life of a renunciate? When will I rest in the actions of the community, the action of purifying and nurturing vows, the action of lifting restrictions, and the action of veneration?" In this way they should delight in the thought of being a renunciate.

This passage states that such bodhisattvas should principally aspire to full ordination.

Furthermore, the *Ornament for the Mahāyāna Sūtras* says:[563]

> The class of renunciates
> Has limitless virtues.
> Therefore, the bodhisattva who observes vows
> Is superior to the one who is a householder.

This being the case, the life of a renunciate is praised for achieving the freedom that is liberation from cyclic existence. In addition, it is taught that it is the best life even for the accomplishment of omniscience by way of the perfection and mantra vehicles. Furthermore, among the three sets of vows, it is the vows of the renunciate that are the vows of individual liberation. Therefore, you should respect the vows of individual liberation, the root of the teaching.

ii) **The kind of path you cultivate to halt cyclic existence**

There are three parts to this explanation:

1. The certainty of the enumeration of the three trainings
2. The determination of the order of the three trainings
3. The nature of the three trainings (Chapter 24)

Train in the path which is the threefold precious training. The *Friendly Letter*:[564]

> Were your head or clothing suddenly to catch fire,
> You should still set aside extinguishing these fires
> And strive to eradicate birth—
> There is no purpose higher than this.
>
> Through ethical discipline, concentration, and wisdom,
> Achieve nirvāṇa, an undefiled state of peace and restraint:
> Ageless, deathless, inexhaustible;
> Free from earth, water, fire, wind, sun, and moon.

a′ **The certainty of the enumeration of the three trainings**

This is explained in terms of three aspects: (1) the stages of disciplining the mind, (2) their results, and (3) the objects that they eliminate.

1′ **The stages of disciplining the mind**

The three trainings bring to completion all the tasks of yogis and yoginīs as follows. The training in ethical discipline makes a distracted mind undistracted. **[268]** The training in concentration—or mental training—balances an unbalanced mind. The training in wisdom liberates an unliberated mind.

2′ **Their results**

The results of ethical discipline that have not degenerated are the two happy rebirths of the desire realm [either as a human or a deity]. The result of ethical discipline that has degenerated is rebirth in the miserable realms. The results of the training of the mind are the two happy rebirths of the higher [deities' form or formless] realms. The result of the training in wisdom is liberation. In brief, the results of the three trainings are the two goals: high status [as a human or deity] and certain goodness [of liberation or omniscience]. Since the former is twofold—happy rebirth in the higher [deities'] realms and happy rebirth in the lower [that is, desire] realm—the trainings that accomplish these are threefold. These first two certainties of enumeration are mentioned in the *Levels of Yogic Deeds*.

3′ **The objects that they eliminate**

The former teachers asserted that, in relation to the objects they eliminate—the afflictions—the trainings are threefold, according to whether they eliminate afflictions by (1) weakening them, (2) suppressing their manifest forms, or (3) eradicating their seeds.

b′ **The determination of the order of the three trainings**

The order of the three trainings is demonstrated in a passage from the *Sūtra Requested by Brahmā (Brahma-paripṛcchā-sūtra)* quoted in the *Levels of Yogic Deeds*:[565]

> Ethical discipline is a very steady root;
> Concentration is the delight in a serene state of mind;
> In wisdom the views of noble beings and the views of sinners
> Are acquired and forsaken respectively.

Among these, ethical discipline is the root because the other two grow out of it. Concentration, the second of the three trainings, depends on ethical discipline and takes pleasure in putting the mind into meditative equipoise. Wisdom, the third of the three trainings, depends on meditative equipoise and forsakes the view of sinners while acquiring the view of noble beings in order to see reality exactly.

24

The Nature of the Three Trainings

The nature of the three trainings is as the *Sūtra Requested by Brahmā* states:[566]

> Ethical discipline has six branches;
> Concentration is the four blissful abodes;
> The four aspects of the four noble truths
> Are always pure sublime wisdoms. **[269]**

With respect to this, the training in ethical discipline has six branches:

1-2) Both (1) the possession of ethical discipline and (2) restraint by the vows of individual liberation demonstrate the pure ethical discipline that certainly leads to liberation.

3-4) Both (3) rites and (4) possession of the range of support demonstrate unimpeachable, pure ethical discipline.

5) Dread of even the smallest misdeed demonstrates pure ethical discipline that is unspoiled.

6) Correctly undertaking and training in the fundamental trainings demonstrates flawless, pure ethical discipline.

"Four abodes" of mind refers to the four meditative stabilizations. It means the training of mind, which is "blissful" because the mind abides blissfully in this lifetime. The four [where the *Sūtra Requested by Brahmā* reads "The four aspects of the four"] are the four [noble] truths. The four aspects of these four are the four aspects of each of the four truths:

(1) for the truth of suffering: impermanent, suffering, empty, and selfless;
(2) for the truth of the origin: cause, origin, arising, and condition;
(3) for the truth of cessation: cessation, pacification, excellence, and freedom;
(4) for the truth of the path: path, correctness, achievement, and deliverance.

The sixteen aspects—the knowledge of these sixteen aspects—constitute the training in wisdom.

If I were explaining here the path of persons of medium capacity alone, I would have to give a lengthy explanation of the three trainings. However, since this is not the case, I will explain the trainings in wisdom (insight) and in mind (meditative serenity) in the section on persons of great capacity and will not elaborate at this point. Thus, I will briefly discuss the training in ethical discipline here.

In the beginning, reflect repeatedly on the benefits of ethical discipline and develop enthusiasm for it from the depths of your heart. As the *Great Final Nirvāṇa Sūtra* states:[567]

> Ethical discipline is the ladder to all virtues. It is their foundation, just as the earth is the foundation for plants and the like. Just as a master trader goes first among all traders, so ethical discipline goes first among all virtues. **[270]** Like the hoisted banner of Indra, ethical discipline is the banner of all teachings. It cuts down all sins and eliminates the paths to the miserable realms. Since it cures all the illnesses of the sins, it is like a medicinal plant. Ethical discipline is the stock of provisions for the terrible road of cyclic existence. It is the weapon that destroys the afflictions, the enemies. It is the spell destroying the poisonous snakes of the afflictions. It is the bridge to cross over the waters of sin.

The protector Nāgārjuna as well says:[568]

> Ethical discipline—like the ground supporting the animate and inanimate worlds—
> Is said to be the foundation of all good qualities.

And the *Tantra Requested by Subāhu* says:[569]

> Just as every harvest grows without fault
> In dependence on the earth,
> So too do the highest virtues depend on ethical discipline,
> And grow by being moistened with the water of compassion.

You should reflect on the benefits of keeping ethical discipline in accordance with the above-cited passages.

There are very grave consequences for you if you undertake an ethical discipline and then fail to keep it. The *Sutra Beloved of Monks* (*Bhikṣu-prareju-sūtra*) says that, once you undertake a training, it will proceed in either an advantageous or disadvantageous direction:[570]

> The ethical discipline of some leads to pleasure;
> The ethical discipline of others leads to pain.
> Those who possess ethical discipline are happy,
> Whereas those who break ethical discipline suffer.

Therefore, you should also think about the drawbacks of not keeping to ethical discipline and thereby generate great respect for the training.

There are four causes of an infraction: not knowing the precept, carelessness, disrespect, and various afflictions. As a remedy for not knowing the precept, listen to and understand the precepts. As a remedy for carelessness, train in attitudes such as mindfulness, which does not forget which ends to adopt and which to cast aside; vigilance, which immediately examines the three doors of body, speech, and mind and understands the right or wrong in which you are engaged; shame, which shuns faults committed with respect to oneself or the teaching; embarrassment, which shuns wrongdoing and thinks, "Others will criticize me"; **[271]** and trepidation, which fears the future karmic fruition of wrongdoing. As a remedy for disrespect, have respect for the Teacher, his rules, and your fellow practitioners. As a remedy for various afflictions, examine your mind and energetically apply the remedies for whatever afflictions predominate.

Those who fail to make an effort in this way, who follow the rules in a lax fashion thinking that even though they have transgressed, "it is merely a small fault," will gain only suffering. For, as the *Exegesis of the Discipline* says:[571]

> Those who take lightly and slightly transgress
> The teaching of the compassionate Teacher
> Thereby come under the power of suffering—
> Just as one who cuts a grove of small bamboo and spoils a
>   whole grove of mango.
>
> Here, those who transgress the king's pronouncements
> Would not be punished for a few such transgressions.
> But were they to transgress improperly the edicts of the Sage,
> They would become animals, as did the *nāga* Elapatra.[572]

Therefore, strive not to be polluted by faults and infractions. However, if you should become polluted by these, do not heedlessly ignore such sins and infractions, but strive to redress them in accordance with the Buddha's teachings. As the *Sūtra Requested by Brahmā* says:[573]

> Rely upon the trainings;
> Undertake them earnestly, from the heart.
> Do not give them up later,
> Or break them even to save your life.
> Always maintain them diligently
> And engage in the discipline.

Moreover, as the Buddha decreed in the *Sūtra on Having Pure Ethical Discipline (Śīla-saṃyukta-sūtra)* using reasons, you should keep your ethical discipline, even at the risk of your life:[574]

> O monks, to lose your life and die is excellent, but to ruin and lose your ethical discipline is not. Why? Losing your life and dying expends only the life span of this rebirth, but if you ruin and lose your ethical discipline, you will experience a great downfall—separating from your lineage and giving up happiness over ten million lifetimes. **[272]**

You should think, "If this need to keep my ethical discipline at all costs were not the case, then shaving off my hair and donning monastic robes was pointless." For, as the *King of Concentrations Sūtra* says:[575]

> After you have renounced the world and gone forth into the
> Buddha's teachings,
> You engage in sinful actions,
> And, attached to mounts, oxen, and chariots
> Have the idea that wealth and grain are essential.
> Why did you who make no effort to train in anything
> Bother to shave your heads?

You who seek to escape from cyclic existence—the composite—and to reach the city of liberation will not succeed if the feet of your ethical discipline are unsteady. Not only that, you will return again to cyclic existence and be destroyed by suffering. The Buddha spoke of this, with an example, in the *King of Concentrations Sūtra*:[576]

> When a man was attacked by a gang of robbers,
> He tried to escape because he wished to live.
> But when he set out, his feet could not move or run,
> And so the robbers caught and subdued him.

Likewise, a confused person whose ethical discipline is impaired,
Though wanting to escape from the composite,
Cannot escape because of impaired ethical discipline
And is destroyed by illness, old age, and death.

Therefore, as this sūtra says:[577]

I set forth trainings
For householders wearing secular clothing.
At that time these monks
Did not have even these trainings.

The Buddha says that in these times when even monks do not completely maintain the five fundamental trainings he taught to lay practitioners, effort in the trainings has an even greater fruit. Therefore, you should strive to maintain the trainings. The same sūtra says:[578]

For ten million eons—as many as there are sands in the Ganges—**[273]**
I served with a pure mind
Food and drink, umbrellas,
Banners, and processions of lamps to ten quadrillion buddhas.

So much greater is the merit of whoever practices
A single training night and day
At a time when the sublime teaching is perishing
And the Sugata's teaching is coming to an end.

Furthermore, you might think that, even were you to incur an infraction, you could confess it afterwards. However, in this case you lack an attitude of restraint that prevents you from committing the action again. So engaging in this infraction is like eating poison and telling yourself that you could always take the antidote later. For, as the *Lion's Roar of Maitreya Sūtra (Maitreya-mahā-siṃha-nāda-sūtra)* states:[579]

Maitreya, in the future, in the final five-hundred-year period of the teaching, certain renunciates and householder bodhisattvas will claim that sinful karma is completely extinguished through confessing the fault. They will disclose the infraction, saying, "After we have become involved in sin, we will confess it." But they will not restrain themselves from doing it again. I tell you that they possess fatal karma.

What do I mean by fatal? For example, it is like people who ingest poison. They create their time of death, and then end up in a misguided descent into a miserable realm.

And also:

> Maitreya, what I call poison in the noble teaching of the discipline is transgressing the fundamental trainings as I have prescribed them. Therefore, do not eat such poison.

Given that maintaining vows in such a way applies to one who has taken the vows of individual liberation, it is also similar for one who practices the mantra vehicle. For, the *Tantra Requested by Subāhu* states that even householder practitioners of mantra must act in accordance with the texts on discipline, except for the matters concerning the marks [robes] of renunciates, the ceremonial activities, and some factors which are merely regulatory:[580]

> Of the entire discipline that I, the Conqueror, taught—
> The pure ethical discipline of individual liberation—
> A householder practitioner of mantra should set aside
> The signs and rituals, and practice the rest. **[274]**

If this is the case, then it goes without saying that renunciate practitioners of mantra must act in accordance with the texts on discipline.

Ethical discipline is the root of practicing the mantra vehicle as well. The *Tantra Requested by Subāhu* says:[581]

> The root of the mantra vehicle is, in the first place, ethical discipline.
> From it come joyous perseverance, patience,
> Faith in the Conqueror, the spirit of enlightenment,
> The mantra vehicle, and the absence of laziness.
>
> Just as a lord possessing the seven treasures
> Tames all beings without disillusionment,
> So a mantra practitioner controls sins
> When possessing these seven.

And, the *Root Tantra of Mañjuśrī* (*Mañjuśrī-mūla-tantra*) says:[582]

> If these persons who recite mantras spoil their ethical discipline,
> They would lose the highest of attainments,
> Also middling attainments,
> And the least of attainments.
>
> The Master of the Sages does not say that faulty
> Ethical discipline achieves the tantric path.
> Breaking ethical discipline is neither a situation nor a destination
> For those going to the city of nirvāṇa.
>
> For these miserable children,
> Where is the achievement of the tantric path?

> For beings who have faulty ethical discipline,
> Where are the happy realms?
>
> Since they will attain neither high status
> Nor the highest bliss,
> What need is there to speak of their attaining
> The knowledge of the mantra vehicle taught by the Conqueror?

Kam-lung-ba said:

> When a famine occurs, everything depends on barley. In the same way everything revolves around ethical discipline in the practice of the teaching. Therefore, apply yourself to this! Those who have not thought about karma and its effects will not achieve pure ethical discipline. Therefore thinking about this is a personal imperative.

And Sha-ra-wa said:

> In general, whatever good or ill happens to you depends on religion. Moreover, within religion, if you depend on what the texts on discipline say, you will not even have to repeat things; you will be confidently pure, consistent, sure, and steadfast. **[275]**

Geshe Drom-dön-ba said:

> One group holds that when you rely upon the discipline, you discard the practice of mantra and that when you rely upon the mantra vehicle, you discard the rules of the discipline. The teaching that the discipline is the companion of the mantra vehicle and the mantra vehicle is the companion of the discipline exists only in my guru Atisha's lineage.

Also, the Elder said:

> When things of great import or unexpected events befell us Indians, those who upheld the scriptural collections would assemble and determine whether these things were proscribed in the three scriptural collections or were at odds with them. Based on this, we made decisions. In addition to that, those of us from Vikramalaśila were concerned that there be no proscription among the bodhisattvas' activities and no contradiction with them. Nonetheless, those who upheld the texts on discipline made the final determinations.

Further, with regard to keeping a pure ethical discipline in this way, Neu-sur-ba said:

> Right now, only this internal struggle with the afflictions is important. If you do not struggle with the afflictions, you will not achieve a pure ethical discipline, in which case, you will not attain the

concentration and wisdom that, respectively, suppress and uproot the afflictions. Hence, as the Buddha says, you will have to wander continually through cyclic existence. Therefore, as I explained before, once you have identified the afflictions, reflected on their faults and on the benefits of separating from them, and planted the spies of mindfulness and vigilance, you must repeatedly fend off whatever affliction raises its head.

Further, you must see any affliction as an enemy and attack it as soon as it arises in your mind. Otherwise, if you acquiesce when it first appears, and then nurture it with improper thoughts, you will have no way to defeat it, and it will conquer you in the end.

Even if you fail to arrest the afflictions through such efforts, you must not allow them to linger, but must immediately disperse them, as though they were drawings in water. Do not let them be like drawings in stone. But with regard to religious matters, you should do the opposite, as Nāgārjuna's *Friendly Letter* says:[583] **[276]**

Know that the mind can be like a drawing
Made in water, in earth, or in stone.
When afflictions arise, it is best to have the first,
But when aspiring to religion, the last is best.

This is said in *Engaging in the Bodhisattva Deeds* as well:[584]

We should be obsessed with these afflictions.
Resenting them, we do battle
While making an exception for only those afflictions
That are destroyers of other afflictions.

Better that I be burnt or killed,
Or that my head be cut off,
Than that I should ever bow
Before my enemies, the afflictions.

Also, Geshe Pu-chung-wa said, "Even when I am buried under the afflictions, I can still clench my teeth beneath them." Upon hearing what Pu-chung-wa said, Bo-do-wa stated, "If you do this, you will instantly stop them."

When you rout ordinary enemies, they can take over another country, seize power, and then return again to challenge you. The afflictions are not like this. Once you expel them completely from your mind, there is no other country to which they can retreat; nor can they return. However, we fail to overcome the afflictions because we lack joyous perseverance. *Engaging in the Bodhisattva Deeds* says:[585]

Ordinary enemies, expelled from a country,
Settle in other countries and take them over;
Recouping their strength, they then return.
The afflictions are enemies of a different sort.

The eye of wisdom eradicates the various afflictions.
Once cleared from my mind, where can they go?
From where can they regroup and counterattack?
Of weak mind, I have no joyous perseverance at all.

Nyuk-rum-ba (bsNyug-rum-pa) said:

> When an affliction appears, do not be indolent, but counter it immediately with its remedy. If you cannot overcome it, stop thinking about it, set up a maṇḍala and other offerings, offer these to the guru and the chosen deities, and make supplications to them to overcome it. Focusing on the affliction, recite the mantras of wrathful deities. Doing these things will cause the affliction to disappear. **[277]**

Lang-ri-tang-ba (Glang-ri-thang-pa) said:

> Even changing the place where you sit or merely turning your head will make the afflictions disappear.

It is said that he struggled with his afflictions.

Such disappearance of the afflictions as Lang-ri-tang-ba describes occurs when you do as Gön-ba-wa said: "What is there to do except to stand guard over your mind day and night?" Furthermore, no matter how many times the Great Elder met someone in a day, he would always ask, "Meanwhile, have you had a good mind?"

The way to eliminate the afflictions is as follows, beginning with the six root afflictions. Among the great misdeeds, ignorance is the most tenacious, and serves as the basis of all other afflictions. Therefore, as a remedy for ignorance, you should meditate a great deal on dependent-arising and become knowledgeable about the progression and cessation of cyclic existence. If you have habitually cultivated this, none of the bad views such as the five afflicted views will occur.

Hostility is the enemy who brings suffering both in this and in future lives, and who destroys the accumulated roots of virtue. As *Engaging in the Bodhisattva Deeds* says, "There is no sin like hatred."[586] Therefore, never give hostility an opportunity, and make every effort to be patient. If hostility does not arise, you will be very happy, even in this lifetime. *Engaging in the Bodhisattva Deeds:*[587]

Those who persistently defeat anger,
Will be happy in this and other lives.

Attachment—that is, craving—strengthens all previously accumulated virtues and nonvirtues and enhances their power to create cyclic existence. For those in the desire realm, craving arises from the feelings caused by the mental process of contact, which involves sensory objects. Therefore, you should meditate a great deal on what is externally or internally unpleasant and on the faults of being attached to desirable objects, and thereby overcome your craving and attachment. The great master Vasubandhu says:

The five beings—deer, elephants, butterflies,
Fish, and bees—are overcome by five desirable objects. **[278]**
If a single desirable object can overwhelm each one of them, why shouldn't
All five destroy someone who constantly dwells on them?

Moreover, the four cravings for gain, fame, praise, and pleasure and the dislike for their four opposites are quick to occur and difficult to get rid of. Strive to remedy this, and stop these eight worldly concerns by meditating on the faults of cyclic existence in general and by cultivating the mindfulness of death in particular.

Eliminate pride, as it is the chief obstacle to the development of the path in this lifetime and causes future rebirth as a servant and so forth. The way to do this is stated in the *Friendly Letter*:[588]

If you reflect again and again, "Just as I have not transcended
Illness, aging, death, and loss of the pleasant,
So my karma and its results are my own doing,"
You will overcome arrogance because you will be applying its remedy.

Once you have achieved certainty about the truths, the three jewels, and karma and its effects, the affliction of doubt will not arise.

The secondary afflictions—those called sleep, lethargy, excitement, laziness, carelessness, shamelessness, lack of embarrassment, forgetfulness, and lack of vigilance—are quick to occur and hinder your cultivation of the virtuous group of phenomena. You should understand their faults and get used to reducing their strength through an immediate application of their remedies. With respect to their faults the *Friendly Letter* says:[589]

Excitement and regret, malice, lethargy
And sleep, longing for the desirable, and doubt—

Understand that these five obscurations
Are robbers who steal the riches of virtue.

Also, the *Exhortation to Wholehearted Resolve* discusses the faults at length:[590]

Phlegm, wind, and bile
Occur to a great extent in the bodies
Of those who take pleasure in sleep and lethargy;
Their constituents are in disorder. **[279]**

For those who take pleasure in lethargy and sleep
Their stomachs are unclean because of poor food,
Their bodies are heavy and their complexions unhealthy,
Even their words are unclear.

And:[591]

Those who take pleasure in lethargy and sleep
Are confused and their aspirations toward religion fade.
These children lose all of their good qualities,
Their virtues degenerate, and they fall into darkness.

The *Mindfulness of the Excellent Teaching* says:[592]

The one foundation of all the afflictions
Is laziness. Those who have it,
Those who have a single moment of laziness,
Will have no practice at all.

The *Collection of Indicative Verses* says:[593]

Those involved in carelessness
Are childish people who ruin their minds.
As master traders guard their wealth,
So should the wise take care.

The *Garland of Birth Stories* says:[594]

O Prince of the Deities, rather than cast aside your shame
And act at odds with the teaching in your mind,
You would do better to take up an earthen vessel, put on poor clothing,
And be seen arriving at the home of an enemy.

The *Friendly Letter* says:[595]

Lord, mindfulness of that within the sphere of the body, speech, and mind
Is taught to be the one path by which the *sugatas* traveled.

Apply yourself to this and maintain it well;
All virtues will disintegrate with deterioration of mindfulness.

Engaging in the Bodhisattva Deeds says:[596]

Even the faithful, the learned,
And those who undertake joyous perseverance
Will be polluted by infractions
Through the fault of a lack of vigilance.

Thus, even if you cannot arrest the afflictions or the secondary afflictions, it is indispensable to see them as enemies right now, without strengthening them or taking their side. Hence, side with the remedies and strive to overcome the afflictions. After you have accomplished this, completely purify whatever ethical discipline you have assumed. As the glorious Gön-ba-wa, disciple of the Great Elder, said to Neu-sur-ba **[280]**:

> Ye-shay-bar (Ye-[shes]-'bar), if, tomorrow or the next day, someone were to ask all your disciples, "What are you practicing as the core of your personal instructions?" they would answer that it was to attain superknowledges or a vision of their chosen deity. However, they should answer, "It is becoming more and more definite about the causes and effects of karma and, consequently, keeping purely whatever vows I have assumed."

Therefore, you should understand this to indicate that the phrase "attainments which result from meditation" refers to the achievement of a reduction in afflictions such as ignorance.

When people fight with others—something that yields only sins and suffering both in this and in other lives—they endure all manner of suffering for however long it takes, even at the cost of their lives. Then they show off the scars of their wounds, etc., and boast, "I received this one at that time." This being the case, it is even more appropriate for us to endure the hardships undergone while persevering joyously in destroying the afflictions. *Engaging in the Bodhisattva Deeds*:[597]

Since even a scar inflicted by an enemy for no reason
Is worn as if it were a decoration for the body,
Why should suffering bother me,
When I truly strive to accomplish a great purpose?

Thus, the one who struggles against the enemy of the afflictions and defeats them should be called a true hero, whereas the one who fights against ordinary enemies kills only a corpse, since these enemies will die naturally anyway even if they are not slain. *Engaging in the Bodhisattva Deeds*:[598]

> They are conquering heroes
> Who scorn all sufferings
> And defeat enemies like hostility;
> The rest are killers of corpses.

Consequently, as the same text says:[599]

> When I dwell amidst the horde of afflictions,
> I must withstand them in a thousand ways;
> Just as foxes and their like cannot harm the lion,
> So the hosts of afflictions will not hurt me.

Thus, do not allow the factors incompatible with the path to inflict harm on you, and conquer them all.

This concludes the explanation of the stages of the path shared with persons of medium capacity.

Appendix 1
Outline of the Text

[Chapter One *Atisha* 35]

I. Showing the greatness of the teaching's author in order to establish that it is of noble origin 35
A. How he took rebirth in an excellent lineage 36
B. How upon that basis he gained good qualities 36
1. How, knowing many texts, he gained the good qualities of scriptural knowledge 36
2. How, engaging in proper practice, he gained the good qualities of experiential knowledge 38
a. That Atisha possessed the training in ethics 38
1) How Atisha possessed superior vows of individual liberation 38
2) That Atisha possessed the bodhisattva vows 38
3) That Atisha possessed the vows of the Vajrayāna 39
b. That Atisha possessed the training in concentration 40
1) The training in concentration common to sūtra and tantra 40
2) The training in the uncommon concentrations 40
c. That Atisha possessed the training in wisdom 40
1) The common training in wisdom 40
2) The uncommon training in wisdom 40
C. Having gained those good qualities, what Atisha did to further the teachings 40
1. What he did in India 40
2. What he did in Tibet 41

[Chapter Two *The Greatness of the Teaching* 45]

II. Showing the greatness of the teaching in order to engender respect for the instructions 46
A. The greatness of enabling one to know that all of the teachings are free of contradiction 46
B. The greatness of enabling one to understand that all of the scriptures are instructions for practice 50

[Chapter Ten *Reflecting on Your Future Life* 161]

[Chapter Eleven *Going for Refuge to the Three Jewels* 177]

[Chapter Fifteen *Cultivating Ethical Behavior* 247]

[Chapter Sixteen *The Attitude of a Person of Small Capacity* 261]

[Chapter Seventeen *The Eight Types of Suffering* 265]

Appendix 2
Glossary

actualized factors	*mngon par grub pa'i yan lag*
actualizing factors	*mngon par 'grub par byed pa'i yan lag*
adepts	*mkhas pa, mkhas grub*
affliction	*nyon mongs*
aggregate	*phung po*
ambrosial state	*bdud rtsi'i go 'phang*
analysis	*dpyad pa, dpyod pa*
analytical meditation	*dpyad sgom*
appropriated	*nyer len*
aspirational prayers	*smon lam*
aspirational spirit of enlightenment	*smon pa'i byang chub kyi sems*
attachment	*mngon par zhen pa, 'dod chags*
attainment	*dngos grub*
awareness	*blo*
beings	*skye bo, 'gro ba*
Bhagavan	*bcom ldan 'das*
bodhisattva	*byang chub sems pa*
buddha	*sangs rgyas*
caring	*brtse ba*
causally concordant behavioral effect	*byed pa rgyu mthun gyi 'bras bu*
causally concordant experiential effect	*myong ba rgyu mthun gyi 'bras bu*
certain goodness	*nges legs*

cessation	*'gogs*
chosen deity	*yi dam*
classic texts	*gzhung che ba rnams*
community	*dge 'dun*
completing karma	*yongs su rdzogs par byed pa'i las*
compositional actions	*'du byed kyi las*
concentration	*ting nge 'dzin*
conditioning	*goms pa*
conduct	*brtul zhugs*
confession	*bshags pa*
confidence	*dad pa, yid ches pa*
confusion	*rmongs pa*
conqueror	*rgyal ba*
conqueror's children	*rgyal sras*
consciousness	*shes pa, rnam shes*
consolidation	*bsgril*
constituent	*khams*
contemplation	*thug dam*
craving	*sred pa*
cyclic existence	*'khor ba, srid pa*
deeds of proficient conduct	*rig pa brtul zhugs*
deeds wrong by nature	*rang bzhin gyi kha na ma tho ba*
deeds wrong by prohibition	*bcas pa'i kha na ma tho ba*
delusion	*gti mug*
dependent arising	*rten 'brel*
desire realm	*'dod khams*
determination to be free	*nges 'byung gi bsam pa*
discerning wisdom	*so sor rtog pa'i ye shes/ so sor rtog pa'i shes rab*
discernment	*so sor rig pa*
disciples	*gdul bya*
discipline	*'dul ba*
discrimination	*'du shes*
disenchantment	*skyo shas*
disgust	*yid 'byung*
dysfunctional tendency	*gnas ngan len*
embodiment of form	*gzugs sku*
embodiment of truth	*chos sku*
emptiness	*stong pa nyid*
engaged spirit of enlightenment	*'jug sems*
enlightened activities	*'phrin las*

enlightenment	*byang chub*
ethically neutral	*lung ma bstan*
explication	*bjes su bstan pa*
faculties	*dbang po*
faith	*dad pa*
familiarization	*goms pa*
fault	*skyon, nyes pa, nyes dmigs*
focusing	*gtad pa*
form realm	*gzugs khams*
formless realm	*gzugs med khams*
freedom	*rnam grol*
full ordination	*bsnyen par rdzogs pa*
fully ordained monks and nuns	*dge slongs pa dang ma*
fundamental consciousness	*kun gzhi*
grasping	*rab tu 'dzin pa, len pa*
great compassion	*snying rje chen po*
happy realm	*bde 'gro*
hearing	*thos pa*
high status	*mtho ris*
Hīnayāna	*theg dman*
hostility	*sdang ba*
householder	*khyim pa*
ignorance	*ma rig pa*
image of the Buddha	*ston pa'i sku*
inclination	*bag chags*
infraction	*ltung ba*
insight	*lhag mthong*
instruction	*gdams ngag*
intelligence	*shes rab*
intended meaning	*dgongs pa*
internalize	*gong du chud pa*
invariable karma	*mi g.yo ba'i las*
joyful perserverance	*brtson 'grus*
karma that is intention	*sems pa'i las*
karma that is the intended action	*bsam pa'i las*
knowledge	*mkhyen pa*
latent propensity	*bag chags, bag la nyal ba*
leisure	*dal ba*
liberation	*thar pa*
living beings	*sems can*

Mahāyāna	*theg chen*
meditation	*sgom pa*
meditative equipoise	*mnyam par 'jog pa, mnyam bzhag*
meditative session	*thun*
meditative stabilization	*bsam gtan*
mental process	*sems byung*
merit	*bsod nams*
mindfulness	*dran pa*
misdeed	*kha na ma tho ba*
miserable realm	*ngan 'gro*
mistakenly superimpose	*sgro 'dogs*
motivation	*kun slong*
neutral	*lung ma bstan*
nirvana	*mya ngan las 'das pa*
noble being	*'phags pa*
non-virtue	*mi dge ba*
novice monks and nuns	*dge tshul pa dang ma*
obeisance	*phyag tshal*
object of meditation	*sgom bya*
obscuration	*sgrib pa*
omniscience	*rnam mkhyen, kun mkhyen*
one-day vow	*bsnyen gnas*
opportunity	*'byor ba*
oral transmission	*lung*
path	*lam*
patience	*bzod pa*
peak of cyclic existence	*srid rtse*
perfection vehicle	*par phyin theg pa*
person of great capacity	*skyes bu chen po*
person of medium capacity	*skyes bu 'bring*
person of small capacity	*skyes bu chung ngu*
personal instruction	*man ngag*
pervasive suffering of conditionality	*khyab pa 'du byed kyi sdug bsngal*
pledge	*dam tshig*
powers	*stobs*
pratyekabuddha	*rang sangs rgyas, rang rgyal*
precept	*bslab bya*
prerequisite	*sngon 'gro*
projected factors	*'phangs pa'i yan lag*
projecting factors	*'phen pa'i yan lag*
projecting karma	*'phen pa'i las*

real nature and diversity of phenomena	*ji lta ba dang ji snyed pa*
reality	*chos nyid, de bzhin nyid, de kho na nyid, yang dag nyid*
realized teaching	*rtogs pa'i bstan pa*
reflection	*bsam pa*
reifying view of the perishing aggregates	*'jig tshog la lta ba*
religion	*chos*
renunciate	*rab tu byung ba*
retention	*gzungs*
rite	*cho ga*
sage	*thup ba, drang srong*
scholar	*mkhas pa*
scriptural collection	*sde snod*
scriptural teaching	*lung gi bstan pa*
selflessness of persons	*gang zag gi bdag med*
sensory faculties	*dbang po*
serenity	*zhi gnas*
service	*rim gro*
serviceable	*las su rung ba*
sin	*sdig pa*
sources	*skyed mched*
spirit of enlightenment	*sems bskyed, byang chub kyi sems*
spiritual attainments	*dngos grub*
śravaka	*nyan thos*
stabilizing meditation	*'jog sgom*
stage of generation	*bskyed pa'i rim pa*
study	*thos pa*
subjective aspects	*rnam pa*
suffering	*sdug bsngal*
superknowledge	*mngon par shes pa*
sustain	*skyong*
sustain the meditation	*skyong, dmigs rnam skyong*
Tantra	*rgyud*
Teacher	*ston pa*
teacher	*dge ba'i bshes gnyen*
teaching	*chos*
texts on knowledge	*chos mngon pa*
three billion world systems	*'jigs rten gyi stong gsum*
three mental poisons	*dug gsum*
trailblazer	*shing rta chen po*

training	*bslab pa*
true aspectarian	*rnam bden pa*
view	*lta ba*
view of the perishing aggregates	*'jig tshogs la lta ba*
virtue	*dge ba*
vows of individual liberation	*so so thar pa'i sdom pa*
vow	*sdom pa*
what to adopt and what to cast aside	*blang dor*
wisdom	*shes rab*
wrong view	*lta ngan, log lta*

NOTES

The citation reference in the notes first supplies the Sanskrit reference if extant, giving first the chapter and then the verse, or simply the page number(s). This is followed by the Suzuki (1955-61) reference (identified by the abbreviation P), giving the page, folio, and line numbers.

Introduction

1. In the following, dates for persons and texts have been indicated according to the conventional conversion of years given in our sources in terms of a Tibetan sexagenary or duodenary cycle. Exact dating will of course depend on extensive research in Tibetan historical and biographical literature, and it may lead to corrections of one year at least in terms of the Gregorian calendar. In several cases no reliable information for dating has been available. As for the Tibetan sources and the translations and studies in European languages cited in this introduction, they do not of course represent a complete bibliography of the *lam rim* literature.

2. The name dGa'/dGe-ldan-pa is connected with the name of the chief monastery of this religious order and philosophical school, 'Brog-ri-bo dGa'/dGe-ldan-rnam-par-rgyal-ba'i-gling, founded near Lhasa by Tsong-kha-pa himself. This school's more familar name is dGe-lugs-pa, said to be a euphonic variant of dGa'-lugs-pa by Thu'u-bkvan Blo-bzang-Chos-kyi-nyi-ma at the beginning of his history of this school in the *Grub mtha' shel gyi me long* (pp. 235-36 of the Kansu reprint of 1984). Being a continuation of the earlier bKa'-gdams school going back to Atisha in the eleventh century, this school is also known as the bKa'-gdams-gsar-ma.

On the life of Tsong-kha-pa, in addition to E. Obermiller's still useful article "Tsoṅ-kha-pa le pandit" in *Mélanges chinois et bouddhiques* 3 (1935), pp. 319-38, see R. Thurman (ed.), *The Life and Teachings of Tsong Khapa* (Dharamsala, 1982) and R. Kaschewsky, *Das Leben des lamaistischen Heiligen Tsongkhapa Blo-bzaṅ-grags-pa* (Wiesbaden, 1971).

3. Bracketed numbers throughout this work are page references to the reprint in book form of the Bya-khyung edition of the *Lam rim chen mo* published in Qinghai (mTsho sngon) in 1985.

4. On the *blo sbyong* or mind-training literature properly speaking, which is closely connected with the *lam rim* literature, see n. 13 below.

5. On the central place in Tsong-kha-pa's Madhyamaka thought of the principle of origination in dependence, *pratītyasamutpāda*, see his very famous metrical "Hymn to the Teacher" (i.e. the Buddha), the *sTon pa bla na med pa la zab mo rten cing 'brel bar byung ba gsung ba'i sgo nas bstod pa Legs par bshad pa'i snying po*. An English translation of this work is found in R. Thurman (ed.), *Life and Teachings of Tsong Khapa*, pp. 99-107; and French translations have been published by G. Driessens, *L'entrée au Milieu par Candrakīrti* (Anduz, 1988), pp. 402-11, and D. Seyfort Ruegg, "La pensée tibétaine," in A. Jacob (ed.), *Encyclopédie philosophique universelle* (Vol. 1, "L'univers philosophique," Paris, 1989), pp. 1589-91. See in general J. Hopkins, *Meditation on Emptiness* (London, 1983); E. Napper, *Dependent-Arising and Emptiness* (Boston, 1989); and H. Tauscher, *Die Lehre von den zwei Wirklichkeiten in Tsoṅ kha pa's Madhyamaka-Werken* (Vienna, 1995).

6. See E. Napper, *Dependent-Arising and Emptiness*, pp. 44 ff., 81; H. Tauscher, *Die Lehre von den zwei Wirklichkeiten in Tsoṅ kha pa's Madhyamaka-Werken*, pp. 75 ff., 86-88.

7. Cf. D. Seyfort Ruegg, "On *Pramāṇa* Theory in Tsoṅ kha pa's Madhyamaka Philosophy," in E. Steinkellner (ed.), *Studies in the Buddhist Epistemological Tradition* (Vienna, 1991), pp. 281-310; and id., "On the Thesis and Assertion in the Madhyamaka/dBu ma," in E. Steinkellner and H. Tauscher (eds.), *Contributions on Tibetan and Buddhist Religion and Philosophy* (Vienna, 1983), pp. 205-41. Enlarged and updated versions of these two articles are now to be found in *Three Studies in the History of Indian and Tibetan Madhyamaka Philosophy* (Vienna, 2000).

8. In his "Small Graded Path," the *Lam gyi rim pa mdo tsam du bstan pa* (see below), Tsong-kha-pa also discusses the Vajrayāna/Mantrayāna in addition to the Pāramitāyāna. For some further texts of the *lam rim* genre that link Pāramitāyāna and Vajrayāna, see below.

9. On this theme and its many religious, philosophical and historical problems, see recently D. Seyfort Ruegg, *Buddha-nature, Mind and the Problem of Gradualism in a Comparative Perspective* (London, 1989).

10. See the second article cited in n. 7 above.

11. Gro-lung-pa's larger *bstan rim* is entitled *bDe bar gshegs pa'i bstan pa rin po che la 'jug pa'i lam gyi rim pa rnam par bshad pa*. On this *bstan rim* and other related works, see D. Jackson, "The *bsTan rim* ("Stages of the Doctrine") and Similar Graded Expositions of the Bodhisattva's Path," in J. Cabezón and R. Jackson (eds.), *Tibetan Literature* (Ithaca, 1996), pp. 229-43.

12. This work by sGam-po-pa has been translated by H. V. Guenther, *The Jewel Ornament of Liberation* (London, 1959).

Another early work of the *bstan rim* category is the *Sangs rgyas kyi bstan pa la rim gyis 'jug pa'i tshul* by sGam-po-pa's disciple Phag-mo-gru-pa rDo-rje-rgyal-po (1110-1170) (reprinted at Bir in 1977).

13. Concerning this *blo sbyong* literature, beside A-khu Shes-rab-rgya-mtsho's *dPe rgyun dkon pa 'ga' zhig gi tho yig* (ed. Lokesh Chandra, *Materials for a History of Tibetan Literature*, Part 3 [New Delhi, 1963]), p. 418 ff., the *Catalogue of the Tohoku University Collection of Tibetan Works on Buddhism* (Sendai, n.d.), pp. 508 ff., and the *Bod kyi bstan bcos kha cig gi mtshan byang* (Qinghai, 1985), pp. 630 ff., see e.g. Geshe Ngawang Dhargyey, *The Wheel of Sharp Weapons* (Dharamsala, 1981) (for the *Theg pa chen po'i blo sbyong mtshon cha 'khor lo* translated into Tibetan by Atisha and 'Brom ston); id., *Tibetan Tradition of Mental Development* (Dharamsala, 1978); Geshe Rabten and Geshe Ngawang Dhargyey, *Advice from a Spiritual Friend* (New Delhi, 1977); Geshe Ngawang Dhargyey with A. Berzin, *An Anthology of Well-spoken Advice* (Dharamsala, 1982). See also K. McLeod, *A Direct Path to Enlightenment* (Vancouver, 1974) (for Kong-sprul's *Blo sbyong don bdun ma'i khrid yig*). A short sketch of the *blo sbyong* literature has been provided by M. Sweet, "Mental Purification," in J. Cabezón and R. Jackson (eds.), *Tibetan Literature*, pp. 244-60.

14. See Thutop Tulku and Ngawang Sonam Tenzin, *The Manjushri Tradition and the Zenpa Zidel* (Sārnāth, 1968). An example of a relevant manual is Go-rams-pa bSod-nams-seng-ge's (1429-1489) *Blo sbyong zhen pa bzhi bral gyi khrid yig zab don gnad kyi lde'u mig* (in volume 8 of his bKa' 'bum).

15. On the *Thub pa'i dgongs gsal*, see Geshe Wangyal and B. Cutillo, *Illuminations* (Novato, 1988).

16. See Sonam T. Kazi, *Kün-zang La-may Zhal-lung: The Oral Instruction of Kün-zang la-ma on the Preliminary Practices of Dzog-ch'en Long-ch'en Nying-tig*, 2 vols. (Montclair, 1989 and 1993); and *The Words of My Perfect Teacher*, translated by the Padmakara Translation Group (San Francisco, 1994).

17. See *The Light of Wisdom*, translated, along with a commentary by Kong-sprul Blo-gros-mtha'-yas (1813-1899), by Erik Pema Kunsang (Boston, 1995).

18. See Lopon Tenzin Namdak, *Heart Drops of Dharmakaya: Dzogchen Practice of the Bön Tradition* (Ithaca, 1993).

19. See the *dPe rgyun dkon pa 'ga' zhig gi tho yig* (cited above, n. 13), pp. 514-22. See also the list of works in the *lam rim* and *blo sbyong* section of the *Catalogue of the Tohoku University Collection of Tibetan Works on Buddhism*, pp. 505-19.

20. See P. V. Bapat, *Vimuktimārga, Dhutaguṇanirdeśa: Tibetan text critically edited and translated into English* (Delhi University Buddhist Studies, 1, Delhi, 1964). This short text of some twelve folios entitled *rNam par grol ba'i lam las sbyangs pa'i yon tan bstan pa*, which was translated into Tibetan by Vidyākaraprabha and dPal-brtsegs, is no. 972 in the Beijing bKa'-'gyur and no. 4143 in the sDe-dge bsTan-'gyur. See also P. V. Bapat, *Vimuttimagga and Visuddhimagga: A Comparative Study* (Poona, 1937); and N. R. M. Ehara, Soma Thera and Kheminda Thera, *The Path of Freedom (Vimuttimagga)* (Colombo, 1961).

An older (non-canonical or, in Burma, semi-canonical) survey of Buddhist thought in Pali which served as a source for the *Visuddhimagga* is the *Peṭakopadesa* (Bapat, op. cit., p. xxv), a work divided into eight chapters termed *bhūmis* that has links with the *Nettipakaraṇa*; both these texts are connected with Mahākaccāna. In still another very important work which might be described as an encyclopedia of Buddhist thought, the *Ta-chih-tu-lun (*Mahāprajñāpāramitopadeśa)* ascribed to Nāgārjuna having the form of a commentary on the *Pañcaviṃśatisāhasrikā prajñāpāramitā*, there is a note by Kumārajīva referring to a "Pi-le" (or "Peṭaka") by Kātyāyana, a text that has been (dubiously) linked with the *Peṭakopadesa*; see E. Lamotte, *Le traité de la Grande Vertu de Sagesse (Mahāprajñāpāramitāśāstra) de Nāgārjuna*, i (Louvain, 1944), p. 109 n. 2, and *Histoire du bouddhisme indien*, i (Louvain, 1958), pp. 207-08, together with P. V. Bapat, op. cit., p. xlii f. The *Ta-chih-tu-lun* has been transmitted in Chinese only, and it was not used by Tsong-kha-pa.

21. For this work see R. Thurman (ed.), *Life and Teachings of Tsong Khapa*, pp. 108-85.

22. See ibid., pp. 67-89.

23. See *Lines of Experience* (Dharamsala, 1973) and *Life and Teachings of Tsong Khapa*, pp. 59-66; and Dagpo Rimpoche, *L'ode aux réalisations* (L'Hay-les-Roses, 1989).

24. This is the first text of the *bKa' 'bum thor bu*, or Miscellaneous Works, contained in the second volume of Tsong-kha-pa's gSung-'bum. Cf. G. Mullin, *Selected Works of the Dalai Lama III; Essence of Refined Gold* (Ithaca, 1983), pp. 199-201; Lobsang Dargyay and Tenzin Chhöphel, *Yon-tan gžir-gyur-ma (Fundament der guten Qualitäten)* (Rikon, 1971); and Khen Rinpoche Geshe Lobsang Tharchin with Michael Roach, *Preparing for Tantra: The Mountain of Blessings* (Howell, 1995).

25. The earliest such *sa lam* work in Tsong-kha-pa's school is perhaps the *Sa lam gyi rnam gzhag mkhas pa'i yid 'phrog* by his pupil Mkhas-grub dGe-legs-dpal-bzang (1385-1438). This author also composed a graded path of both Mantra and Pāramitā, the *sNgags dang pha rol tu phyin pa'i sa lam bgrod tshul gsal sgron dang sbyor ba*, as well as a manual of the path based on Dharmakīrti's Pramāṇa school of epistemology, the *Tshad ma'i lam 'khrid*. There is also a *Tshad ma'i lam khrid* among the writings of Tsong-kha-pa's other great disciple, Rgyal-tshab Dar-ma-rin-chen (1364-1432), Tsong-kha-pa's successor on the abbatial seat of dGa'-ldan Monastery. A short sketch of the *sa lam rnam bzhag* literature has been given by J. Levinson, "Metaphors of Liberation: Tibetan Treatises on Grounds and Paths," in J. Cabezón and R. Jackson (eds.), *Tibetan Literature*, pp. 261-74.

26. On bSod-nams-rgya-mtsho's *lam rim* work, see G. Mullin, *Selected Works of the Dalai Lama III: Essence of Refined Gold*. And on the *Yon tan gzhir gyur ma* see above.

27. See J. Hopkins, *Practice of Emptiness: The Perfection of Wisdom Chapter of the Fifth Dalai Lama's "Sacred Word of Mañjuśrī"* (Dharamsala, 1976).

28. See the already cited (n. 13) *Catalogue of the Tohoku University Collection of Tibetan Works on Buddhism*, no. 6986. Other works by the same author have been translated by H. V. Guenther, *Tibetan Buddhism Without Mystification* (Leiden, 1966).

Yongs-'dzin Ye-shes-rgyal-mtshan also produced a collection of biographies of the masters who transmitted the *lam rim*: the *Byang chub lam gyi rim pa'i bla ma brgyud pa'i rnam par thar pa*. On this and similar works, including the *Byang chub lam gyi rim pa'i bla ma brgyud pa'i rnam par thar pa padma dkar po'i 'phreng ba* by this author's teacher Paṇchen Blo-bzang-ye-shes, see A. Vostrikov, *Tibetan Historical Literature* (Calcutta, 1970), pp. 180-82.

29. Another *sa bcad* or synoptic table of the *Lam rim chen mo*, the *Byang chub lam rim chen mo'i shar sgom bya tshul gyi man ngag*, was composed by Klong-rdol-bla-ma Ngag-dbang-blo-bzang (1719-1794/5), who in addition wrote a *sa bcad* of the *Lam rim chung ba*.

30. There exists a guidance-transmission (*'khrid rgyun*) of the graded path to awakening known as the *lho brgyud*, or "Southern Tradition," *lam rim* which derives from the Fifth Dalai Lama's above-mentioned *'Jam dpal zhal lung* and is connected with the Lho-kha region and with the Dvags-po-grva-tshang monastery; this is the *Byang chub lam gyi rim pa'i dmar khrid 'jam dpal zhal lung gi 'khrid rgyun bsdus pa lho brgyud du grags pa* (see no. 6984 in *A Catalogue of the Tohoku University Collection of Tibetan Works on Buddhism* cited above in n. 13). Following a transmission (*gsung rgyun*) from the Grub-pa'i dbang-phyug Ngag-dbang-blo-bzang-bstan-pa-dar-rgyas-dpal-bzang-po, dGe-'dun-'jam-dbyangs wrote down this *dmar khrid*. A xylograph of it was prepared in 1913 by Blo-bzang-ngag-dbang-bstan-'dzin-rgya-mtsho, it having been received as a guiding instruction (*bka' 'khrid*) from the aforementioned Dvags-po-bla-ma-rin-po-che Blo-bzang-'Jam-dpal-lhun-grub-rgya-mtsho. A sketch of the history of this "Southern Tradition" *lam rim* is provided in the *lHo brgyud lam rim gyi khrid rgyun 'dzin pa'i mkhas grub phyis byon rnams la nyer mkho ba'i mna' gtam gser gyi phreng ba* printed at the Zhol-par-khang at Lhasa. Details concerning this *lho brgyud lam rim* are to be found in vol. 10 (*tha*) of the gSung-'bum of Pha-bong-kha-pa Byams-pa-bstan-'dzin-'phrin-las (1878-1941). As indicated earlier, significant *lam rim* texts are found already in the gSung-'bum of the above-mentioned earlier master of the Dvags-po-grva-tshang, (Dvags-po) Mkhan-chen Ngag-dbang-grags-pa (born in the fifteenth century); see the *Zhva ser bstan pa'i sgron me ... Dri med zla shel gtsaṅ ma'i me long* ("gSung-'bum dkar- chag," Lha sa and Zi ling, 1990), p. 182. But these latter works do not form part of the *lho brgyud lam rim* tradition deriving from the Fifth Dalai Lama's *'Jam dpal zhal lung*.

31. On this work see Khen Rinpoche Geshe Lobsang Tharchin with Artemus Engle, *Liberation in Our Hands*, 2 Parts (Howell, 1990 and 1994); and Michael Richards, *Liberation in the Palm of Your Hand* (Boston, 1991). See also Geshe Ngawang Dhargyey with A. Berzin, *An Anthology of Well-spoken Advice* (Dharamsala, 1982).

32. See Khen Rinpoche Geshe Lobsang Tharchin with Michael Roach, *Preparing for Tantra: The Mountain of Blessings* (Howell, 1995).

33. On this last work see Lokesh Chandra (ed.), *Buryat Annotations on the Lam-rim* (New Delhi, 1973). For several other works in this list and for further titles, see the already cited (n. 13) *Catalogue of the Tohoku University Collection of Tibetan Works on Buddhism*, pp. 505 ff., A-khu Shes-rab-rgya-mtsho's *dPe rgyun dkon pa 'ga' zhig gi tho yig*, pp. 514

ff., and the *Bod kyi bstan bcos kha cig gi mtshan byang* (Qinghai, 1985), pp. 625 ff., as well as the bibliography in Geshe Ngawang Dhargyey with A. Berzin, *An Anthology of Well-spoken Advice*. Many of the works included in this paragraph have been unavailable for consultation and have therefore been listed here following standard bibliographic sources.

34. Cf. Geshe Wangyal, *The Door of Liberation* (New York, 1973), pp. 191-235; and R. Thurman, *Life and Teachings of Tsong khapa*, pp. 57-58. Tsong-kha-pa's relevant *Lam gyi gtso bo* work is found among the *bKa' 'bum thor bu* in the second volume of his gSung 'bum.

35. On this commentarial work (listed e.g. in the *Catalogue of the Tohoku University Collection of Tibetan Works on Buddhism*, no. 6977), see Pha-bong-kha-pa's *Byang chub lam rim chen mo mchan bu bzhi sbrags kyi skor dran gso'i bsnyel byang mgo smos tsam du mdzad pa* (in vol. 5 of *The Collected Works of Pha-boṅ-kha-pa*, New Delhi, 1973). Cf. A. Wayman, *Calming the Mind and Discerning the Real* (New York, 1978), p. 70; and E. Napper, *Dependent-Arising and Emptiness*, p. 219 ff.

36. See L. Petech, *Il nuovo Rasmusio II: I missionari italiani nel Tibet e nel Nepal – Ippolito Desideri S.I.* (Parts V-VII, Rome, 1954-56); and F. de Filippi (ed.), *An Account of Tibet: The Travels of Ippolito Desideri of Pistoia, S.J., 1712-1727* (London, 1932). Cf. C. Wessels, *Early Jesuit Travellers in Central Asia* (The Hague, 1924); G. M. Toscano, *La prima missione cattolica nel Tibet* (Istituto Missioni Estere, Parma, and M. Nijhof, The Hague, 1931; Hong Kong, 1951); and R. Sherburne, "A Christian-Buddhist Dialog? Some Notes on Desideri's Tibetan Manuscripts," in L. Epstein and R. Sherburne (eds.), *Reflections on Tibetan Culture: Essays in Memory of Turrell V. Wylie* (Lewiston, 1990), pp. 295-305.

37. On the Mongolian translation of the *Lam rim chen mo*, see W. Heissig, *Pekinger lamaistische Blockdrucke* (Wiesbaden, 1954), pp. 67-68.

38. For an early tribute and appreciation of Geshe Wangyal relating to the 1930s and 1940s, see M. Pallis, *Peaks and Lamas* (3rd ed., London, 1974). On the Buddhist clergy and hierarchy among one group of the Oirats (Oyirads or West Mongols), see A. Bormanshinov, *The Lamas of the Kalmyk People: The Don Kalmyk Lamas* (Bloomington, 1991); cf. id., "Kalmyk Pilgrims in Tibet and Mongolia," *Central Asiatic Journal* 42 (1998), pp. 1-23.

Chapter One *Atisha*

1. In Buddhist cosmology, Jambudvīpa is the southern of the four continents surrounding Mount Meru, the mountain in the center of the world. It is the continent on which humans have the best inner and outer conditions for religious practice.

2. "Mother of Conquerors" is the *Prajñāpāramitā-sūtras* (*Perfection of Wisdom Sūtras*). Wisdom is the mother of all the conquerors, i.e. buddhas, in the sense that through developing the wisdom which knows emptiness and so forth one can finally attain buddhahood.

3. Text corrected from "Vrikāmalaśīla" in accordance with A-kya: 92.5-93.3, who discusses the spelling of this name and says that in spite of its appearing in many old and new editions of Tsong-kha-pa's text as *Vrikamalaśīla*, the correct form is *Vikramalaśīla*.

4. This outline is part of the Tibetan text. The translators have included the outline for each chapter's content at the beginning of the chapter, and the subsequent headings that occur throughout the chapter repeat this outline. When an outline entry covers future chapters, the translators have indicated the chapters to which it refers. When an outline entry covers material included in the next two volumes, they have indicated the chapter in which it begins and added the words "and on."

5. *Abhisamayālaṃkāra-prajñāpāramitopadeśa-śāstra-kārikā* (AA), P5184. This text sets forth the hidden meaning of the *Prajñāpāramitā-sūtras*, detailing the path to enlightenment.

6. 'Jam-dbyangs-bzhad-pa (*mChan*: 18.5-6) explains that the *Bodhi-patha-pradīpa* is the root text for Tsong-kha-pa's text, and since Atisha is the author of that, implicitly he can be considered the author of this text. 'Jam-dbyangs-bzhad-pa sees his interpretation as supported by the fact that when Tsong-kha-pa discusses the greatness of the teaching to be explained, he speaks of the greatness of the *Bodhi-patha-pradīpa*.

7. Nag-tsho-lo-tsā-ba-tshul-khrims-rgyal-ba (Nak-tso-lo-dza-wa-tsul-trim-gyel-wa) was born in 1011, in the Gung-thang region of mNga'-ris (Nga-ri), in present-day Ladakh. Nag-tsho successfully invited and accompanied Atisha to Tibet and then stayed with him for many years as his student.

The full name of this short verse praise of Atisha by Nag-tsho is the *Khams gsum chos kyi rgyal po dpal ldan mar me mdzad ye shes la bstod pa'i rab tu byed pa tshigs bcad brgyad cu pa*. It is found in the *Legs par bshad pa bka' gdams rin po che'i gsung gi gces btus nor bu'i bang mdzod (bKa' gdams bces btus)* compiled by Ye-shes-don-grub-bstan-pa'i-rgyal-mtshan, pp. 30-39. A longer biography, *Jo bo rje dpal ldan mar me mdzad ye shes kyi rnam thar rgyas pa* (*rNam thar rgyas pa*) (*Long Biography of Atisha)*, is based largely on Nag-tsho's account of the life of Atisha.

This citation and the following citations from Nag-tsho's *bsTod pa brgyad cu pa* are, with one possible exception, all found within his *rNam thar rgyas pa (Jo bo rje dpal ldan mar me mdzad ye shes kyi rnam thar rgyas pa)*, and Tsong-kha-pa's prose elaborations often also closely follow it. Tsong-kha-pa's following citations from these verses of praise will be cited from the *rNam thar rgyas pa*. The stanzas cited here (with a few variations) are in the *rNam thar rgyas pa:* 48.8-12 and 49.9-16, but there they are attributed to one of Atisha's foremost Indian disciples, the paṇḍita Kṣitigarbha (Sa'i-snying-po). For more on the *rNam thar rgyas pa*, see Eimer 1979. For more on the *bsTod pa brgyad cu pa*, see *The Blue Annals* (Roerich: 242), and Eimer 1977: 142-146.

8. The Tibetan for eastern emperor is *stong khun*. A-kya-yongs-'dzin in his *Brief Explanation of Terminology in the "Lam rim chen mo"* (A-kya: 97.2-4) reports that lCang-skya-rol-pa'i-rdo-rje (Jang-gya-rol-bay-dor-jay, 1717-1786) said that *stong khun* stands for the Chinese *tūng kus* with *tūng* meaning "east" and *kus* being a polite way of referring to a

king or minister. Thus the meaning is that Atisha's father's wealth, etc., were like that of the emperor of eastern China. Stein (1961: note 70) states that *stong khun* is perhaps a transcription of the Chinese "T'ang kiun" or "sovereign of T'ang." Tashi Tsering of the Library of Tibetan Works and Archives, in a personal communication, identifies *stong khun* as a stock expression meaning "Chinese emperor of legendary wealth."

9. Ba-so-chos-kyi-rgyal-mtshan (*mChan*: 20.5) says this is Dhanaśrīmitra.

10. *rNam thar rgyas pa*: 51.2-51.5.

11. *sGyu rtsal*. A-kya-yongs-'dzin (A-kya: 98.1-2) gives a breakdown of the sixty-four arts that he says comes from the *Mahā-vibhāṣā*, the compendia of orthodox Sarvāstivāda Abhidharma. These are also listed in the *Bod rgya tshig mdzod chen mo* (*Tibetan Chinese Dictionary*) (People's Publishing House 1984). Thirty include skills (*bzo*), such as writing, astrology, martial arts, riding and training animals, and athletics; eighteen refer to aspects of music (*rol mo'i bye brag*), primarily different types of instruments as well as vocal and physical accompaniment with hands and feet; seven types of pitch (*glu dbyangs kyi nges pa*), which are sounds like various types of animals and birds to show different emotions; and nine refer to moods of dance (*gar gyi cha byad*), showing different mannerisms of body (fierce, courageous), speech, and mind (compassionate, peaceful). Ganguly (1962) has a description of these from the viewpoint of the Indian tradition.

12. *rNam thar rgyas pa:* 35-45 details what Atisha studied.

13. Kṛṣṇagiri or Kālaśilā (Chattopadhyaya 1981: 73); the more probable, Kālaśila, also given by Roerich (1979: 242), which in B.C. Law's view is one of the famous seven hills near Rājagṛha. The information that Tsong-kha-pa gives in this paragraph can be found in *rNam thar rgyas pa*: 51.5-10 and 33.16-34.7.

14. The mantra vehicle (*gsang sngags kyi theg pa*), or vajra vehicle (*rdo rje theg pa*) is the practice of what is taught in the tantric texts, tantras, or classes of tantra (*rgyud sde*).

15. All editions of the the text say *ḍākima*, a variation on the Indian word *ḍākinī* usually rendered into Tibetan as *mkha' 'gro ma*, "sky-goer," rather than given in a transliterated form.

16. A-kya: 101.5. This refers to the attainment of the forbearance level of the path of preparation, the third of its four levels. The five Buddhist paths or stages of attainment are the paths of accumulation, preparation, seeing, meditation, and no-more-learning.

17. *rNam thar rgyas pa*: 61.12. The material in this and the following paragraph is found in *rNam thar rgyas pa:* 60.3-62.6. There is a slight variation in the citation of the second line: as cited by Tsong-kha-pa, the line ends *rab tu grags;* as found in the *rNam thar rgyas pa* it reads *grags pa yin*. The meaning is the same.

18. This is a variant spelling of the name; the usual form seen in secondary literature is Odantapuri. Chattopadhyaya (1981: 119-120) says that the exact site of Odantapuri has not been identified. However, she cites dGe-'dun-chos-'phel, who locates it to the north of Nālanda, somewhere between Patna and Rājgir. Sukumar Dutt (1962: 344-346) says that Odantapuri was built by the founder of the Pāla Dynasty, Gopāla, in the mid-eighth

century about six miles from Nālanda and was completely destroyed around 1198. See also Ngag-dbang-rab-brtan (*mChan*: 23.2-6).

19. The great systematization of Sarvāstivāda Buddhism used by the Vaibhāṣikas, preserved in three Chinese translations but not in Tibetan (Dessein and Cox 1998).

20. Ngag-dbang-rab-brtan (*mChan*: 23.6) identifies these as Sarvāstivāda (*gzhi thams cad yod par smra ba)*, Mahāsaṃghika (*phal chen po)*, Sthāvira (*gnas brtan pa*), and Saṃmitīya (*mang pos bkur ba*).

21. That is, the discourses (*mdo sde, sūtra*), discipline (*'dul ba, vinaya*), and knowledge (*mngon pa, abhidharma*).

22. The three precious trainings are the trainings in ethics, concentration, and wisdom. The Tibetan for "the teachings as they are realized" is *rtogs pa'i bstan pa.*

23. This heading is not spelled out explicitly in Tsong-kha-pa's text, but is found in the separate listing of the outline of the text called *Byang chub lam rim chen mo'i sa bcad* and in 'Jam-dbyangs-bzhad-pa et al.'s *mChan* (*Four Interwoven Annotations*): 24.5. Its appropriateness is demonstrated by the parallelism with the sections that follow, "b. That Atisha possessed the training in concentration," and "c. That Atisha possessed the training in wisdom."

24. *rNam thar rgyas pa*: 94.15-18.

25. This refers to the fact that the monastic vows are taken in accordance with the scriptures of the *śrāvaka* vehicle, not that Atisha was a *śrāvaka* in the sense of having a Hīnayāna motivation.

26. *rNam thar rgyas pa:* 95.9-12.

27. Sauvarṇadvīpa or Suvarṇadvīpiya ("the Sumatran"). He is also known by the name Dharmakīrtiśrī and Maitripāda (*rNam thar rgyas pa*: 26.1 and 26.5).

28. *rNam thar rgyas pa:* 87.2-3.

29. "Conquerors' children" (*rgyal sras*) means bodhisattvas.

30. *rNam thar rgyas pa:* 95.16-96.1.

31. "Saw yourself as a deity" means that Atisha practiced deity yoga.

32. Avadhūtipa, an epithet for Atisha, means "one engaged in practices involving the central channel."

33. *rNam thar rgyas pa*: 96.17-97.1

34. The three vows are the *śrāvaka*, bodhisattva, and tantric vows.

35. Lochö Rimbochay says that "the deeds of proficient conduct" (*rig pa brtul zhugs*) refers to conduct of a higher tantric practitioner that is so contrary to that of ordinary persons that the practitioner appears to be crazy.

36. *rNam thar rgyas pa*: 40.13-16. The last four lines are also cited at 21.7-8.

37. Ibid.: 92.13-93.1. Roerich (1979: 43) cites this verse as a source showing how much Buddhism had already diminished in India by the time of Atisha.

38. See note 20.

39. Ngag-dbang-rab-brtan (*mChan*: 28.5) identifies these four as monks, nuns, and male and female lay practitioners.

40. Ye-shes-'od (Ye-shay-ö), who lived in the late tenth and early eleventh century, and Byang-chub-'od (Jang-chup-ö), who lived in the early to mid-eleventh century, were kings of Western Tibet.

41. That is, brGya-brtson-'grus-seng-ge, who died in 1041 enroute to Tibet with Atisha.

42. Ngag-dbang-rab-brtan (*mChan:* 29.4-6) mentions that there are two traditions on how long Atisha spent in Tibet, one stating that he spent eleven years there, the other, also followed by Tsong-kha-pa, that he spent seventeen years; both concur that he died at age seventy-three. Chattopadhyaya (1981: 307-366) discusses the chronology of Atiśa's trip to Tibet and the duration of his stay there.

43. That is, one should be a scholar who has mastered the five topics of knowledge: Buddhist (*nang rig pa*), non-Buddhist (*phyi'i rig pa*), grammar and logic (*sgra gtan tshigs*), the arts (*bzo*), and medicine (*gso ba*). The list of five also appears as Buddhist knowledge, grammar, logic, the arts, and medicine.

44. *rNam thar rgyas pa:* 4.4-8. The fifth line, the "venerable Tārā, and so forth," is omitted there in what appears to be a copying error. In the commentary following the verse, the *rNam thar rgyas pa* lists as Atisha's six main deities (*thugs dam gyi gtso bo*) Tārā (Jo-mo sGrol-ma), Avalokiteśvara ('Phags-pa sPyan-ras-gzigs), Acala (Mi-g.yo-ba), Trisamayavyūharāja (Dam-tshig-gsum-bkod-pa'i-rgyal-po), Cakrasaṃvara (bDe-mchog-'khor-lo), and Hevajra (dPal dGyes-pa-rdo-rje).

45. 'Jam-dbyangs-bzhad-pa (*mChan*: 32.2) lists these five as: the lineage of all of Tantra (*sngags mtha' dag gi brgyud pa*); the lineage of Guhyasamaja, the lineage of the mother tantras, the lineage of Action and Yoga (*kriyā* and *yoga*), and the lineage of Yamāri (gShin-rje-gshed). A-kya's list (A-kya: 106.2-3) has the first as the lineage of all Secret Tantra (*gsang sngags mtha' dag gi brgyud pa*), and includes Performance along with Action and Yoga tantras in the fourth (*bya spyod dang rnal 'byor rgyud kyi brgyud pa*), giving as a source the *rNam thar chen mo (Great Biography)*, which may be the *Jo bo rin po che rje dpal ldan a ti sha'i rnam thar rgyas pa yongs grags* (*Renowned Biography*) by mChims-thams-cad-mkhyen-pa (Chim-tam-jay-kyen-ba) or the *rNam thar rgyas pa*. This same information is in the *rNam thar rgyas pa:* 7.11-14.

46. This is cited in the *rNam thar rgyas pa:* 21.17-22.2. The preceding paragraph is a very condensed version of 6-21 of the *rNam thar rgyas pa*. Corresponding passages to the following three paragraphs can be found in the *rNam thar rgyas pa*: 6.3 ff., 28.16 ff., and 225.1-226.8.

47. For brief biographies of many of these individuals, see Tshe-mchog-gling-Ye-shes-rgyal-mtshan (Ye-shay-gyen-tsen, 1713-1793), *Byang chub lam gyi rim pa'i bla ma brgyud pa'i rnam par thar pa* (*Lives of the Teachers of the Lam-rim Precepts*), vol. 1, pp. 359-385. Known dates not previously given for those above are: Rin-chen-bzang-po (958-1055);

rNal-'byor-ba-chen-po (1015-1077); dGon-pa-ba (1016-1082); Khu-ston-brtson-'grus-g.yung-drung (1011-1075); 'Brom-ston-pa-rgyal-ba'i-'byung-gnas (1005-1064).

48. *rNam thar gyi yi ge chen mo rnams*. There is no known standard biography of Atisha by this name. It may refer to the *rNam thar rgyas pa* or to the biographies known in Tsong-kha-pa's time, including the *rNam thar rgyas pa* and the *rNam thar rgyas pa yongs grags* (see above note 45).

Chapter Two *The Greatness of the Teaching*

49. The two great trail-blazers are gSer-gling-pa, learned in the system of Asaṅga, and the younger Vidyākokila (Rig-pa'i-khu-byug-chung-ba), also known as Avadhūtipa, who was learned in the system of Nāgārjuna. gSer-gling-pa and Vidyākokila were Atisha's two main teachers (*mChan*: 34.2-3, A-kya: 106.5-6).

50. *Prajñā-pradīpa-ṭīkā*, P5259: 275.3.7-8.

51. An epithet of a buddha that means "one who has overcome (*bhagna*) the four demons" and "one who has (*vat*) the six goodnesses (*bhaga*)—beauty, fame, power, glory, wisdom, and joyous perseverance."

52. This is *Bodhicitta-vivaraṇa*: 38, following the translation by Rab-zhi-chos-kyi-bshes-gnyen (Rap-shi-chö-gyi-shay-nyen) et al. (P5470: 273.3.4-5). Lindtner (1982: 196-197) reads *rang la de bzhin gzhan dag la/ nges pa bskyed par bya ba'i phyir*, however the reading *nges* is supported by Smṛtijñānakīrti's *Bodhicitta-vivaraṇa-ṭīkā (Commentary on the "Essay on the Spirit of Enlightenment"*) (P2694: 140.2.3), which says *de bas na rang gi nges pa gzhan rnams la nges pa bskyed pa'i don du ni*.... This verse comes in the middle of a section in which Nāgārjuna is refuting the Vijñānavāda, and its relation here to that context is not obvious.

53. *Pramāṇa-vārttika-kārikā*, Shastri 1968: 50.3; P5709: 85.5.1-2.

54. AA: 1.1; P5184: 3.1.1-2. The "paths" are the paths of *śrāvakas*, *pratyekabuddhas*, and bodhisattvas.

55. *Ārya-aṣṭādaśasāhasrikā-prajñāpāramitā-nāma-mahāyāna-sūtra*, P732: 129.3.4-6. The words are somewhat different from Tsong-kha-pa's quotation but the meaning is the same.

56. Some activities that are proscribed in the shared practices, such as avoiding killing, not telling lies, not engaging in sexual conduct, not drinking beer, and so forth, are prescribed in the tantric vehicle, and thus these two would seem to be contradictory.

57. *Vajra-śikhara-mahā-guhya-yoga-tantra*, P113: 7.2.7; 26.3.8-26.4.1; 31.2.5.

58. Ba-so-chos-kyi-rgyal-mtshan (*mChan*: 38.6) identified the three types of ethics as (1) restraining bad activities (*nyes spyod sdom pa*); (2) gathering virtuous qualities (*dge ba chos bsdus*), and (3) accomplishing the welfare of living beings (*sems can don byed*).

59. When taking the tantric vows there are nineteen pledges (*samaya*, *dam tshig*) enumerated, among which is this pledge of Amitābha, found in the *Śrī-vajra-ḍāka-nāma-*

mahā-tantra-rāja (P18: 107.3.7) as *phyi nang gsang ba'i theg pa gsum / dam chos yang dag gsung bar bgyi;* in the *Saṃpuṭi-nāma-mahā-tantra* (P26: 255.2.8-255.3.1) as *phyi dang gsang ba theg pa gsum/ dam pa'i chos kyang so sor gsung;* and in the *Vajra-śikhara* (P113: 19.2.8) as *phyi nang gsang ba'i theg pa gsum/ dam pa'i chos ni gzung bar bgyi.* The *Vajra-śikhara* and *Vajra-ḍāka* are the more straightforward and say the teachings to be upheld are "the three vehicles: external, internal, and secret." Tsong-kha-pa's reading is closest to the *Saṃpuṭi* version, however, which he cites in his *rTsa ltung rnam bshad* (*Root Downfalls in Tantra*): 3b2. According to Ba-so-chos-kyi-rgyal-mtshan (*mChan*: 39.2), "external" refers to Action and Performance Tantras, "secret" refers to Yoga and Highest Yoga Tantras, and "three vehicles" refers to these two and the Perfection Vehicle.

60. *Ārya-prajñāpāramitā-ratna-guṇa-sañcaya-gāthā,* Conze 1973: 22.3; P735: 192.2.5.

61. A-kya-yongs-'dzin (A-kya: 107.4-108.6) presents a variety of explanations for this passage on the "four," such as the three trainings plus the tantric paths, but then seems to settle on the idea that it expresses an analogy with something four-sided, like dice, which are complete just as they are, no matter what angle they are viewed from. Just so, no matter what facet of the stages of the path to enlightenment you are practicing, it contains within it the complete teachings.

62. *Mahāyānottara-tantra-śāstra,* Johnston 1950 (RGV): 5.20; P5525: 31.5.2-3. The Tibetan tradition considers Maitreya to be the author of this work but the Chinese tradition considers Sāramati the author. On this question see Takasaki 1966: 6-9 and Ruegg 1969: 32-55.

63. *Abhidharma-kośa-kārikā,* Shastri 1972 (AK): 8.39; P5590: 127.1.8.

64. *Bhāvanā-krama,* P5312: 40.1.2-3.

65. *Sad-dharma-puṇḍarīka-nāma-mahāyāna-sūtra,* Vaidya 1960a (SP): 2.54; P781: 10.1.5-15.4.5.

66. The *Satyaka-parivarta* is the fourth chapter of the *Ārya-bodhisattva-gocaropāya-viṣaya-vikurvāṇa-nirdeśa-nāma-mahāyāna-sūtra.*

67. *Ārya-sarva-vaidalya-saṃgraha-nāma-mahāyāna-sūtra,* P893: 124.5.4-7. The first line as cited by Tsong-kha-pa does not appear in the Tibetan version of the sūtra, but is in the Skt. version cited in chapter four of Śāntideva's *Śikṣā-samuccaya* (*Compendium of Trainings*), Vaidya 1960b: 56. Here and elsewhere Tsong-kha-pa is citing from this text, not the original sūtras.

68. *Tathāgata* is an epithet for a buddha. It means "one who has reached (*gata*/*āgata*) enlightenment in the same way (*tathā*) that former buddhas have."

69. *Sarva-dharma-svabhāva-samatā-vipañcita-samādhi-rāja-sūtra,* Vaidya 1961 (SR): 18.31-32; P795: 300.3.7-8.

70. A *stūpa* is a memorial to a buddha's enlightenment, symbolizing a buddha's enlightened mind. It also serves as a reliquary, often containing the remains of greatly revered religious persons, though it can be used by families for their deceased members.

Chapter Three *How to Listen to and Explain the Teachings*

71. *Udāna-varga*, Bernhard 1965 (Ud): 22.6, 22.3-5; P992: 97.2.1-3. *Verses about Hearing* is the title for Chapter 22 of the *Collection of Indicative Verses.*

72. *Jātaka-mālā*, Vaidya 1959a (Jm): 31.31-34ab, 31.38cd; P5650: 56.5.6-57.1.2, 57.1.5-6. The author of this *Jātaka-mālā* is Āryaśūra according to the P catalogue.

73. *Yoga-caryā-bhūmaubodhisattva-bhūmi*, Dutt 1966 (Bbh): 165; P5538: 190.1.6-190.2.2. The *Bodhisattva-bhūmi* is section 15 of the *Yoga-caryā-bhūmi* (*Level of Yogic Deeds*), a long collection of works all attributed to Asaṅga in the Tibetan tradition.

74. *Daśa-cakra-kṣitigarbha-nāma-mahāyāna-sūtra*, P905: 96.3.6-7. *Kṣitigarbha* ("Earth-womb") is the name of a bodhisattva.

75. Bbh: 73, 165; P5538: 158.4.4-158.5.2, 190.2.2-8. The discussion of the five conditions not to be brought to mind is in chapter 16.

76. Jm: 31.69-70; P5650: 58.2.6-8.

77. This general exhortation to listen well before giving a teaching is found in numerous sūtras such as the *Ārya-suvikrānta-vikrami-paripṛcchā-prajñāpāramitā-nirdeśa* (*Questions of Suvikrānta*) cited in the *Mahāyāna-sūtra-saṃgraha* (*Collection of Mahāyāna Sūtras*) (Vaidya 1964: 3), the *Sāgaramati-paripṛcchā-sūtra* (*Questions of Sāgaramati*) (P819: 91.2.8-91.3.1) and *Daśa-cakra-kṣitigarbha-nāma-mahāyāna-sūtra* (P905: 47.4.7-8, 53.2.4).

78. Bbh: 74; P5538: 158.5.1-2.

79. *Bodhisattva-caryāvatāra*, Bhattacharya 1960 (BCA): 2.54.

80. Conze 1973: 22.1; P735: 192.2.3-5.

81. *Deśanā-stava*, P2048: 98.3.8-98.4.1.

82. SR: 9.43-46, 4.24; P795: 284.2.1-4, 278.3.1.

83. BCA: 5.109.

84. Ud: 22.7-10, 22.18-19; P992: 97.2.3-6, 97.3.2-3.

85. The *Āryādhyāśaya-saṃcodana-nāma-mahāyāna-sūtra* is chapter 25 of the *Ratna-kūṭa* (*Ratna-kūṭa Collection*). The Skt. is found in Vaidya 1960b: 63; P760: 60.1.6-7; 60.1.8-60.2.1; 60.2.6-7.

86. Jm: 31.68-70; P5650: 58.2.4-5.

87. Vaidya 1960b: 187; P760.25: 55.4.6-55.5.3.

88. Conze 1990: 38ff.

89. *Ārya-sāgaramati-paripṛcchā-nāma-mahāyāna-sūtra*, P819: 92.1.1-2. The Skt. is given in Vaidya 1960b: 190. The list of ideas is the same as those given for how you should listen to the teachings, with one exception: the idea that earnest practice clears away the illness of the afflictions has been omitted, because this idea is for students alone to contemplate.

90. This mantra can be found in Vaidya 1960b: 190; P819: 92.1.1.

91. SP: 13.30, 13.32-35; Vaidya 1960a: 189; P781: 50.5.8-51.1.5.

92. *Vinaya-sūtra*, P5619: 222.3.7.

93. SR: 24.44-46. The wording in P795: 308.4.8-308.5.2 is quite different from the way Tsong-kha-pa cites the passage. His citation accords very closely with the way the sūtra appears in chapter 19 of the *Śikṣā-samuccaya*, Vaidya 1960b: 189; P5336: 270.3.6-8.

94. *Vinaya-sūtra*, P5619: 218.3.3-7.

Chapter Four *Relying on the Teacher*

95. *Hṛdaya-nikṣepa-nāma*, P5346: 47.2.8-47.3.1.

96. The *Ārya-bodhisattva-piṭaka-nāma-mahāyāna-sūtra* is chapter 12 of the *Ratna-kūṭa*, P760.

97. *Mahāyāna-sūtrālaṃkāra-kārikā*, Bagchi 1970 (MSA): 17.10; P5521: 13.4.5-6.

98. *Prātimokṣa-sūtra*, P1031: 143.2.2. Codification of the discipline (*vinaya*) rules of monks and nuns recited at the bi-monthly confession ceremony. The Tibetan title *So sor thar pa'i mdo* means *Sūtra on Individual Liberation*.

99. *Vinaya-vibhaṅga*, P1032: 149.5.1. Tsong-kha-pa refers to the scripture as *Lung rnam 'byed (Āgama-vibhaṅga, Exegesis of the Tradition)*. This is the second section of the discipline.

100. Ud: 25.5-6; P992: 98.3.3-7. *Verses about Friends* is the title for Chapter 25 of the *Collection of Indicative Verses*.

101. mChims-thams-cad-mkhyen-pa (Chim-tam-jay-kyen-ba) in his *mChims mdzod gyi 'grel pa mngon pa'i rgyan* (*mChim's Abhidharma-kośa Commentary*): 145-150, quotes this verse (LRCM: 36.7) and says that it is in Prajñāvarman's explanation of *Mārga-varga:* 12.10 in his *Udāna-varga-vivaraṇa* (*Explanation of the Udāna-varga*), but it is not found there.

102. SR: 2.21-22ab, 3.24-27; P795: 277.2.5-6, 277.2.7-277.3.1.

103. *Ārya-subāhu-paripṛcchā-nāma-tantra*, P428: 34.3.8-34.4.3.

104. *Catuḥ-śataka-śāstra-kārikā-nāma*, Lang 1986 (Cś): 12.1; P5246: 138.1.1-2.

105. *Bodhisattva-yoga-caryā-catuḥ-śataka-ṭikā* (*Commentary on the "Four Hundred Stanzas"*), P5266: 252.5.8-253.1.7.

106. *Madhyamaka-hṛdaya-kārikā*, P5255: 4.2.3-4.

107. *Bodhisattva-prātimokṣa-catuṣka-nirhāra-nāma-mahāyāna-sūtra*. The word *prātimokṣa* refers to the codification of the rules of bodhisattvas.

108. *Bodhisattva-yoga-caryā-catuḥ-śataka-ṭikā*, P5266: 253.1.1-2.

109. The *Gaṇḍa-vyūha-sūtra* is section 45 of the *Buddhāvataṃsaka-nāma-mahā-vaipulya-sūtra* (*Flower Ornament Sūtra*). This part (P761: 292.3.5-292.4.4) describes Subhadra's quest for and devotion to his guru Dharmottara. The Tibetan title used by Tsong-kha-pa, *sDong po bkod pa*, is different from the title at P761, vol. 26, *sDong po brgyan pa*.

110. *Ārya-pratyutpanna-buddha-saṃmukhāvasthita-samādhi-nāma-mahāyāna-sūtra*, P801: 126.2.8.

111. Ibid.: 126.3.1.

112. dGe-shes ['Brom]-ston-pa had three principal disciples, called the three "brothers" (*sku mched*): Po-to-ba (Bo-do-wa), sPyan-snga-ba (Jen-nga-wa), and Phu-chung-ba (Pu-chung-wa) (Roerich: 263-264). Geshe Nawang Lhundup points out that they were very close spiritual friends. Po-to-ba, in saying "my *geshe*" in reference to sPyan-snga-ba, uses the term as an endearment and is calling him a bodhisattva as praise. Thus, *geshe* (*dge bshes*) in this instance is not translatable as "teacher," but rather indicates respect for someone who has earned a degree of learning, much like "doctor."

113. A maṇḍala in this context is an offering that symbolizes the entire universe, which the one who makes the offering imagines as being filled with many wondrous things.

114. *Ah-ray* (*ah re*) is an expression of great pleasure.

115. *Āryāṣṭa-sāhasrikā-prajñāpāramitā-sūtra*, Vaidya 1960d: 239; P734: 172.3.2-3.

116. *Ārya-ratnolka-nāma-dhāraṇī-mahāyāna-sūtra*, cited in Vaidya 1960b: 4; P5336: 184.1.1-3.

117. The *Ārya-daśa-dharmaka-nāma-mahāyāna-sūtra* is section 9 of the *Ratna-kūṭa*, cited in Vaidya 1960b: 1.11-14; P760: 202.2.4-6.

118. *Ārya-vajrapāṇy-abhiṣeka-mahā-tantra*, P130: 90.5.1-2.

119. Ibid.: 50.3.5-6.

120. *Ārya-ratna-megha-nāma-mahāyāna-sūtra*, P897: 215.1.4-8.

121. The *Ārya-gṛha-paty-ugra-paripṛcchā-nāma-mahāyāna-sūtra* is section 19 of the *Ratna-kūṭa*, cited in Vaidya 1960b: 2.9-13; P760: 271.4.4-8.

122. *Daśa-dharmaka-sūtra*, P760: 204.2.2-6.

123. *Gaṇḍa-vyūha-sūtra*, Vaidya 1960c: 131; P761: 184.1.7-184.2.4.

124. Ibid., Vaidya 1960c: LIV.70, 72-74, 71, 75; P761: 297.4.1-6.

125. *Guru-pañcāśikā:* 46-47; P4544: 206.1.7-8.

126. MSA: 17.11; P5521: 13.4.6-8.

127. *Guru-pañcāśikā:* 17, 21; P4544: 205.4.4, 205.4.6-7

128. Ibid.: 20; P4544: 205.4.6.

129. Jm: 17.32a-b; P5650: 28.5.4-28.5.5.

130. *Vinaya-sūtra*, P5619: 201.2.6.

131. *Ratna-megha-sūtra*, P897: 215.1.8.

132. The twelfth birth story recounts one of the Buddha's births in India as a brahmin. It is as follows: one day the teacher of a group of young brahmins decided to test his students. He first elicited their sympathy by telling them of his financial problems. Then he stated, "It is said, 'When a brahmin is declining in his fortune, it is virtuous to steal.' Brahma, the creator of the universe, is the father of all brahmins. When a brahmin is declining in fortune, it is all right to steal, because everything is Brahma's creation, and the brahmins own those creations. Therefore, please go and steal something." Most of the students replied that they would do just as the teacher said, but the student who was to become Śākyamuni Buddha remained silent. When the teacher asked him to

explain his silence, he replied, "You, my teacher, have instructed us to steal, but according to the general teachings stealing is completely improper. Although you have said to do it, it doesn't seem right." The teacher was very pleased and said, "I said this in order to test you all. He is the one who has actually understood my teaching. He has not been led foolishly anywhere like a rivulet of water, but has examined what his teacher has said, and made his own determination. He is the best among my students."

133. *Guru-pañcāśikā:* 24cd; P4544: 205.4.8-205.5.1.

134. MSA: 17.14; P5521: 13.5.1.

135. *Gaṇḍa-vyūha-sūtra*, cited in Vaidya 1960b: 23; cf. Vaidya 1960c: 364; P761: 291.5.7-292.1.8, which has some extra lines.

136. Ibid., Vaidya 1960c: 131; P761: 184.2.6-8. The Tibetan translation differs, but is identical with the citation in the *Śikṣā-samuccaya* (Vaidya: 1960b: 23; P5336: 194.4.8-194.5.3).

137. The *Ārya-tathāgatācintya-guhya-nirdeśa-nāma-mahāyāna-sūtra* is section 3 of the *Ratna-kūṭa*, P760.

138. *Kṣitigarbha-sūtra,* cited in Vaidya 1960b: 51.06, 51.12.

139. Jm: 31.72; P5650: 58.3.4-5.

140. *Vajrapāṇy-abhiṣeka-mahā-tantra*, P130: 90.4.6-90.5.1.

141. *Guru-pañcāśikā:* 11-12; P4544: 205.3.7-205.4.2.

142. Although *ḍākās* can refer to beings who are beyond cyclic existence and who assist Buddhist practitioners, in this context they are harmful spirits.

143. *Śrī-kṛṣṇa-yamāri-mahā-tantra-rāja-pañjikā-ratna-pradīpa-nāma*, P2782: 257.3.4-5.

144. *Pratyutpanna-buddha-saṃmukhāvasthita-samādhi-sūtra*, P801: 107.1.6-8.

145. Lochö Rimbochay explains this to be referring to bodhisattvas.

146. *Ārya-sad-dharmānusmṛty-upasthāna*, P953: 309.5.23.

147. *'Phags pa yongs su mya ngan las 'das pa chen po'i mdo*, P787: 9.2.2-7. No Skt. title is given for this work in P. This version of the sūtra was translated from Chinese.

148. *Satyaka-parivarta*, P813: 247.1.1-2.

149. Ud: 25.1, 25.9-10; P992: 98.2.8-98.3.1; 98.3.6-7.

150. Kensur Yeshe Thupten defines the practice of guru yoga as keeping the mind in single-pointed meditation on the method of reliance on the teacher, and employing that method in practice.

151. For the story of Sadāprarudita see Conze 1973, chapter 30, and for the story of Sudhana see Cleary 1985-87, vol. 3, where Sudhana seeks out and learns from innumerable teachers.

Chapter Five *The Meditation Session*

152. *Yoga-caryā-bhūmauśrāvaka-bhūmi* (Śbh), P5537: 58.4.2-58.5.8. The *Śrāvaka-bhūmi* is section 13 of the *Yoga-caryā-bhūmi*.

153. Geshay Nawang Lhundup comments that "those who abide in the Buddha's word" refers to the remainder of the field for accumulating the collections of merit and sublime wisdom—the heroes and heroines, the ḍakas and ḍakinis, and the protectors of the teaching. To "abide" here means that they are following and achieving the Buddha's advice.

154. This and the following well-known twelve verses from the beginning of the *bZang spyod smon lam* ([*Samanta*]*bhadra-caryā-praṇidhāna*) (also known as *King of Prayers*) are at the end of *Gaṇḍa-vyūha-sūtra* (P761: 320.1.7-320.3.2), the last section of the *Buddhāvataṃsaka-nāma-mahā-vaipulya-sūtra*. Tsong-kha-pa cites only the opening words of each verse, which have been rendered here in full for clarity.

155. *Mi yi seng ge*, lions-among-humans. This is an epithet for the buddhas.

156. *bZang spyod kyi 'grel pa bzhi'i don bsdus nas brjed byang du byas pa* (*Notes Summarizing the Topics in the Four Commentaries on the Prayer of Samantabhadra*), P5846: 89.4.5-6.

157. Ibid., P5846: 89.5.6-7.

158. *Sugata* (*bde bar gshegs pa*) is an epithet for a buddha meaning "one who has reached the highest bliss" and also "the one who is gone well."

159. Kensur Yeshe Thupten comments that there would be five types of persons if you group together as *śrāvakas* those with more to learn and those with no more to learn.

160. *bZang spyod kyi 'grel pa bzhi'i don bsdus nas brjed byang du byas pa*, P5846: 92.2.3-4.

161. This is the sixth and last aspect of the preparation for the meditation session. The other five were numbered and listed above. Usually the offering of the maṇḍala is included with the fifth aspect of preparation, offering the seven branches of worship, but here, according to 'Jam-dbyangs-bzhad-pa (*mChan*: 126.3) the maṇḍala is offered at the occasion of the final aspect.

162. This prayer is known as the *Don chen po gsum la gsol ba 'debs pa* (*Supplication for the Three Great Purposes*).

163. In this context, the object's subjective aspect (*yul gyi rnam pa*) is the guru's being a buddha and your mind's subjective aspect (*yul can gyi rnam pa*) is your faith of conviction that the guru is a buddha.

164. The *Praṇidhāna-saptati-nāma-gāthā* attributed variously to gZhan-la-phan-pa'i-dbyangs dGon-pa-pa and Āryasūra/Āryaśūrya (Beresford 1979).

165. The outline details under this heading were not in the text's original outline but have been added by the editors to make the translation easier to read.

166. Perception in Buddhist psychology consists of three aspects: the sensory faculty (which includes the mental sensory faculty along with the five sensory faculties), the object, and the consciousness which arises in dependence on the sensory faculty and its object. The six sensory objects are the five of the sensory consciousnesses—forms, sounds, odors, tastes, and tangible objects—and the one of the mental consciousness—phenomena.

167. 'Jam-dbyangs-bzhad-pa (*mChan*: 135.5) lists the five places as a place that sells liquor, a brothel, a bad slaughterhouse, the king's palace, and a regular slaughterhouse.

168. Vaidya 1960b: 72; P5336: 216.5.7.

169. *Suhṛl-lekha:* 38; P5682: 236.2.3-4.

170. Ibid.: 39; P5682: 236.2.4-5.

171. Ibid.: 44 sets forth five obscurations: excitement and regret, malice, lethargy and sleepiness, longing for desires, and doubt.

172. The two kinds of joyous perseverance are the joyous perseverance of constant practice (*rtag sbyor*) and the joyous perseverance of reverent practice (*gus sbyor*). The first is as it sounds, and the second is taking delight in that and making intense effort.

173. 'Jam-dbyangs-bzhad-pa (*mChan*: 141.2-3) comments that the hungry ghost way of sleeping is with face down, the deity way is on the back, and the way for those who are involved in desires is on the left side.

174. This follows the Ganden Bar Nying (33a.2) which reads *mi nyal ba*, as does the *mChan* (142.4). The LRCM (68.11) reads *nyal stangs*.

Chapter Six *Refuting Misconceptions About Meditation*

175. MSA; P5521: 3.3.2.

176. The three wisdoms are those arising from study, from reflection, and from meditation.

177. "Access" to the level of meditation called the "first meditative stabilization" is attained through specific types of attention, such as meditative serenity.

178. The term translated here as "good quality that results from meditation," *bsgoms byung*, has a specific meaning. Such good qualities are only associated with the form and formless realms. However, you can attain them in the desire realm; there are just no good qualities that result from meditation which are associated with the desire realm itself.

179 *Abhisamayālaṃkāra-kārikā-prajñā-pāramitopadeśa-śāstra-ṭikā-prasphuṭa-padā-nāma*, P5194: 104.1.1-2.

180. AA: 4; P5184: 6.1.5-6.

181. Ibid.: 4.53; P5184: 6.3.1.

182. The *nirveda-bhāgīya* (also rendered "aids to penetration") is the name of the path of preparation.

183. BCA: 1.2d; and Śs, P5336: 183.4.8.

184. Śs: 4; P5336: 188.4.8-188.5.1.

185. Lochö Rimbochay comments that this means that the mind becomes serviceable and pliant.

186. Śbh, P5537: 108.5.7-109.1.5.

Chapter Seven *A Human Life of Leisure and Opportunity*

187. *Ratna-guṇa-sañcaya-gathā*, Conze 1973: 32.2; P735: 192.2.5.

188. *Suhṛl-lekha* 63-64; P5682: 236.5.2-4.

189. *Vyakta-padā-suhṛl-lekha-ṭīkā*, P5690: 264.3.5.

190. *Aṣṭākṣaṇa-kathā*, P5423: 103, 234.4.8-234.5.2.

191. Great Fruit (Skt. *Vṛtaphala*) is one of eight lands in the fourth meditative stabilization. Some of the deities of this region are without leisure because they are in a meditative absorption lacking discrimination (*asaṃjñisamāpatti, 'du shes med pa'i snyoms 'jug*), which is much like our dreamless deep sleep. When they are born, they have the idea that they have been born, and when they are about to die, they have the idea that they are about to die. This description of the location of their region refers to a monastery's being set off from any lay settlement by a distance of five hundred cubits.

192. Ba-so-chos-kyi-rgyal-mtshan (*mChan*: 158.2-3) comments that Tsong-kha-pa is pointing out that only the deities of the desire and formless realms who are ordinary persons and not noble beings are without leisure.

193. *Vyakta-padā-suhṛl-lekha-ṭīkā*, P5690: 264.3.5.

194. Śbh, P5537: 37.5.2-38.1.5.

195. The five deeds of immediate retribution are the heinous acts of killing one's father, killing one's mother, killing an arhat, purposely shedding the blood of a buddha, and causing a schism in the community.

196. Śbh, P5537: 38.1.5-38.2.1.

197. Ibid.

198. *Śiṣya-lekha:* 76 (Minareff: 1890); P5683: 240.2.8-240.3.1.

199. Ibid., P5683: 240.1.1-2.

200. *Nāgas* are dragon-like creatures, *vidyādharas* are bewitching women, *garudas* are bird-like creatures that overcome snakes, and *kinnaras* (literally "Are these human?") are demigods of the Himālaya.

201. The *Ārya-nanda-garbhāvakrānti-nirdeśa-[nāma-mahāyāna-]sūtra*, P760: 110.5.5-6. This is section 14 of the *Ratna-kūṭa*, translated from Chinese. There is another version, the *Āryāyuṣman-nanda-garbhāvakrānti-nirdeśa-[nāma-mahāyāna-]sūtra* that is section 13.

202. That is, you cannot attain the path of seeing and become a noble being as a deity of the form or formless realm.

203. In the *Subhāṣita-ratna-karaṇḍaka-kathā* (*Talk Which Is Like a Jeweled Receptacle of Good Explanations*), verse 15; P5424: 235.4.2-3 and P5668: 208.2.3-4.

204. BCA: 4.23-27; P5272: 248.1.3-7.

205. *Madhyamakāvatāra-nāma:* 2.5; P5262: 100.4.7-8.

206. *Subhāṣita-ratna-karaṇḍaka-kathā:* 16-18b; P5424: 235.4.3-5.

207. BCA: 5.69, 8.14; P5272: 249.5.1-2, 253.3.6.

208. The first two analogies represent the difficulty of attaining leisure and opportunity. It is rare for an insect to make obeisance, as it is for a blind cripple to ride a wild

ass. Kensur Yeshay Tupden says that there is a story about a worm coming up out of the earth and bowing down to the Buddha. Just so, it is very difficult for us to come up out of the miserable realms and be reborn as a human being with leisure and opportunity. In the story about the wild ass, a cripple sings a song after he has fallen by chance onto an ass's back. When asked why he sang, he replies, "It was so amazing for me to be on the back of a wild ass that if I didn't sing then, when should I sing?"

The last two examples illustrate the great importance of leisure and opportunity. A construction worker from Tsang visits a family, and they serve him fish for the first time in his life. It tastes so good that he greedily eats too much, and when he is about to vomit, he ties his sash around his neck. When asked why he did such, he replies, "The fish is so good that to vomit it out would be a great loss!" The final example refers to the story of a poor young boy who goes to a party and eats a lot of food, forcing it down well beyond his appetite. When asked by his friends what he was doing, he replies, "This may be the only chance I have to get such wonderful food. I must eat it now!"

A slightly different explanation for the first three examples is found in lCe-sgom-pa's *dPe chos rin chen spungs pa'i 'bum 'grel* (62.2-6); the last example (65.1) is given as *byis pa'i nas zan* rather than the LRCM's *sme'u zan*. There is a different story given to illustrate this last example.

The *dPe chos rin chen spungs pa'i 'bum 'grel*, Ganden Bar Nying, and LRCM give the spelling of Tsang as *rtsang* rather than *gtsang*.

209. *Vinaya-vastu*, P1030: 37.1.5-37.5.5. Tsong-kha-pa refers to the scripture as *Lung gzhi (Āgama-vastu), Bases of the Tradition*. This is the first section of the discipline.

210. Cś, P5246: 135.4.8-135.5.1.

211. BCA: 4.17-21; P5272: 247.5.7-248.1.3.

212. Ibid.: 4.22; P5272: 248.1.3.

213. *Suhṛl-lekha:* 59-60; P5682: 236.4.7-8.

214. *Śiṣya-lekha:* 64a; P5683: 240.1.2-3.

215. A-kya-yongs-'dzin (A-kya: 119.2) says that this refers to dGe-bshes 'Brom-ston-pa.

Chapter Eight *The Three Types of Persons*

216. *Bodhi-patha-pradīpa*, P5343: 20.4.5-6.

217. Ibid., P5343: 103, 20.4.5.

218. *Caryā-saṃgraha-pradīpa*, P5379: 186.3.6-7.

219. *Bodhi-patha-pradīpa*, P5343: 20.4.6.

220. *rNal 'byor spyod pa'i sa rnam par gtan la dbab pa bsdu ba* (Vs), P5539: 9.2.4-5. P5539, vol. 110 is cited variously as *gTan la dbab pa bsdu pa* (*Viniścaya-saṃgrahaṇī*) and *rNam par nges pa bsdu pa* (*Nirṇaya-saṃgraha*). The full name in the P catalogue is *Yoga-caryā-bhūmau-nirṇaya-saṃgraha*.

221. *Abhidharma-kośa-bhāṣya* (AKbh), P5591: 189.1.4-6.

222. *Saṃvṛti-bodhicitta-bhāvanopadeśa-varṇa-saṃgraha*, P5307: 18.3.4-7.

223. *Madhyamaka-hṛdaya-kārikā*, P5255: 3.4.2-4.

224. BCA: 1.9a-c; P5272: 245.2.3-4.

225. Ibid.: 1.24; P5272: 245.3.6-7.

226. *Bodhi-patha-pradīpa*, P5343: 21.2.6-7.

227. *Bodhi-mārga-pradīpa-pañjikā-nāma*, P5344, vol. 103.

228. *Madhyamakāvatāra-nāma*: 6.226; P5262: 106.2.4-5.

229. *Mahāyāna-patha-sādhana-saṃgraha*, P5352: 51.5.23.

230. *Mahāyāna-patha-sādhana-varṇa-saṃgraha*, P5351: 50.3.3-5.

231. Ibid., P5351: 50.4.8-50.5.2.

232. Ibid., P5351: 51.3.5-6.

233. *Samādhi-sambhāra-parivarta*, P3288: 257.5.2-5.

234. The *gZungs kyi dbang phyug rgyal pos zhus pa (Dhāraṇīśvara-rāja-paripṛcchā)* is the *Ārya-tathāgata-mahā-karuṇā-nirdeśa-nāma-mahāyāna-sūtra*, P814: 300.5.4

235. *Rāja-parikathā-ratnāvalī*, Rā: 1.3-4; P5658: 173.5.7-8.

236. Bbh, P5538: 186.1.3-6.

237. *Caryā-melāpaka-pradīpa*, P2668: 295.3.8-295.4.1.

238. Cś: 8.15; P5246: 136.3.2-3.

239. In the *Śata-pañcāśatka-nāma-stotra* (*Praise in One Hundred and Fifty Verses*): 12.5; P2038. The author is Aśvaghoṣa according to P.

Chapter Nine *Mindfulness of Death*

240. These are the five misdeeds that are secondary to the five deeds of immediate retribution: (1) committing incest with your mother if she is an arhat; (2) murdering a bodhisattva or (3) a noble being on the Hīnayāna path of meditation; (4) stealing the resources of the community; and (5) with hatred, destroying a monastery or a *stūpa*.

241. Cś: 1.1; P5246: 131.2.3-5.

242. BCA: 2.34; P5272: 246.3.4.

243. *'Phags pa yongs su mya ngan las 'das pa chen po'i mdo*, P787: 147.3.5, 147.3.7-8.

244. Ud: 18.19; P992: 95.5.7-8.

245. Ibid.: 1.27; P992: 90.1.2-3. Instead of *lus* in line 3, Bernhard 1965 reads *'jig rten*.

246. Jm: 31.60-62; P5650: 58.1.2-6.

247. Cś: 1.25; P5246: 133.3.4-5.

248. Ud: 1.25; P992: 90.1.1-2. This verse is not in Bernhard's Skt. edition.

249. Ibid.: 1.26-27 (1.25-26 in Bernhard's edition); P992: 90.1.2-3.

250. *Ārya-rājāvavādaka-nāma-mahāyāna-sūtra*, cited in Vaidya 1960b: 114; P887: 79.5.4-80.1.2.

251. *Garbhāvakrānti-sūtra*, P760: 108.4.7-8.

252. BCA: 2.40; P5272: 246.3.7-8.

253. Ud: 1.13-17; P992: 89.5.1-4.

254. *Ārya-lalitavistara-nāma-mahāyāna-sūtra,* Vaidya 1958: 13.70; P763: 195.1.6

255. *Bodhisattva-yoga-caryā-catuḥ-śataka-ṭikā,* P5266: 184.5.2-3.

256. *Catur-viparyaya-[parihāra]-kathā,* P5669: 213.3.2-3. The author according to the P catalogue is Mātricitra.

257. *Garbhāvakrānti-sūtra,* P760: 108.4.7-8. Tsong-kha-pa appears to have had a different translation of this passage before him.

258. *Catur-viparyaya-[parihāra]-kathā,* P5669: 213.4.2-3.

259. Jm: 32.7-9; P5650: 59.5.7-60.1.2.

260. *Mahā-rāja-kaniṣka-lekha,* P5411: 221.1.5-7. The author according to the P catalogue is Maticitra.

261. AK: 3.78cd; P5590: 120.2.5.

262. Ud: 1.7-10; P992: 89.4.6-8

263. *Rāja-parikathā-ratnāvalī* (Rā): 4.17; P5658, 179.5.2.

264. *Suhṛl-lekha:* 55; P5682: 236.4.3-4.

265. Cś: 2.41; P5246: 133.4.7.

266. The five impurities (*snyigs ma lnga*) are the impurity of (1) living beings, (2) afflictions, (3) persons, (4) philosophical view, and (5) resources.

267. Rā: 3.79; P5658: 179.1.5.

268. *Suhṛl-lekha:* 57; P5682: 236.4.5-6.

269. *Mahā-rāja-kaniṣka-lekha,* P5411: 221.1.4-5.

270. *Candra-rāja-lekha* (*Letter to Candra-rāja*), P5689: 251.2.2-4. The P catalogue lists as author Jagata-mitrānanda.

271. *Mahā-rāja-kaniṣka-lekha,* P5411: 242.4.8-242.5.2.

272. *Candra-rāja-lekha,* P5689: 251.4.8-251.5.2.

273. BCA: 8.81; P5272: 256.2.2-3.

274. Ba-so-chos-kyi-rgyal-mtshan, *mChan:* 223.6, comments that Po-to-ba is being asked condescendingly by a philosopher what his system asserts with regard to appearance and exclusion, and positive and negative phenomena. He skillfully answers by using the terms in the context of his religious experience, rather than in the context of philosophical discussion. His play on the words appearance and exclusion is clear in translation, but not so for positive (*sgrub pa*) and negative (*dgag pa*) phenomena. He takes the word for negative phenomenon and makes a pun by using a similar sounding word that means "to block" (*'gags pa*).

275. Lochö Rimbochay says that these two exchanges mean that you must stay with one object of meditation.

276. Lochö Rimbochay comments that this means that your intelligence is clear enough to contemplate what has been explained above.

Chapter Ten *Reflecting on Your Future Life*

277. BCA: 6.12cd, 6.21, 2.50ab; P5272: 250.5.1, 250.5.8., 246.4.7.

278. Tsong-kha-pa uses the title *Sa'i dngos gzhi*, according to Thurman (1984: 410), to refer to sections of the *Yoga-caryā-bhūmi* other than the Bbh and Śbh. This long excerpt (P5536: 230.3.8-231.5.6) is from the first part of the *Yoga-caryā-bhūmi.*

279. *Suhṛl-lekha:* 87; P5682: 237.2.8-237.3.1.

280. AK: 3.79, 3.82-83b; P5590: 120.2.5-7.

281. *Yoga-caryā-bhūmi* (*Sa'i dngos gzhi*), P5536: 230.3.8.

282. Jm: 29.22; P5650: 52.2.3-4.

283. *Śiṣya-lekha:* 52-53; P5683: 239.4.3-5.

284. *Yoga-caryā-bhūmi* (*Sa'i dngos gzhi*), P5536: 230.4.1-2.

285. AKbh, P5591: 187.1.4-6.

286. *Vinaya-vastu,* P1030: 42.5.2.

287. The *Saṃgharakṣitāvadāna* is story 67 in Kṣemendra's *Bodhisattvāvadāna-kalpalatā,* P5655: 83.4.3-85.1.6; cf. Vaidya 1959b: 204-212.

288. AKbh: 717; P5591: 184.2.3-5.

289. BCA: 8.12cd; P5272: 253.3.5.

290. *Suhṛl-lekha:* 83; P5682: 237.2.4-6.

291. Ibid.: 84-86, 88; P5682: 237.2.6-8, 237.3.1-2.

292. AKbh, P5591: 184.2.5-6.

293. *Suhṛl-lekha:* 89-90; P5682: 237.3.2-4.

294. *Vyakta-padā-suhṛl-lekha-ṭikā,* P5690: 267.3.5-268.1.1.

295. AK: 3.83c; P5590: 120.7.8.

296. AKbh: 517; P5591: 184.2.6-7.

297. *Suhṛl-lekha:* 91-95; P5682: 237.3.4-8.

298. *Vyakta-padā-suhṛl-lekha-ṭikā,* P5690: 267.3.1-6.

299. *Śiṣya-lekha:* 35-40; P5683: 239.2.1-7.

300. *Yoga-caryā-bhūmi* (*Sa'i dngos gzhi*), P5536: 230.2.8-230.4.1.

301. AK: 3; P5590: 187.1.3.

302. *Suhṛl-lekha:* 96; P5682: 237.3.8-237.4.1.

303. *Vyaktapadā-suhṛl-lekha-ṭikā,* P5690: 268.1.1-2.

304. *Vinaya-vastu* (*Lung gzhi*), P1030: 36.3.3-37.1.3.

305. BCA: 4.18, 2.46-48; P5272: 247.5.8-248.1.1, 246.4.4-6.

306. *Sad-dharmānusmṛty-upasthāna*, P953.

Chapter Eleven *Going for Refuge to the Three Jewels*

307. BCA: 1.10; P5272: 245.1.5-245.2.1.

308. This is *Miśraka-stotra-nāma* (*Interwoven Praise*): 1; P2041: 87.5.2-3, attributed both to Mitraciṭa and Dignāga in P.

309. *Śata-pañcāśatka-nāma-stotra:* 1.1-2; P2038: 53.5.4-5.

310. *Tri-śaraṇa-gamana-saptati*, P5478: 281.1.3.

311. Vs, P5539: 17.2.2-3.

312. *Varṇārha-varṇebhagavato-buddhasyastotreśakya-stava*, P2029: 46.3.4-8. P includes the first section of the praise, the *Aśakya-stava* (*Praise That Falls Short*), in the title. The author is Maticitra according to P.

313. The text (134.11) states, "the four subdivisions of this topic are taught in the [*Viniścaya-*] *Saṃgrahaṇī*," P5539: 17.2.4.

314. *Varṇārha-varṇa-stotra*, P2029: 48.5.3-7.

315. *Satyaka-parivarta*, P813: 261.5.5-7.

316. *Śata-pañcāśatka-nāma-stotra:* 3.72-78; P2038: 55.1.8-55.2.5.

317. Tib. *skyu ru ra*; Skt. *dhātrī* fruit; Latin *Emblica offinalis.*

318. *Varṇārha-varṇa-stotra*, P2029: 43.5.4, 43.4.1-3

319. *Śata-pañcāśatka-nāma-stotra:* 13.138-139; P2038: 54.5.6-7.

320. *Satyaka-parivarta*, P813: 263.2.1-2, 263.3.1-4.

321. *Śata-pañcāśatka-nāma-stotra*, P2038, 56.3.4-5.

322. *Varṇārha-varṇa-stotra*, P2029: 46.2.2.

323. SR: 4.16-18, 4.20-21; P795: 278.2.3-5, 278.2.6-7.

324. *Ārya-dharma-saṃgīti-nāma-mahāyāna-sūtra*, P904: 23.4.6-7. Skt. appears in Vaidya 1960b: 171.

325. Ibid., Vaidya 1960b: 172; P904: 24.2.1-3.

326. Vs, P5539: 17.3.2-17.4.2.

327. This begins the *Ārya-buddhānusmṛti* or *'Phags pa sang rgyas rjes su dran pa (Recollection of the Buddha)*, P5433: 247.4.7. It begins, "*'Di ltar bcom ldan 'das de ni....*"

328. *Vinaya-sūtra-ṭīkā*, P5622, vols. 124-126.

329. *Viśeṣa-stava*, P2001: 1.2.3-4, 4.2.6-7.

330. Ibid., P2001: 4.2.8.

331. *Varṇārha-varṇa-stotra*, P2029: 45.3.5-8.

Chapter Twelve *The Precepts of Refuge*

332. Vs, P5539: 17.2.4-5; cf. below LRCM: 156.19.

333. *Mahā-parinirvāṇa-sūtra*, P787: 184.1.1-2.

334. *Suhṛl-lekha:* 2; P5682: 235.3.2.

335. *Vinaya-vibhaṅga* (*Lung rnam 'byed*), P1032: 205.2.7-8.

336. The *Vinaya-kṣudraka-vastu* (*Lung phran tshegs*) (*Lesser Parts of the Tradition*) is section 3 of the discipline. This story is also found in the *mDzang lun zhe bya ba'i mdo* (*Damamūko-nāma-sūtra*), P1008: 106.3.6-107.1.3, where the king's name is Kri kri, rather than Cārumat.

337. *Āryādhyāśaya-saṃcodana-nāma-mahāyāna-sūtra*, P760: 59.4.2-4. Skt. appears in Vaidya 1960b: 62-63.

338. SR: 24.41ab; P795: 308.4.6-7.

339. Ibid.: 9.58cd; P795: 284.3.5-6.

340. *Ārya-ratna-megha-nāma-mahāyāna-sūtra*, P897: 218.5.6-7; *Tri-samaya-vyūha-rāja-tantra*, P134: 101.2.8-101.3.3. Cited in Vaidya 1960b: 152, where the name is just *Tri-samaya-rāja*.

341. The *udumvara* flower is a very large and pervasively fragrant flower that came into existence upon the Buddha's birth and disappeared following his final nirvāṇa.

342. Bbh: P5538: 187.4.4-190.2.2

343. *Varṇārha-varṇa-stotra*, P2029: 48.3.4-5.

344. Ibid., P2029: 48.5.1-2. The Tibetan name is *dPal ldan ma khol*.

345. BCA: 2.7ab; P5272: 245.5.6.

346. *Ratna-megha-sūtra*, P897: 183.5.8-184.1.1.

347. The *'Chi med rnga sgra'i gzungs* (P359, vol. 7) is recited along with the the *Triratnānusmṛti* before beginning a meal.

348. *Pāramitā-samāsa-nāma*, P5340: 11.5.1.

349. Ud: 15.9; P992: 94.5.1-3.

350. AKbh: 630; P5591: 201.3.5.

351. *Tri-śaraṇa-[gamana]-saptati*; P5478: 281.1.2-3.

352. The eight vows are monk, nun, novice monk, novice nun, layman, laywoman, and male and female one-day vow holder.

353. Vaidya 1960b: 98; P5336: 228.5.4. The tale is also found in the *Sūkarikāvadāna-nāma-sūtra* (*The Edifying Tale of the Pig Sūtra*), P1014: 251.1.6, and is section 14 of the *Divyāvadāna* (Vaidya 1959b).

354. These verses, similar to those found in the Ud, are cited AKbh: 3.32 (Shastri 1973: 630); P5591: 201.1.1-5.

355. Lochö Rimbochay relates the story of a non-Buddhist who overcame anyone he disliked with a magic rope, but when he tried it on a Buddhist who then went for refuge to the three jewels, his rope was rendered useless.

356. *Ārya-siṃha-paripṛcchā-nāma-mahāyāna-sūtra*, Vaidya 1960b: 6; P760: 149.2.5. This is section 37 of the *Ratna-kūṭa*.

357. *Saḍ-aṅga-śaraṇa-[gamana]*, P5367: 176.2.5.

358. Vs, P5539: 17.2.1-17.4.2.

359. Ud: 12.10; P992: 93.5.3.

Chapter Thirteen *The General Characteristics of Karma*

360. *Las, karma. Karma* is a term that most often means action, but occasionally means effect. As "karma" has become a common term in the English language, we have used it as a translation for *las* in some contexts; in others, we have translated *las* with "action(s)."

361. The outline starts with the second of the two parts of 2′, "Relying on the means for achieving happiness in the next life," the first entry in the outline for chapter eleven. The first part of 2′ is "Training in going for refuge, the excellent door for entering the teaching," the second entry in the outline for chapter eleven.

362. Rā: 2.21; P5658: 174.2.5-6.

363. According to theistic Sāṃkhyas, the supreme deity (*dbang phyug, īśvara*) initiates and oversees the creation of the world out of "fundamental nature" (*rang bzhin, prakṛti*), otherwise known as "primal essence" (*gtso bo, pradhāna*).

364. Ud: 28.24-25; P992: 100.4.4-5.

365. The Indian title given in parentheses for the *mDzang lun zhe bya ba'i mdo* is *Dama-mūko-nāma-sūtra*. Fry 1981 has Skt. *Dama-mūrkha-sūtra*. P1008.

366. *Vinaya-vastu* (*Lung gzhi*), P1030: 174.3.8-176.4.1.

367. *Ārya-sāgara-nāga-rāja-paripṛcchā*, P820: 109.5.7-110.1.4. Sāgara-nāga is a king of the *nāgas*, very wealthy dragon-like creatures associated with water.

368. With the exception of the last two verses (Ud: 17.5-6; P992: 95.3.8-95.4.1), the exact wording does not exactly match either of the Tibetan versions or Bernhard's Skt. version of the *Udāna-vārga*.

369. Jm: 15.1, 28.16-17, 29.2; P5650: 26.4.5, 40.2.3-5, 51.3.6-7. For the context see *mChan*: 309.3-6.

370. *Viśeṣa-stava*, P2001: 3.5.2.

371. *Samādhirāja-sūtra:* 37.35; P795: 1.3.5.

372. *Vinaya-vastu* (*Lung gzhi*), P1030: 19.1.6.

Chapter Fourteen *The Varieties of Karma*

373. AK: 4.66b-d; P5590: 121.4.8.

374. *Vinaya-vibhaṅga* (*Lung rnam 'byed*), P1032: 149.3.3-4.

375. *Sāgara-nāga-rāja-paripṛcchā*, P820: 114.1.6-7, 115.4.1-3.

376. *Madhyamakāvatāra:* 2.7; P5262: 100.5.1-2, summarizing *Daśa-bhūmika-sūtra*, Vaidya 1960c: 15-16; P761: 250.5.4-251.3.4. The entire chapter discusses morality.

377. *Kṣitigarbha-sūtra*, Vaidya 1960c: 11; P905: 94.2.6-94.3.1.

378. The first category is literally the "basis," although the reference is clearly to the object of the action—in the sense of that person or thing toward whom the action is directed. The third category—the performance—refers to the actual commission of the action.

379. *Yoga-caryā-bhūmi*, P5536: 254.2.5.

380. For there to be a culmination, the victim must die before the killer, as Tsong-kha-pa mentions below.

381. When Tsong-kha-pa says "there is no actual sin," he is saying that there is no complete infraction with all its aspects fullfilled. The action will still give rise to negative effects for the perpetrator.

382. AK: 4.72ab; P5590: 121.5.4.

383. *Yoga-caryā-bhūmaunirṇaya-saṃgraha*, P5539: 289.4.6.

384. Ibid., P5539: 290.4.2.

385. *Daśākuśala-karma-patha-nirdeśa* (*Explanation of the Ten Virtuous Paths of Action*), P5678: 232.3.8-232.4.1 (identical to P5416: 226.3.4-5).

386. The words Tsong-kha-pa puts in the mouth of the Great Elder (*jo bo chen po*), usually Atisha, are found in the *Daśākuśala-karma-patha-nirdeśa* itself, P5678: 232.3.7-8.

387. *Daśākuśala-karma-patha-nirdeśa*, P5678: 232.3.5-6.

388. Ibid., P5678: 232.3.7.

389. *Yoga-caryā-bhūmaunirṇaya-saṃgraha*, P5539: 289.4.7.

390. This is a paraphrase of AKbh on AK: 4.74; P5591: 211.2.5-6.

391. *Yoga-caryā-bhūmaunirṇaya-saṃgraha*, P5539: 290.4.6.

392. AKbh on AK: 4.74; P5591: 209.1.4.

393. Ibid. on AK: 4.78; P5591: 209.1.2.

394. *Yoga-caryā-bhūmaunirṇaya-saṃgraha*, P5539: 289.5.3.

395. Ibid.; P5539: 289.5.4.

396. *Yoga-caryā-bhūmi* (*Sa'i dngos gzhi*), P5536: 255.5.1-2.

397. *Suhṛl-lekha:* 42; P5682, 236.2.7-8.

398. *Sad-dharmānusmṛty-upasthāna*, P953: 123.1.7-123.2.1.

399. *Ārya-sūrya-garbha-nāma-vaipulya-sūtra*, P923: 234.4.7-234.5.2.

400. This is a paraphrase of *Ārya-śraddhā-balādhānāvatāra-mudrā-nāma-mahāyāna-sūtra,* cited in Vaidya 1960b: 51; P5336: 207.4.3-8.

401. Ibid., Vaidya 1960b: 52; P5336: 207.4.8-208.2.7.

402. *Ārya-niyatāniyata-gati-mudrāvatāra-nāma-mahāyāna-sūtra* according to P868; *Niyatāniyatāvatāra-mudra-sūtra* according to Bendall and Rouse (1971: 89). This is a paraphrase of the passage cited in Vaidya 1960b: 52; P5336: 208.1.4-6.

403. *Ārya-praśānta-viniścaya-prātihārya-samādhi-nāma-mahāyāna-sūtra,* P797: 45.4.6-7. Cited in Vaidya 1960b: 50.

404. This is not in the *'Phags pa yongs su mya ngan las 'das pa chen po'i mdo,* P787.

405. *Ārya-ratna-rāśi-nāma-mahāyāna-sūtra,* Vaidya 1960b: 165. This is not in section 45 of the Tibetan version of the *Ratna-kūṭa.*

406. *Buddha-piṭaka-duḥśila-nigrahī-nāma-mahāyāna-sūtra,* P886: 61.3.4-5.

407. The Tibetan for "monk's robes" here is *drang srong gi rgyal mtshan,* literally "the sage's victory banner."

408. *Vinaya-vibhaṅga* (*Lung rnam 'byed*), P1032: 1.4.4-5.

409. *Ratna-rāśi-sūtra,* Vaidya 1960b: 165. This is not in section 45 of the Tibetan version of the *Ratna-kūṭa.*

410. BCA: 6.1; P5272: 250.3.8-250.4.1.

411. SR: 35.52; P795: 14.1.3-14.3.4.

412. BCA: 1.34; P5272: 245.4.5-6.

413. Throughout this section, Tsong-kha-pa's use of the term *Sa'i dngos gzhi* refers to the opening section of the *Yoga-caryā-bhūmi.*

414. *Satyaka-parivarta,* P813: 252.4.6-252.5.8, 253.1.1-6. The phrasing here is not identical.

415. *Daśa-bhūmika-sūtra,* Vaidya 1960c: 21-28; P761: 251.3.1-251.4.2.

416. *Abhidharma-samuccaya,* P5550: 257.1.2-4.

417. AK: 4.95ab; P5590: 122.2.4-5.

418. *Abhidharma-samuccaya,* P5550: 257.1.4-5.

419. *Yoga-caryā-bhūmi,* P5536: 256.3.8-256.4.1.

420. Ibid., P5536: 256.3.4-7.

421. Vs, P5539: 292.3.8-292.4.8.

422. This section paraphrases the AKbh, P5591: 220.4.3-8. It is also cited by Atisha in the *Karma-vibhaṅga-nāma,* P5356: 56.2.3.

423. In chapter seven above, on the precious human life of leisure and opportunity (LRCM: 78.4), Tsong-kha-pa says that having incomplete sensory faculties means "having incomplete limbs, ears, and so on."

424. The six superknowledges (*mngon shes, abhijña*) are the divine eye/clairvoyance, divine ear/clairaudience, knowledge of others' minds, remembrance of former lives,

miraculous power, and a sixth, knowledge of the removal of defilements, which is attainable only at liberation. The first five are accepted by non-Buddhist schools as well.

Chapter Fifteen *Cultivating Ethical Behavior*

425. BCA: 2.63, 7.40; P5272: 246.5.8-247.1.1, 254.1.1.

426. SR: 14.9; P795: 292.4.1-2.

427. Ibid.: 22.2cd-4ab; P795: 302.3.6-7.

428. *Sāgara-nāga-rāja-paripṛcchā*, P820: 114.1.4-5.

429. Ud: 25.22ab; P992: 98.4.7.

430. To carry a corpse it is easiest to bind it up and put its back upon your back. Thus, you and the corpse would be facing away from each other.

431. Ud: 25.22cd; P992: 98.4.7.

432. Jm: 31.75; P5650: 58.3.8-58.4.1.

433. *Satyaka-parivarta*, P813: 253.1.8-253.2.1.

434. Ud: 9.3-5, 9.13-16, 9.18-20; P992: 92.5.6-8, 93.1.4-6, 93.1.7-93.2.1.

435. *Ārya-catur-dharma-nirdeśa-nāma-mahāyāna-sūtra,* cited in Vaidya 1960b: 89; P102: 224.3.5-6.

436. *Ārya-suvarṇa-prabhāsottama-sūtrendra-rāja-nāma-mahāyāna-sūtra*, Bagchi 1967: 11-23; P176: 78.5.8-80.5.4.

437. See the *Ārya-tri-skandha-nāma-mahāyāna-sūtra* (*Sūtra of the Three Aggregates [of Obeisance, Confession, and Dedication]*). The thirty-five buddhas of confession are buddhas whose names you recite and before whom you then make obeisance and rejoice in virtue.

438. *Subāhu-paripṛcchā-tantra*, P428: 41.5.5-7.

439. *Āryāṣṭa-sāhasrikā-prajñāpāramitā-vyākhyāna Abhisamayālaṃkārālokā-nāma,* P5189: 501.14-19.

440. *Madhyamaka-hṛdaya-vṛtti-tarka-jvālā*, P5256: 82.5.6.-83.1.3.

441. Ibid., P5256: 83.1.3-83.2.1.

442. Angulimāla, though a murderer, stopped his violence, became a monk and attained arhatship. Thus he escaped rebirth and did not experience the effects of killing in the sufferings of the hell realms. Ajataśatru was the son of King Bimbisara; he usurped the throne and imprisoned his father, who died in prison. Later he became a devoted, virtuous follower of the Buddha. As a result, after death he was reborn in a hell realm but only briefly due to his good karma. Aśoka was one of the most important monarchs in Buddhist history, who ruled most of the Indian subcontinent in the third century B.C.E. Following a battle against the Kingdom of Kaliṅga, he felt great remorse and then dedicated himself to following and propagating the teaching; he renounced violence and set about creating a just and peaceful society. His pillar edicts and rock inscriptions give evidence for his social projects and encouragment of ethical behavior, tolerance of

different religions, as well as support of the Buddhist community. Svaka (A-kya: 136.4) killed his own mother.

443. This is in the account of King Śūradatta in SR (chapter 35) (Vaidya 1961: 239; P795: 14.1.4-14.2.8). Supuṣpacandra was King Śūradatta's queens' guru and a bodhisattva.

444. Bbh, P5538: 171.1.2.

445. *Sarva-vaidalya-saṃgraha-sūtra:* 13; P893: 125.3.4-6. Cited in Vaidya 1960b: 56.

446. Ud: 28.39-40; P992: 100.5.8-101.1.2.

447. Ibid.: 4.22-23, 4.27-28; P992: 91.3.2-6.

448. *Suhṛl-lekha:* 47; P5682: 236.3.4.

449. The *rTogs brjod rgya pa* (literally, *One Hundred Stories*) is the *Bodhisattvāvadāna-kalpalatā*, which has 107 stories, and the *'Dul ba lung gi rgyud gleng* are the different sections prefacing explanations of rules in the discipline.

Chapter Sixteen *The Attitude of a Person of Small Capacity*

450. MSA: 16.2ab; P5521: 11.5.3.

451. BSA: 7.14ab; P5272: 253.3.6.

Chapter Seventeen *The Eight Types of Suffering*

452. The pervasive suffering of conditionality is one of three types of suffering discussed in more detail below. The other two are the suffering of pain and the suffering of change.

453. BCA: 9.156; P5272: 260.5.8-261.1.1.

454. *Śiṣya-lekha:* 18; P5683: 238.4.8-238.5.1.

455. Cś: 7.14; P5246: 135.5.6.

456. *Ratna-guṇa-sañcaya-gāthā*, P735: 192.2.8.

457. *Śiṣya-lekha:* 87-88cd; P5683: 240.4.5-7.

458. Cś: 8.12; P5246: 136.2.8-136.3.1.

459. Ibid.: 7.1; P5246: 135.4.5.

460. RGV: 4.52; P5525: 30.3.6-7.

461. *Suhṛl-lekha:* 65; P5682: 236.5.4.

462. Read *des* for *nges* at LRCM: 211, line 5; *des pa* = "your highness." *Suhṛl-lekha* is addressed to a King bDe-spyod, who is sometimes identified as Gautamīputra Śatkarṇī of the Śātavāhana dynasty.

463. These four are mentioned later on in the text. They are the suffering of (1) birth, (2) encountering what is unpleasant, (3) seeking yet not getting what you want, and (4) the five appropriated aggregates.

464. This is a reference to the five faults that impede meditation: laziness, forgetting the personal instructions, excitement and laxity, not applying the remedies, and overapplying the remedies.

465. BCA: 5.16; P5272: 248.5.4.

466. This translation follows the Tibetan translation. However the Skt. text has *sarvavit*, "all-knowing," which is corroborated by Prajñākaramati, who glosses it *sarvajña*.

467. *Ārya-mahāyāna-prasāda-prabhāvanā-nāma-mahāyāna-sūtra* is the title in P. According to Namdol (1985: 205-206), Kamalaśīla, in his *Bhāvanā-krama* (P5310: 31.5.6-7) uses the title *Mahāyāna-śraddhā-bhāvanā-sūtra*.

468. *Ārya-saṃdhi-nirmocana-nāma-mahāyāna-sūtra:* 8.12; P774: 17.3.3-4.

469. "Dysfunctional tendencies" renders *dauṣṭulya, gnas ngan len*. As this paragraph makes clear, this term refers to the presence of the seeds, or predisposing latencies, for afflicted karma, and the way in which these predisposing latencies make it hard to use the body and mind for the practice of the path.

470. *Śiṣya-lekha:* 19; P5683: 238.5.1-2.

471. *Garbhāvakrānti-sūtra*, P760: 107.4.2-107.5.7. Tsong-kha-pa appears to have had a different translation of this passage before him.

472. The five bonds are the two arms, two legs, and head.

473. *Śiṣya-lekha* 20-21; P5683: 238.5.2-4.

474. *Garbhāvakrānti-sūtra*, P760: 110.2.6-110.3.3. Tsong-kha-pa appears to have had a different translation of this passage before him.

475. *Lalita-vistara-sūtra*, Vaidya 1958: 13.83-85; P763: 195.2.8-195.3.3.

476. Ibid., Vaidya 1958: 13.86-88; P763: 195.3.3-5

477. Ibid., Vaidya 1958: 13.89-91; P763: 195.3.6-8.

478. *Nidāna-saṃyukta*, Tripāṭhī 1962: 194.

479. LRCM: 227ff.

Chapter Eighteen *The Six Types of Suffering*

480. *Suhṛl-lekha:* 66; P5682: 236.5.5.

481. *Subāhu-paripṛcchā-tantra*, P428: 35.3.5-6.

482. *Suhṛl-lekha:* 67; P5682: 236.5.5-6.

483. The wording (*so so yi skye bo'i rjes su 'brangs pa'i 'khor ba pa*) suggests that some ordinary beings may be following the ways of noble beings and thus, by approximating their behavior, approaching their condition.

484. *Suhṛl-lekha:* 26; P5682: 235.5.8-236.1.1.

485. *Pāramitā-samāsa:* 27; P5340: 16.3.4.

486. *Śiṣya-lekha:* 90-91; P5683: 240.5.2-3.

487. *Śoka-vinodana,* P5677: 232.1.6-232.2.1. Attributed to Aśvaghoṣa in P.

488. Tsong-kha-pa cites a version of the *Gaṇḍa-vyūha-sūtra* somewhat different from P761: 299.3.1-3. Cf. Vaidya 1960c: 390.

489. *Suhṛl-lekha:* 68ab; P5682: 236.5.6-7.

490. Ibid.: 68ab; P5682: 236.5.7.

491. *Vyakta-padā-suhṛl-lekha-ṭīkā,* P5690: 264.5.2-4.

492. Cś: 7.10; P5246: 135.5.3-4.

493. *Bodhisattva-yoga-caryā-catuḥ-śataka-ṭīkā,* P5266: 226.2.1-5.

494. *Suhṛl-lekha* 69-75; P5682: 236.5.7-237.1.7.

495. The Brahmā-type deities live beyond the desire realm, where there is no sensual desire and there are no women. Zahler et al. (1983) says that these deities are in the first concentration level of the form realm (*rūpadhātu*); other sources (Kloetzli 1983: 29-30, 45-50) suggest that all of the levels of the form realm may be known collectively as the world of Brahmā (*Brahmaloka*). One source (Lozang Jamspal et al. 1981: 42, n.15) states that the word "Brahmā" in this particular line refers to all the beings of the form and formless (*arūpadhātu*) realms.

496. *Vinaya-vastu* (*'Dul ba lung*), P1030: 50.2.5.

497. *Suhṛl-lekha:* 76; P5682: 237.1.6-7.

498. BCA: 8.32-33; P5272: 255.2.3-4.

Chapter Nineteen *Further Meditations on Suffering*

499. The subheadings for this are not explicitly in the text, but are taken from the *mChan*, where they were added by 'Jam-dbyangs-bzhad-pa.

500. In the context of mental processes, the phrase "similar to it" refers to the five ways in which mental processes are similar to the main mind which they accompany. The five, as given in the AK, are the sameness of (1) base, (2) observed object, (3) aspect, (4) time, and (5) substantial entity.

501. *Garbhāvakrānti-sūtra,* P760: 109.3.3-6. Tsong-kha-pa appears to have had a different translation of this passage before him. The following citation is also found here.

502. Cś: 2.12; P5246: 133.4.4-5.

503. The text here (LRCM: 229.17) reads *tshol kro* and has been corrected to read *tshol 'gro* (*mChan*: 444.01; A-kya: 139.02).

504. The remaining items in this list of seven are three from the above list of eight: the suffering of encountering what is unpleasant, the suffering of separation from what is pleasant, and the suffering of seeking yet not getting what you want. The eighth in the list, the suffering of the appropriated aggregates, is a synoptic addition and is left out when listing human sufferings.

505. *Sambhāra-parikathā*, P5422: 233.2.8-233.3.3.

506. Cś: 2.8; P5246: 133.4.2.

507. *Suhṛl-lekha:* 102; P5682: 237.4.6.

508. Ibid.: 98; P5682: 237.4.2-3.

509. Ibid.: 99-100; P5682: 237.4.3-5.

510. Ibid.: 101; P5682: 237.4.5-6.

511. *Sambhāra-parikathā*, P5422: 233.3.3-5, 233.3.6-7.

512. Ibid., P5422: 233.3.7-233.4.1.

Chapter Twenty *The Origin of Suffering*

513. *Pramāṇa-vārttika*: 105d-196b, 276ab; P5709: 86.5.4, 88.2.3.

514. *Abhidharma-samuccaya*, P5550: 253.3.5-6.

515. Literally, the view of the perishing aggregates (*'jig tshogs la lta ba*) is "the view of the perishing collection." Here, in breaking down the term into its parts, Tsong-kha-pa literally says, "*Collection* indicates plurality."

516. Some Hindu philosophical systems regard God (Īśvara) as the creator of the world; others (in particular the Sāṃkhya school) see the transformation of primal matter as involved in the creation of the world. According to theistic Sāṃkhyas, the supreme deity initiates and oversees the creation of the world out of "fundamental nature" (*rang bzhin, prakṛti*), otherwise known as "primal essence" (*gtso bo, pradhāna*).

517. *Pañca-skandha-prakaraṇa*, P5560, vol. 113.

518. *Pramāṇa-vārttika*: 221cd-222ab; P5709: 87.2.5-6.

519. MSA: 27.25-26; P5521: 14.1.2-3.

520. BCA: 4.28-33; P5272: 248.1.7-248.2.3.

521. *Abhidharma-samuccaya*, P5550: 256.4.7.

522. AK: 4.46b; P5590: 120.4.5.

523. See AK, Shastri 1972: 576-589 and Pruden 1988 on la Vallée Poussin 1971: 12-25.

524. AK: 4.46ab; P5590: 121.3.2.

525. Ibid.: 4.46cd; P5590: 121.3.2-3.

526. *Prajña-nāma-mūla-madhyamaka-kārikā:* 26.10; P5224.

527. *Pratītya-samutpādādi-vibhaṅga-nirdeśa (Explanation of the Divisions of Dependent-Arising)*, P5496: 302.3.8. Tucci 1934 gives the title as *Pratītya-samutpāda-vyākhyā* (*Explanation of Dependent-Arising*).

528. Vs, P5539: 38.5.8-39.1.2.

529. Paraphrasing AKbh on AK: 3.43; P5591: 182.1.3-4.

530. AK: 3.13b-14; P5590: 119.2.4-5.

531. *Garbhāvakrānti-sūtra*, P760: 103.5.4-6.

532. AKbh, Shastri 1972: 429; P5591: 172.5.2.

533. *Garbhāvakrānti-sūtra*, P760: 107.3.1-5. Tsong-kha-pa appears to have had a different translation of this passage before him.

534. AK: 3.15c; P5590: 119.2.5.

535. AKbh, Shastri 1972: 429; P5591: 172.4.5-6.

536. The title used for the *Yoga-caryā-bhūmi* is again *Sa'i dngos gzhi*.

Chapter Twenty-one *The Twelve Factors of Dependent-Arising*

537. AK: 3.28; P5590: 119.3.5.

538. *Śālistamba-sūtra*, P876: 303.4.1-2.

539. Ibid., P876: 303.4.2.

540. *Abhidharma-samuccaya*, P5550: 246.5.7-247.1.2.

541. *Yoga-caryā-bhūmi* (*Sa'i dngos gzhi*), P5536: 263.4.4-6, 263.4.8-263.5.2.

542. This *rTen 'brel mdo 'grel* in P is *Pratītya-samutpādādi-vibhaṅga-nirdeśa*, P5496.

543. *Pratītya-samutpāda-hṛdaya-kārikā* (*Heart of Dependent-Arising*): 2; P5467: 270.5.1. The next citation of this text is the verse following this one: 3; P5467: 270.5.2.

544. *Ārya-śālistamba-nāma-mahāyāna-sūtra*, P876; see Vaidya 1964: 104.

545. *Subāhu-paripṛcchā-tantra*, P428: 35.3.5.

546. *Suhṛl-lekha:* 112a; P5682: 237.5.7.

547. The Tibetan is *'Dul ba lung* as above, note 496.

Chapter Twenty-two *The Attitude of a Person of Medium Capacity*

548. LRCM: 95.3.

549. *Tathāgatācintya-guhya-nirdeśa-sūtra*, P760: 87.4.1-2, 87.4.8, 87.5.2-3.

550. *Madhyamaka-hṛdaya-kārikā*, P5255: 3.3.2-3.

551. *Bodhisattva-yoga-caryā-catuḥ-śataka-ṭīkā*, P5266: 194.4.7-194.5.1.

552. *Caryā-melāpaka-pradīpa*, P2668: 315.1.7-315.2.1.

Chapter Twenty-three *Ascertaining the Nature of the Path Leading to Liberation*

553. *Candra-rāja-lekha*, P5689: 251.3.1-2, 251.4.3-4.

554. *Sapta-kumārikāvadāna*, P5419: 228.5.5-7.

555. *Suhṛl-lekha:* 103; P5682: 237.4.7.

556. Ibid.: 63-64; P5682: 236.5.2-5.

557. Jm: 18.10-12; P5650: 29.3.5-7.

558. Ibid.: 18.13-15, 18.20; P5650: 29.3.8-29.4.2, 29.4.7-8.

559. *Sapta-kumārikāvadāna*, P5419: 231.4.7-231.5.2.

560. Ibid., P5419: 231.5.2-3.

561. Ibid., P5419: 231.5.4-6.

562. *Gṛha-paty-ugra-paripṛcchā-sūtra*, P760: 265.4.6-8.

563. MSA: 20.5; P5521: 18.3.4-5.

564. *Suhṛl-lekha:* 104; P5682: 237.4.7-237.5.1.

565. *Yoga-caryā-bhūmi* (*Sa'i dngos gzhi*), P5536: 309.3.3-4; cf. *Ārya-brahma-paripṛcchā-nāma-mahāyāna-sūtra,* P825.

Chapter Twenty-Four *The Nature of the Three Trainings*

566. *Yoga-caryā-bhūmi* (*Sa'i dngos gzhi*), P5536: 309.3.2-3.

567. *Mahā-parinirvāṇa-sūtra*, P787: 71.5.2-6.

568. *Suhṛl-lekha:* 7cd; P5682: 235.3.7.

569. *Subāhu-paripṛcchā-tantra*, P428: 34.3.4-5.

570. *Bhikṣu-prareju-sūtra-nāma* is the original title given for the *dGe slong la rab tu gces pa'i mdo shes bya ba*, P968: 55.1.1. The word *plareju* (*sic*) has been changed to *prareju* and then to *priyā* in the catalogues.

571. *Vinaya-vibhaṅga* (*Lung rnam 'byed*), P1032: 149.5.3.

572. This *nāgā* had a small tree growing out of its head, which caused great pain whenever the wind blew. This was the karmic result of its former life as a monk who disregarded the lesser vows.

573. Cited in *Yoga-caryā-bhūmi* (*Sa'i dngos gzhi*), P5536: 309.4.6-7.

574. *Śīla-saṃyukta-sūtra*, P969: 55.2.3-6.

575. SR: 16.15b-16; P795: 295.1.6-7.

576. Ibid.: 9.38-39; P795: 284.1.6-7.

577. Ibid.: 24.28; P795: 308.3.6-7.

578. Ibid.: 35.3-4; P795: 15.2.8-15.3.1.

579. *Ārya-maitreya-mahā-siṃha-nāda-nāma-mahāyāna-sūtra*, P760: 34.1.2-3, 34.1.7-8.

580. *Subāhu-paripṛcchā-tantra*, P428: 34.3.5-6.

581. Ibid., P428: 41.5.8-42.1.1.

582. *Ārya-mañjuśrī-mūla-tantra.* The translation follows the Tibetan translation used by Tsong-kha-pa, but cf. Vaidya 1964: 85-88, which suggests *vidiśa* should be construed not as "direction" but as a verb meaning "to show."

583. *Suhṛl-lekha:* 17; P5682: 235.4.8.

584. BCA: 4.43-44; P5272: 248.3.3-4.

585. Ibid.: 4.45-46; P5272: 248.3.4-6.

586. Ibid.: 6.2a; P5272: 250.4.1.

587. Ibid.: 6.6b; P5272: 250.4.5.

588. *Suhṛl-lekha:* 46; P5682: 236.3.3.

589. Ibid.: 44; P5682: 236.3.1-2.

590. *Āryādhyāśaya-saṃcodana-sūtra,* P760: 60.4.5-6.

591. Ibid., P760: 60.5.5-6, cited in Vaidya 1960b: 64.

592. *Sad-dharmānusmṛty-upasthāna,* P953: 138.1.7.

593. Ud: 5.10; P992: 91.2.1-2.

594. Jm: 12.19; P5650: 22.4.3-4. This is the story about the teacher testing his disciples by asking them to steal, cited earlier (LRCM: 49ff) in the section on reliance upon the teacher.

595. *Suhṛl-lekha:* 54; P5682: 236.4.2-3.

596. BCA: 5.26; P5272: 249.1.3-4.

597. Ibid.: 4.39; P5272: 248.2.8-248.3.1.

598. Ibid.: 4.20; P5272: 250.5.7-8.

599. Ibid.: 8.60; P5272: 254.2.8-254.3.1.

ABBREVIATIONS

A-kya	A-kya-yongs-'dzin, *Lam rim brda bkrol*
AA	*Abhisamayālaṃkāra-nāma-prajñāpāramitopadeśa-śāstra-kārikā*
AK	*Abhidharma-kośa-kārikā*
AKbh	*Abhidharma-kośa-bhāṣya*
Bbh	*Yoga-caryā-bhūmaubodhisattva-bhūmi*
BCA	*Bodhisattva-caryāvatāra*
Cś	*Catuḥ-śataka-śāstra-kārikā-nāma*
Jm	*Jātaka-mālā*
LRCM	Tsong-kha-pa (1985) *sKyes bu gsum gyi rnyams su blang ba'i rim pa thams cad tshang bar ston pa'i byang chub lam gyi rim pa*
mChan	'Jam-dbyangs-bzhad-pa, et al. *Lam rim mchan bzhi sbrags ma*
MSA	*Mahāyāna-sūtrālaṃkāra-kārikā*
P	Suzuki (1955-61)
RGV	*Uttara-tantra* (*Ratna-gotra-vibhāga*)
rNam thar rgyas pa	Nag-tsho, *Jo bo rje dpal ldan mar me mdzad ye shes kyi rnam thar rgyas pa*
Rā	*Rāja-parikathā-ratnāvalī*
Śbh	*Yoga-caryā-bhūmauśrāvaka-bhūmi*
Skt.	Sanskrit
SP	*Sad-dharma-puṇḍarīka-nāma-mahāyāna-sūtra*
SR	*Sarva-dharma-svabhāva-samatā-vipañcita-samādhi-rāja-sūtra*
Ud	*Udāna-varga*
Vs	*Viniścaya-saṃgrahaṇī*

Bibliography

Indian sūtras and tantras are listed alphabetically by title in the first section; Indian śāstras are listed alphabetically by title in the second section; Tibetan commentaries are listed alphabetically by author in the third section; works by modern writers are listed alphabetically by author in the fourth section.

A. Sūtras and Tantras

Avataṃsaka. See *Buddhāvataṃsaka-nāma-mahā-vaipulya-sūtra.*

Aṣṭa-sāhasrikā: Āryāṣṭa-sāhasrikā-prajñā-pāramitā-sūtra, 'Phags pa shes rab kyi pha rol tu phyin pa brgyad stong pa. Skt. ed. Vaidya 1960d. English trans. Conze 1973. P734, vol. 21.

Ārya-aṣṭādaśasāhasrikā-prajñāpāramitā-nāma-mahāyāna-sūtra, 'Phags pa shes rab kyi pha rol tu phyin pa khri brgyad stong pa. English trans. Conze 1979. P732, vol.20.

Ārya-tri-skandha-nāma-mahāyāna-sūtra, 'Phags pa phung po gsum pa shes bya ba theg pa chen po'i mdo. English trans. Beresford 1980. P950, vol. 37.

Ārya-laṅkāvatāra-mahāyāna-sūtra, 'Phags pa lang kar gshegs pa'i mdo. Skt. ed. Vaidya 1963. P775, vol. 29.

Ārya-suvikrānta-vikrami-paripṛcchā-prajñā-pāramitā-nirdeśa, 'Phags pa rab kyi rtsal gyis rnam par gnon pas shus pa shes rab kyi pha rol tu phyin pa bstan pa. P736, vol. 21.

Āryādhyāśaya-saṃcodana-nāma-mahāyāna-sūtra, 'Phags pa lhag pa'i bsam pa bskul pa shes bya ba theg pa chen po'i mdo. Section 25 of the *Ratna-kūṭa.* P760, vol. 24.

Āryāyuṣman-nanda-garbhāvakrānti-nirdeśa-[*nāma-mahāyāna-*]*sūtra, 'Phags pa tshe dang ldan pa dga' bo mngal du gnas pa bstan pa shes bya ba theg pa chen po'i mdo.* Section 13 of the *Ratna-kūṭa.* P760, vol. 23.

Udāna-varga, Ched du brjod pa'i tshoms. Skt. ed. Bernhard 1965. English trans. Rockhill 1982. P992, vol. 39.

Karma-śataka-sūtra, Las brgya tham pa'i mdo. P1007, vol. 39.

Kṣitigarbha-sūtra: Daśa-cakra-kṣitigarbha-nāma-mahāyāna-sūtra, 'Dus pa chen po las sa'i snying po'i 'khor lo bcu pa'i mdo. P905, vol. 36.

Gaṇḍa-vyūha-sūtra, sDong pos brgyan pa/ sDong po bkod pa'i mdo. Section 45 of the *Buddhāvataṃsaka-nāma-mahā-vaipulya-sūtra, Sangs rgyas phal po che shes bya ba shin tu rgyas pa chen po'i mdo.* Skt. ed. Vaidya 1960c. English trans. Cleary 1985-87. P761, vol. 26.

Garbhāvakrānti-sūtra: Ārya-nanda-garbhāvakrānti-nirdeśa-[nāma-mahāyāna-]sūtra, 'Phags pa dga' bo mngal du 'jug pa bstan pa shes bya ba theg pa chen po'i mdo. Section 14 of the *Ratna-kūṭa.* P760, vol. 23.

Gṛha-paty-ugra-paripṛcchā-sūtra: Ārya-gṛha-paty-ugra-paripṛcchā-nāma-mahāyāna-sūtra, 'Phags pa khyim bdag drag shul can gyis zhus pa shes bya ba theg pa chen po'i mdo. Section 19 of the *Ratna-kūṭa.* P760, vol. 23.

Catur-dharma-nirdeśa-sūtra: Ārya-catur-dharma-nirdeśa-nāma-mahāyāna-sūtra, 'Phags pa chos bzhi bstan pa shes bya ba theg pa chen po'i mdo. P915, vol. 36.

Tathāgatācintya-guhya-nirdeśa-sūtra: Ārya-tathāgatācintya-guhya-nirdeśa-nāma-mahāyāna-sūtra, 'Phags pa de bzhin gshegs pa'i gsang ba bsam gyis mi khyab pa bstan pa shes bya ba theg pa chen po'i mdo. Section 3 of the *Ratna-kūṭa.* P760, vol. 22.

Tri-samaya-vyūha: Tri-samaya-vyūha-rāja-nāma-tantra, Dam tshig gsum bkod pa'i rgyal po shes bya ba'i rgyud. P134, vol. 6.

Dama-mūrkha-nāma-sūtra, mDzang lun zhe bya ba'i mdo. English trans. Fry 1981. P1008, vol. 40.

Daśa-dharmaka-sūtra: Ārya-daśa-dharmaka-nāma-mahāyāna-sūtra, 'Phags pa chos bcu pa shes bya ba theg pa chen po'i mdo. Section 9 of the *Ratna-kūṭa.* P760, vol. 22.

Daśa-bhūmika-sūtra, Sa bcu pa'i mdo. Section 31 of the *Avataṃsaka.* English trans. Cleary 1985-87. P761, vol. 26.

Duḥśīla-nigraha-sūtra: Buddha-piṭaka-duḥśīla-nigrahī-nāma-mahāyāna-sūtra, Sangs rgyas kyi sde snod tshul khrims 'chal ba tshar gcod pa shes bya ba theg pa chen po'i mdo. P886, vol. 35.

Dharma-saṃgīti: Ārya-dharma-saṃgīti-nāma-mahāyāna-sūtra, 'Phags pa chos yang dag par sdud pa shes bya ba theg pa chen po'i mdo. P904, vol. 36.

Dhāraṇīśvara-rāja-paripṛcchā: Ārya-tathāgata-mahā-karuṇā-nirdeśa-nāma-mahāyāna-sūtra, 'Phags pa de bzhin gshegs pa'i snying rje chen po nges par bstan pa shes bya ba theg pa chen po'i mdo/gZungs kyi dbang phyug rgyal pos zhus pa. P814, vol. 32.

Niyatāniyata-mudrāvatāra-sūtra: Ārya-niyatāniyata-gati-mudrāvatāra-nāma-mahāyāna-sūtra, 'Phags pa nges pa dang mi nges par 'gro ba'i phyag rgya la 'jug pa shes bya ba theg pa chen po'i mdo. P868, vol. 34.

Pratyutpanna-buddha-saṃmukhāvasthita-samādhi-sūtra: Ārya-pratyutpanna-buddha-saṃmukhāvasthita-samādhi-nāma-mahāyāna-sūtra, 'Phags pa da ltar gyi sangs rgyas mngon sum du gshugs pa'i ting nge 'dzin ces bya ba theg pa chen po'i mdo. P801, vol. 32.

Praśānta-viniścaya-prātihārya-sūtra: Ārya-praśānta-viniścaya-prātihārya-samādhi-nāma-mahāyāna-sūtra, Rab tu zhi ba rnam par nges pa'i cho 'phrul gyi ting nge 'dzin ces bya ba theg pa chen po'i mdo. P797, vol. 32.

Prātimokṣa-sūtra, So sor thar pa'i mdo. P1031, vol. 42.

Buddhāvataṃsaka-nāma-mahā-vaipulya-sūtra, Sangs rgyas phal po che shes bya ba shin tu rgyas pa chen po'i mdo. English trans. Cleary 1985-87. P761, vols. 25-26.

Bodhisattva-piṭaka: Ārya-bodhisattva-piṭaka-nāma-mahāyāna-sūtra, 'Phags pa byang chub sems dpa'i sde snod ces bya ba theg pa chen po'i mdo. Section 12 of the *Ratna-kūṭa.* P760, vol. 22.

Bodhisattva-prātimokṣa: Bodhisattva-prātimokṣa-catuṣka-nirhāra-nāma-mahāyāna-sūtra, Byang chub sems dpa'i so sor thar pa chos bzhi sgrub pa shes bya ba theg pa chen po'i mdo. P914, vol. 36.

Brahma-paripṛcchā-sūtra, Tshang pas zhus pa'i mdo. P825, vol. 33.

Bhikṣu-prareju-sūtra-nāma, dGe slong la rab tu gces pa'i mdo shes bya ba. P968, vol. 39.

Mañjuśrī-mūla-tantra: Ārya-mañjuśrī-mūla-tantra, 'Phags pa 'jam dpal gyi rtsa ba'i rgyud. Skt. ed. in Vaidya 1964. P162, vol. 6.

Mahā-parinirvāṇa-sūtra: Ārya-mahā-parinirvāṇa-sūtra, 'Phags pa yongs su mya ngan las 'das pa chen po'i mdo. P787, vol. 31.

Mahāyāna-prasāda-prabhāvanā-sūtra: Ārya-mahāyāna-prasāda-prabhāvanā-nāma-mahāyāna-sūtra, 'Phags pa theg pa chen po la dad pa rab tu sgom pa shes bya ba theg pa chen po'i mdo. P812, vol. 32.

Maitreya-mahā-siṃha-nāda-sūtra: Ārya-maitreya-mahā-siṃha-nāda-nāma-mahāyāna-sūtra, 'Phags pa byams pa seng ge'i sgra chen po shes bya ba theg pa chen po'i mdo. Section 23 of the *Ratna-kūṭa*. P760, vol. 24.

Ratna-kūṭa: Ārya-mahā-ratna-kūṭa-dharma-paryāya-śata-sāhasrika-grantha, dKon mchog brtsegs pa chen po'i chos kyi rnam grangs le'u stong phrag brgya pa. P760, vols. 22-24.

Ratna-guṇa-sañcaya-gāthā: Ārya-prajñāpāramitā-ratna-guṇa-sañcaya-gāthā, 'Phags pa shes rab kyi pha rol tu phyin pa sdud pa tshigs su bcad pa. Skt. ed. Yuyama 1976. English trans. Conze 1973. P735, vol. 21.

Ratna-megha-sūtra: Ārya-ratna-megha-nāma-mahāyāna-sūtra, 'Phags pa dkon mchog sprin ces bya ba theg pa chen po'i mdo. P897, vol. 35.

Ratna-rāśi-sūtra: Ārya-ratna-rāśi-nāma-mahāyāna-sūtra, 'Phags pa rin po che'i phung po shes bya ba theg pa chen po'i mdo. Section 45 of the *Ratna-kūṭa*. P760, vol. 24.

Ratnolka-dhāraṇī: Ārya-ratnolka-nāma-dhāraṇī-mahāyāna-sūtra, 'Phags pa dkon mchog ta la'i gzungs shes bya ba theg pa chen po'i mdo. P472, vol. 11.

Rājāvavādaka: Ārya-rājāvavādaka-nāma-mahāyāna-sūtra, 'Phags pa rgyal po la gdams pa shes bya ba theg pa chen po'i mdo. P887, vol. 35.

Lalita-vistara-sūtra: Ārya-lalitavistara-nāma-mahāyāna-sūtra, 'Phags pa rgya cher rol pa shes ya ba theg pa chen po'i mdo. Skt. ed. Vaidya 1958. P763, vol. 27.

Vajra-ḍāka: Śrī-vajra-ḍāka-nāma-mahā-tantra-rāja, rGyud kyi rgyal po chen po dpal rdo rje mkha' 'gro zhes bya ba. P18, vol. 2.

Vajrapāṇy-abhiṣeka-mahā-tantra: Ārya-vajrapāṇy-abhiṣeka-mahā-tantra, 'Phags pa lag na rdo rje dbang bskur ba'i rgyud chen mo. P130, vol. 6.

Vajra-śikhara: Vajra-śikhara-mahā-guhya-yoga-tantra, gSang ba rnal 'byor chen po'i rgyud rdo rje rtse mo. P113, vol. 5.

Vinaya-kṣudraka-vastu, 'Dul ba phran tshegs kyi bzhi. Section 3 of the *Vinaya*. P1035, vol. 44.

Vinaya-vastu, 'Dul ba gzhi. Section 1 of the *Vinaya*. P1030, vol. 41.

Vinaya-vibhaṅga, 'Dul ba rnam par 'byed pa. Section 2 of the *Vinaya*. P1032, vols. 42-43.

Śāli-stamba-sūtra: Ārya-śālistamba-nāma-mahāyāna-sūtra, 'Phags pa sā lu'i ljang ba shes bya ba theg pa chen po'i mdo. P876, vol. 34.

Śīla-saṃyukta-sūtra, Tshul khrims yang dag par ldan pa'i mdo. P969, vol. 39.

Śraddhā-balādhānāvatāra-mudrā-sūtra: Ārya-śraddhā-balādhānāvatāra-mudrā-nāma-mahāyāna-sūtra, Dad pa'i stobs bskyed pa la 'jug pa'i phyag rgya shes bya ba theg pa chen po'i mdo. P867, vol. 34.

Saṃdhi-nirmocana-sūtra: Ārya-saṃdhi-nirmocana-nāma-mahāyāna-sūtra, 'Phags pa dgongs pa nges par 'grol pa shes bya ba theg pa chen po'i mdo. English trans. Powers 1995b. P774, vol. 29.

Saṃpuṭi-nāma-mahā-tantra, Yang dag par sbyor ba zhes bya ba'i rgyud chen po. P26, vol. 2.

Satyaka-parivarta, bDen pa po'i le'u. The fourth chapter of the *Ārya-bodhisattva-gocaropāya-viṣaya-vikurvāṇa-nirdeśa-nāma-mahāyāna-sūtra, 'Phags pa byang chub sems dpa'i spyod yul gyi thabs kyi yul la rnam par 'phrul ba bstan pa shes bya ba theg pa chen po'i mdo.* English trans. Jamspel 1991. P813, vol. 32.

Sad-dharma-puṇḍarīka-nāma-mahāyāna-sūtra, Dam pa'i chos pa dma dkar po shes bya ba theg pa chen po'i mdo. Skt. ed. Vaidya 1960a. English trans. Hurvitz 1976. P781, vol. 30.

Sad-dharmānusmṛty-upasthāna: Ārya-sad-dharmānusmṛty-upasthāna, 'Phags pa dam pa'i chos dran pa nye bar gzhag pa. P953, vols. 37-38.

Samantabhadra-caryā-praṇidhāna. Section 62 of the *Gaṇḍa-vyūha-sūtra.* Skt. also in Pandeya 1994:139-143 under the title *Bhadra-carī-praṇidhāna-stotra.* P761, vol. 26.

Samādhi-rāja-sūtra: Sarva-dharma-svabhāva-samatā-vipañcita-samādhi-rāja-sūtra, Chos tham cad kyi rang bzhin mnyam pa nyid rnam par spros pa ting nge 'dzin gyi rgyal po'i mdo. Skt. ed. Vaidya 1961. P795, vol. 31.

Sarva-vaidalya-saṃgraha-sūtra: Ārya-sarva-vaidalya-saṃgraha-nāma-mahāyāna-sūtra, 'Phags pa rnam par 'thag pa thams cad bsdus pa shes bya ba theg pa chen po'i mdo. P893, vol. 35.

Sāgara-nāga-rāja-paripṛcchā: Ārya-sāgara-nāga-rāja-paripṛcchā-nāma-mahāyāna-sūtra, 'Phags pa klu'i rgyal po rgya mtshos zhus pa shes bya ba theg pa chen po'i mdo. P820, vol. 33.

Sāgaramati-paripṛcchā-sūtra: Ārya-sāgaramati-paripṛcchā-nāma-mahāyāna-sūtra, 'Phags pa blo gros rgya mtshos zhus pa shes bya ba theg pa chen po'i mdo. P819, vol. 33.

Siṃha-paripṛcchā-sūtra: Ārya-siṃha-paripṛcchā-nāma-mahāyāna-sūtra, 'Phags pa seng ges zhus pa shes bya ba theg pa chen po'i mdo. Section 37 of the *Ratna-kūṭa.* P760, vol. 24.

Subāhu-paripṛcchā-tantra: Ārya-subāhu-paripṛcchā-nāma-tantra, 'Phags pa dpung bzang gis zhus pa shes bya ba'i rgyud. P428, vol. 9.

Suvarṇa-prabhāsa-sūtra: Ārya-suvarṇa-prabhāsottama-sūtrendra-rāja-nāma-mahāyāna-sūtra, 'Phags pa gser 'od dam pa mdo sde'i dbang po'i rgyal po shes bya ba theg pa chen po'i mdo. Skt. ed. Bagchi 1967. P176, vol. 7.

Sūkarikāvadāna-nāma-sūtra, Phag mo'i rtogs pa brjod pa shes bya ba'i mdo. Skt. ed. in Section 14 of the *Divyāvadāna,* Vaidya 1959b. P1014, vol. 40.

Sūrya-garbha-sūtra: Ārya-sūrya-garbha-nāma-vaipulya-sūtra, 'Phags pa shin tu rgyas pa chen po'i sde nyi ma'i snying po shes bya ba'i mdo. P923, vol. 36.

Smṛty-upasthāna. See *Sad-dharmānusmṛty-upasthāna.*

B. Śāstras

Abhidharma-kośa: Abhidharma-kośa-kārikā, Chos mngon pa'i mdzod kyi tshig le'ur byas pa. Vasubandhu. Skt. ed. Gokhale 1946. English trans. Pruden 1988 from French trans. of la Vallée Poussin 1971. P5590, vol. 115.

Abhidharma-kośa-bhāṣya, Chos mngon pa'i mdzod kyi bshad pa. Vasubandhu. Skt. ed. Shastri 1972. English trans. Pruden 1988 from French trans. of la Vallée Poussin 1971. P5591, vol. 115.

Abhidharma-samuccaya, Chos mngon pa kun las btus pa. Asaṅga. Partial Skt. ed. Gokhale 1947. French trans. Rahula 1980. P5550, vol. 112.

Abhisamayālaṃkāra: Abhisamayālaṃkāra-nāma-prajñāpāramitopadeśa-śāstra-kārikā. Maitreyanātha. Skt. ed. Wogihara 1973. English trans. Conze 1954. P5184. vol. 88.

Abhisamayālaṃkārālokā: Āryāṣṭa-sāhasrikā-prajñāpāramitā-vyākhyāna Abhisamayālaṃkārālokā-nāma, 'Phags pa shes rab kyi pha rol tu phyin pa brgyad stong pa'i bshad pa mngon par rtogs pa'i rgyan gyi snang ba shes bya ba. Haribhadra. Skt. ed. Wogihara 1973. P5189, vol. 90.

Aṣṭākṣaṇa-kathā, Mi khom pa brgyad kyi gtam. Aśvaghoṣa. P5423, vol. 103.

Ārya-buddhānusmṛti, 'Phags pa sangs rgyas rjes su dran pa. P5433, vol. 103.

Uttara-tantra: Mahāyānottaratantra-śāstra, Theg pa chen po rgyud bla ma'i bstan bcos. Also called *Ratna-gotra-vibhāga, dKon mchog gi rigs rnam par dbye ba.* Maitreyanātha. Skt. ed. Johnston 1950. English trans. Obermiller 1931. P5525, vol. 108.

Udāna-varga: Udāna-varga-vivaraṇa, Ched du brjod pa'i tshoms kyi rnam gyi 'grel pa. Prajñāvarman. P5601, vol. 119.

Karma-vibhaṅga-nāma, Las rnam par 'byed pa. Atisha. P5356, vol. 103

Kṛṣṇa-yamāri-pañjikā: Śrī-kṛṣṇa-yamāri-mahā-tantra-rāja-pañjikā-ratna-pradīpa-nāma, dPal gshin rje'i dgra nag po'i rgyud kyi rgyal po chen po'i dka' 'grel rin po che'i sgron ma shes bya ba. Ratnākaraśānti. P2782, vol. 66.

Guru-pañcāśikā, Bla ma lnga bcu pa. Aśvaghoṣa. Skt. partial ed. Levi 1929. English trans. Sparham 1999. P4544, vol. 81.

Catur-viparyaya-[parihāra]-kathā, Phyi ci log bzhi spangs pa'i gtam. Mātricitra. P5669, vol. 129.

Catuḥ-śataka: Catuḥ-śataka-śāstra-kārikā-nāma, bsTan bcos bzhi brgya pa zhes bya ba'i tshig le'ur byas pa. Āryadeva. Skt. and Tibetan ed. Lang 1986. English trans. Rinchen and Sonam 1994. P5246, vol. 95.

Candra-rāja-lekha, rGyal po zla ba la springs pa'i phrin yig. Śrī Jagan-mitrānanda. P5689, vol. 129.

Caryā-melāpaka-pradīpa, sPyod pa bsdus pa'i sgron ma. Āryadeva. P2668, vol. 61.

Caryā-saṃgraha-pradīpa, sPyod pa bsdus pa'i sgron ma. Atisha. P5379 and P5357, vol. 103.

Jātaka-mālā, sKyes pa'i rabs kyi rgyud. Āryaśūra. Skt. ed. Vaidya 1959a. English trans. Speyer 1971. P5650, vol. 128.

Nyāya-bindu-prakaraṇa: Nyāya-bindu-nāma-prakaraṇa, Rigs pa'i thigs pa shes bya ba'i rab tu byed pa. Dharmakīrti. English trans. Stcherbatsky 1962. P5711, vol. 130.

Tarka-jvālā: Madhyamaka-hṛdaya-vṛtti-tarka-jvālā, dBu ma'i snying po'i 'grel pa rtog ge 'bar ba. Bhāvaviveka. P5256, vol. 96.

Triśaraṇa-[gamana]-saptati, gSum la skyabs su 'gro ba bdun cu pa. Candrakīrti. P5478, vol. 103.

Daśākuśala-karma-patha-nirdeśa, Mi dge ba bcu'i las kyi lam bstan pa. Aśvaghoṣa. P5416, vol. 103, and P5678, vol. 129.

Deśanā-stava, bShags pa'i bstod pa. Candragomin. P2048, vol. 46.

Dharmānusmṛti, Chos rje su dran pa. P5434, vol. 103.

Pañca-skandha-prakaraṇa, Phung po lnga'i rab tu byed pa. Vasubandhu. P5560, vol. 113.

Pāramitā-samāsa-nāma, Pha rol tu phyin pa bsdus pa shes bya ba. Āryaśūra. Skt. partial ed. Ferrari 1946. English trans. Meadows 1986. P5340, vol. 103.

Prajñā-pradīpa-ṭīkā, Shes rab sgron ma'i rgya cher 'grel pa. Avalokitavrata. P5259, vols. 96-97.

Praṇidhāna-saptati: Praṇidhāna-saptati-nāma-gāthā, sMon lam bdun cu pa shes bya ba'i tshigs su bcad pa. The author of both versions according to P is gZhan la phan pa'i dbyangs dGon pa pa. Beresford says the author is Āryaśūrya (*sic*). English trans. Beresford 1979. P5430, vol. 103, and P5936, vol. 150.

Pratītya-samutpādādi-vibhaṅga-nirdeśa, rTen cing 'brel bar 'byung ba dang po dang rnam par dbye ba bshad pa. Vasubandhu. P5496, vol. 104.

Pratītya-samutpāda-hṛdaya-kārikā, rTen cing 'brel par 'byung ba'i snying po'i tshig le'ur byas pa. Nāgārjuna. Skt. ed. Gokhale and Dhadphale 1978. P5467, vol. 103.

Pramāṇa-vārttika-kārikā, Tshad ma rnam 'grel gyi tshig le'ur byas pa. Dharmakīrti. Skt. ed. Shastri 1968. Partial English trans. Mookerjee and Nagasaki 1964. P5709, vol. 130.

Prasphuṭa-padā: Abhisamayālaṃkāra-kārikā-prajñā-pāramitopadeśa-śāstra-ṭīkā-prasphuṭa-padā-nāma, Shes rab kyi pha rol tu phyin pa'i man ngag gi bstan bcos mngon par rtogs pa'i rgyan gyi tshig le'ur byas pa'i 'grel bshad tshig rab tu gsal ba zhes bya ba. Dharmamitra. P5194, vol. 91.

Bodhicitta-vivaraṇa, Byang chub sems kyi 'grel pa. Nāgārjuna. Tibetan ed. Lindtner 1982 with English trans. P2665 and P2666, vol. 61.

Bodhicitta-vivaraṇa-ṭīkā, Byang chub sems kyi 'grel pa'i rnam par bshad pa. Smṛtijñānakīrti. P2694, vol. 62.

Bodhi-patha-pradīpa, Byang chub lam gyi sgron ma. Atisha. English trans. Sherbourne 1983. P5343, vol. 103.

Bodhi-mārga-pradīpa-pañjikā-nāma, Byang chub lam gyi sgron ma'i dka' 'grel. Atisha. English trans. Sherbourne 1983. P5344, vol. 103.

Bodhisattva-caryāvatāra, Byang chub sems dpa'i spyod la 'jug pa. Śāntideva. Skt. and Tibetan ed. Bhattacharya 1960. English trans. Crosby and Skilton 1995. P5272, vol. 99.

Bodhisattva-yoga-caryā-catuḥ-śataka-ṭīkā, Byang chub sems dpa'i rnal 'byor spyod pa bzhi brgya pa'i rgya cher 'grel pa. Candrakīrti. P5266, vol. 98.

Bodhisattvāvadāna-kalpalatā, Byang chub sems dpa'i rtogs pa brjod pa'i dpag bsam gyi 'khri shing. Kṣemendra. P5655, vol. 129.

Bhāvanā-krama, sGom pa'i rim pa. Kamalaśīla. Partial ed. and trans. in Tucci 1956: 467-592. P5310-5312, vol. 102.

Madhyamaka-hṛdaya-kārikā, dBu ma'i snying po'i tshig le'ur byas pa. Bhāvaviveka. P5255, vol 96.

Madhyamakāvatāra-nāma, dBu ma la 'jug pa shes bya ba. Candrakīrti. Tibetan ed. la Vallée Poussin 1970. Partial English trans. Hopkins 1980, Klein 1994. P5262, vol. 98.

Mūla-madhyamaka-kārikā: Prajñā-nāma-mūla-madhyamaka-kārikā, dBu ma rtsa ba'i tshig le'ur byas pa shes rab ces bya ba. Nāgārjuna. Skt. ed. de Jong 1977. English trans. Garfield 1995. P5224, vol. 95.

Mahāyāna-patha-sādhana-varṇa-saṃgraha, Theg pa chen po'i lam gyi sgrub thabs yi ger bsdus pa. Atisha. P5351, vol. 103.

Mahāyāna-patha-sādhana-saṃgraha, Theg pa chen po'i lam gyi sgrub thabs shin tu bsdus pa. Atisha. P5352, vol. 103.

Mahāyāna-sūtrālaṃkāra-kārikā, Theg pa chen po'i mdo sde'i rgyan gyi tshig le'ur byas pa. Maitreyanātha. Skt. ed. Bagchi 1970. P5521, vol. 108.

Mahā-rāja-kaniṣka-lekha, rGyal po chen po ka ni ka la springs pa'i spring yig. Maticitra. P5411, vol. 103.

Miśraka-stotra-nāma, sPel mar bstod pa shes bya ba. Dignāga. P2041, vol. 46.

Yukti-ṣaṣṭikā-vṛtti, Rigs pa drug cu pa'i 'grel pa. Candrakīrti. P5265, vol. 98.

Yoga-caryā-bhūmi, rNal 'byor spyod pa'i sa. Asaṅga. P5536-5543, vols. 109-111. *Sa'i dngos gzhi,* the Tibetan name for the first part of the *Yoga-caryā-bhūmi* (P5536), and perhaps for all parts except the *Viniścaya-saṁgrahaṇī, Śrāvaka-bhūmi,* and *Bodhisattva-bhūmi,* is rendered *Yoga-caryā-bhūmi* in the translation.

Yoga-caryā-bhūmaunirṇaya-saṃgraha, rNal 'byor spyod pa'i sa rnam par gtan la dbab pa bsdu ba. Asaṅga. This is the *Viniścaya-samgrahaṇī.* The Skt. title here suggests *rNal 'byor spyod pa'i sa rnam par nges pa bsdu pa.* P5539, vol. 110.

Yoga-caryā-bhūmaubodhisattva-bhūmi, rNal 'byor spyod pa'i sa las Byang chub sems dpa'i sa. Asaṅga. Skt. ed. Dutt 1966. P5538, vol. 110.

Yoga-caryā-bhūmauśrāvaka-bhūmi, rNal 'byor spyod pa'i sa las Nyan thos kyi sa. Asaṅga. Skt. ed. Shukla 1973. P5537, vol. 110.

Ratnāvalī: Rāja-parikathā-ratnāvalī, rGyal po la gtam bya ba rin po che'i phreng ba. Nāgārjuna. English trans. Dunne and McClintock 1998. P5658, vol. 129.

Varṇārha-varṇa-stotra: Varṇārha-varṇebhagavato-buddhasyastotreśakya-stava, Sangs rgyas bcom ldan 'das la bstod pa bsngags par 'os pa bsngags pa las bstod par mi nus par bstod pa. Āryaśūra/Maticitra. P2029, vol. 46.

Vinaya-sūtra, 'Dul ba'i mdo. Guṇaprabha. P5619, vol. 123.

Vinaya-sūtra-ṭīkā, 'Dul ba'i mdo'i rgya cher 'grel pa. Dharmamitra. P5622, vols. 124-126.

Viniścaya-saṃgrahaṇī. See *Yoga-caryā-bhūmi-nirṇaya-saṃgraha.*

Viśeṣa-stava, Khyad par du 'phags pa'i bstod pa. Udbhaṭasiddhasvāmin. P2001, vol. 46.

Vyakta-padā-suhṛl-lekha-ṭīkā, bShes pa'i spring yig gi rgya cher bshad pa tshig gsal ba. Mahāmati. P5690, vol. 129.

Śata-pañcāśatka-stotra: Śata-pañcāśatka-nāma-stotra, brGya lnga bcu pa shes bya ba'i bstod pa. Aśvaghoṣa. P2038, vol. 46.

Śikṣā-samuccaya, bSlab pa kun las btus pa. Śāntideva. Skt. ed. Vaidya 1960b. English trans. Bendall and Rouse 1971. P5336, vol. 102.

Śiṣya-lekha, Slob ma la springs pa'i spring yig. Candragomin. Skt. partial ed. Minareff 1890. P5683, vol. 129, and P5410, vol. 103.

Śoka-vinodana, Mya ngan bsal ba. Aśvaghoṣa. P5677, vol. 129.

Saṃghānusmṛti, dGe 'dun rje su dran pa. P5435, vol. 103.

Saṃvṛti-bodhicitta-bhāvanā: Saṃvṛti-bodhicitta-bhāvanopadeśa-varṇa-saṃgraha, Kun rdzob byang chub kyi sems bsgom pa'i man ngag yi ger bris pa. Aśvaghoṣa. P5307, vol. 102.

Saḍ-aṅga-śaraṇa-[gamana], sKyabs 'gro yan lag drug pa. Vimalamitra. P5367, vol. 103.

Sapta-kumārikāvadāna, gZhon nu ma bdun gyi rtogs pa brjod pa. Guhyadatta. P5419, vol. 103.

Samādhi-sambhāra-parivarta. Ting nge 'dzin gyi tshogs kyi le'u. Bodhibhadra. P3288, vol. 69, and P5398, vol. 103

Sambhāra-parikathā, Tshogs kyi gtam. Vasubandhu. English trans. Nakatani 1987. P5422, vol. 103.

Subhāṣita-ratna-karaṇḍaka-kathā, Legs par bshad pa rin po che za ma tog lta bu'i gtam. [Ārya]śūra. P5668, vol. 129, and P5424, vol. 103.

Suhṛl-lekha, bShes pa'i spring yig. Nāgārjuna. English trans. Jamspal 1981. P5682, vol. 129.

Hṛdaya-nikṣepa-nāma, sNying bo nges par bsdu ba zhes bya ba. Atisha. P5346, vol. 103.

C. Tibetan Works

Anonymous. *Byang chub lam rim chen mo'i sa bcad.* Dharamsala: Shering Parkhang, 1964.

dGe-bshes-rong-pa-phyag-sor-ba. See Nag-tsho, *rNam thar rgyas pa.*

dGe-bshes-zul-phu-ba. See Nag-tsho, *rNam thar rgyas pa.*

Ngag-dbang-rab-brtan (sDe-drug-mkhan-chen-ngag-dbang-rab-brtan). See 'Jam-dbyangs-bzhad-pa, et al.

lCe-sgom-pa-shes-rab-rdo-rje. *dPe chos rin chen spungs pa'i 'bum 'grel.* Delhi: 1975.

mChims-thams-cad-mkhyen-pa. *mChims mdzod gyi 'grel pa mngon pa'i rgyan.* No date. No place.

'Jam-dbyangs-bzhad-pa, et al. *mNyam med rje btsun tsong kha pa chen pos mdzad pa'i byang chub lam rim chen mo'i dka' ba'i gnad rnams mchan bu bzhi'i sgo nas legs par bshad pa theg chen lam gyi gsal sgron* (abbreviated title *Lam rim mchan bzhi sbrags ma*). New Delhi: Chophel Lekden, 1972.

Dol-pa-rog-shes-rab-rgya-mtsho/Dol-pa-dmar-zhur-pa. *Be'u bum sngon po.*

Nag-tsho (Nag-tsho-lo-tsā-ba-tshul-khrims-rgyal-ba). *Khams gsum chos kyi rgyal po dpal ldan mar me mdzad ye shes la bstod pa'i rab tu byed pa tshigs bcad brgyad cu pa.* In *Legs par bshad pa bka' gdams rin po che'i gsung gi gces btus nor bu'i bang mdzod* (abbreviated title *bKa' gdams bces btus*). Compiled by Ye-shes-don-grub-bstan-pa'i-rgyal-mtshan. Delhi: D. Tsondu Senghe, 1985.

———. *Jo bo rje dpal ldan mar me mdzad ye shes kyi rnam thar rgyas pa.* Varanasi: E. Kalsang, 1970. The Tibetan tradition attributes this work to Nag-tsho, although the colophon states that Nag-tsho's account was gathered by dGe-bshes-rong-pa-phyag-sor-ba and written down by dGe-bshes-zul-phu-ba.

Pha-bong-kha (Pha-bong-kha-pa-byams-pa-bstan-'dzin-'phrin-las-rgya-mtsho). *Byang chub lam rim chen mo mchan bu bzhi sbrags kyi skor dran gso'i bsnyel byang mgo smos tsam du mdzad pa.* In *The Collected Works of Pha-boṅ-kha-pa Byams-pa-bstan-'dzin-phrin-las-rgya-mtsho.* Vol. 5. New Delhi: Chophel Legdan, 1973.

Ba-so-chos-kyi-rgyal-mtshan. See 'Jam-dbyangs-bzhad-pa, et al.

Bra-sti (Bra-sti-dge-bshes-rin-chen-don-grub). See 'Jam-dbyangs-bzhad-pa, et al.

Tsong-kha-pa. 1985. *sKyes bu gsum gyi rnyams su blang ba'i rim pa thams cad tshang bar ston pa'i byang chub lam gyi rim pa/ Byang chub lam rim che ba.* Zi-ling (Xining): Tso Ngön (mTsho sngon) People's Press. Also, Ganden Bar Nying, early fifteenth century, and Dharamsala, 1991, editions.

———. *Byang chub sems dpa'i gsang sngags kyi sgo nas byang chub sems dpa'i spyad pa spyod pa rnams kyi tshul khrims kyi bslab pa yongs su dag par bya ba'i tshul rnam par bshad pa dngos grub kyi snye ma shes bya ba.* (Abbreviated name *rTsa ltung rnam bshad.*) In *The Complete Works of Tsong-kha-pa.* P6188, vol. 160.

Ye-shes-rgyal-mtshan (Tshe-mchog-gling Ye-shes-rgyal-mtshan). *Byang chub lam gyi rim pa'i bla ma brgyud pa'i rnam par thar pa rgyal bstan mdzes pa'i rgyan mchog phul byung nor bu'i phreng ba*. Published as *Lives of the Teachers of the Lam-rim Precepts*. Vol. 1. New Delhi: Ngawang Gelek Demo, 1970.

Ye-shes-don-grub-bstan-pa'i-rgyal-mtshan. See Nag-tsho, *bKa' gdams bces btus*.

Ye-shes-sde. *bZang spyod kyi 'grel pa bzhi'i don bsdus nas brjed byang du byas pa*. The Skt. title *Bhadra-caryā-catuṣṭikā-piṇḍārthābhismaraṇa* is given in parentheses. P5846, vol. 145.

A-kya-yongs-'dzin, dByangs-can-dga'-ba'i-blo-gros. *Byang chub lam gyi rim pa chen mo las byung ba'i brda bkrol nyer mkho bsdus pa* (abbreviated title *Lam rim brda bkrol*). In *The Collected Works of A-kya Yoṅs-ḥdzin*, vol. l. New Delhi: Lama Guru Deva, 1971.

D. Modern Works

Bagchi, S., ed. 1967. *Suvarṇaprabhāsottamasūtra*. Darbhanga: Mithila Institute.

———., ed. 1970. *Mahāyāna-Sūtrālaṅkāra of Asaṅga*. Darbhanga: Mithila Institute.

Bareau, André. 1955. *Les Sectes bouddhiques du Petit Véhicule*. Paris: École française d'Extrême-Orient.

Bendall, C. and W.H.D. Rouse, 1971. *Śikṣā Samuccaya*. London, 1922; reprint, Delhi: Motilal Banarsidass.

Beresford, Brian C., with L.T. Doboom Tulku et al. 1979. *Āryaśūrya's Aspiration and A Meditation on Compassion*. Dharamsala: Library of Tibetan Works and Archives.

———. 1980. *Mahayana Purification*. Dharamsala: Library of Tibetan Works and Archives.

Bernhard, Franz, ed. 1965. *Udānavarga, Sanskrit Text*. 2 vols. Akademie der Wissenschaftengottingen. Göttingen: Vandenhoeck & Ruprecht.

Bhattacharya, Vidhushekhara, ed. 1960. *Bodhicaryāvatāra*. Calcutta: The Asiatic Society.

Chandra, Lokesh. 1982. *Tibetan-Sanskrit Dictionary*. Indo-Asian Literature, 3. New Delhi: International Academy of Indian Culture, 1959-61; reprint ed., Kyoto: Rinsen.

Chattopadhyaya, Alaka. 1981. *Atiśa and Tibet*. Delhi: Motilal Banarsidass.

Cleary, Thomas. 1985-87. *The Flower Ornament Scripture: A Translation of the Avatamsaka Sutra*. 3 vols. Boston and London: Shambhala Publications.

Conze, Edward. 1954. *Treatise on Reunion with the Absolute*. Serie Orientale Roma, 6. Rome: Istituto Italiano per il Medio ed Estremo Oriente.

———. 1973. *The Perfection of Wisdom in 8,000 Lines and Its Verse Summary*. Bolinas: Four Seasons Foundation.

———, ed. and trans. 1990. *The Large Sūtra on Perfect Wisdom*. Delhi: Motilal Banarsidass.

Crosby, Kate and Andrew Skilton. 1995. *The Bodhicaryāvatāra*. Oxford and New York: Oxford University Press.

Das (Bahadur), Sarat Chandra. 1985. *Tibetan-English Dictionary*. Calcutta, 1902; reprint ed., New Delhi.

de Jong, J.W., ed. 1977. *Madhyamaka-kārikā*. Adyar: Theosophical Society.

———. 1987. *A Brief History of Buddhist Studies in Europe and America*. 2nd rev. ed. Bibliotheca Indo-Buddhica, no. 33. Delhi: Sri Satguru Publications.

Dessein, Bart, Collett Cox, et al. 1998. *Sarvāstivāda Buddhist Scholasticism*. Handbuch der Orientalistik. Zweite Abteilung Indien; 11 Bd. Leiden: Brill.

Dhargyey, Geshe Ngawang. 1982. *An Anthology of Well-Spoken Advice*. Vol. 1. Dharamsala: Library of Tibetan Works and Archives.

Driessens, Georges. 1990 and 1992. *Le grand livre de la progression vers l'Éveil*. Jujurieux and Saint-Jean-le-Vieux.

Dunne, John and Sara McClintock. 1998. *Precious Garland*. Boston: Wisdom Publications.

Dutt, Nalinaksha, ed. 1966. *Bodhisattva-bhūmi*. Tibetan Sanskrit Works Series, vol. 7. Patna: K.P. Jayaswal Research Institute.

Dutt, Sukumar. 1962. *Buddhist Monks and Monasteries of India*. London: George Allen & Unwin.

Edgerton, F. 1972. *Buddhist Hybrid Sanskrit Grammar and Dictionary*. New Haven: Yale University Press, 1953; reprint ed., Delhi: Motilal Banarsidass.

Eimer, Helmut. 1977. *Berichte über das Leben des Atiśa (Dīpaṃkaraśrījñāna)*. Wiesbaden: Otto Harrassowitz.

———. 1979. *rNam thar rgyas pa, Materialien zu einer Biographie des Atiśa (Dīpaṃkaraśrījñāna)*. In *Asiatische Forschungen* 67. Wiesbaden: Otto Harrassowitz.

Ferrari, A., ed. 1946. *Pāramitā-samāsa*. Annali Laterenesi, X. Rome.

Fry, Stanley. 1981. *Sutra of the Wise and the Foolish*. Dharamsala: Library of Tibetan Works and Archives.

Ganguly, Anil Baran. 1962. *Sixty-Four Arts in Ancient India*. New Delhi: The English Book Store.

Garfield, Jay. 1995. *The Fundamental Wisdom of the Middle Way*. New York: Oxford.

Gokhale, V.V. 1946. "The Text of the *Abhidharmakośa* of Vasubandhu." *Journal of the Bombay Branch, Royal Asiatic Society* 22: 73-102.

———. 1947. "Fragment of the *Abhidharma-samuccaya* of Asaṅga." *Journal of the Bombay Branch, Royal Asiatic Society* 23: 13-38.

Gokhale, V.V. and M. G. Dhadphale. 1978. "The *Pratītyasamutpādahṛdaya-Kārikā* of Nāgārjuna." *Principal V.S. Apte Commemoration Volume*. Ed. by Dr. M.G. Dhadphale. Poona: Poona Deccan Educational Society.

Guenther, Herbert V. 1971. *The Jewel Ornament of Liberation*. Berkeley: Shambhala.

Gyatso, Geshe Kelsang. 1980. *Meaningful to Behold*. London and Boston: Wisdom Publications.

Hirakawa, A. 1990. *A History of Indian Buddhism*. Asian Studies at Hawaii, 36. Honolulu: University of Hawaii.

Hopkins, Jeffrey. 1980. *Compassion in Tibetan Buddhism*. London: Ryder and Co.

———. 1996. *Meditation on Emptiness*. London: Wisdom Publications.

Horner, I.B. 1938-1966. *The Book of Discipline*. Vols. 1-3. London: Humphrey Milford. Vols. 4-6. London: Luzac and Company, Ltd.

Hurvitz, Leon. 1976. *Scripture of the Lotus Blossom of the Fine Dharma*. New York: Columbia University Press.

Jamspal, Lozang, et al. 1981. *Nāgārjuna's Letter to King Gautamīputra*. Delhi: Motilal Banarsidass.

Jamspal, Lozang. 1991. "The Range of the Bodhisattva: A Study of an Early Mahāyāna-sūtra, 'Āryasatyakaparivarta' Discourse of Truth Teller." Ph.D. dissertation, Columbia University.

Johnston, E.H., ed. 1950. *Ratna-gotra-vibhāga-mahāyānottara-tantra-śāstra. Journal of the Orissa and Bihar Research Society* 26, part I.

Jones, J.J. 1956. *The Mahāvastu.* Vol. 3. London: Luzac and Company, Ltd.

Klein, Ann. 1994. *Path to the Middle.* Albany: State University of New York Press.

Kloetzli, Randy. 1983. *Buddhist Cosmology.* Delhi: Motilal Banarsidass.

la Vallée Poussin, Louis de, ed. 1970. *Madhyamakāvatāra par Candrakīrti.* Bibliotheca Buddhica IX [St. Petersburg 1907]. Osnabruck: Biblio Verlag.

———. 1971. *L'Abhidharmakośa de Vasubandhu.* Vol. III. Brussels: Institut Belge des Hautes Études Chinois.

Lang, Karen. 1986. *Āryadeva's Catuḥśataka.* Copenhagen: Akademisk Forlag.

Lévi, Sylvain. 1929. "Autour d'Aśvaghoṣa." *Journal asiatique* 214 (Oct.-Dec.): 259-267.

Lindtner, Christian. 1982. *Nagarjuniana.* Indiske Studier 4. Copenhagen: Akademisk Forlag.

Meadows, Carol. 1986. *Ārya-śūra's Compendium of the Perfections: Text, Translation and Analysis of the Pāramitāsamāsa.* Indica et Tibetica 8. Ed. by Michael Hahn. Bonn: Indica et Tibetica Verlag.

Minareff, I.P., ed. 1890. *Śiṣya-lekha.* Ruselenied Zappiski. Vol. 4. St. Petersburg.

Monier-Williams, M. 1984. *A Sanskrit-English Dictionary.* Oxford: University Press, 1899; reprint ed., Delhi: Motilal Banarsidass.

Mookerjee, S. and H. Nagasaki. 1964. *The Pramāṇa-vārttikam of Dharmakīrti.* Patna.

Nagatomi, M. 1957. "A Study of *Dharmakīrti*'s *Pramāṇa-vārttika.*" Ph.D. dissertation, Harvard University.

Nakamura, Hajime. 1989. *Indian Buddhism: A Survey with Bibliographical Notes.* [1980]. Delhi: Motilal Banarsidas.

Nakatani, H., trans. 1987. *Sambhāra-parikathā.* Paris.

Namdol, Gyaltsen. 1985. *Bhāvanā-krama.* Varanasi: Institute of Higher Tibetan Studies.

Obermiller, E. 1931 "Sublime Science of the Great Vehicle to Salvation." *Acta Orientalia* 9: 81-306.

Pabongka Rinpoche. 1990. *Liberation in Our Hands, Part One: the Preliminaries.* Geshe Lobsang Tharchin and Artemus Engle, trans. Howell, N.J.: Mahayana Sutra and Tantra Press.

Pandeya, J.S., ed. 1994. *Bauddhastotrasaṃgraha,* Varanasi: Motilal Banarsidass.

People's Publishing House. 1984. *Bod rgya tshig mdzod chen mo. (Tibetan Chinese Dictionary.)* 3 vols. Beijing.

Pfandt, Peter. 1983. *Mahāyāna Texts Translated into Western Languages: A Bibliographical Guide.* Køln: E.J. Brill.

Powers, John. 1995a. *Introduction to Tibetan Buddhism.* Ithaca, N.Y.: Snow Lion Publications.

———. 1995b. *Wisdom of Buddha: The Saṁdhinirmocana Mahāyāna Sūtra.* Berkeley: Dharma Publishing.

Pruden, Leo M., trans. 1988. *Abhidharmakośabhāṣyam by Louis de la Vallée Poussin.* Berkeley: Asian Humanities Press.

Rahula, Walpola. 1980. *Le compendium de la super-doctrine (philosophie) (Abhidharmasamuccaya) d'Asaṅga.* Publications de l'École française d'Extrême-Orient, 78. Paris: École française d'Extrême-Orient [1971].

Richards, Michael, trans. 1991. *Liberation in the Palm of Your Hand*. Boston: Wisdom Publications.

Rinbochay, Lati and Jeffrey Hopkins. 1979. *Death, Intermediate State and Rebirth in Tibetan Buddhism*. London: Rider and Company.

Rinchen, Geshe Sonam, and Ruth Sonam. 1994. *Yogic Deeds of Bodhisattvas*. Ithaca: Snow Lion Publications.

Rockhill, W. Woodville. 1982. *Udanavarga: A Collection of Verses from the Buddhist Canon*. Calcutta: Trübner's Oriental Series [1892]; reprint ed. New Delhi: D.K. Publishers' Distributors.

Roerich, George N. 1979. *The Blue Annals*. Calcutta, 1949; reprint ed., Delhi: Motilal Banarsidass. [This is a translation of 'Gos-lo-tsā-ba-gzhon-nu-dpal's *Bod kyi yul du chos dang chos smra ba ji ltar byung ba'i rim pa deb ther sngon po*.]

Ruegg, David Seyfort. 1969 *La Théorie du Tathāgathagarbha et du Gotra*. Paris: École française d'Extrême-Orient.

Shastri, Swami Dwarikadas, ed. 1968. *Pramāṇavārttika of Āchārya Dharmakīrti*. Varanasi: Bauddha Bharati.

———. 1972. *Abhidharma-kośa and Bhāṣya of Ācārya Vasubandhu with Sphūṭārthā Commentary of Ācārya Yaśomitra*. Varanasi: Bauddha Bharati.

Sherbourne, Richard. 1983. *A Lamp for the Path and Commentary*. London: George Allen & Unwin.

Shukla, Karunesha, ed. 1973. *Śrāvakabhūmi of Ārya Asaṅga*. Patna: K.P. Jayaswal Research Institute.

Snellgrove, David, and T. Skorupski. 1977. *The Cultural History of Ladakh*. Vol. 2. Boulder, CO: Prajñā Press.

Sopa, Geshe Lundrup, and Jeffrey Hopkins. 1976. *Practice and Theory of Tibetan Buddhism*. New York: Grove Press.

Sparham, Gareth. 1999. *Fulfillment of All Hopes of Disciples*. Boston: Wisdom Publications.

Speyer, J.S. 1971. *The Jātakamālā: Garland of Birth-Stories of Āryaśūra*. Reprint edition. Delhi: Motilal Banarsidass.

Stcherbatsky, Th. 1962. *Buddhist Logic*. New York: Dover Books.

Stcherbatsky, Th. and E. Obermiller, eds. 1970. *Abhisamayālaṃkāra-prajñāpāramitā-upadeśa-śāstra: The Work of the Bodhisattva Maitreya*. Fasc. I, Introduction, Skt. Text and Tib. Trans. Bibliotheca Indica 23. St. Petersburg 1929; reprint ed., Osnabrück: Biblio Verlag.

Stein, R.A. 1961. *Les Tribus Anciennes des Marches Sino-Tibetaines*. Paris: Presses Universitaires de France.

Suzuki, D.T., ed. 1955-61. *The Tibetan Tripiṭaka, Peking Edition*. Reprinted under the supervision of the Otani University, Kyoto. 168 volumes. Tokyo and Kyoto.

———. 1973. *The Lankavatara Sutra*. London: Routledge and Kegan Paul.

Takasaki, Jikido. 1966. *A Study on the Ratnagotravibhāga (Uttaratantra)*. Rome: Istituto Italiano per il Medio ed Estremo Oriente.

Tatz, Mark. 1987. *Asanga's Chapter on Ethics with the Commentary of Tsong-Kha-Pa,* The Basic Path to Awakening: *The Complete Bodhisattva*. Lewiston/Queenston: The Edwin Mellen Press.

Thurman, Robert A.F. 1984. *Tsong Khapa's Speech of Gold in the Essence of True Eloquence.* Princeton: Princeton University Press.

Tripāthī, Chandrabhal, ed. 1962. *Fünfundzwangzig Sūtras des Nidānasaṃyukta.* Berlin: Akademie-Verlag.

Tucci, Giuseppe. 1934. "A Fragment from the *Prātitya-samutpāda-vyākhyā.*" *Journal of the Royal Asiatic Society* (1934): 611-623.

———. 1986. *Minor Buddhist Texts Parts I and II.* Delhi: Motilal Banarsidass [1956].

———. 1988. *Rin-chen-bzaṅ-po and the Renaissance of Buddhism in Tibet Around the Millenium.* Indo-Asian Literatures, 348. New Delhi: Aditya Prakashan [1932].

Vaidya, P.L., ed. 1958. *Lalitavistara.* Darbhanga: Mithila Institute.

———. 1959a. *Jātakamāla by Āryaśūra.* Darbhanga: Mithila Institute.

———. 1959b. *Divyāvadāna.* Darbhanga: Mithila Institute.

———. 1960a. *Saddharmapuṇḍarīkasūtra.* Darbhanga: Mithila Institute.

———. 1960b. *Śikṣāsamuccaya.* Darbhanga: Mithila Institute.

———. 1960c. *Gaṇḍhavyūhasūtra.* Darbhanga: Mithila Institute.

———. 1960d. *Aṣṭasāhasrikā Prajñāpāramitā.* Darbhanga: Mithila Institute.

———. 1961. *Samādhirājasūtra.* Darbhanga: Mithila Institute.

———. 1963. *Laṅkāvatārasūtra.* Darbhanga: Mithila Institute.

———. 1964. *Mahāyānasūtrasaṃgraha.* 2 vols. Darbhanga: Mithila Institute.

Verdu, Alfonso. 1979. *Early Buddhist Philosophy in the Light of the Four Noble Truths.* Washington, D.C.: University Press of America.

Vitali, Roberto. 1996. *The Kingdoms of Gu.ge Pu.hrang. According to mNga'.ris rgyal.rabs by Gu.ge mkhan.chen Ngag.dbang grags.pa.* Asian edition. Dharamsala, India: Tho.ling gtsug.lag.khang lo.gcig.stong 'khor.ba'i rjes.dran.mdzad sgo'i go.sgrig tshogs.chung.

Wangyal, Geshe. 1978. *The Door of Liberation.* New York: Lotsawa.

Wayman, Alex. 1980. "The Sixteen Aspects of the Four Noble Truths and Their Opposites." *Journal of the International Buddhist Association* 3: 67-76.

Wogihara, Unrai, ed. 1973. *Abhisamayālaṃkārālokā Prajñā-pāramitā-vyākhyā: The Work of Haribhadra.* Tokyo: The Toyo Bunko, 1932-35; reprint ed., Tokyo: Sankibo Buddhist Book Store.

Wylie, T. 1959. "A Standard System of Tibetan Transcription." *Harvard Journal of Asiatic Studies.* 22: 261-267.

Yuyama, A., ed. 1976. *Prajñā-pāramitā-ratna-guṇa-sañcaya-gāthā.* (Skt. Recension A.) Cambridge: University Press.

Zahler, Leah et al. 1983. *Meditative States in Tibetan Buddhism.* London and Boston: Wisdom Publications.

Index

Nag-tsho-tshul-khrims-rgyal-ba (Nag-tso Tshul-trim-gyal-wa), 41, 43

Nag-tso Tshul-trim-gyal-wa. *See* Nag-tsho-tshul-khrims-rgyal-ba.

Nālanda (Nā-lendra), 34

Nā-lendra. *See* Nālanda.

Nal-jor-ba-chen-bo. *See* rNal-'byor-pa-chen-po.

Nanda, 211, 291

Neu-sur-ba. *See* sNe'u-zur-pa.

Nga-ri. *See* mNga'-ris.

Ngog-legs-pa'i-shes-rab (Ngok Lek-bay-shay-rap), 43

Ngok Lek-bay-shay-rap. *See* Ngog-legs-pa'i-shes-rab.

Nirṇaya-saṃgraha. See Yoga-caryā-bhumi.

nirvāṇa 46, 56, 57, 60, 98, 120, 170, 189, 193, 195, 197, 199, 204, 205, 212, 301, 328, 330, 331, 339, 346

Niyatāniyata-mudrāvatāra-sūtra (Seal of Engaging in Certain and Uncertain Destinies Sūtra), 232

Nyag-mo-ba (Nyak-mo-wa), 79

Nyak-mo-wa. *See* Nyag-mo-ba.

Nyāya-bindu-prakaraṇa (Drop of Reasoning) [Dharmakīrti], 37

Nyen-dön. *See* gNyan-ston.

Nye-tang. *See* sNye-thang.

Nyuk-rum-ba. *See* bsNyug-rum-pa.

Oḍḍiyāna, 40, 43

Ornament for Clear Knowledge. See Abhisamayālaṃkāra.

Ornament for the Mahāyāna Sūtras. See Mahāyāna-sūtrālaṃkāra.

Padmasambhava, 41

Pañca-skandha-prakaraṇa (Explanation of the Five Aggregates) [Vasubandhu], 300, 302

'Pan-[po] (Pen-bo), 126

Pāramitā-samāsa (Compendium of the Perfections) [Āryaśūra], 202, 282

Parinirvāṇa-sūtra. See Mahā-parinirvāṇa-sūtra.

path of preparation, 37, 40, 257, 304, 305, 388, n. 182

Pen-bo. *See* 'Pan-po.

perception, in Buddhist psychology, n. 166

Perfection of Wisdom in Eight Thousand Lines. See Aṣṭa-sāhasrikā.

Phu-chung-ba (Pu-chung-wa), 72, 201, 251, 323, 348, n. 112

Phyag-dar-ston-pa (Chak-dar-dön-ba), 43

Po-to-ba (Bo-do-wa), 70, 73, 77, 78, 86-87, 89, 249

Po to ba'i gsung sgros (Bo-do-wa's Method of Explaining) [Dol-ba], 70, 75

Praise by Example. See Upamā-stava.

Praise in Honor of One Worthy of Honor. See Varṇārha-varṇa-stotra.

Praise in One Hundred and Fifty Verses. See Śata-pañcāśatka-stotra.

Praise of Confession. See Deśanā-stava.

Praise of the Exalted One. See Viśeṣa-stava.

Prajñā-nāma-mūla-madhyamaka-kārikā. See Mūla-madhyamaka-kārikā.

Prajñāpāramitā (Perfection of Wisdom sūtras), 252. *See also Abhisamayālaṃkārālokā; Aṣṭādaśasāhasrikā; Aṣṭa-sāhasrikā;* Mother of Conquerors; *Ratna-guṇa-sañcaya-gāthā.*

Prajñāpāramitā-ratna-guṇa-sañcaya-gāthā. See Ratna-guṇa-sañcaya-gāthā.

Prajñā-pradīpa-ṭīkā (*Commentary on the "Lamp for Wisdom"*) [Avalokitavrata], 46

Prajñāvarman. *See Udāna-varga.*

Pramāṇa-vārttika (Commentary on the "Compendium of Valid Cognition") [Dharmakīrti], 46, 298, 300

Praṇidhāna-saptati (Aspiration in Seventy Verses), 100

Praśānta-viniścaya-prātihārya-sūtra (Sūtra on the Magic of Final Peace), 233

Prasphuṭa-padā (Clear Words Commentary) [Dharmamitra], 111

prātimokṣa, n. 107

Prātimokṣa-sūtra (Sūtra on the Vows of Individual Liberation), 71

Pratītya-samutpāda-hṛdaya-kārikā (Heart of Dependent-Arising) [Nāgārjuna], 322, 323

Pratītya-samutpādādi-vibhaṅga-nirdeśa (Explanation of the Divisions of Dependent-Arising) [Vasubhandu], 304, 321

pratyekabuddha, 46, 47, 54, 94, 97, 130, 149, 217, 228, 229, 239, 245

Pratyutpanna-buddha-saṃmukhāvasthita-samādhi-sūtra (Sūtra on the Concentration